"Iarussi offers a timely and comprehensive text that impressively situates the integration of MI and CBT in psychotherapy. Case examples, practice exercises, and annotated transcripts engage the reader in a joint excursion of the four options for MI and CBT integration. A centerpiece of this work is the application of an integrative method with diverse populations. Iarussi provides feasible recommendations for resolving potential dilemmas in today's practice settings. A highly useful text for students and practitioners alike."

—**Cynthia J. Osborn, PhD,** *Professor of Counselor Education and Supervision, Kent State University, Ohio, USA*

"Written with the practitioner in mind, Dr. Iarussi outlines in superb detail how to properly integrate two of the most well-researched counseling approaches: MI and CBT. Readers will find a firm grounding in each approach, followed by a treasure trove of applications to enhance their practice. With increasing calls for therapeutic integration, I cannot think of a timelier and more relevant resource on MI and CBT."

—**Todd F. Lewis, PhD,** *Professor of Counselor Education at North Dakota State University, USA*

"In this book's preface, Melanie Iarussi promises an integration of two popular, evidenced-based approaches to counseling in clinical settings. She succeeds admirably! Her integration provides clinicians with a fresh, practical perspective of MI and CBT that encourages creative new approaches to working with mental health issues. This is a great addition to any mental health practitioner's library!"

—**Charles F. Gressard, PhD, LPC, NCC,** *Chancellor Professor of Education at the College of William and Mary, Virginia, USA*

Integrating Motivational Interviewing and Cognitive Behavior Therapy in Clinical Practice

Integrating Motivational Interviewing and Cognitive Behavior Therapy in Clinical Practice shows counseling and other mental health professionals how the theoretical bases and evidence-based practices of motivational interviewing (MI) and cognitive behavior therapy (CBT) can be used together to maximize client outcomes.

Chapters outline effective methods for integrating MI and CBT and show how these can be applied to clients in a diverse range of mental health, substance use and addiction, and correctional settings. Written in a clear and applicable style, the text features case studies, resources for skill development, and "Voices From the Field" sections, as well as chapters devoted to specific topics such as depression, anxiety, and more.

Building on foundational frameworks for integrative practice, this is a valuable resource for counseling and psychotherapy practitioners looking to incorporate MI and CBT into their clinical practices.

Melanie M. Iarussi, PhD, is an associate professor in the Department of Counseling at Nova Southeastern University, Florida, USA. She is a member of the Motivational Interviewing Network of Trainers, and she routinely teaches and presents on MI and CBT, including on empirical findings related to this integrated practice.

Integrating Motivational Interviewing and Cognitive Behavior Therapy in Clinical Practice

Melanie M. Iarussi

Routledge
Taylor & Francis Group
NEW YORK AND LONDON

First published 2020
by Routledge
52 Vanderbilt Avenue, New York, NY 10017

and by Routledge
2 Park Square, Milton Park, Abingdon, Oxon, OX14 4RN

Routledge is an imprint of the Taylor & Francis Group, an informa business

© 2020 Melanie M. Iarussi

The right of Melanie M. Iarussi to be identified as author of this work has been asserted by her in accordance with sections 77 and 78 of the Copyright, Designs and Patents Act 1988.

All rights reserved. No part of this book may be reprinted or reproduced or utilised in any form or by any electronic, mechanical, or other means, now known or hereafter invented, including photocopying and recording, or in any information storage or retrieval system, without permission in writing from the publishers.

Trademark notice: Product or corporate names may be trademarks or registered trademarks and are used only for identification and explanation without intent to infringe.

Library of Congress Cataloging-in-Publication Data
Names: Iarussi, Melanie M., author.
Title: Integrating motivational interviewing and cognitive behavior therapy in clinical practice / Melanie M. Iarussi.
Description: New York, NY : Routledge, 2020. | Includes bibliographical references and index. Identifiers: LCCN 2019036207 (print) | LCCN 2019036208 (ebook) | ISBN 9780815375838 (hbck) | ISBN 9780815375845 (pbk) | ISBN 9781351203234 (ebk)
Subjects: LCSH: Interviewing in psychiatry. | Motivation (Psychology) | Cognitive therapy.
Classification: LCC RC480.7 .I27 2020 (print) | LCC RC480.7 (ebook) | DDC 616.8900835—dc23
LC record available at https://lccn.loc.gov/2019036207
LC ebook record available at https://lccn.loc.gov/2019036208

ISBN: 978-0-8153-7583-8 (hbk)
ISBN: 978-0-8153-7584-5 (pbk)
ISBN: 978-1-351-20323-4 (ebk)

Typeset in Minion
by Apex CoVantage, LLC

*To Adam, my incredible partner in life, and
to Evelyn and Avery, I am so lucky to be your mommy*

Contents

Preface	xi
Acknowledgments	xiv

Section I: The Foundations   1

1. The Growing Trend of Integrative Practice   3
2. Motivational Interviewing   17
3. Cognitive Behavior Therapy   34
4. An Introduction to Integrating MI and CBT   46
5. Integrating MI and CBT With Diverse Clients   65

Section II: Methods of Integration   81

6. MI as a Precursor to CBT   83
7. Assimilating MI Into CBT   96
8. Assimilating CBT Into MI   116
9. Seamless Blending of MI and CBT   131

Section III: Clinical Applications — 151
10 Substance Use and Addictive Disorders — 153
11 Mental Health–Related Concerns — 189
12 Criminal Behaviors and Correctional Settings — 222

Section IV: Clinical Practice Issues — 245
13 Reconciling Potential Dilemmas — 247
14 Training and Supervision — 257

Index — 267

Preface

Welcome to a journey of exploring the integrative practice of motivational interviewing (MI) and cognitive behavior therapy (CBT). Both MI and CBT are popular, evidence-based approaches with wide applicability in clinical practice. CBT has been characterized as "the most well-established evidence-based psychotherapy," and it is vastly disseminated (Dozois, Dobson, & Rnic, 2019, p. 3). MI also boasts strong empirical support, and as a style of counseling that explicitly addresses discord (formerly known as "resistance") and client motivation, MI is a sensible choice for integrating with other approaches. However, methods of doing so are still developing (Miller & Rollnick, 2013).

At various professional conferences, after conducting presentations on integrating MI and CBT, I would commonly receive enthusiastic requests from participants: "How can I learn more?" Until Naar and Safren published their text on combining MI and CBT in 2017, there were unfortunately few resources to which to point professional counselors, social workers, psychologists, and other helping professionals who were eager to learn more. When I was approached about writing this book, I considered if another book was needed in addition to Naar and Safren's (2017), and I developed the desire to write a book that provided information about integrating MI and CBT in a variety of ways that were already established in general psychotherapy literature (e.g., Norcross, 2005). I also wanted to make the connections explicit of how MI and CBT can be used together to help treat clients with a range of presenting concerns, including substance use and addictive disorders, mental health disorders, and criminal behavior. Therefore, in this book, I present various methods of integrating MI and CBT with explanations for how each type of integration might work in clinical practice considering the client, presenting concerns, and the settings in which we work.

This book was written for students and clinicians who provide mental health, substance use, correctional, or other types of counseling and psychotherapy services. Throughout the book, I use terms such as "counselor," "therapist," "clinician," and "practitioner" interchangeably. It is my hope and understanding that professionals of various disciplines, including counseling, social work, criminal justice, and psychology, find this information useful and applicable. Therefore, I used a variety of terms in an effort to set the tone of inclusivity and applicability for various professionals. I hope you will find this book applicable regardless of where you place yourself on the continuum of experience from novice to seasoned professional and regardless of your familiarity with MI or CBT—you might know one or both approaches well separately or not at all.

In Section I, we start by exploring the clinical trend of using integrated practice in general (as opposed to the singular practice of one theory). This book is aligned with the trajectory of the helping professions to be trained in and to practice more than one approach to counseling. Then we visit the foundations of MI and CBT separately. You may be familiar with or even extensively trained in one, both, or neither. The purpose of these chapters is to provide you with enough information about the approaches separately so that you have a foundation for their integration as discussed in the remainder of the book, regardless of your preexisting knowledge or training. Of course, there is a wealth of information available on these approaches that is beyond the scope of this book. Therefore, resources to learn more are included in Chapters 2 and 3. In Chapter 4, we dive into the rationale for integrating MI and CBT in clinical practice and envision its practice through a case example. To close Section I, Chapter 5 describes the value and practice of integrating MI and CBT with diverse populations.

Section II explores various methods to integrate MI and CBT in practice. There is no "right" or "wrong" approach to integrating MI and CBT, but rather there are options from which to make sensible choices. First, we explore using MI as a precursor to CBT treatment, which can be especially useful in settings where clients are referred to CBT treatment that is offered by another provider. Then, we will explore two forms of assimilative integration (Norcross, Goldfried, & Arigo, 2016): 1) assimilating MI into an existing CBT practice in which CBT remains the foundational or primary theory, and 2) assimilating CBT into MI as the foundational or primary approach. If you are currently practicing MI or CBT alone, you might choose to begin with an assimilated approach, either as your integrative practice goal or as a stepping stone to full integration. Theoretical integration, or a true blending of MI and CBT, is described in the final chapter of Section II. In this type of practice, MI and CBT are no longer considered separate approaches, but rather they have become a single, unified approach.

In Section III, we explore clinical applications of MI+CBT in three broad areas of practice: substance use and addictive disorders, mental health–related concerns, and criminal behaviors and correctional settings. Each of these chapters also includes specific case examples to illustrate its use. These areas were chosen due to each being discussed in the literature, although to varying degrees. Literature on MI+CBT is most robust in substance use treatment, and applications in mental health have been on the rise in the past decade. Applications of MI and CBT are often discussed separately in correctional treatment. My hope is that these chapters can help encourage the integration of these practices in their respective settings and within the context of existing frameworks (i.e., Risk-Need-Responsivity in correctional settings). My own experience in clinical practice and in providing trainings also supported the development of these chapters. Although only these three broad areas were chosen for this text, the application of MI+CBT can expand beyond these areas to very worthy topics, such as intimate partner violence and rehabilitation counseling, and be applied more specifically to disorders and concerns within each area (e.g., specific to gambling addiction and obsessive-compulsive disorder). The information provided is only a start to many possible expansions.

Section IV wraps up our exploration of this integrated practice. Chapter 13 describes common dilemmas that providers integrating MI and CBT experience and guidance to navigate these challenges. Finally, Chapter 14 provides information about training and supervision to strive toward competence in practice in MI+CBT.

References

Dozois, D. J. A., Dobson, K. S., & Rnic, K. (2019). Historical and philosophical bases of the cognitive-behavioral therapies. In K. S. Dobson & D. J. A. Dozois (Eds.), *Handbook of cognitive-behavioral therapies* (4th ed., pp. 3–31). New York, NY: Guilford Press.

Miller, W. R., & Rollnick, S. (2013). *Motivational interviewing: Helping people change* (3rd ed.). New York, NY: Guilford Press.

Naar, S., & Safren, S. A. (2017). *Motivational interviewing and CBT: Combining strategies for maximum effectiveness*. New York, NY: Guilford Press.

Norcross, J. C. (2005). A primer on psychotherapy integration. In J. C. Norcross & M. R. Goldfried (Eds.), *Handbook of psychotherapy integration* (2nd ed., pp. 3–23). New York, NY: The Oxford University Press, Inc.

Norcross, J. C., Goldfried, M. R., & Arigo, D. (2016). Integrative theories. In J. C. Norcross, G. R. VandenBos, D. K. Freedheim, & B. O. Olatunji (Eds.), *APA handbook of clinical psychology: Theory and research* (Vol. 2, pp. 303–332). Washington, DC: American Psychological Association.

Acknowledgments

This book would be not be possible without the incredible work of the theorists, researchers, and writers who are cited in these pages. It has been my privilege and pleasure to bring a breadth of research and scholarship together with the intention of further disseminating the practice of MI+CBT.

I am incredibly grateful for the opportunity to share this information that has been shaped and supported through innumerable conversations with professional colleagues, trainees, various stakeholders, and students about how to teach and learn these approaches, as well as how to apply MI and CBT in clinical counseling and supervision. This book essentially began with my dissertation work, and I wholeheartedly appreciate my continuing mentor, Cynthia Osborn, for her support in pursuing this topic and in general. I am also incredibly grateful to my colleagues and former students who collaborated with me on various writing and research projects related to this topic.

This book was enriched by first-person accounts of students and professionals who shared their own experiences of practicing, learning, and teaching MI and CBT in the "Voices From the Field" insets. A very special thank you to Vivian Hariton, whose integrity in work ethic and in character assisted me in proofreading this book and with references, and to Karli Gallo whose diligent work assisted with the references at the end of each chapter.

I must also acknowledge my dear colleagues (past and present), friends, and family who supported me throughout this process. Thank you for believing in me and for being patient with me.

Finally, I am grateful to you, the reader, for being interested in learning more to serve your clientele in ways that effectively meet their individualized needs. Because in the end, isn't that what it's all about?

SECTION I
The Foundations

CHAPTER 1

The Growing Trend of Integrative Practice

When we first learn to practice counseling or psychotherapy, we are introduced to a number of counseling theories that offer ideas about the etiology of clients' presenting concerns as well as related propositions of how to facilitate change. These theories are commonly grouped in categories based on their foundational concepts, such as psychodynamic approaches, experiential and relationship-oriented therapies, cognitive behavioral approaches, and systems and postmodern approaches (Corey, 2017). Students and beginning helping professionals are also typically introduced to atheoretical components of the therapeutic process, such as the stages of change (Norcross, Krebs, & Prochaska, 2011) and the common factors (Wampold, 2015). After learning the basics of these various theories and approaches, students are encouraged to choose one or two to learn more deeply: first in coursework and then applied to their clinical practice with clients. Therefore, students who are enrolled in early clinical experience courses (e.g., practicum, internship) and counseling professionals who are at the start of their careers commonly strive to further develop a theoretical basis for their clinical work. Progress in achieving this goal occurs over time and with intentionality. Common activities include engaging in self-directed reading of original sources from a theorist(s), attending workshops or trainings, and engaging in supervised practice, including working with a supervisor to conceptualize clients through the lens of a theory and then implement interventions that are derived from or congruent with the theoretical conceptualization. In these early training experiences, it is common for students and new professionals to experience a gap between theory and the practice they witness in their clinical settings. However, modeling after a supervisor or aligning with a theoretical model can aid in the new practitioner's development (Skovholt & Trotter-Mathison, 2011).

Regardless of early training experiences, *any clinician can choose to pursue additional growth and development related to counseling theory and practice* in order to enhance the quality and effectiveness of counseling services they provide to clients. Given that you have chosen to read this book on integrating MI and CBT, you might be embarking on your own intentional efforts to learn more about and practice this specific integration. In this first chapter, we explore the value of theoretical integration within the current milieu of counseling and therapy practices.

We begin with a description of the shift toward integrative practice and gain an overview of the various methods to implement integrative practice. Then we will examine the function of counseling theory in clinical practice, using the case example of Maria. We will briefly compare counseling theories, including conceptualizations and interventions, and then apply multiple theoretical and atheoretical approaches (i.e., stages of change, common factors) in an integrative fashion.

Movement Toward Integrative Practice

Historically, therapists were trained in and then practiced with a single theoretical approach. The various forces of psychotherapy were born from theorists who did not agree with the available theories at the time, resulting in siloed and competing approaches to therapy. To illustrate, Carl Rogers, founder of person-centered therapy, wrote of behavior therapists of the mid-20th century, "the majority . . . are so committed to seeing the individual solely as an object, that what I have to say often baffles if it does not annoy them" (Rogers, 1961, p. viii). Approaches to psychotherapy have also evolved due to outcome research and increasingly sophisticated methods, including use of technology (e.g., neuroscience). Jones-Smith (2016) categorized the five forces of psychotherapy as follows: (1) psychoanalytic and psychodynamic theories, (2) behavior therapy and cognitive therapy, (3) existential and humanistic theories, (4) social constructivism and postmodernism, and (5) neuroscience and pharmacology. When practicing counseling and psychotherapy today, counselors have robust options to guide their methods, many of which have comparable empirical support. For instance, the American Psychological Association (APA) concluded that "comparisons of different forms of psychotherapy most often result in relatively nonsignificant difference, and contextual and relationship factors often mediate or moderate outcomes" (APA, 2013, p. 321). If indeed various theories provide a valid basis for therapy and have comparable empirical support, clinicians may have the luxury to have an open mind to consider other factors when choosing their theoretical approach, such as the unique characteristics of a particular client, the client's presenting concern and the circumstances in which they are experiencing that concern, and the setting in which services are being provided (Norcross & Wampold, 2011). At this point, it seems unreasonable to believe that a single treatment approach will work for all clients, for every presenting concern, and in all settings. For instance, Norcross, Goldfried, and Arigo (2016) reported that studies have found only 2% to 12% of therapists use a pure, single theoretical approach. As such, we have moved beyond a siloed, single theory approach and into a new era in which multiple therapeutic approaches are used in a systematic way to tailor treatment to client needs. In recent times, integrative practice in counseling and therapy has become the norm.

Methods of Integrative Practice

So, what does it mean to practice an integrative approach? Integrating therapeutic approaches involves combining elements from traditionally stand-alone theories in an organized and systematic way in order to enhance client outcomes (Holmes & Bateman, 2002). For example, CBT itself is an integration of two formerly stand-alone treatments—behavior therapy and cognitive therapy. Acceptance and commitment therapy (ACT) is an integration of CBT with acceptance and mindfulness therapy, and dialectical behavior therapy is another example in which CBT is integrated with mindfulness and emotional regulation.

Norcross and colleagues (2016) described four approaches to integrative practice: (a) common factors, (b) technical eclecticism, (c) assimilative integration, and (d) theoretical integration. Two of these—assimilative integration and theoretical integration—are described in this book related to MI and CBT (see Chapters 7–9). Assimilative integration involves the therapist using one therapeutic approach as their foundation, while selectively incorporating one or more approaches into the foundational approach. For instance, Chapter 7 describes practicing with CBT as the primary or foundational approach while selectively incorporating MI as needed to address motivational issues. Chapter 8 describes using MI as the primary or foundational approach and then selectively adding cognitive or behavioral interventions as needed to address problematic thoughts or behaviors. Although this is not a comprehensive integration of the approaches, it does provide a structured way to use more than one approach in therapy. Theoretical integration involves a blending of two (or more) approaches. This type of integration is essentially seamless, as the underlying theories about change and the techniques to facilitate change are melded together. The goal of theoretical integration remains to enhance client outcomes in a way that neither theoretical approach could do alone. Therefore, theoretical integration is intended to be synergistic or more than the sum of its parts. This approach to MI+CBT is described in Chapter 9.

Common factors and technical eclecticism are the two remaining approaches to integrative practice identified by Norcross et al. (2016). The common factors approach identifies the components of therapy that are consistent across theoretical approaches. In the historical argument surrounding which was the most effective theoretical approach to treatment, another conflict arose in the field of psychotherapy—Which was more important in therapy: the treatment method or the therapeutic relationship (Norcross & Lambert, 2011)? Subsequent research has supported that both the theoretically driven treatment and the therapeutic relationship and processes that comprise the common factors are important (Laska, Gurman, & Wampold, 2014). Wampold (2015) described a contextual model of the common factors, which consisted of the therapeutic relationship, expectations, and specific actions in therapy. The relationship involves the client experiencing trust, empathy, caring, and counselor genuineness. Expectations involves the counselor discussing the diagnosis and treatment plan with the client and the counselor and client agreeing on the goals and tasks for therapy. Finally, the therapist implements treatment methods and interventions that are tailored to client characteristics (not solely the diagnosis) and that consider the client holistically. The contextual model of the common factors acknowledges the importance of specific treatment methods in therapy. However, it considers it to be only one of three essential components, and the previous two components—therapeutic relationship and expectations—must be established in order for the treatment methods to be optimally effective.

Another atheoretical approach, the transtheoretical stages of change model, is also commonly integrated into therapy. This model draws attention to the client's readiness for change and clinician behaviors that can assist clients in progressing through the stages (Prochaska, DiClemente, & Norcross, 1992). This model cautions clinicians about assuming that all clients are ready for active changes, as only an estimated 20% of clients are ready for action (Norcross et al., 2011). Instead, this model suggests that clinicians need to first assess the client's stage of change and then respond with appropriate goals, treatment methods, and approaches to establishing the therapeutic relationship (Norcross et al., 2011). Table 1.1 describes the five stages of change identified by Norcross et al. (2011) as well as therapeutic processes research has found to be helpful each stage of change. The stages appear to be sequential; however, it is common for clients to recycle through earlier stages of change. Therefore, Norcross et al. (2011) encouraged clinicians to anticipate nonlinear movement between stages to avoid their own feelings of guilt or exacerbating a client's feelings of shame and embarrassment when recycling occurs. Instead, it should be seen as a common experience of the process of change. MI and CBT both involve some of these common factors, and MI is especially designed to approach clients in their current degree of readiness for change. As such, elements of the common factors approach and the stages of change will be included in later chapters in this book within the context of combining MI+CBT.

Technical eclecticism focuses on identifying interventions that have research support when treating similar concerns among people with similar characteristics (Norcross et al., 2016). Eclecticism is not included further in this book due to this approach lacking a consistent theoretical underpinning, which can lead to a lack of continuity in therapy; in essence, it is not consistent with practicing MI+CBT. Although eclecticism gained some popularity a few decades ago, concerns have emerged related to haphazardly combining techniques with little regard for an organized, intentional approach to treatment as a whole. These concerns have resulted in a negative connotation of eclecticism (Norcross et al., 2016). In my experience teaching and supervising, counseling students and early professionals can become hyperfocused on interventions and what they can "do" with a client. Especially in earlier stages of counselor development, it is easy to adopt an eclectic counseling "toolbox" without a coherent foundational theory of change. Instead of simply filling a toolbox, it is essential for students and early professionals to learn to conceptualize client concerns through the lens of a theory and then identify interventions that stem from or are consistent with the theory's ideas about how to facilitate change. In addition to being consistent with counseling theory, interventions should be chosen with consideration to the client's characteristics, concerns, and context. This promotes a holistic approach to treatment that involves clear goals or direction in therapy and interventions with continuity to help clients strive toward their goals.

Table 1.1 Stages of Change Model

Stage of Change	Characteristics	Therapeutic Components
Precontemplation	• No intention to change • Presents for treatment at the urging of others (e.g., family, court)	• Relationship: Nurturing • Interventions: Empathy and positive regard
Contemplation	• Have awareness that they have a problem but are not sure if they want to or can change it • Ambivalent about change—if someone voices one side of the ambivalence, the client will likely voice the alternative side	• Relationship: Socratic teacher • Interventions: Using intentional questioning to explore the client's ambivalence to help the client arrive at his or her own conclusions
Preparation	• Committed to making the change • Developing a plan and setting the stage for change	• Relationship: Experienced coach • Interventions: Offer suggestions for client's plan for change, review client's plan
Action	• Changes are implemented, requires the most time and energy • Efforts are observed by others	• Relationship: Consultant • Interventions: Provide support and advice, counterconditioning, cognitive restructuring, coping skill development
Maintenance	• Changes have been ongoing for six-plus months	• Relationship: Sporadic consultant • Interventions: Promote client autonomy, relapse prevention

Selecting a Theoretical Approach

Theory serves as the roadmap for counseling practice (Corey, 2019). Counseling theories provide counselors with key concepts used to conceptualize client's concerns, goals of therapy, roles of the therapist and client to achieve the goals, techniques used to facilitate change, and the importance of the counseling relationship and multicultural factors in therapy. Although it is beyond the scope of this book to describe a multitude of counseling theories, there are various books that offer robust descriptions of counseling theories. Some also offer a description of theoretical integration, and others focus on guiding integrated practice, such as Corey (2019) and Jones-Smith (2016).

When counselors decide which theoretical approach to use with a specific client, they take into consideration the following questions: "What is/are my personal guiding theoretical approach(es)?" and "Which approach, executed by me, would be most helpful for this particular client at this time, given the client's circumstances?" (Norcross & Wampold, 2011). As Corey (2019) stated, "Attempting to practice without an explicit theoretical rationale is like trying to build a house without a set of blueprints" (p. 3). Counseling theories provide the framework for counselors to make sense of how clients' concerns came to be and how to diminish distress, enhance wellness, and, other mental health, relationship, academic, and career goals. Prior to clinicians choosing which approaches they will use in treatment, they need to consider their own ideas about how people grow and change. Often, student counselors will recognize that one or more of the counseling theories resonate with their own ideas about how problems come to be and how people can change. Then students are encouraged to learn more deeply about at least one counseling theory and then begin to use it in practice. Such learning occurs through reading original works written by the theorist or others, watching videos of theories being applied with clients, and engaging in supervised practice that includes conceptualizing clients through the lens of the theory and implementing techniques and interventions that are consistent with the theory of change.

Prior to conceptualization and treatment, counselors gather information about client's presenting concerns and histories and often provide a diagnosis. Assessment embedded in integrative counseling casts a wide net of information gathering, including individual experiences, strengths, personality, culture, readiness to change, and coping styles, as well as systemic and familial influences (Norcross et al., 2016). Integrative clinicians then use this information to develop a unique conceptualization and to tailor treatment—selecting from more than one theory—to best fit the client, taking into consideration empirically supported treatments for the client's presenting concerns along with the client's personal and contextual factors. During and following the initial assessment, counselors apply counseling theory to conceptualize or make sense of how the client's presenting concerns came to be and then develop a plan for treatment.

Further, treatment should be tailored to the client in light of the client's characteristics, presenting concern and diagnosis, and individual context (Norcross & Wampold, 2011). Having knowledge of empirically supported treatments for specific disorders can help inform decisions about which approach to use; however, it is essential that counselors consider the client holistically and within the client's context, including relevant history, culture, and circumstances, and adapt or tailor the treatment to this specific client in a way that will optimize its effectiveness (Norcross & Lambert, 2011; Norcross & Wampold, 2011). In Chapter 5, we explore how MI+CBT can be tailored for diverse clients as well as examine cultural adaptations of each approach. Finally, the setting in which you are providing services will also likely influence your decision when selecting a counseling approach. It is not uncommon for agencies to include CBT as a core component of treatment due to its known empirical support as well as it being readily available in manualized approaches that are easily disseminated. However, these expectations and possibilities will vary depending on if you are practicing in a private clinic, hospital, substance use treatment agency, correctional setting, domestic violence shelter, and so on.

Clinical Application

Maria, a 30-year-old woman, presents with symptoms of anxiety, including racing thoughts, sleeplessness, and worrying about her relationship. Maria is Mexican American and has had stable, long-term employment as a customer service agent at a bank. Through an integrative assessment, the counselor learns that her previous relationship of six years ended when she discovered her boyfriend was cheating on her with other women. Maria was devastated over the "time lost" in a relationship that did not lead to marriage. She feels tremendous pressure from her parents to marry and have a family. Her parents often remind her that she is the oldest woman in her family who is not yet married, and the tension surrounding this topic intensified after Maria's 21-year-old cousin recently became engaged.

Maria entered a relationship with a new boyfriend two weeks after her breakup, and her symptoms of anxiety intensified quickly upon entering this new relationship. Conflicts often arise in their relationship due to Maria compulsively checking and scrutinizing the calls and messages on her boyfriend's phone. She obsesses over where he is when they are apart. She recently became irate and had a panic attack after he took one hour to respond to her call while he was at work. This episode led her to schedule a counseling appointment. Maria's fear of losing another relationship is motivating her to want to change. In the next section, we conceptualize Maria's case and consider possible plans for treatment through the lens of counseling theories and then apply one theory, CBT, to the counselor's work with Maria. Then, the counselor applies the common factors and stages of change approaches. Finally, the counselor executes an integrated approach to best meet Maria's needs within her specific context.

Applying Counseling Theory

Table 1.2 provides an example of how Maria's presenting concerns can be conceptualized and her treatment can be approached through the lens of various counseling theories (Corey, 2017). It becomes obvious that there are multiple legit approaches to assist Maria with her concerns. For the sake of this example, let us imagine that Maria came to a counselor who practiced CBT, and the counselor

Table 1.2 Theoretical Conceptualizations and Plans for Counseling with Maria

Theory	Key Concepts Applied	Maria's Conceptualization and Plan for Counseling
Psychodynamic	• Structure of Personality: Id, ego, superego • Defense mechanisms	• Maria's anxiety is due to repressed emotions and memories from her previous relationship (repression is a defense mechanism). Maria's id is too strong, causing her to obsess over her boyfriend's behaviors and compulsively check his phone and whereabouts to reduce the tension she feels from worrying. Her ego is telling her something is wrong with these behaviors. In therapy, Maria will develop an increased awareness and understanding of her current behavior, including how her past relationship has influenced her present behavior.
Existential	• Existential anxiety • Neurotic anxiety	• After the breakup with her previous boyfriend, Maria was confronted with being isolated and having a meaningless life if she is not married, causing existential anxiety. Her failure to move through this anxiety caused her to experience neurotic anxiety, or anxiety that is disproportionate to the given situation. In therapy, Maria can learn to tolerate ambiguity in her relationship and in her life and move from dependence to autonomy.
Gestalt	• Field theory: • Figure and ground • Unfinished business • Introjection	• Maria's unfinished business with her ex-boyfriend is manifesting in her anxiety. Her current relationship is acting as the figure (most prominent at this time), while the past relationship is serving as the ground (out of her awareness but affecting her). In counseling, Maria can work toward increasing her awareness about how the parts fit together and strive for holism by attending to her thoughts, feelings, and behaviors. Maria might also be experiencing introjection in that she is accepting of her parents' belief that she should be married already without analyzing it or restructuring this cultural norm for herself.

(Continued)

Table 1.2 (Continued)

Theory	Key Concepts Applied	Maria's Conceptualization and Plan for Counseling
CBT	• Cognitive Conceptualization • Cognitive model • Collaborative Empiricism • Coping skills training	• Maria's past experience left her with a cognitive schema consisting of maladaptive beliefs and thoughts that cause mistrust and anxiety in her current relationship. In therapy, Maria can become aware of how her thoughts and beliefs affect her emotions and behaviors, and then through the counselor's use of collaborative empiricism, she can evaluate and modify her existing dysfunctional thought processes. Maria might also benefit from learning coping skills, such as breathwork or mindfulness, to help her manage the physiological manifestations of her anxiety.
Feminist Therapy	• Social identity analysis • Power analysis • Bibliotherapy	• Maria has been socialized to believe that she should be married already and that it is a problem that she is not. Maria identifies as a woman who is of Mexican heritage and who has adopted the traditional cultural values of her family. In therapy, Maria can learn how these identities led her to believe that there is something wrong with her. Maria can then decide what messages she would like to accept and be aware of the messages that are not helpful to her. Power analysis can be useful for Maria to become aware of the power differences between men and women in relationships, especially in regard to her cultural context. The therapist can empower Maria to take actions that are helpful to her, including considering alternative actions to her current behaviors that can help her exercise healthy power and gain self-confidence based on her strengths and positive attributes. Maria can read books, especially autobiographies of other Mexican American women, and discuss her reactions to their stories in therapy.

(Continued)

Table 1.2 (Continued)

Theory	Key Concepts Applied	Maria's Conceptualization and Plan for Counseling
Narrative Therapy	• Social construction • Externalization • Reauthoring/restorying	• Through consistent socially constructed narratives, Maria has come to believe that she—due to not being married and experiencing relationship difficulties—is the problem. In narrative therapy, the counselor and Maria will title the problem-saturated story as a means of externalizing the problem from the person. Maria can identify how this story has caused her trouble, including her symptoms of anxiety and distress. Maria will then develop an alternative story and make a choice of which story she chooses to live in.

developed a conceptualization and treatment plan consistent with the theoretical foundation and key concepts of CBT (such as those described in Table 1.2). With the philosophy that Maria developed distorted beliefs and automatic thoughts that cause mistrust and anxiety in her current relationship, the counselor educated Maria about the cognitive model and attempted to help Maria become aware of how her thoughts and beliefs affect her emotions and behaviors.

Let us stop here for a moment and consider possible outcomes if the counselor approaches Maria solely through the lens of CBT. Although the counselor could clearly connect Maria's automatic thoughts, such as "he's cheating on me" and "he's found someone younger," to her intense experiences of anxiety and subsequent behaviors and physiological responses, when the counselor presents the theory to Maria, she rejects it saying,

> No, it's not a problem with how I'm thinking. My parents expect me to get married, and that's not in my head. That's real! And I wasted so much time with my ex. I don't have any more time to waste, and I don't think he's committed to me!

This is important feedback for the counselor, and perhaps it suggests that using CBT alone was too limited and did not account well enough for Maria's contextual factors or stage of change. She brought attention to the cultural expectation her family placed on her to be married, which was not accounted for in the intervention of applying the cognitive model. Maria's feedback indicates that she felt the counselor was missing essential components of the context in which she was experiencing her anxiety and perhaps not viewing her holistically.

Integrating Atheoretical Approaches

After receiving Maria's important feedback, the counselor might then integrate the common factors approach. First, the counselor strives to develop a strong alliance with the client by expressing empathy. Then, after revising the counselor's explanation of the cause of her distress to include a holistic understanding, including the cultural context of her situation, the counselor facilitates an open discussion of the cognitive conceptualization to see if Maria will or will not agree with this explanation. Within the context of a strong therapeutic alliance, Maria agrees with the explanation and commits to a minimum of six weeks of CBT for anxiety. However, four weeks into treatment, the counselor observes that Maria is not completing the thought logs or using the breathing exercises between sessions. By applying the stages of change model, the counselor suspects that Maria is ambivalent about changing her behaviors. Although Maria has expressed her desire to change, there might be some underlying ambivalence to explore to help Maria progress from contemplation to preparation. Overall, she does not appear to be benefiting from the therapy, as each week her anxiety levels remain unchanged, and she experienced another panic attack. This might be a time to consider exploring her ambivalence about changing or engaging in CBT work and integrating another therapeutic approach to enhance Maria's outcome through integrative practice.

In this example, the common factors and stages of change models were applied after CBT was attempted. Instead, integrative practice with Maria might have been more effective if the counselor initially conceptualized Maria's concerns by using an integration of CBT, common factors, and stages of change. We can also consider using theoretical integration at the onset of treatment or integrating another theory-based approach that might assist with Maria's case, such as feminist theory, as described in the next section.

Theoretical Integration in Practice

Now, let's consider how practicing theoretical integration could impact a counselor's work with Maria. Using CBT alone was not effective in reducing her anxiety, and she did not engage in the CBT work in between sessions. Given Maria's experiences as a woman in her culture and the power disadvantages she has experienced in her family of origin and her intimate relationships, feminist therapy might be especially beneficial for Maria. CBT and feminist therapy would be used simultaneously by blending both conceptualizations and techniques (such as those described in Table 1.2) to enhance the effectiveness of therapy. For example, exploring Maria's social and gender identities could be a means to understand how she developed her current cognitive schemas, and empowerment can be used to help Maria evaluate the usefulness of her current cognitions and to develop new, more functional ways of thinking. Further attention to the gender and cultural components would likely shed light on Maria's ambivalence about changing her beliefs about these significant components of her identity.

Challenges of an Integrative Practice

Compared to using a single approach to therapy, integrative practice is more complex to execute competently. Determining which essential components of the approaches to include in clinical practice and how to include them can be challenging with little explicit direction or guidelines to inform these decisions. Using clinical judgment, including responsiveness to client characteristics and contexts, is essential when making such decisions (Lampropoulos, 2009). Further, it is a substantial undertaking to learn two or more approaches to therapy compared to a single approach.

Learning to effectively implement an integrated counseling practice requires intentionality and diligence. Considering assimilative integration and theoretical integration as the goals of integrated practice, Norcross and Halgin (2005) provided a six-step model for ideal training. In the first step, students are trained in fundamental communication and relationship-building skills. We often see this built into graduate-level curriculum as an introduction to counseling techniques or a counseling skills course. This information is typically presented in an atheoretical format, often consistent with the relationship components of the common factors approach. In the second step, trainees are exposed to various theories of counseling. This often occurs by many counseling theories being described in a single course. The exposure to various theories is followed by the third step in which trainees apply and compare the various theoretical models in depth and detail. This might be accomplished in an initial or advanced counseling theories course. Applying at least two theory-based treatments in clinical practice is the fourth step, often occurring in practicum or internship experiences. However, this might also occur when one is an early professional. Lampropoulos (2009) noted that training directors of programs accredited by the APA differed in that some believed that students should master two theories simultaneously, while others believed that one approach should be mastered before training to integrate additional approaches, with the former belief being endorsed by the majority of APA training directors surveyed. Norcross and Halgin (2005) suggested that after applying at least two approaches in clinical practice, a formal course in psychotherapy integration should follow (step five). However, in reality, this step might be difficult to accomplish as a stand-alone course depending on the training program. One study showed that 90% of APA-accredited programs included psychotherapy integration as part of one or more courses (Lampropoulos & Dixon, 2007); however, these were often part of advanced theories courses, as opposed to a course solely dedicated to integrative practice. Alternatives might include self-directed learning through books, webinars, or workshops focused on psychotherapy integration. Professional organizations such as the Society for the Exploration of Psychotherapy Integration (www.sepiweb.org) and peer-reviewed publications such as the *Journal of Psychotherapy Integration*, published by the APA, may also aid in clinicians striving to develop an integrated practice. In the sixth and final step, trainees practice the integration in a supervised clinical experience. If you are a student, this might be an internship or even an advanced internship. However, for professionals, this might mean consulting with an expert who reviews actual samples of your practice (e.g., video or audio recordings acquired with client permission for training purposes) or participating in a learning community that includes group supervision or coaching. In Norcross and Halgin's (2005) ideal model, the trainee is evaluated for mastery of each step prior to moving forward to the next step in the training module. In reality, such evaluation rarely occurs in this pure form (Lampropoulos & Dixon, 2007; Norcross et al., 2016); instead, engaging in honest self-evaluation of achieving the learning goals in each step prior to pursuing subsequent steps would behoove the trainee in the goal of an integrated practice.

Summary

Whether you are a student in the midst of training in a master's or doctoral degree program or you are a seasoned professional, with intentionality and persistence, you can create your own path in realizing your goals related to integrative practice. Given that this is a relatively newer area of research and practice, not all training opportunities are embedded in degree programs or explicitly encouraged in professional practice settings, but that does not mean that you cannot build and expand on these experiences to grow as an integrative clinician. As we explored in this chapter, integrative practice is becoming the expectation. Between assimilative integration, theoretical integration, and atheoretical integration, there are essentially infinite ways to execute integrative practice. The remainder of this book explores the integrative practice of MI and CBT.

References

American Psychological Association. (2013). Recognition of psychotherapy effectiveness. *Journal of Psychotherapy Integration, 23*(3), 320–330. doi:10.1037/a0033179

Corey, G. (2017). *Theory and practice of counseling and psychotherapy* (10th ed.). Boston, MA: Cengage Learning.

Corey, G. (2019). *The art of integrative counseling* (4th ed.). Alexandria, VA: American Counseling Association.

Holmes, J., & Bateman, A. (2002). *Integration in psychotherapy: Models and methods*. Oxford and New York, NY: Oxford University Press.

Jones-Smith, E. (2016). *Theories of counseling and psychotherapy: An integrative approach* (2nd ed.). Thousand Oaks, CA: Sage.

Lampropoulos, G. K. (2009). Issues in the development, practice, training, and research of integrative therapies. *Pragmatic Case Studies in Psychotherapy, 5*(1), doi:10.14713/pcsp.v5i1.960

Lampropoulos, G. K., & Dixon, D. N. (2007). Psychotherapy integration in internships and counseling psychology doctoral programs. *Journal of Psychotherapy Integration, 17*(2), 185–208. doi:10.1037/1053-0479.17.2.185

Laska, K. M., Gurman, A. S., & Wampold, B. E. (2014). Expanding the lens of evidence-based practice in psychotherapy: A common factors perspective. *Psychotherapy, 51*(4), 467–481. doi:10.1037/a0034332

Norcross, J. C., Goldfried, M. R., & Arigo, D. (2016). Integrative theories. In J. C. Norcross, G. R. VandenBos, D. K. Freedheim, & B. O. Olatunji (Eds.), *APA handbook of clinical psychology: Theory and research* (Vol. 2, pp. 303–332). Washington, DC: American Psychological Association. doi:10.1037/14773-011

Norcross, J. C., & Halgin, R. P. (2005). *Training in psychotherapy integration* (Vol. 1). Oxford University Press. doi:10.1093/med:psych/9780195165791.003.0021

Norcross, J. C., Krebs, P. M., & Prochaska, J. O. (2011). Stages of change. *Journal of Clinical Psychology, 67*(2), 143–154. doi:10.1002/jclp.20758

Norcross, J. C., & Lambert, M. J. (2011). Psychotherapy relationships that work II. *Psychotherapy, 48*(1), 4–8. doi:10.1037/a0022180

Norcross, J. C., & Wampold, B. E. (2011). What works for whom: Tailoring psychotherapy to the person. *Journal of Clinical Psychology, 67*(2), 127–132. doi:10.1002/jclp.20764

Prochaska, J. O., DiClemente, C. C., & Norcross, J. C. (1992). In search of how people change. *American Psychologist, 13.*

Rogers, C. (1961). *On becoming a person.* New York, NY: Houghton Mifflin Company.

Skovholt, T. M., & Trotter-Mathison, M. (2011). *The resilient practitioner* (2nd ed.). New York, NY: Routledge.

Wampold, B. E. (2015). How important are the common factors in psychotherapy? An update. *World Psychiatry, 14*(3), 270–277. doi:10.1002/wps.20238

CHAPTER 2

Motivational Interviewing

Motivational interviewing (MI) is an empirically supported counseling method with wide applicability. It can be used as a stand-alone intervention; however, the founders of MI, Miller and Rollnick (2009, 2013), clearly noted that MI is not a panacea, and they encouraged its practice with other treatment methods. MI does not provide a theory of change, but rather it is a style of counseling that can be integrated with theoretical approaches. The foundations of MI are rooted in humanistic, Rogerian concepts, and yet MI is unique in that it offers counselors methods to conceptualize and to address discord in the counseling relationship (known to many as "resistance") and client ambivalence. MI offers explicit strategies to engage clients who might not be interested in talking with a counselor and to address low levels of motivation, including uncertainty or hesitancy about change or about engaging in treatment. The MI approach encompasses specific skills clinicians use to address situations where they might otherwise throw up their hands and exclaim, "Well, there's nothing I can do; the client is just not ready!" In this chapter, we learn about the foundational components of MI, including its spirit, core skills, and processes. Further explanations and examples of how MI can be used to address client ambivalence about change and to engage clients who are not motivated to partake in counseling or to pursue change are provided throughout this text. This chapter also includes information about learning to practice MI.

A Brief History of MI

William Miller initially developed MI in his work with clients who experienced problematic drinking. The first published description of MI (Miller, 1983) introduced a counseling method that contrasted the authoritarian approach that was common in substance use counseling at that time, which relied heavily on confrontation and resulted in power struggles within the therapeutic relationship (Miller, 2008). Miller partnered with Steve Rollnick to publish the first book on MI in 1991. This text remained focused on the use of MI to address substance use and addictive disorders. Over the next decade, in addition to gaining popularity in addressing substance use, MI was applied more broadly, such as to treatment for comorbid disorders, to medical and public health settings, and to group therapy.

18   The Foundations

Further, MI was applied to work with specific populations, including adolescents and young adults, people in the criminal justice system, and couples (Miller & Rollnick, 2002). Hundreds of articles were published on various applications of MI during the 2000s. Advances from such research and literature were used to inform Miller and Rollnick's emendations of MI for their third edition of the MI book (Miller & Rollnick, 2013), which applied MI to behavior change in general. This edition included slight revisions to the spirit of MI, reconceptualized the MI principles, and added four distinct yet overlapping processes. This edition also brought attention to training considerations for individuals or agencies that wish to adopt MI into practice.

Since its origination in 1983, MI has been found to be an effective, versatile, and evolving counseling approach. In this chapter, I describe MI largely from Miller and Rollnick's (2013) third edition of the MI text as well as from recent research and seminal studies with the goal of providing the reader with a sound understanding of the basics of MI and the value of this approach in nurturing change. This basic understanding will aide in understanding the remainder of the book in which MI is integrated with CBT.

What Is Motivational Interviewing?

It is common for people who are unfamiliar with MI to hear the terms "motivational" and "interviewing" and assume that this approach requires the practitioner to act as motivational speaker or emphatic coach (i.e., motivational) and to ask lots of questions (i.e., interviewing). However, these misconceptions are far from the actual practice of MI. Instead, the MI practitioner acts as a guide to the client— one who neither pushes nor pulls the client along but who rather walks beside the client on his or her journey of personal change. Miller and Rollnick (2013) defined MI as follows:

> A collaborative, goal-oriented style of communication with particular attention to the language of change. It is designed to strengthen personal motivation and commitment to a specific goal by eliciting and exploring the person's own reasons for change within an atmosphere of acceptance and compassion.
> (p. 29)

Let us pause and dissect this definition a bit. MI is *collaborative* in that it requires a partnership between the client and counselor, with both parties bringing assets to the relationship. Although the professional has a good deal of knowledge and experience with helping others, truly no one knows more about the client's problem or his or her potential solutions than the client him/herself. MI is a *style of communication* in that it permeates how the practitioner interacts with the client. It is not a technique a counselor pulls out of a toolbox and then dismisses. Rather, it is a foundational "way of being" with clients. It is *goal-oriented* in that the client and counselor focus their joint attention on specific, desired outcomes that they have discussed and agreed upon. In using MI, the counselor is trained to listen for and hone in on the *language of change* or client statements that are in favor of change or against the status quo (i.e., change talk). Counselors using MI understand that *clients have their own reasons for change*. Therefore, they do not attempt to install motivation in clients or to provide reasons for clients to change, but rather MI counselors elicit, reinforce, and strengthen clients' personal motivations for change. Counselors using MI also understand that clients have reasons why they have not yet changed or factors that are causing them to be hesitant to change, and they do not pathologize clients when they express their desire, reason, or need for the status quo (i.e., sustain talk). Finally, in order to execute MI, counselors must create *an atmosphere of acceptance and compassion*. In such environments, clients are more likely to trust and feel understood, and therefore, they are more willing to explore and verbalize the various facets of their change process. Without this environment, clients can remain cautious or disengaged, inhibiting therapeutic conversations about change.

MI is practiced with a humanistic spirit that involves developing a partnership with clients, accepting where clients are in their unique process of change, exercising compassion, and evoking clients' perspectives, strengths, and motivations. With the spirit as an essential foundation, MI provides four overlapping and recursive processes (engaging, focusing, evoking, and planning). In each of these processes, the counselor employs the core skills of MI, including open questions, reflections, paraphrases, affirmations, summarizations (known as OARS), and provides information with permission. Each of these essential components of MI is discussed in further depth in this chapter, including MI's conceptualizations and methods to explore and resolve client ambivalence about change and to diminish relationship discord.

The Spirit of MI

MI contains an indispensable humanistic spirit that is essential to its practice. The spirit is the foundation on which the core skills of MI are employed in each of the four processes (further described later in this chapter). The MI spirit involves four components: partnership, acceptance, compassion, and evocation (Miller & Rollnick, 2013). Within the client-counselor partnership, collaboration is emphasized in that the counselor is not doing anything "to" the client, but rather he or she is working "with" the client. The counselor values the knowledge and experience the client brings to the therapeutic alliance, and together the client and counselor work toward mutually determined goals. In this way, the counselor avoids the expert role as the client is considered the "expert" on his or her own life, and the counselor assumes the role of a guide in the client's journey of change (Miller & Rollnick, 2013).

Acceptance, the second component of the MI spirit, is an extension of Rogers's (1957) unconditional positive regard. The counselor accepts the client as a human being who is in his or her unique process of change, including the client's current degree of readiness (or lack thereof) to change. Miller and Rollnick (2013) further deconstructed acceptance into the four following constructs: absolute worth, accurate empathy, autonomy, and affirmation. Concerning absolute worth, counselors who practice MI recognize the inherent worth and potential of every human being. They avoid defining or labeling clients by their behaviors, disorders, or histories. Further, absolute worth acknowledges each client's potential to grow and change and the counselor's responsibility to create a therapeutic environment to encourage client growth.

In the second component of acceptance, the practice of MI heavily emphasizes counselors expressing accurate empathy (Miller & Rollnick, 2013), another of Rogers's (1957) critical conditions for change. Accurate empathy requires the counselor to see the world through the eyes of the client, including within the context of the client's experiences, traumas, family, upbringing, values, goals, beliefs, and inherent components of diversity, such as race, ethnicity, gender identity, sex, religion, sexual identity, education, income, ability, and so on. After striving to understand the perspectives of the client, the counselor then offers empathic statements, such as paraphrases or reflections, that express a sincere understanding of the client's perspective.

Concerning autonomy, the third component of acceptance, counselors who use MI respect and support clients' freedom to make choices and to govern their own lives, including making their own decisions about change (e.g., whether to change and if so how to go about doing it). Counselors using MI avoid the notion of "making" clients change or "getting them" to engage in therapeutic activities. Instead, counselors who use MI support client autonomy by emphasizing clients' personal choice and control in their unique process of change. The fourth and final component of acceptance within the MI spirit is affirmation. Counselors who use MI recognize and highlight clients' strengths, positive attributes, and efforts. They do not search for what is wrong, and they refrain from pathologizing clients. Instead, the MI counselor looks for what the client is doing well, his or her positive attributes, and efforts the client is making and then offers the client statements of affirmation to highlight and reinforce these strengths and positive efforts (affirmation is also a core skill of MI, which is further described later in this chapter).

In addition to partnership and acceptance, compassion and evocation round out the MI spirit. Compassion emphasizes that the counselor acts in the best interest of the client with a sincere desire to help. Counselors using MI refrain from prioritizing their personal self-interest ahead of client welfare. In regard to evocation, MI counselors offer clients an opportunity to recognize and cultivate their own personal motivations for change, and they elicit clients' ideas about how to implement the change. Throughout the processes of MI, the counselor elicits information from the client—information about the problem and potential solutions from the client's perspective and information about the client's goals, values, strengths, and struggles. In this way, the counselor seeks to understand and empathize with the client's experiences related to the presenting issues, explore the client's ambivalence about change, and evoke the client's personal motivations to change. The MI counselor avoids "installing" motivation from an outside perspective, and he or she honors and respects that the client has a good deal of knowledge, wisdom, and experience in addition to his or her own values and goals from which motivation is often derived. When sufficient motivation appears to be present, counselors elicit the client's ideas about how he or she might engage in the identified behavior change and guide the client in developing *the client's* plan for change. The counselor honors the client's knowledge and experience related to the change and acknowledges that the client likely knows best which plan will work, or what might not work, and what he or she is willing to try as he or she pursues change. Using evocation encourages the counselor to avoid prescribing a plan to pursue change. For instance, consider a client who is newly sober and who you believe might benefit from attending an Alcoholics Anonymous (AA) or other mutual help group meeting. In a directive approach, the counselor risks prescribing a plan without knowledge of the client's history or experiences with AA meetings. Using MI, instead of telling a client she should attend an AA meeting, a counselor might ask, "What do you think would be helpful for you to do in between sessions to help you in your sobriety, especially related to finding sober social support?" By focusing on evocation, the counselor remains grounded in the client's perspective and is more likely to help the client develop a plan that she will act on because it is indeed *her* plan.

Illustrating the humanistic nature of this approach, the founders of MI have emphasized the importance of its spirit over techniques (Miller & Rollnick, 2013). The components of MI described next in this chapter must be used with the presence of the MI spirit in order for it to be called MI. Without the presence of the spirit, it is not MI.

The Core Skills of MI

The practice of MI includes five core skills. Four of these skills are known by the acronym OARS, including (a) **O**pen questions, (b) statements of **A**ffirmation, (c) **R**eflections/paraphrases, and (d) **S**ummarizations. The fifth skill involves providing information with the client's permission (Miller & Rollnick, 2013). Table 2.1 briefly describes each of these skills, along with examples of each. By nature of MI's client-responsive approach, there is no prescribed way of using these skills. Rather, the art of MI involves making decisions in the moment to implement these skills in a strategic way for the benefit of the client.

Counselors practicing MI use open questions to invite the client to share with them, including opening the door for client exploration of his or her own knowledge, values, goals, and ideas about how to pursue change. Open questions often begin with "how," "what," or "tell me about." Using open questions helps set the tone for the conversation by inviting clients to share openly and sending the implicit message of "I want to hear what you have to say." Ideally, the client talks more than the counselor in MI practice. In contrast, closed questions result in single word responses. These questions commonly begin with "have/had/has," "do/did/does," "could/would," "is/are," and "when." In MI, closed questions are used sparingly and only when the counselor truly intends to receive a brief and specific response from the client. As illustrated in Practice Box 2.1, using several closed questions in a row can have a negative effect on the counseling relationship as

Table 2.1 Core Skills of MI

Core Skill	Purpose and Benefits	Opposite of	Examples
Open questions	• Invites the client to consider his/her perspective and share it • Sets the tone for the client talking more than the counselor	• Closed questions • Limiting client's responses • Setting the tone of an interrogation • The question-answer trap	• "What would you like to get out of our time here together?" • "Tell me more about . . ." • "What have you tried?" • "How did that work out for you?"
Affirmations	• Identifies strengths • Highlights what is going well • Aids in movement away from the problem and toward positive alternatives	• Searching for what is wrong with people or looking for deficits • Keeping clients stuck in the problem • "One-size-fits-all" affirmations must be genuine and unique to that client	• "Even with some setbacks, you are proving to persevere through this." • "Your work ethic is shining through." • "You're incredibly resourceful and resilient."
Reflections (paraphrases)	• Expresses empathy • Helps the client feel heard and understood • Clients hear themselves through the counselor—she or he is, in essence, holding a mirror for clients to "see" themselves • Encourages the client to think and talk further	• A question—the counselor's voice must go down to signify a statement • Making suggestions • Judgments • Parroting—the counselor must put the statement in her or his own words instead of simply repeating what the client said	• "You are really fed up with the way things have been going for you." • "You feel like a different person when you're on the medication." • "You believe there is nothing wrong with what you're doing, and yet the judge seems to be telling you otherwise."

(Continued)

Table 2.1 (Continued)

Core Skill	Purpose and Benefits	Opposite of	Examples
	• Reinforces and strengthens client's ideas in favor of change	• Pushing the client toward change	• "You know you're capable of changing, and it would mean a lot to your kids if you did kick this habit."
Summaries	• Collects information to show evidence of good listening and to ensure that the counselor has an accurate understanding • Links current dialogue with a previous conversation • Transitions between topics	• Counselor's judgments or opinions • Not listening well	• "You've tried a number of things that haven't seemed to work to help you manage your anxiety: you found you don't like taking medications, and reading or watching TV to take your mind off things just isn't working anymore. You're looking for other options and hoping that counseling might work for you."
Providing information with permission	• Honors what the client already knows • Respects client autonomy by asking for permission prior to giving information	• Providing the client with information she or he already has • Giving unsolicited advice • Lecturing the client	• "What are your thoughts about the importance of staying on your medication as the doctor prescribed it for you?" *(elicit)*

(Continued)

24 The Foundations

Table 2.1 (Continued)

Core Skill	Purpose and Benefits	Opposite of	Examples
	• Provides information that is new and relevant to the client • The client considers how she or he can apply the information		• "Would you mind if I shared some information I have about medication compliance?" *(ask for permission, then provide the information)* • "With the information I've just shared with you, what do you think about the importance of medication compliance now?" *(elicit)*

well as limit the information received from clients. Asking more than two or three questions sequentially is avoided in MI to refrain from imposing an interrogation feel to the conversation. Instead, reflections are the dominant skill in MI practice, with competent practice involving using twice as many reflections as questions in our dialogue with clients.

Affirmations are a core skill of MI as well as part of the MI spirit. This skill involves highlighting specific observations of the client's strengths, positive attributes, and her or his efforts. However, affirmations are not mere compliments (i.e., "I like your shirt"). Instead, they are unique to the particular individual and based on the counselor's attentiveness to and familiarity with the client. Statements of affirmation are sincere expressions used to help empower clients to strengthen existing efforts and capacities to move toward their goals. Examples include, "Your determination to get a job and to stay out of jail is unwavering." "In these six weeks of treatment, you have put in tremendous effort," or "Despite there not being enough time or money to get everything you need to do done, you're certainly making the best effort you can." In MI, affirmations are used sporadically and in culturally appropriate ways so that clients' strengths and positive attributes are received as sincere, believable statements without sarcasm or hyperbole.

> ***Practice Box 2.1   Question-and-Answer Trap***
>
> We rarely intend to ask multiple closed questions in a row, but many clinicians find themselves falling into a question-answer trap. This is an exercise you can do with a partner to illustrate the challenge created by using serial closed questions:
>
> *Using only closed questions, find out what your partner ate for dinner last night.*
>
> Many people find this exercise to be frustrating or even silly. It starts to feel like you are playing the game 20 questions. Of course, we would never intentionally ask our clients 20 closed questions when one open question would elicit a fruitful response (e.g., "What did you eat for dinner last night?"). However, this exercise highlights the importance of catching ourselves if we fall into MI-inconsistent behavior and begin asking the client multiple, sequential, closed-ended questions (e.g., "Have you tried this?" "Did you talk to ____?" "Have you called X?"). By falling into the question-answer trap, you are likely doing much more work than your client, which can be frustrating and perpetuate discord in the counseling relationship. Further, when the Q&A trap is occurring, the client is not provided opportunities to be thoughtful and to share his or her ideas or perspectives. Instead, he or she can just sit back and wait for the counselor to ask the next question. Needless to say, this is not the dynamic we wish to set or maintain in counseling. Therefore, we limit our use of closed questions when practicing MI. Further, we avoid asking three or more (open or closed) questions in a row.

In MI, the term "reflection" encompasses paraphrases, reflections of emotion, and reflections of meaning. Reflections are the skills used most frequently in MI, as they are considered the key to empathy and good listening, which is fundamental to MI. Further, reflections allow clients to hear themselves through the counselor, as if the counselor is holding a mirror up for the client to see him/herself. This encourages the client to think more deeply about the content and to continue the dialogue. The recommendation is to use twice as many reflections compared to questions for proficient practice and a one-to-one ratio of reflections-to-questions for beginning practice. Various types of reflections, including simple, complex, double-sided, and amplified, are strategically used in each of the four processes of MI (see Miller & Rollnick, 2002, 2013; Rosengren, 2018 for more detailed descriptions of the types of reflections used in MI). When we deliver reflections, they must not be confused with questions—your voice tone goes down with a reflection compared to going up when delivering a question. For instance, say aloud, "You're angry about that?" With the question mark, your voice tone likely went up. Now try, "You're angry about that." With the period, your voice tone should go down. Reflections are statements, not questions, and therefore, our voice tone must go down when delivering reflections. Reflections are also not parroting or saying the exact same words the client said. Instead, we might retain key words that the client used, but we largely put what he or she said into our own words and give it back to the client in a reflection for him or her to consider further.

A typical concern I hear from trainees who are first learning or beginning to increase their use of reflections in practice is, "What if I am wrong?" First, we form reflections with content we gathered from listening to the client and that we have a pretty good hunch is true. If you do not have a good hunch, then you may need to ask a question first and then reflect the client's response to your question. After all, we are aiming to express *accurate* empathy. Asking yourself the questions in Practice Box 2.2 might initially aid in developing reflections. Second, if you do deliver an inaccurate reflection, the client will most often correct you. By correcting you, the client is further considering and verbalizing his or her perspective, and you are still showing that you are trying to understand by listening to the correction, modifying your understanding, and then delivering a more accurate reflection that provides evidence of your listening and openness to revising your initial (mis)understanding. Ultimately, our task is to gain an understanding of the client's perspective and demonstrate our understanding of that in our own words in a reflection back to the client.

Summaries are used in MI to recap what has occurred in all or a part of the conversation. By using a summary, counselors communicate interest and understanding in addition to calling attention to important elements of the discussion. Counselors should selectively decide what to include in the summary so that it is succinct and organized. Summaries are used with three different purposes in MI: (a) gathering information to present it back to the client, such as at the end of a session (collecting summary); (b) linking an idea shared in the current conversation with an idea shared previously (linking summary); and (c) shifting attention from conversation that appears to be unproductive or exhausted (transitional summary).

In addition to OARS, the fifth core skill of MI is providing information with permission. It is common for helping professionals to provide information to clients about various topics relevant to the client's concern. For example, counselors might wish to share information about strategies to manage anxiety, what to expect at a 12-step meeting, or how to express a concern to a work supervisor using effective communication. To provide such information, counselors who use MI employ the strategy known as elicit-provide-elicit (EPE) to provide information relevant to the client's concern without imposing unwanted information or diminishing client engagement. Using EPE, the counselor first elicits what the client already knows about the topic. For example, a counselor might ask a client who is struggling with anxiety, "In your experience, what has helped you to manage the anxiety?" or, "What have you already tried?" Next, the *counselor asks for the client's permission* to provide the information that builds on what the client shared with him or her. Asking for the client's permission is a small step that honors the client's autonomy to choose whether he or she wants to receive additional information. For example, the counselor might say, "I have some ideas about what might be helpful based on what I've seen work for other clients with similar concerns.

> **Practice Box 2.2   Practicing Reflections**
>
> Reflective listening can be a challenging skill to learn and to execute well. When I was first gaining competency in MI, I had difficulty not asking questions. I can still remember my MI trainer pausing my recorded counseling session and saying, "Melanie, you asked the client another question. How could you turn that into a reflection?" Through this training, I (slowly) became accustomed to using reflections as my first response to clients. As a general guideline, I learned to first reflect and then, if needed, ask a question. I learned to gauge the client's response to see if my reflection was accurate and if it was not to listen further to get a more accurate understanding. Today (after more than a decade of practice), it has simply become second nature. But that indeed took some intentional effort.
>
> As reflective listening is in essence good communication skills, you can practice this in your everyday conversations, as well as in professional helping conversations. Your conversations with clients will likely benefit from intentional reflective listening, as will your conversations with friends, family members, and colleagues. We can also practice by listening to lyrics of a song and reflecting the content, emotion, and meanings we hear. In order to form and deliver accurate reflections, we must actually listen to what the other person is saying. Then we can ask ourselves the following questions to help us form reflective statements:
>
> - Simple reflections can be formed by asking, "What is the essence of what he/she said?"
> - Reflections of emotion can be formed by asking, "How is he/she feeling about this?"
> - Reflections of meaning, or complex reflections, can be formed by asking, "What does he/she mean by this?"
> - Double-sided reflections can be formed by asking the following when developing discrepancies: "What are the two sides of her ambivalence?" or "What are the two things that seem to conflict?"
>
> Examples of reflections are provided in Table 2.1 in this chapter and throughout the dialogue in the following text, and there is a specific opportunity for skill development in Chapter 7. I encourage you to practice forming and delivering reflections to help develop or strengthen this skill, as it is essential to MI and therefore to an integration of MI and CBT.

Would you be interested in hearing about them?" Upon an affirmative response, the counselor would provide the information (e.g., information about mindfulness, relaxation exercises, identifying automatic thoughts). Finally, the counselor then elicits what the client thinks about or how the client might use the information provided; for instance, "What do you think about these strategies?" or, "How do you think these strategies might work for you?" Providing information is a common therapeutic activity, and the applications of EPE are broad. In addition to presenting information about coping skills or interventions, other common uses include providing information about various treatment options, resources, social services, medication information, assessment feedback, risks associated with specific behaviors, or information about policies.

The Method of MI

While the spirit and core skills of MI are the essential nuts and bolts of its practice, the method of MI provides the practitioner with four therapeutic processes to facilitate client change: engaging, focusing, evoking, and planning (Miller & Rollnick, 2013). The processes are sequential, yet they build on each other so that the preceding process must remain as a foundation for the subsequent processes to be effective. Further, phases are often revisited depending on the needs of the client or the counseling relationship. For instance, if a client who was once engaged in the therapeutic process now appears disengaged, the counselor would return to the engaging process, or if the client describes a new concern after three sessions together, the counselor would return to the focusing process. Each of these processes is briefly described in this section. Miller and Rollnick (2013) offer a full description.

Engaging, the first process of MI, involves establishing an effective therapeutic alliance. For some clients, this occurs easily and with little time; however, for others, practitioners must work to diminish any relationship discord (formerly known as "resistance") that might inherently be present in the counseling relationship. For example, consider an adolescent client who was told she must attend counseling by her parent after receiving a notice from the school that the client engaged in self-injurious behaviors or a client who comes for court-mandated substance use assessment despite claiming he does not use substances and that he was "set up." When clients feel forced to attend counseling or have had negative experiences with helping professionals in the past, practitioners might have to work harder to overcome preexisting barriers to engage clients in conversation in the therapeutic process. MI is based on the premise that the client's level of engagement is influenced by counselors' responses to the client. In other words, our responses to these barriers can increase or decrease client engagement. Using the MI spirit as the foundation, the MI counselor employs the core skills of MI in intentional ways to reduce any discord that exists and to establish an effective working relationship. Common strategies include reflective listening, "rolling with resistance," offering affirmations, and emphasizing client autonomy.

In the second phase of MI, *focusing*, the client and counselor establish a clear direction for their work together. In some cases, it might be easy for the counselor to assume what "should" be the focus of treatment. Considering the case of the adolescent, upon talking with the parent and hearing about the concern from the school administrators, the counselor could easily assume that self-injury behaviors should be the focus of treatment. However, the process of focusing in MI requires the counselor to partner with the client to collaboratively discuss and determine the focus of treatment. In using MI, the counselor will hear the concerns of the parent and school and then discuss with the client, "What do you think is important to discuss in counseling?" If there is a conflict between agendas (e.g., that of the parent and that of the client), the counselor can openly discuss the conflict with the client, and together they can negotiate the focus of treatment to continue to foster the client's engagement as well as include the focus of any stakeholders (e.g., address both self-injury behavior and the client's concerns). Without having this collaborative conversation about the focus of treatment, the counselor risks client disengagement and may lose the sense of partnership due to an imposed goal on the client. Further, without completing the focusing process of MI, the counselor may be missing important information about the client's concerns in the case that the counselor acts solely on the concerns of the stakeholder (e.g., the client is being bullied, which is leading to her cutting behaviors).

After an effective therapeutic relationship and focus for counseling are established, the counselor proceeds to the *evoking* process. While evoking, the counselor aims to assist the client in exploring and resolving his or her ambivalence about change and to enhance the client's readiness to change. To do so, the MI practitioner evokes *the client's* arguments in favor of change and against the status quo—also known as change talk—and guides the client in further developing and strengthening these arguments based on the client's personal beliefs, values, and goals. Specific strategies used in the evoking process include asking evocative questions (e.g., "How do you want your life to be different one year from now?" "What do you think you might be able to change?" "What do you think needs to change?"), using the importance ruler (e.g., "On a scale of 0 to 10, how important is it to you to ____? Why a ___ and not a 0?"), looking forward questions (e.g., "If you decide to continue on this path and not make any changes, what do you think might happen?"), looking back questions (e.g., "Tell me about a time when you didn't have these problems. What was different about that time?"), and exploring personal values and goals (e.g., "What is most important to you in your life?" "What do you hope to accomplish?"). Although client change talk is elicited by the counselor, counselors can also expect to hear client statements arguing against change (sustain talk), as change talk and sustain talk together constitute ambivalence. Sustain talk is understood by the counselor as normal (not pathological), and the counselor seeks to empathize with these counter-change arguments. Change talk is typically followed by the use of OARS to further explore and develop the client's motivations for change.

In the final process of MI, *planning*, the counselor and client collaboratively develop a plan for change. This plan includes actions to be taken by the client and can include engagement in a specific type of treatment (e.g., CBT, group counseling). The counselor continues to use evocation and collaboration in the planning process to ensure that a plan is developed that the client is capable of and motivated to implement.

Research Support

MI has been the subject of extensive outcome research. It is considered an evidence-based practice, especially in the treatment of substance use disorders. Its applications have been investigated beyond substance use to a wide variety of mental and behavioral health issues, as well as health care and public health. To illustrate, at the time of this writing a list of systematic and meta-analyses of research on MI is provided on the MI website (www.motivationalinterviewing.org/sites/default/files/mi_research_reviews_2017.pdf). This list includes more than 100 systematic and meta-analyses published as of 2017. About one-quarter of these were in the realm of substance use and addictive behaviors. Four were specific to mental illness (i.e., schizophrenia, dual diagnosis), while others focused on eating disorders, education, medication compliance, offenders, and a variety of health-care issues (e.g., diabetes, HIV/AIDS, smoking cessation, physical activity). Although findings of this breadth of meta-analyses vary, average effect sizes range from small to medium. Specific meta-analyses and research studies have shown MI to have efficacy across diverse populations, symptoms, and behaviors, including chronic mental disorders management, treatment adherence, problem gambling, smoking cessation, generalized anxiety disorder, co-occurring disorders, and various health issues (Barrowclough et al., 2010; Burke, Arkowitz, & Menchola, 2003; Cleary, Hunt, Matheson, & Walter, 2009; Hettema, Steele, & Miller, 2005; Lundahl, Kunz, Brownell, Tollefson, & Burke, 2010; Westra, Arkowitz, & Dozois, 2009).

Although MI has demonstrated usefulness and efficacy as a stand-alone approach, Miller and Rollnick have been clear that MI is not a panacea, and they have encouraged its use with other treatments (Miller & Rollnick, 2009, 2013). Arkowitz and Burke (2008) conceptualized MI as "an integrative framework into which almost any therapy methods or theories can be incorporated" (p. 149). When MI is used with another approach (e.g., CBT), the overall effects have been characterized as synergistic (i.e., Arkowitz & Westra, 2004; Burke, Dunn, Atkins, & Phelps, 2004; Flynn, 2011). The purpose of this text is to illustrate how MI and CBT can be used in an integrative fashion to promote synergistic outcomes.

Learning to Practice MI

Although MI might appear to be simple in its concepts and approach, MI is complex and can be difficult to learn and practice with fidelity (Hall, Staiger, Simpson, Best, & Lubman, 2016; Miller & Mount, 2001). Learning MI often requires in-depth training, including practice feedback (Hall et al., 2016; Miller & Mount, 2001; Miller, Yahne, Moyers, Martinez, & Pirritano, 2004; Schwalbe, Oh, & Zweben, 2014). MI trainings take place in face-to-face workshops or courses, as well as in online formats. According to the Motivational Interviewing Network of Trainers (MINT; www.motivationalinterviewing.org), introductory workshops include two to three days of training during which the trainee learns about MI and how to practice it. In order to achieve competency, additional training is often necessary, including follow-up consultation or supervision or through an advanced training, which can range between two to three days.

Competency benchmarks are necessary to assess for fidelity of practice (Hall et al., 2016), and several instruments have been developed and used to evaluate trainees' practice, including the *Motivational Interviewing Treatment Integrity* manual (*MITI* 4.2.1; Moyers, Manuel, & Ernst, 2015) and the *Manual for the Motivational Interviewing Skill Code* (*MISC*; Miller, Moyers, Ernst, & Amrhein, 2008). It is common for trainees to achieve MI competency after completing a training; however, these gains are often not maintained without ongoing consultation or supervision focused on MI practice. From their meta-analysis of studies focused on MI training, Schwalbe et al. (2014) found that three to four consultation sessions over a six-month period were largely sufficient for trainees to sustain MI skills learned in the initial training. They also noted that attrition in follow-up consultation or supervision is a barrier to trainees maintaining their MI skills.

Summary

MI is a humanistic, evidence-based approach with wide applicability. The spirit, core skills, and processes are essential to its practice. Despite the positive impact MI alone can have, especially in regard to diminishing discord and addressing ambivalence, counselors who practice MI are not expected to abandon prior methods or to only use MI. Instead, they are encouraged to incorporate MI into existing practices or other theoretical approaches. Overall effects of MI and another approach (e.g., CBT) have been characterized as synergistic (Miller & Rose, 2009). Chapter 4 in this text provides an introduction to MI+CBT integration, and Section II provides descriptions of various methods to integrate MI and CBT.

Resource Box 2.1 Resources to Learn More about MI

MI website: www.motivationalinterviewing.org

Arkowitz, H., Westra, H. A., Miller, W. R., & Rollnick, S. (2015). *Motivational interviewing in the treatment of psychological problems* (2nd ed.). New York, NY: Guilford Press.

Herman, K. C., Reinke, W. M., Frey, A. J., & Shepard, S. A. (2014). *Motivational interviewing in schools: Strategies for engaging parents, teachers, and students.* New York, NY: Springer Publishing.

Hohman, M. (2012). *Motivational interviewing in social work practice.* New York, NY: Guilford Press.

Miller, W., & Rollnick, S. (2013). *Motivational interviewing: Helping people change* (3rd ed.). New York, NY: Guilford Press.

Murphy, C. M., & Maiuro, R. D. (2009). *Motivational interviewing and stages of change in intimate partner violence.* New York, NY: Springer Publishing Company.

Naar-King, S., & Suarez, M. (2011). *Motivational interviewing with adolescents and young adults*. New York, NY: Guilford Press.

Rosengren, D. B. (2018). *Building motivational interviewing skills: A practitioner workbook* (2nd ed). New York, NY: Guilford Press.

Stinson, J. D., & Clark, M. D. (2017). *Motivational interviewing with offenders*. New York, NY: Guilford Press.

Wagner, C. C., & Ingersoll, K. S. (2012). *Motivational interviewing in groups*. New York, NY: Guilford Press.

References

Arkowitz, H., & Burke, B. L. (2008). MI as a framework for the treatment of depression. In H. Arkowitz, H. A. Westra, W. R. Miller, & S. Rollnick (Eds.), *Motivational interviewing in the treatment of psychological problems* (pp. 145–172). New York, NY: Guilford Press.

Arkowitz, H., & Westra, H. A. (2004). Integrating motivational interviewing and cognitive behavioral therapy in the treatment of depression and anxiety. *Journal of Cognitive Psychotherapy, 18*, 337–350. doi:10.1891/jcop.18.4.337.63998

Barrowclough, C., Haddock, G., Wykes, T., Beardmore, R., Conrod, P., Craig, T., . . . Tarrier, N. (2010). Integrated motivational interviewing and cognitive behavioral therapy for people with psychosis and comorbid substance misuse: Randomised controlled trial. *British Medical Journal, 341*(3), 1–12. doi:10.1136/bmj.c6325

Burke, B. L., Arkowitz, H., & Menchola, M. (2003). The efficacy of motivational interviewing: A meta-analysis of controlled clinical trials. *Journal of Consulting and Clinical Psychology, 71*(5), 843–861. https://doi.org/10.1037/0022-006X.71.5.843

Burke, B. L., Dunn, C. W., Atkins, D. C., & Phelps, J. S. (2004). The emerging evidence base for motivational interviewing: A meta-analytic and qualitative inquiry. *Journal of Cognitive Psychotherapy: An International Quarterly, 18*, 309–322.

Cleary, M., Hunt, G. E., Matheson, S., & Walter, G. (2009). Psychosocial treatments for people with co-occurring severe mental illness and substance misuse: Systematic review. *Journal of Advanced Nursing, 65*(2), 238–258. https://doi.org/10.1111/j.1365-2648.2008.04879.x

Flynn, H. A. (2011). Setting the stage for the integration of motivational interviewing with cognitive behavioral therapy in the treatment of depression. *Cognitive and Behavioral Practice, 18*, 46–54. doi:10.1016/j.cbpra.2009.09.006

Hall, K., Staiger, P. K., Simpson, A., Best, D., & Lubman, D. I. (2016). After 30 years of dissemination, have we achieved sustained practice change in motivational interviewing? *Addiction, 111*, 1144–1150. doi:10.1111/add.13014

Hettema, J., Steele, J., & Miller, W. R. (2005). Motivational interviewing. *Annual Review of Clinical Psychology, 1*, 91–111. doi:10.1037/a0016830

Lundahl, B. W., Kunz, C., Brownell, C., Tollefson, D., & Burke, B. L. (2010). A meta-analysis of motivational interviewing: Twenty-five years of empirical studies. *Research on Social Work Practice, 20*, 137–159. doi:10.1177/1049731509347850

Miller, W. R. (1983). Motivational interviewing with problem drinkers. *Behavioural Psychotherapy, 11*, 147–172. doi:10.1017/S0141347300006583

Miller, W. R. (2008). The first description of motivational interviewing. *MINT Bulletin, 14*, 1–38.

Miller, W. R., & Mount, K. A. (2001). A small study of training in motivational interviewing: Does one workshop change clinician and client behavior? *Behavioural and Cognitive Psychotherapy, 29,* 457–471.

Miller, W. R., Moyers, T. B., Ernst, D., & Amrhein, P. (2008). *Manual for the motivational interviewing skill code 2.1.* Retrieved from https://casaa.unm.edu/download/misc.pdf

Miller, W. R., & Rollnick, S. (2002). *Motivational interviewing: Preparing people for change* (2nd ed.). New York, NY: Guilford Press.

Miller, W. R., & Rollnick, S. (2009). Ten things that motivational interviewing is not. *Behavioural and Cognitive Psychotherapy, 37,* 129–140. doi:10.1017/S1352465809005128

Miller, W. R., & Rollnick, S. (2013). *Motivational interviewing: Helping people change* (3rd ed.). New York, NY: Guilford Press.

Miller, W. R., & Rose, G. S. (2009). Toward a theory of motivational interviewing. *American Psychologist, 64,* 527–537. doi:10.1037/a0016830

Miller, W. R., Yahne, C. E., Moyers, T. B., Martinez, J., & Pirritano, M. (2004). A randomized trial of methods to help clinicians learn motivational interviewing. *Journal of Clinical and Consulting Psychology, 72,* 1050–1062.

Moyers, T. B., Manuel, J. K., & Ernst, D. (2015). *Motivational interviewing treatment integrity 4.2.1.* Retrieved from https://casaa.unm.edu/download/miti4_2.pdf

Rogers, C. R. (1957). The necessary and sufficient conditions of therapeutic personality change. *Journal of Consulting Psychology, 21,* 95–103.

Rosengren, D. B. (2018). *Building motivational interviewing skills: A practitioner workbook* (2nd ed.). New York, NY: Guilford Press.

Schwalbe, C. S., Oh, H. Y., & Zweben, A. (2014). Sustaining motivational interviewing: A meta-analysis of training studies. *Addiction, 109,* 1287–1294. doi:10.1111/add.12558

Westra, H. A., Arkowitz, H., & Dozois, D. J. A. (2009). Adding a motivational interviewing pretreatment to cognitive behavioral therapy for generalized anxiety disorder: A preliminary randomized controlled trial. *Journal of Anxiety Disorders, 23*(8), 1106–1117. doi:10.1016/j.janxdis.2009.07.014

CHAPTER 3

Cognitive Behavior Therapy

CBT encompasses a wide range of practices that incorporate both cognitive and behavioral conceptualizations and interventions with the goals of cognitive and behavioral change (Dozois, Dobson, & Rnic, 2019). CBT approaches are highly popular and known for having an extensive research base (Dobson, McEpplan, & Dobson, 2019). The structure and interventions common in CBT allow for these approaches to be disseminated through manualized protocols and for client outcomes to be evaluated using randomized controlled trials. In this chapter, we take a brief look at the history of CBT and then learn about common components, conceptualizations, and interventions included in these approaches. This information will help inform the remainder of the book in which we explore integrating CBT with MI in clinical practice. Suggestions for learning more about CBT are provided at the end of the chapter in Resource Box 3.1.

A Brief History of CBT

The origins of CBT provide an example of theoretical integration in itself, as behavior therapy and cognitive therapy existed separately as stand-alone treatments prior to their integration to form CBT (Dozois et al., 2019). Behavior theories emerged as part of the movement to understand behavior differently than the preceding psychodynamic approaches. Concepts such as classical and operant conditioning were developed through research grounded in behaviorism, and psychological distress was believed to be caused by learning maladaptive behaviors. The goal of behavior therapy was to unlearn the maladaptive behaviors and then to learn new behaviors. In the 1950s and 1960s, versions of cognitive therapy emerged, such as Albert Ellis's rational emotive behavior therapy, Aaron Beck's cognitive therapy, and Donald Meichenbaum's stress inoculation training (Dozois et al., 2019). These theories asserted that dysfunctional thoughts and beliefs caused psychological distress. The focus of therapy was therefore on developing awareness of dysfunctional cognitions and modifying them to be healthy, functional thoughts and beliefs, which then allowed for changes in behaviors and emotional responses. The merging of behavior therapy and cognitive therapy to form CBT began in the 1970s, and today CBT is practiced a variety of ways, all beneath the umbrella of "cognitive behavior therapy" or "cognitive-behavioral therapy" (and the acronym CBT). The umbrella of CBT continues to expand as more contemporary approaches have emerged as the "third wave" of CBT (Dozois et al., 2019, p. 15), such as dialectical behavior therapy (Linehan, 2015), acceptance and commitment therapy (Hayes, Strosahl, & Wilson, 2012), and mindfulness-based cognitive therapy (Segal, Williams, & Teasdale, 2002).

Processes of CBT

Before we discuss conceptualization and interventions used in CBT, let us first understand the processes of CBT. CBT is often valued for being a structured approach, and yet many versions of CBT emphasize the therapeutic relationship, with trust and rapport being essential elements in CBT (Beck, 2011). Typical components of developing and maintaining a sound therapeutic alliance in CBT include effective counseling skills (including empathic expressions), transparency in client conceptualization and treatment planning, collaboration, receptivity to client feedback, and reflectively adjusting the style of the counselor to best meet the client's needs (Beck, 2011). Kendall (2012) described the therapeutic relationship in CBT with children and adolescents to be similar to a coach who does not have all the answers and who is primarily interested in collaborating with the client as opposed to telling them what to do and how to do it.

Assessment is also an essential process of CBT. Interventions focused on change cannot begin until clients complete a thorough evaluation, including a clinical interview. As part of initial and ongoing assessments in CBT, functional analysis is often used to identify patterns or associations between the client's behavior and occurrences in the client's environmental context (Drossel, Rummel, & Fisher, 2009). For example, consider a client who uses alcohol to manage anxiety in social situations. The client's alcohol use is reinforced, as it is effective in reducing his or her anxiety and promoting his or her social interaction and a feeling of connectedness with others. Through this exploration, functional analysis provides information about the causes and consequences of behaviors. Outcomes of assessment overall include the therapist arriving at a diagnosis and conceptualizing a client's concerns, both of which enable the therapist to recommend possible courses of treatment (Beck, 2011; Ledley, Marx, & Heimberg, 2010). Although a full assessment must be completed initially, assessment is also typically part of every counseling session, either formally or informally, to evaluate the client's progress.

In order to maximize efficiency and effectiveness, CBT counseling sessions often follow a specific structure. According to Beck (2011), the client's diagnosis and goals for counseling are discussed in the first therapy session following assessment. Each subsequent session begins with a mood check; an update since the previous session, including a review of homework; setting the agenda for the current session; addressing the problem using relevant interventions; establishing homework; and eliciting feedback on the session. CBT is meant to be a time-limited therapy, in which client and counselor contract for a specific number of sessions and then reevaluate periodically and adjust the projected number of sessions before termination as appropriate.

Common CBT Strategies and Techniques

Within CBT, psychological distress is considered to be a result of dysfunctional cognitive processes, and change is believed to occur by identifying and restructuring irrational beliefs or distorted ways of thinking. The core assumptions of CBT postulate that changes in cognitions will cause different emotional and behavioral reactions. In order to facilitate change, counselors target clients' thoughts and beliefs using cognitive conceptualization to guide their work, while they also implement interventions targeted at specific behaviors (Beck, 2011; Mennin, Ellard, Fresco, & Gross, 2013).

The Cognitive Model

The cognitive model is the starting point of CBT conceptualization. Beck (2011) described the cognitive model as beginning with a situation or event that triggers the individual's automatic thoughts. The automatic thoughts then influence the person's reactions, including emotions, behaviors, and physiological changes. Figure 3.1 presents an example of the cognitive model. This example describes Janie, a 24-year-old woman who becomes extremely anxious when left alone at night. She is coming to counseling at the urging of her boyfriend, Shane, who feels as though he cannot leave her alone. The last several times he went out with friends or to work in the evening and left Janie home, she called him crying with intense anxiety and fear, and she was angry with him for leaving her alone. The cognitive model presented in Figure 3.1 illustrates how the event—hearing a noise when home alone—triggered Janie's automatic thoughts that created her distress. Because Janie relies on others to keep her safe, emotionally she experiences fear and panic and then anger at the person who "left" her alone. Physiologically, her sympathetic nervous system is activated, and behavioral responses include calling her boyfriend.

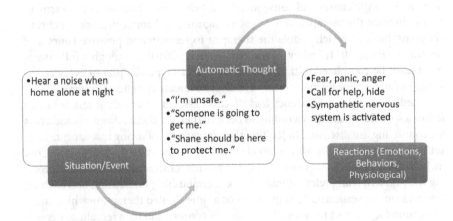

Figure 3.1 Example of the Cognitive Model

Cognitive Hierarchy

Understanding the cognitive hierarchy is an essential component in CBT conceptualization. In the cognitive hierarchy, core beliefs are the base from which individuals develop their intermediate beliefs, and automatic thoughts are derived from these deeper belief systems (Beck, 2011). Core beliefs are individuals' fundamental beliefs about themselves, others, and the world. These are typically rigid, overgeneralized beliefs with varying degrees of accuracy. Personality and environment are believed to shape core beliefs early in life, often as children, and they are especially activated during times of stress. Intermediate beliefs then serve as the rules by which we live, including assumptions and attitudes about ourselves, others, and the world. Automatic thoughts are the most accessible in the hierarchy of cognition. These are spontaneous and often repetitive thoughts that have little empirical support. Continuing the example of Janie described earlier, Figure 3.2 illustrates an example of the cognitive hierarchy in a cognitive conceptualization.

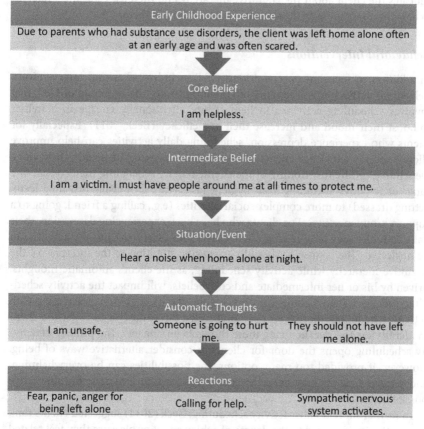

Figure 3.2 Example of Cognitive Conceptualization

Altering Cognitions

Given that cognitions are typically considered to be the root of the problem in CBT, they are also the focus of the change process. To begin the process of change, according to Beck (2011), the counselor first provides information to the client about the cognitive model so that the client understands how his or her current way of thinking impacts his or her emotional, behavioral, and physiological reactions. The counselor then works to elicit the client's automatic thoughts. Once identified, these thoughts are evaluated for accuracy, and if the client determines that they are not accurate, or if they are accurate but ultimately unhelpful, the counselor assists the client in developing responses to the automatic thoughts that are grounded in evidence and that are helpful thoughts to the client. Although the counselor guides the client in counseling sessions, the work that facilitates change in CBT is largely conducted by the client outside of counseling sessions in which the client completes thought records, logs, or worksheets as homework in between counseling sessions. A similar process is pursued when client and counselor aim to identify and modify the client's intermediate and core beliefs. The counselor educates the client about the cognitive hierarchy and then uses specific strategies to help the client identify these cognitions and modify them.

Behavioral Interventions

In addition to focusing on cognitions, CBT includes behavioral interventions. Behavioral activation is a specific intervention under the umbrella of CBT that involves scheduling activities to help clients intentionally engage in activities to boost their mood and increase their self-efficacy (Beck, 2011). Especially for clients who experience depression, scheduling daily activities can help improve clients' moods and keep clients on track with engaging in healthy behaviors. Depending on the functioning of the client, activity scheduling may consist of a range of activities, including basic hygiene tasks (e.g., showering, brushing teeth, getting dressed) to more complex social activities (e.g., calling a friend, going to a support group meeting). For clients who have been experiencing depression, their daily activities may have been limited, causing necessary and healthy activities to be neglected. The counselor should pay specific attention to the interplay of the cognitive hierarchy while activity scheduling, as the client's automatic thoughts, driven by his or her intermediate and core beliefs, will impact the activity scheduling process. When a counselor observes the client's cognitions interfering with activity scheduling, there are opportunities for the counselor to assist the client in identifying and restructuring these thoughts and beliefs. The process of activity scheduling opens the door for clients to consider alternative ways of being. However, if provided too many options, the possibilities can be overwhelming, and yet some clients may need the counselor's assistance to generate alternative possibilities.

To further individualize activity scheduling, Beck (2011) suggested clients rank their activities in regard to the degree of achievement or pleasure they feel related to these activities, as depression is believed to be due to a lack of activities that provide a sense of mastery or pleasure to the client. When developing a schedule with new possibilities, the client will want to include a balance of activities that result in the client feeling a sense of achievement and pleasure. In addition to considering mastery and pleasure, Knaus (2012) suggested clients reward themselves after completing an activity in their new daily schedule. Clients may even use activities they already engage in that they find pleasurable to serve as the reward, as in the Premack principle. Further, what the client considers to be rewarding will likely evolve over time, and so rewards must be flexible. As a client's depression improves, she or he may no longer enjoy watching television as much as the client did at the start of treatment, and therefore, the client may choose a different reward after experiencing a reduction in symptoms.

Beyond behavioral activation, clients can benefit from engaging in behavioral experiments that provide opportunities for clients to try out different behaviors and to observe the outcomes (Beck, 2011; Dobson & Hamilton, 2009). For example, consider the woman who is scared to be alone at night. She and her counselor might set up a behavioral experiment for her to be alone for one hour and then observe the outcome to assist in restructuring her belief system. Additional interventions such as guided relaxation and mindfulness, exposure, behavior rehearsal, and role-playing are often implemented in CBT (Beck, 2011). CBT also includes a range of skills training, such as relaxation skills, assertiveness skills, social skills, and problem-solving skills. A sample of behavioral interventions commonly used in CBT approaches is provided in Table 3.1. This table is an amalgamation of information from Beck (2011); DeRubeis, Keefe, and Beck (2019); and Mennin et al. (2013).

Table 3.1 Sample of Behavioral Interventions

Intervention	Description	Purposes
Self-monitoring	• Client keeps records of activities and associated moods, thoughts, and behaviors	• Serve as baseline and subsequent assessments • Identify patterns and associations • Use as data to test hypotheses • Record noteworthy events to discuss in next session
Behavioral activation/scheduling activities	• Scheduling activities in the therapist's office to be carried out by the client in between sessions	• Increase probability that the client will engage in activities associated with mastery, pleasure, or enhanced mood (especially for clients with depression) • Identify associated cognitions

(Continued)

Table 3.1 (Continued)

Intervention	Description	Purposes
Exposure	• Intentional exposure to an anxiety-producing conditioned stimulus after learning relaxation and cognitive coping skills	• Extinguish fear by unpairing the conditioned stimulus and developing new pairings
Relaxation skills/ mindfulness	• Intentional calming and relaxation of mind and body • Intentional, nonjudgmental attention paid to the client's present experience and the senses	• Increase awareness of current state • Slow physiological processes (heart rate, breathing) • Increase focus and attention
Behavioral rehearsal/ role-playing	• Practicing behaviors in session for the client to use out of session	• Learn effective communication and assertiveness skills • Attain therapist feedback before using new behaviors • Build self-efficacy

Research Support of CBT

CBT is one of the most extensively researched and endorsed empirically supported therapeutic approaches (Dobson et al., 2019). More specifically, various CBT-based programs and practices have been found to be efficacious when applied to the treatment of mood disorders, anxiety disorders, eating disorders, attention deficit/hyperactivity disorder, substance use disorders, gambling disorder, conduct disorder, and oppositional defiant disorder, as well as others (Dobson et al., 2019; Nathan & Gorman, 2015). In general, CBT has been found to produce outcomes that are superior to or on par with other theoretical approaches in regard to treatment efficacy (Baardseth et al., 2013; Tolin, 2010). More specifically, CBT has resulted in superior outcomes in studies in which the outcome was defined as symptom reduction or improvements in functioning, whereas CBT was not found to be more effective compared to other treatments when the outcomes were defined as improvements in self-concept, social adjustment, well-being, or non-disorder-related symptoms (Baardseth et al., 2013; Tolin, 2010).

Limitations of CBT

There is no question that many clients benefit from CBT. However, despite its popularity and strong research support, CBT is not always successful. As Naar and Safren (2017) stated, "CBT is hard work for clients!" (p. 2). In CBT treatment, some clients fail to respond to the treatment and do not improve while others only partially respond. Some clients drop out of treatment prematurely. As homework is often a required component of CBT work, noncompliance with homework completion can cause setbacks in treatment. One study found that 63% of clients completed homework as assigned, meaning 37% either did not complete it or only partially completed homework (Helbig & Fehm, 2004). Motivation is often cited as a reason for why clients do not complete CBT treatment or related work.

The strategies used in CBT often promote active change, therefore assuming the client is ready for "action." In reality, clients who seek counseling services present in varying degrees of readiness for change. Some clients are ready to actively engage in change behaviors, whereas others are contemplating change but have not yet committed, and still others are only attending due to a third party's request (e.g., parent, teacher, judge) and have no or limited intentions to change. For instance, Norcross, Krebs, and Prochaska (2011) found that about 40% of clients who enter substance use treatment present in the precontemplation stage, 40% in contemplation, and 20% in preparation or action. Client readiness to change is not restricted to substance use treatment, however, as clients present with varying degrees of readiness to change related to mental health concerns as well. For example, three people might attend counseling for help with anxiety. One is tired of feeling anxious and ready to do "whatever it takes" to improve her symptoms. The second client identifies how her anxiety negatively affects her, including avoiding social situations, yet she is comfortable with the status quo; she is hesitant to change her behaviors, and she is ambivalent about whether she needs to change. The third client is coming after having a panic attack and being referred by her doctor for counseling. She does not believe counseling will be helpful, especially now that the doctor gave her medication to assist with her anxiety and panic attacks. For the first client, CBT would likely be a helpful approach. However, when clients present to counseling with lower levels of motivation, therapist adherence to structured or manualized approaches can lead to poorer outcomes (Huppert, Barlow, Gorman, Shear, & Woods, 2006), and CBT is commonly disseminated in treatment manuals, as its structure and methods lend itself well for this type of approach. If the counselor approaches the second and third clients as if they are ready to make changes, the clients will likely not fully comply with or benefit from the treatment or even fail to return. In addition, therapists might become frustrated with clients who are not fully engaging in the therapy process. Counselor style can also have an impact on client motivation. Some counselors who use CBT take a directive approach that can elicit resistance, especially with clients who have lower degrees of readiness to change (e.g., Miller, Benefield, & Tonigan, 1993; Patterson & Chamberlain,

1994). Further, some counselors have misunderstood CBT to believe that the therapist leads the client to a "correct" way of thinking or to the "right" solution (Mansell, 2008). However, CBT encourages clients to identify a solution that they believe will work for them, and the counselor assists them in exploring options in a collaborative fashion.

Learning to Practice CBT

According to Beck (2011), developing competency in CBT occurs in three stages. In the first stage, students learn to conceptualize client cases using CBT, structure counseling sessions, plan treatment, and help clients problem solve and become aware of their dysfunctional thinking. In the second stage, students become competent in integrating case conceptualizations with CBT techniques, expand their repertoire of techniques, and become more proficient in implementing techniques. In stage three, students automatically integrate new information into case conceptualization, and they are able to adjust session structure and techniques as needed to meet clients' needs. In addition to these recommendations by Beck (2011), there has been a growing body of research examining the development of CBT competence, and within counseling and related professions, various pedagogical methods for teaching CBT have been studied (Barnfield, Mathieson, & Beaumont, 2007). Research has suggested that successful training in CBT involves experiential group interaction in the form of role-play simulations and in-class discussions to allow students to discover skills, deficiencies, and consequences of clinical decisions. This learning occurs in a safe and supportive environment that can also provide the opportunity for feedback from different perspectives (Stroessner, Beckerman, & Whittaker, 2009). Through such exercises, students learn how to tactfully assist clients in identifying and modifying problematic cognitions, as well as to engage in in-session behaviors and attitudes to be effective in clinical work (Gerber & Solari, 2005). Previous studies have evaluated the transfer of CBT practice from training programs, and it has been found that the majority of trainees successfully transfer skills from training into clinical practice (Barnfield et al., 2007).

The Cognitive Therapy Scale (CTS; Young & Beck, 1980) is a measure widely used to assess CBT competency (Mansell, 2008). The CTS is organized into four parts: (a) general therapeutic skills; (b) conceptualization, strategy, and technique; (c) additional considerations; and (d) overall ratings and comments. General therapeutic skills include setting the agenda, feedback, understanding, interpersonal effectiveness, collaboration, and pacing and efficient use of time. Conceptualization, strategy, and technique include guided discovery, focusing on key cognitions or behaviors, strategy for change, application of cognitive-behavioral techniques, and homework. Additional considerations involve any special problems and unusual factors of the session. Finally, overall ratings involve the rater's overall perceptions of the therapist and the difficulty of the client's presentation. The rater uses a 0 to 6 scale (0 being poor and 6 being excellent) to assess each of the areas in the first two parts of the CTS. Parts three and four include a variety of items, including yes/no questions and scaling questions. Counselors learning to practice CBT competently might seek a supervisor skilled in using the CTS. Audio recordings of actual counseling sessions are then evaluated, and feedback is provided to the supervisee.

Summary

CBT is a widely popular, empirically supported treatment. The basis of CBT theory is applicable to a broad range of disorders and client concerns. The umbrella of CBT includes a range of cognitive and behavioral interventions to facilitate change and alleviate symptoms. Despite its strengths, counselors who use CBT typically assume the client is ready to make changes, which can lead to frustration of the client and the counselor.

Resource Box 3.1 **Resources to Learn More About CBT**

Websites:
https://beckinstitute.org/get-training/
http://albertellis.org/affiliated-rebt-cbt-training-centers/

Beck, J. S. (2011). *Cognitive behavior therapy: Basics and beyond* (2nd ed.). New York, NY: Guilford Press.
Dobson, K. S., & Dozois, D. J. A. (2019). *Handbook of cognitive-behavioral therapies* (4th ed.). New York, NY: Guilford Press.
Ellis, A., & Dryden, W. (1997). *The practice of rational emotive behavior therapy.* New York, NY: Springer Publishing Company.
Friedberg, R. D., & McClure, J. M. (2015). *Clinical practice of cognitive therapy with children and adolescents: The nuts and bolts* (2nd ed.). New York, NY: Guilford Press.
Knaus, W. J. (2014). *The cognitive behavioral workbook for anxiety: A step by step program.* Oakland, CA: New Harbinger Publications.
Knaus, W. J. (2014). *The cognitive behavioral workbook for depression: A step by step program.* Oakland, CA: New Harbinger Publications.
Leahy, R. L. (2017). *Cognitive therapy techniques: A practitioner's guide* (2nd ed.). New York, NY: Guilford Press.
Meichenbaum, D. (2017). *The evolution of cognitive behavior therapy.* New York, NY: Routledge.
O'Donohue, W. T., & Fisher, J. E. (2009). *General principles and empirically supported techniques of cognitive behavior therapy.* Hoboken, NJ: Wiley & Sons.

References

Baardseth, T. P., Goldberg, S. B., Pace, B. T., Wislocki, A. P., Frost, N. D., Siddiqui, J. R., ... Wampold, B. E. (2013). Cognitive-behavioral therapy versus other therapies: Redux. *Clinical Psychology Review, 33*(3), 395–405. doi:10.1016/j.cpr.2013.01.004

Barnfield, T. V., Mathieson, F., & Beaumont, G. R. (2007). Assessing the development of competence during postgraduate cognitive-behavioral therapy training. *Journal of Cognitive Psychotherapy, 21*(2), 140–147. doi:10.1891/088983907780851586

Beck, J. S. (2011). *Cognitive behavior therapy: Basics and beyond* (2nd ed.). New York, NY: Guilford Press.

DeRubeis, R. J., Keefe, J. R., & Beck, A. T. (2019). Cognitive therapy. In K. S. Dobson & D. J. Dozois (Eds.). *Handbook of cognitive-behavioral therapies* (4th ed., pp. 32–63). New York, NY: Guilford Press.

Dobson, K. S., & Hamilton, K. E. (2009). Cognitive restructuring: Behavioral tests of negative cognitions. In W. T. O'Donohue & J. E. Fisher (Eds.), *General principles and empirically supported techniques of cognitive behavior therapy: General principles and empirically supported techniques of cognitive behavior therapy* (pp. 194–198). Hoboken, NJ: John Wiley & Sons Inc.

Dobson, K. S., McEpplan, A. M., & Dobson, D. (2019). Empirical validation and the cognitive-behavioral therapies. In K. S. Dobson & D. J. Dozois (Eds.), *Handbook of cognitive-behavioral therapies* (4th ed., pp. 32–63). New York, NY: Guilford Press.

Dozois, D. J. A., Dobson, K. S., & Rnic, K. (2019). Historical and philosophical bases of the cognitive-behavioral therapies. In K. S. Dobson & D. J. A. Dozois (Eds.), *Handbook of cognitive-behavioral therapies* (4th ed., pp. 3–31). New York, NY: Guilford Press.

Drossel, C., Rummel, C., & Fisher, J. (2009). Assessment and cognitive behavior therapy: Functional analysis as key process. In W. T. O'Donohue & J. E. Fisher (Eds.), *General principles and empirically supported techniques of cognitive behavior therapy* (pp. 15–41). Hoboken, NJ: John Wiley & Sons.

Gerber, M. M., & Solari, E. L. (2005). Teaching effort and the future of cognitive-behavioral interventions. *Behavioral Disorders, 30*(3), 289–299. doi:10.1177/019874290503000301

Hayes, S. C., Strosahl, K. D., & Wilson, K. G. (2012). *Acceptance and commitment therapy: The process and practice of mindful change* (2nd ed.). New York, NY: Guilford Press.

Helbig, S., & Fehm, L. (2004). Problems with homework in CBT: Rare exception or rather frequent? *Behavioural and Cognitive Psychotherapy, 32*(3), 291–301. doi:10.1017/S1352465804001365

Huppert, J. D., Barlow, D. H., Gorman, J. M., Shear, M. K., & Woods, S. W. (2006). The interaction of motivation and therapist adherence predicts outcome in cognitive behavioral therapy for panic disorder: Preliminary findings. *Cognitive and Behavioral Practice, 13*(3), 198–204. doi:10.1016/j.cbpra.2005.10.001

Kendall, P. C. (2012). Guiding theory for therapy with children and adolescents. In P. C. Kendall (Ed.), *Child & adolescent therapy: Cognitive—behavioral procedures* (4th ed., pp. 3–25). New York, NY: Guilford Press.

Knaus, W. J. (2012). *The cognitive behavioral workbook for depression* (2nd ed.). Oakland, CA: New Harbinger Publication.

Ledley, D. R., Marx, B. P., & Heimberg, R. G. (2010). *Making cognitive-behavioral therapy work: Clinical process for new practitioners* (2nd ed.). New York, NY: Guilford Press.

Linehan, M. M. (2015). *DBT skills training handouts and worksheets* (2nd ed.). New York, NY: Guilford Press.

Mansell, W. (2008). What is CBT really, and how can we enhance the impact of effective psychotherapies such as CBT? In R. House & D. Loewenthal (Eds.), *Against and for CBT: Towards a constructive dialogue* (pp. 19–32). Herefordshire, UK: PCCS Books.

Mennin, D. S., Ellard, K. K., Fresco, D. M., & Gross, J. J. (2013). United we stand: Emphasizing commonalities across cognitive-behavioral therapies. *Behavior Therapy, 44*(2), 234–248. doi:10.1016/j.beth.2013.02.004

Miller, W. R., Benefield, R. G., & Tonigan, J. S. (1993). Enhancing motivation for change in problem drinking: A control comparison of two therapist styles. *Journal of Consulting and Clinical Psychology, 61*(3), 455–461. doi:10.1037/0022-006X.61.3.455

Naar, S., & Safren, S. A. (2017). *Motivational interviewing and CBT: Combining strategies for maximum effectiveness.* New York, NY: Guilford Press.

Nathan, P. E., & Gorman, J. M. (Eds.). (2015). *A guide to treatments that work* (4th ed.). New York, NY: Oxford University Press.

Norcross, J. C., Krebs, P. M., & Prochaska, J. O. (2011). Stages of change. *Journal of Clinical Psychology, 67*(2), 143–154. doi:10.1002/jclp.20758

Patterson, G. R., & Chamberlain, P. (1994). A functional analysis of resistance during parent training therapy. *Clinical Psychology: Science and Practice, 1*(1), 53–70. doi:10.1111/j.1468-2850.1994.tb00006.x

Segal, Z. V., Williams, J. M., & Teasdale, J. D. (2002). *Mindfulness-based cognitive therapy for depression: A new approach to preventing relapse.* New York, NY: Guilford Press.

Stroessner, S. J., Beckerman, L. S., & Whittaker, A. (2009). All the world's a stage? Consequences of a role-playing pedagogy on psychological factors and writing and rhetorical skill in college undergraduates. *Journal of Educational Psychology, 101*(3), 605–620. doi:10.1037/a0015055

Tolin, D. F. (2010). Is cognitive—behavioral therapy more effective than other therapies? A meta-analytic review. *Clinical Psychology Review, 30*(6), 710–720. doi:10.1016/j.cpr.2010.05.003

Young, J. E., & Beck, A. T. (1980). *Cognitive therapy scale.* Philadelphia, PA: University of Pennsylvania.

CHAPTER 4

An Introduction to Integrating MI and CBT

In this chapter, we begin to explore the integration of MI and CBT. First, we examine the differences between these approaches and how they can complement one another, especially considering the limitations of each as a stand-alone approach. Then we explore the rationale for integrating these approaches to facilitate change, including the role of each approach in various methods of integration. A case example is used to illustrate the potential benefit of practicing an integration of MI and CBT, compared to one approach or the other alone. Finally, research support of combining MI and CBT is presented. This chapter serves as the introduction to the MI+CBT integration, whereas subsequent chapters describe using MI+CBT in greater depth specific to the method of integration used (i.e., assimilative, theoretical integration) and for various presenting concerns and settings (i.e., substance use and addictions, mental health–related concerns, and criminal behaviors). This chapter focuses on how the different foci and components of MI and CBT can work together to assist clients in a synergistic fashion. However, considering the complexities involved in integrated practice, clinicians naturally encounter dilemmas in how to implement MI and CBT together. Chapter 13 addresses common challenges in using the MI+CBT integration, including ideas to reconcile common dilemmas.

Comparing and Contrasting MI and CBT

As you learned in Chapters 2 and 3, MI and CBT are both well-known counseling practices, and both have substantial empirical support for their use with a range of presenting concerns. Vast differences exist between MI and CBT, starting with the fact that MI does not present a theory of change (Miller & Rollnick, 2009) whereas CBT does. To be a theory, it must predict observable changes to occur under specific conditions (Laska, Gurman, & Wampold, 2014). Instead, MI is a style of counseling that specifies how to interact with people in ways to enhance motivation to change, whereas CBT is clearly based on cognitive and behavioral theories that explain how problems originate and from which interventions to promote change are derived. Further, MI and CBT address different components of the change process and have different methods to promote change. MI addresses client readiness to change and focuses on eliciting and strengthening the motivation that already exists within the client; in this way, MI does not seek to "install" or "insert" anything into the client but rather awaken it from within the client. MI comes from the perspective of "you have what you need and together we will find it" (Miller & Rollnick, 2013, p. 21). On the other hand, CBT typically comes from the perspective that the client has a deficit and the counselor's job is to identify and provide what the client needs, such as cognitive restructuring or learning new behaviors (e.g., coping skills, anger management skills).

Concerning the relationship, MI requires the clinician to employ the spirit of MI, which encompasses humanistic conditions to foster an environment based in trust and respect. The spirit encourages the MI clinician to express acceptance of the client, including treating the client with absolute worth, expressing accurate empathy, supporting the client's autonomy, and affirming the client's strengths and assets. Further, MI clinicians establish a partnership with the client. The clinician understands that the client has valuable knowledge and experience related to his or her concerns and believes that the solution to the problem lies within the client. The clinician acts as a guide in the client's change process, but with the perception that the client is not an empty vessel to fill. The spirit of MI also includes evocation, which involves the clinician eliciting the client's perceptions of the problem and ideas about change—including their personal motivations for and against changing—as well as evoking the client's goals and values that often factor into motivation for change. The emphases on partnership, acceptance, and evocation essential in MI can differ from the therapeutic relationship in some CBT approaches. The relationship in CBT can vary, with some approaches emphasizing collaboration and empathy more than others, but a common thread across CBT is that the counselor takes the role of an educator. For instance, the counselor teaches the client the cognitive model and conceptualization, coping skills, cognitive distortions, and thought restructuring. In contrast to MI's focus on avoiding the "expert trap" and "righting reflex" (Miller & Rollnick, 2013, p. 16; p. 5), in CBT the clinician embraces the role of the expert and indeed proposes solutions to diminish clients' symptoms and concerns. These differences can be challenging to combine in integrated practice. As such, Chapter 13 provides some guidance on navigating this dilemma. With MI and CBT presenting so differently, it might seem as though they are essentially opposites, and yet these two approaches have been found to be "not only compatible, but complimentary" (Miller, 2017, p. vii).

Rationale for MI and CBT Integration

As we have established, MI and CBT are unique stand-alone treatments, and both have strong empirical support for their efficacy with a variety of presenting problems and clientele. Yet the research on integrative practice suggests that combining treatments in a manner that is responsive to the client in a holistic sense can be even more effective. The question is then, "Why integrate MI and CBT specifically?" Looking deeper into the specific foci of these approaches and how the strengths of one approach can minimize the limitations of the other provides us with a further understanding of the benefits of this integrated practice.

Although both MI and CBT aim to promote client change, they have two different foci in pursuing this goal. MI targets client engagement in the change process and enhancing client readiness to change, whereas CBT focuses on teaching clients tools to change their thoughts and behaviors (Kertes, Westra, Angus, & Marcus, 2011). In other words, MI can help clients find their individualized responses to the question, "Why change?" Whereas CBT can help clients respond to the question, "How do I change?" (Burke, Dunn, Atkins, & Phelps, 2004). Failure to address one or the other can result in less than optimum, or even ineffective, treatment.

Complementary Approaches

Despite their different foci, MI and CBT are indeed compatible in therapy. In fact, they can harmonize in a complementary fashion. When we consider the limitations of MI and CBT as separate approaches, their complementary nature and synergistic effect becomes clearer.

Research on the mechanism of change within therapy has found the therapeutic relationship serves as an important contributor to therapy outcomes (Lambert & Barley, 2001; Norcross & Lambert, 2019). Although CBT has noted the importance of client-counselor collaboration and a sound therapeutic alliance, more explicit attention paid to the process of developing and maintaining this relationship would assist with uniting the method of change with the interpersonal factors in CBT (Norcross, Beutler, & Goldfried, 2019). Integrating MI into CBT would assist with making the interpersonal skills explicit, including the humanistic "way of being" encompassed by the spirit of MI as well as relying on reflective listening.

One of the strengths of CBT is that it is action-based. It provides clients with a range of theory-based, empirically supported ways clients can actively pursue change related to their thoughts and behaviors. However, client action and commitment are essential for CBT to be effective, including investing time and energy into in-session interventions and in between session homework. If a client is not motivated to engage in these therapeutic behaviors, treatment will likely not be successful. Further, it is common for clinicians who use CBT to assume that clients are ready for change and to commit to the treatment process, as it is not a common practice for CBT clinicians to routinely assess or attend to client motivation. Considering that roughly 20% of clients will be ready for action (Norcross, Krebs, & Prochaska, 2011), CBT therapists who do not assess for readiness for change will be providing motivation-appropriate interventions for only one out of five clients. In addition, if therapists approach clients who are in precontemplation as if they are (or should be) ready for action, common ensuing consequences include client termination of treatment, lack of progress, and the perception that the client is "resistant" (Norcross et al., 2011). Further, therapist directiveness, a common characteristic of the teacher-role used in CBT, has been found to elicit client reactance, especially for clients who are not ready to make active changes (Beutler, Harwood, Michelson, Song, & Holman, 2011). In turn, client resistance is correlated with poorer outcomes (Miller, Benefield, & Tonigan, 1993; Norcross, Goldfried, & Arigo, 2016). Therefore, if a client responds in opposition or defiance to the therapy process or counselor, we can expect this client to either terminate treatment prematurely or make limited progress. Optimistically, through a meta-analysis, Beutler et al. (2011) confirmed that matching the counselor's approach to the client's level of resistance or reactance (reactance is similar in presentation to resistance but is considered a product of the environment and interactions with others, such as the therapist, rather than a characteristic of the client as an individual) can have a significant positive impact on counseling outcomes. Clients with higher levels of reactance benefit from a nondirective counseling style in which the client's autonomy is supported in therapy. MI offers this type of therapeutic approach and has traditionally been used with clients who present in the earlier stages of change, including precontemplation and contemplation. In this way, MI can supplement CBT by encouraging counselors to meet clients in their unique process of change and address motivational issues prior to clients being expected to partake in action-oriented interventions and activities. As Geller and Dunn (2011) stated, "A skillful CBT therapist may intuitively manage their pacing and interventions to patient readiness but MI makes these goals explicit and provides a language and set of techniques to assist in the process" (p. 13).

On the other side of the readiness to change continuum, Beutler and colleagues (2011) found that clients who had lower levels of reactance had better outcomes when they experienced more directive counseling methods, such as cognitive restructuring or behavioral contracting. Therefore, CBT can supplement MI by providing action-based interventions to help clients learn how to modify their thoughts and behaviors. For some clients, motivation is not sufficient to successfully implement and sustain change. Some clients will need to change their cognitions, learn specific skills, or take medication to manage symptoms of chronic or serious mental health disorders. Miller and Rollnick (2009, 2013) have long acknowledged that MI is not a panacea and is well suited to be used with other therapeutic approaches, such as CBT. To match client's readiness to change, MI and CBT provide complementary approaches, and MI+CBT integration thus creates a comprehensive, personalized treatment experience that is responsive to the specific needs of each individual.

The stages of change (Norcross et al., 2011) provide a helpful framework for conceptualizing how integrating MI and CBT can assist clients throughout the change process in a complementary fashion. Figure 4.1 shows how the specific foci of MI and CBT can work together to guide clients to make and sustain successful changes.

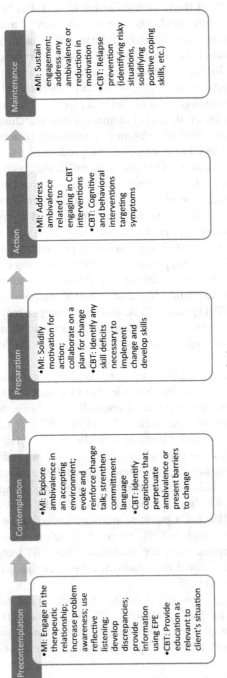

Figure 4.1 Foci of MI and CBT for Clients in Each Stage of Change

Methods of Integration

In Chapter 1, we explored integrative practice in general. The MI and CBT integration is unique in that MI is not a theory but rather an approach to counseling (Miller & Rollnick, 2013). Therefore, although the existing methods of psychotherapy integration can be used to inform an integration of MI and CBT, there might also be distinctions between integrating two theories and integrating one theory and one style of counseling in practice.

Within the scope of this text, we will explore four methods of using MI and CBT together. Section II of this text explores each of these methods of integration in-depth, including examples from clinical settings and research. The first involves using MI as a prelude to CBT in which clients receive a dose of MI (typically one to three sessions) prior to engaging in CBT. In this way, MI and CBT are treated as serial treatments as opposed to blending the approaches. This approach is further delineated in Chapter 6. The second method involves using CBT as the foundational approach into which MI is integrated as needed to address motivational issues. In this method, the counselor begins by using CBT with each client until clients demonstrate a lack of engagement or ambivalence that interferes with treatment progress. At that point, the counselor draws on MI conceptualizations and methods to address the motivational concerns and then returns to CBT once sufficient motivation is again present. This method is further described in Chapter 7. In the third method of integration, the counselor is primarily grounded in MI and then integrates CBT as needed. In this approach, the counselor uses MI with every client until the counselor recognizes that the client would benefit from additional skills or tools. Then the counselor uses CBT for the purpose of meeting those specific needs, but then returns to MI as the foundational approach after the necessary skills are learned. This method is further described in Chapter 8. Finally, Chapter 9 describes a seamless integration of MI and CBT as the fourth possible method of integration. In this approach, the counselor conceptualizes each client using MI and CBT, and the approaches overlap in that the MI style is used to implement CBT techniques (i.e., Naar & Safren, 2017).

Considering that effective integrative practice requires clinicians to consider who they are, who the client is, what the client is struggling with, and within what context (Norcross & Wampold, 2011), decisions about the method of MI and CBT integration should take into account the following: (1) the clinician's philosophy of change and training in each approach; (2) client factors, such as readiness to change, presenting concern, and demographic and cultural factors; and (3) the treatment setting and structure. First, clinicians often naturally align with one approach more than the other, even if they are using some method of integration. Depending on clinicians' beliefs about how change occurs, which is often related to training and supervision experiences, some clinicians subscribe more fully to CBT and some more to MI, while others will buy in to both approaches equally. For example, consider a therapist, Steve, who was trained in CBT 25 years ago and who has been practicing CBT ever since. CBT is what

Steve knows, what he executes in therapy on a daily basis, and what he believes works. Recently, Steve was introduced to MI through a two-day professional development workshop. He now has some training in MI, and he uses it when his clients do not appear to be motivated to engage in CBT interventions. Steve is practicing assimilative integration in which CBT is his primary approach, into which he integrates MI only when needed to address motivational issues (see Chapter 7 for further description of this type of integration). Now consider Jared, who was introduced to both MI and CBT in his master's degree program. He has been implementing components of each since he graduated three years ago. It will be more likely that Jared would practice a true blending of MI and CBT (further described in Chapter 9) compared to Steve. This is not to say that either is right or wrong in his approach to integrate MI and CBT, but rather to speak to the reality that not every clinician will integrate MI and CBT in the same way. It would be remiss to say that all MI+CBT integration has to look a certain way (e.g., a true theoretical integration), as this would contradict the premise of integration in the first place—that the clinician decides the best approach to use with consideration to the client, the context, and his or her own philosophy of change and training.

In regard to the client's factors, the clinician should consider the client's presenting concern and outcome research related to the efficacy of various approaches for that concern or disorder. Further, the client's culture, identity, and development should be considered. When applicable, culturally adapted or culturally responsive interventions should be implemented as well as interventions that are affirming of sexual and gender minority clients. Consideration should also be given to the situation in which the client is experiencing his or her concerns. For instance, treatment that occurs due to a mandate from a third party (e.g., judge, employer, or family member) may need to be approached differently compared to voluntary treatment. Finally, how one integrates MI and CBT will be influenced by the type of treatment and level of care provided. For instance, MI+CBT will be delivered differently in group therapy compared to individual therapy or family therapy. Decisions about how to implement MI and CBT should be made within the scope of practice and the parameters of the agency in which services are being provided. Outpatient services are going to vary from inpatient, residential, partial hospitalization, and intensive outpatient. For example, an inpatient unit that provides short-term, acute crisis stabilization or detoxification might benefit from using MI initially given its success in short-term settings, and this intervention might serve as a prelude to longer-term CBT in the subsequent level of care (e.g., partial hospitalization, intensive outpatient). In another example, a provider who runs ongoing outpatient groups for parents who are required to attend by a child protective agency might benefit from a true blending of MI+CBT, as this population will likely present with a range of levels of motivation and benefit from an approach that values their experience as parents while also striving to enhance parenting skills.

Case Example

The case example of Portia will help illustrate the various methods to integrate MI and CBT in practice. Portia is a graduate student who presents for counseling at the university counseling center. She is behind on her assignments and at risk of failing two of her courses. In this example, I discuss treatment options for using MI only, CBT only, assimilative integration, and theoretical integration. I am presenting the case as if I am the counselor. However, when you read the case, imagine that you are the counselor, and you are faced with making decisions about which approach to use (MI, CBT, or some integration of both) and when. Also, consider how your work with the client might be different based on your identities and the unique relationship you would establish with Portia.

Portia is a 25-year-old African American woman who began a master's program in public health two months ago. At intake, the counselor learns that Portia loves the public health program. She finds the work important and valuable to greater society, and her dream is to pursue a career in public health policy. However, she is overwhelmed with the amount of work she has to do, and she is questioning if she can be successful in a master's program. Portia explains that she has not completed any of her major assignments, and she feels "paralyzed." She describes feeling intense anxiety when she sits down to complete her work, and she is afraid the work she will do is "nowhere near good enough to even turn it in." Portia is still attending her classes, but her motivation is diminishing each week. Portia explains that she feels tremendous pressure to provide for her 4-year-old son and to be a good role model and mother to him. Portia had her son while she was in college, and her relationship with her son's father ended before he was born. Her son's father sends child support payments, but he does not visit often. Portia's mother helps with her son while Portia is at school and while she works her part-time job at the library, but she often does not have childcare when she has homework, projects, and studying to do.

Although she is the first person in her immediate family to pursue a master's degree, her mother and father both have bachelor's degrees and highly value education. Portia explains that her parents are very proud of her, and they tell her they know she is capable of earning her master's degree and getting a "good, stable job." She has two younger brothers, who Portia is tasked with "setting a good example for." Her parents often compared Portia to her cousins, a 30-year-old woman who is earning a Ph.D. in education and a 24-year-old man earning a master's degree in engineering, both without children and both attending Historically Black Colleges and Universities (HBCUs). Portia's parents encouraged her to attend an HBCU, but she chose her dream school, a predominantly white institution, to earn her master's degree.

If I were Portia's counselor, I would first consider our different identities and how to establish a trusting, effective therapeutic relationship. I am a white woman who is older than Portia. As with all counseling, but especially when I am a member of a privileged group (i.e., being white and older) compared to my client, I find it essential to use a humanistic approach to begin to develop a trusting relationship that is grounded in my client's experiences. I believe the spirit of MI sets the stage for an effective multicultural counseling relationship, and therefore, I decide to implement MI initially in my work with Portia. I start by striving to gain an accurate understanding of Portia's perception and experiences of the problem. This begins the engaging process of MI. I use open questions to gather information, but I use more reflections than questions to express empathy and my unfolding understanding of her dilemma, including the context in which she is experiencing her concerns. By employing accurate empathy, I strive to understand the dilemma truly from Portia's perspective, including through the lens of her culture, racial identity, family, values, spirituality, resources, and so on. The reflections I offer also provide Portia with opportunities to consider the content in further depth. I work to establish a partnership with Portia to address her concerns in which she is an essential contributor; after all, she understands the issues and the potential courses of action much better than I do. In addition to developing a partnership and expressing empathy, I also tune in to identify and then make statements of affirmation that highlight Portia's strengths and efforts. For instance, I affirm Portia by stating, "You were successful in finishing your undergraduate degree, even in the midst of becoming a single mother—what strength and perseverance you have."

In addition to learning about how Portia is experiencing anxiety (i.e., racing thoughts, inability to concentrate on schoolwork, difficulty falling asleep, irritability especially with her parents), I assess her readiness to change. I learn that Portia has a desire and reasons to reduce her anxiety, but she is struggling with when and how to reduce her symptoms. When I elicit her ideas about how to manage her anxiety, she responds that listening to music, watching a favorite TV show, and reading novels are what she really loves to do to relax and that she would benefit tremendously from "just a little me time." However, Portia quickly follows these ideas up with "but there is no time!" In which case, the conversation might go something like this:

Counselor: Those activities calm you down; you notice a change in how you feel when you do them. [*paraphrase/reflection of content*]

Portia: Right, but then I start thinking about all the other things I should be doing—my assignments, playing with my son, studying.

Counselor: And then you start to feel anxious again. [*reflection of emotion*]

Portia: Yes, and I cannot get anything done!

Counselor: So, these thoughts about what you should be doing come in, create anxiety for you, and then leave you paralyzed. [*summary of status quo*]

Portia: Right, and now I'm going to fail my classes and let my family down. I can't even get myself to turn in a single assignment.

Counselor: And that feels like a lot of pressure. [*reflection of emotion*]

Portia: Yes!

At this point in my work with Portia, she appears to be engaged in the counseling process, and we have identified the focus of our work together—to find a way to effectively manage anxiety. Considering integrative practice, at this point, let's imagine I need to make a decision about which approach to use to proceed: (1) continue with MI, (2) implement to CBT, or (3) begin to use a seamless blending of the two approaches together. Let's explore each of these options briefly.

Option 1: Continue With MI

If I chose to continue to use MI, I would have the goal of enhancing Portia's motivation to engage in activities to reduce anxiety. Given that she is already engaged, and we have identified the focus of our work, I would enter the evoking process of MI to elicit her reasons, needs, and abilities to engage in activities that she believes will reduce her anxiety. I would ask open questions, such as, "If you look down the road, in a few weeks or so, what will be happening if you are not making time to help yourself calm down and relax some?" or "What difference might it make if you do take this time to engage in these activities that help you relax?" I might also explore all sides of her ambivalence using a decisional balance, including evoking from Portia what she perceives to be benefits and costs of remaining in the status quo compared to the benefits and costs of completing the anxiety-reducing activities; however, I would attend to and reinforce Portia's change talk when using a decisional balance in order to avoid further solidifying her ambivalence.

Once Portia's motivation is sufficient to transition into the planning process of MI, I would help Portia develop a detailed plan to execute anxiety-reducing behaviors, including specifics such as when, with whom, and how to overcome barriers that might arise to impede her plan. An example of a plan is provided in Figure 4.2. However, the process of developing the plan is just as important as the content of the plan. The partnership that I have with Portia transcends into developing a plan together, with me as the guide and Portia as the protagonist who will leave my office and implement the plan. Therefore, Portia's input into the content of the plan is essential, and the plan must ultimately include what Portia believes will work *for her*. For example, let's imagine that I practiced mindfulness, and I found that this strategy worked extremely well for me. It might be natural for me to want to suggest to Portia that she include mindfulness as another strategy to manage her symptoms of anxiety, especially if I really believed in this strategy and personally felt the benefits. Intending to use MI's strategy of EPE, I ask Portia, "I wonder if you're familiar with the practice of mindfulness and how that can be useful to manage some symptoms of anxiety?" She responds, "Oh, yes, I took a class in undergrad, and they made us do mindfulness—the breathing and trying to focus on the moment— I hated that." Regardless of my bias in favor of mindfulness practice, it is essential that I listen to Portia: she tried it, and it did not work for her. Now, I might explore in more detail what she did not like about it exactly and inquire about her interest in learning variations of mindfulness, including using imagery, body scans, mindful movements, and so on, but I avoid

56　*The Foundations*

Change Plan
The change I would like to make is _____ **because** _____. Reduce anxiety by taking time to relax each day, because when I do not do this, I cannot function.
Steps I will take to make this change include the following: 1. Start my day with music I like. Listen to music I enjoy while getting my son ready for the day. 2. Watch a favorite show after my son goes to sleep at night. 3. Read a nonschool book for 10–15 minutes before bed.
Other people can help me by doing the following: 1. Understanding when I say "no" to activities in the evenings because I need time to relax by myself. 2. Respecting my time and space. 3. Avoiding putting additional pressures on me (comparing me to my cousins, asking about my grades).
I will know if my plan is working if the following occurs: 1. I feel more motivated in the mornings when I listen to my favorite music. 2. I watch a TV show three times a week, and I feel happy when watching it. 3. I fall asleep easily because I'm reading to relax before bed.
Some things that can interfere with my plan are as follows: 1. My parents expecting me to be at their house in the evenings instead of at my apartment. 2. My parents asking excessively about school and grades and comparing me to my cousins. 3. My head won't turn off, and I cannot relax even during these activities.
If my plan is not working, I will do the following: 1. Set better boundaries with my parents. 2. Talk with my counselor about other strategies.

Figure 4.2 Portia's Sample Change Plan

convincing, coercing, or pushing Portia in any way to add this to her plan. Ultimately, this is Portia's plan to implement in her life.

In some cases, the enhanced motivation derived from using MI is sufficient for successful changes, and this might be the case for Portia. However, if she continues to struggle with anxiety, additional MI and/or CBT interventions will be needed, such as becoming aware of the influence of her thoughts on her anxiety, time management, and additional coping skills.

An Introduction to Integrating MI and CBT   57

Option 2: Implement CBT

Given that I began my work with Portia using MI, I was operating with MI as my primary framework. If I chose to integrate CBT methods at this point, and I maintain my use of MI, I would be using a form of assimilative integration (see Chapter 8 for more on this method of integration). However, some therapists will use MI as a precursor and then transition completely to CBT, without retaining MI as the foundation (see Chapter 6 for more on this method).

Let's imagine Portia came to session one week after developing her change plan and I found that she implemented it partially, but she noticed only a slight change in her anxiety. She was more relaxed in the morning, but while she attempted to watch TV, she continued to think about all the things she "should" be doing. She is also still having trouble falling asleep at night. Therefore, I could implement CBT in several ways. First, I would hone in on the thoughts she is having that are contributing to and exacerbating her anxiety. For instance, I would ask, "What thoughts go through your mind when you're attempting to relax and watch TV?" Then I would explain the cognitive model to Portia and illustrate for her in session (on a dry-erase board or paper) how the cognitive model might apply to her experience of anxiety, as illustrated in Figure 4.3. Portia and I would discuss various applications of the cognitive model with the goal that she was able to make connections between her thoughts, feelings, and behaviors, as well as further honing in on her automatic thoughts. I would ask Portia to become more aware of these thoughts as she has them in between sessions and to keep record in a thought log. Then in session, we would evaluate her current ways of thinking for how accurate and how helpful they are and then identify alternative, more accurate, and helpful thoughts that are believable to Portia to replace the anxiety-provoking thoughts. Additional sessions would be used to explore Portia's intermediate beliefs and eventually her core beliefs. Through the thought restructuring process, I would go at Portia's pace and integrate behavioral interventions to help alleviate her anxiety as well. For instance, I would ask Portia to try deep breathing with me in session and ask her to complete similar exercises in between sessions. I would also help

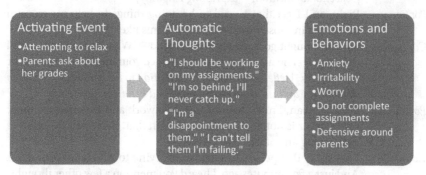

Figure 4.3 Cognitive Model Applied to Portia

58   *The Foundations*

Portia create a weekly schedule to help her manage her time between school, caring for her son, and engaging in therapeutic anxiety-reducing activities.

For some clients, especially those who are ready for active change, cognitive restructuring and behavioral interventions are sufficient for change to occur. However, for others, especially for those who are ambivalent about change, CBT alone might not be fully effective.

Option 3: MI+CBT Integration

When using a seamless blending of MI+ CBT, I conceptualize Portia's concerns through the lens of MI and CBT simultaneously. I assess her readiness to change and understand her ambivalence as a normal part of the change process while I also hear the thoughts and beliefs she has that are likely contributing to her anxiety. Both are equally important, and they likely even interplay. For example, when I am exploring Portia's motivations for doing her assignments, she states, "It's just too hard. I'm way behind everyone else, so what is the point?" I hear her thoughts and beliefs that decrease her motivation and that perpetuate her ambivalence about completing her schoolwork, which results in her work not being completed. In other words, her thoughts are causing a lack of motivation, and modifying these thoughts through cognitive interventions would likely lead to increased motivation. With this simultaneous, complementary conceptualization, the evoking process of MI would involve becoming aware of the automatic thoughts Portia is having that are perpetuating her ambivalence. The following sample dialogue (continued from earlier) is an example of integrating MI and CBT in practice in which I am in the process of engaging Portia in the counseling process by getting a thorough, accurate understanding of her dilemmas:

Portia: I'm so worried I'm going to fail my classes and let my family down. I can't even get myself to turn in a single assignment!

Counselor: And that feels like a lot of pressure. [*reflection of emotion*]

Portia: Yes!

Counselor: And that pressure builds and builds and ultimately causes you to be somewhat "paralyzed" and unable to get your schoolwork done. [*reflection of meaning—expressing empathy*]

Portia: Right, and I get that I need to be doing things to help me to calm down, but in those moments, it just seems like, "What's the point?"

Counselor: So that thought goes through your mind—"What's the point?"—and then you feel no ambition to try to reduce your anxiety or to do your schoolwork. [*reflection that brings attention to the connection between the thought and subsequent emotions and behaviors*]

Portia: Yeah, I mean, I'm so behind in schoolwork and listening to music or whatever is not going to help me with that. So, what's the point of even trying any of it?

Counselor: That really dampers your chances of trying to get some work done. And just a few minutes ago, I heard you mention a few other thoughts

	like, "I'm going to fail my classes and let my family down." I wonder how those thoughts might affect you? [*linking summary and open question to draw attention to similar automatic thoughts Portia mentioned previously*]
Portia:	I mean, they feel true in those moments, so it feels really scary to think about. I've never failed anything. I've always pushed through. So thinking that I could really, actually fail these courses and have to leave the program is like the worst thing ever.
Counselor:	You feel terrified that failing might be a possibility. [*Reflecting emotion to express empathy. I make the decision here to delay going into introducing the cognitive model until the engaging and focusing processes of MI are accomplished. However, I am continuing to conceptualize through the lens of CBT.*]
Portia:	I don't understand why I can't just pull myself together like I usually do. I've never been this far behind before.
Counselor:	So even though you've certainly encountered difficult times in the past, this is the first time you feel afraid that you might not accomplish your goals. [*complex reflection that introduces her past successes*]
Portia:	Yeah and then what does this mean? I have no career then, or at least not in public health like I planned.
Counselor:	When you look into the future, if this doesn't work out, then you wonder, "Then what?". [*reflection*]
Portia:	Right .... [*silence*]
Counselor:	Now, of course undergraduate is different than a master's program, and yet I'm curious, Portia, how have you been able to manage challenges in the past? [*open questions to elicit strategies Portia has used in the past that will encourage her success in the present*]
Portia:	I could just pull it together. My mentality used to be more of "nothing is going to stop me," and I relied on God and prayer for strength through my pregnancy and then coming back to school after having my son. I was just so determined then.
Counselor:	Your determination carried you through. [*simple reflection*]
Portia:	Yeah, but that mentality isn't there now. Now, I look around and I don't feel like I belong. I don't think I can do this. This is too hard. [*conceptualization: these cognitions are part of the source of Portia's anxiety as well as sustain talk describing her perceived lack of ability*]
Counselor:	So those thoughts of "I don't belong; I don't think I can do this" did not happen before, in undergrad, and they seem to be making a big difference in your beliefs about your ability to be successful. [*complex reflection*]

At this point in the conversation, I have used several reflections to express empathy and communicate my understanding of the issues to Portia. By her verbal

60 The Foundations

and nonverbal responses, I assess that Portia feels heard and understood. Portia is engaged in the counseling process, and I have learned that her thoughts are a major cause in her anxiety and connected to her ambivalence. Using an MI lens to conceptualize her ambivalence, I have heard her desire, reasons, and need to manage her anxiety and complete her work, but her belief that she lacks the ability appears to be stopping her from completing her work. The methods she used previously to foster her determination and to succeed in school are no longer working. The thoughts that are detrimental to her have emerged this semester, thus resulting in the onset of her anxiety and academic difficulties.

Next in our work together, I would bring my conceptualization into the focusing process of MI, which can intersect with the treatment planning process of CBT. For example, I might summarize and then collaborate with Portia on the explicit targets of our work together as we work toward her goal of academic success.

Counselor: Well, it sounds like you like the public health profession, and it is a good fit for you, and you would ultimately be excited about a career in that profession, but some of these things that are going through your mind—the negative thoughts about failing and questioning your ability—they seem to be impeding you from getting your schoolwork done, causing you a good deal of anxiety, and stopping you from doing the things that might lessen the anxiety some. Does that sound about right? [*summary of her long-term goal and my conceptualization about how the negative cognitions are interfering with her goals, closed question to check for accuracy*]

Portia: Yes, that sounds right.

Counselor: Ok, well, in our work together, we can focus on these thoughts and how they affect you and then work to find ways of thinking that reduce your anxiety and increase your motivation for schoolwork. How does that sound to you? [*inviting Portia to collaborate on the focus for treatment, including both cognitive and motivational components*]

Portia: Yeah, that sounds good.

Counselor: Ok, and in addition to focusing on these thoughts, what else should we focus on to promote your success in your master's program? [*fostering a partnership with Portia, evocation*]

Portia: I think I need to learn how to stop my parents from making it worse, you know? I mean they help a lot with my son, and that's great, but then they throw in these comments like, "Your cousin called and asked how your program was going. She's almost done with her Ph.D.!" And the comparisons just work me up. After that, I cannot wait to get out of their house, and then I just sit and think about how I'm not my cousin, but my mom wishes I was.

Counselor: Those comments lead you to feeling deflated, like you're not achieving everything your cousin is. [*reflection of emotion—express empathy and understanding*]

Portia:	Right, and again, it comes back to that I had a child. And I don't regret that, but it's almost like she regrets it for me.
Counselor:	So in addition to focusing on your thoughts, perhaps we should also discuss how interactions with your parents also seem to increase your anxiety and diminish your motivation for schoolwork. [*linking summary of the focus of our work together*]
Portia:	Yeah, I think that would help a lot.

In my continued work with Portia, I would strive to use a blending of MI+CBT, meaning that when I use behavioral and cognitive interventions, such as role-playing assertiveness skills to use with her parents or applying the cognitive model, I would maintain the style of MI. The spirit of MI would continue to be evident in my interactions with Portia, and I would continue to assess her level of engagement, ensure that we were focused on the same issue and goals, and address her ambivalence when it surfaced. Further, I would be using OARS and providing information in an MI-consistent way, even when introducing and delivering CBT interventions.

Research Support for MI+CBT Integration

According to Norcross et al. (2016), "Integration converges with the evidence-based movement in emphasizing that different problems require different solutions and that these solutions can increasingly be selected on the basis of outcome research" (p. 324). MI and CBT each have robust outcome research supporting their use as stand-alone treatments; MI for increasing motivation for change, increasing treatment adherence, and resulting in sustained behavior change, and CBT for treating a wide range of disorders, including reducing symptomology. By integrating MI and CBT, clinicians can tailor their style and interventions to each individual client with consideration to the research supporting each of these approaches. For instance, if a client is struggling with motivation to change, MI would be at the forefront of treatment initially. However, if the client was ready for active change, CBT would likely be most helpful.

In some cases, clients will fluctuate in their readiness for change or have different degrees of readiness for separate issues. For example, consider a client who is motivated to improve his relationship with his child but who does not see any problem with his daily marijuana use. For these clients, a blending of MI and CBT is likely warranted, with the clinician essentially creating a custom treatment for this individual client.

There is a growing research base to support the efficacy of combining MI and CBT in the areas of substance abuse and addiction, co-occurring disorders, and mental health. For example, in regard to treating alcohol dependence, the COMBINE Research Study Group (2003) found that MI+CBT with medical management was as efficacious as naltrexone and medical management in reducing drinking (Anton et al., 2006). Research has also supported the use of MI+CBT integration with adolescents who abuse cannabis (Dennis et al., 2004). Beyond substance use disorders, among persons experiencing pathological gambling, MI+CBT has been found to reduce gambling urges and behaviors, lower gambling severity, reduce depression and anxiety symptoms, and improve psychosocial functioning more effectively than Gamblers Anonymous (Grant et al., 2009). Pertaining to co-occurring disorders, Cleary, Hunt, Matheson, and Walter (2009) conducted a systematic review of MI, CBT, MI+CBT, and six other treatment approaches. Findings showed that MI was the most effective in reducing substance use and that MI+CBT led to the greatest improvements in mental health symptoms as well as reductions in substance use problems. Cornelius et al. (2011) investigated treatments for adolescents and young adults (ages 15–20) who were diagnosed with an alcohol use disorder and major depressive disorder. They found that participants improved more with MI+CBT on symptoms of depression and alcohol use compared to fluoxetine and that these differences were maintained at the two-year follow-up.

Among persons with generalized anxiety disorder, research has found that four sessions of MI prior to eight sessions of CBT resulted in greater reduction in worry and increased homework compliance compared to CBT alone (Westra, Arkowitz, & Dozois, 2009) as well as reduced resistance and greater engagement in the CBT treatment (Aviram & Westra, 2011). There has also been some empirical support for the MI+CBT combination for social anxiety (Buckner & Schmidt, 2009), obsessive-compulsive disorder (Meyer et al., 2010), anxiety related to traumatic brain injury (Hsieh et al., 2012), and eating disorders (Dean, Touyz, Rieger, & Thornton, 2008). Applications of CBT+MI have been described for depressed (Flynn, 2011) and suicidal clients (Britton, Patrick, Wenzel, & Williams, 2011), but research is needed in these areas.

Summary

In summary, matching counseling approaches to the client's stage of change increases the effectiveness of treatment across disorders (Prochaska & Norcross, 2013). Integrating MI and CBT enables clinicians to match their client's readiness for change as well as provide cognitive and behavioral interventions relevant to the client's presenting concerns to diminish symptoms and enhance functioning. There are various ways to combine MI and CBT, such as by using MI as a prelude to CBT, using one as the foundational approach and assimilating the other as needed (i.e., assimilating MI into CBT or assimilating CBT into MI), or by blending the two approaches to essentially create a new approach that is a seamless combination of the two. The rationale for integrating MI and CBT and the various methods of integration were introduced in this chapter, and a case example was presented to illustrate various methods of integration in practice. Each of these methods is described and illustrated in further depth in Section II of this book.

References

Anton, R. F., O'Malley, S. S., Ciraulo, D. A., Couper, D., Donovan, D. M., Gastfriend, D. R., ... Zweben, A. (2006). Combined pharmacotherapies and behavioral interventions for alcohol dependence: The COMBINE study: A randomized controlled trial. *Journal of the America Medical Association, 295*(17), 2003–2017. doi:10.1001/jama.295.17.2003

Aviram, A., & Westra, H. A. (2011). The impact of motivational interviewing on resistance in cognitive behavioural therapy for generalized anxiety disorder. *Psychotherapy Research, 21*(6), 698–708. doi:10.1080/10503307.2011.610832

Beutler, L. E., Harwood, T. M., Michelson, A., Song, X., & Holman, J. (2011). Resistance/reactance level. *Journal of Clinical Psychology, 67*(2), 133–142. doi:10.1002/jclp.20753

Britton, P. C., Patrick, H., Wenzel, A., & Williams, G. C. (2011). Integrating motivational interviewing and self-determination theory with cognitive behavioral therapy to prevent suicide. *Cognitive and Behavioral Practice, 18*(1), 16–27. doi:10.1016/j.cbpra.2009.06.004

Buckner, J. D., & Schmidt, N. B. (2009). A randomized pilot study of motivation enhancement therapy to increase utilization of cognitive-behavioral therapy for social anxiety. *Behaviour Research and Therapy, 47*(8), 710–715. doi:10.1016/j.brat.2009.04.009

Burke, B. L., Dunn, C. W., Atkins, D. C., & Phelps, J. S. (2004). The emerging evidence base for motivational interviewing: A meta-analytic and qualitative inquiry. *Journal of Cognitive Psychotherapy, 18*(4), 309–322. doi:10.1891/jcop.18.4.309.64002

Cleary, M., Hunt, G. E., Matheson, S., & Walter, G. (2009). Psychosocial treatments for people with co-occurring severe mental illness and substance misuse: Systematic review. *Journal of Advanced Nursing, 65*(2), 238–258. doi:10.1111/j.1365-2648.2008.04879.x

Cornelius, J. R., Douaihy, A., Bukstein, O. G., Daley, D. C., Wood, S. D., Kelly, T. M., & Salloum, I. M. (2011). Evaluation of cognitive behavioral therapy/motivational enhancement therapy (CBT/MET) in a treatment trial of comorbid MDD/AUD adolescents. *Addictive Behaviors, 36*(8), 843–848. doi:10.1016/j.addbeh.2011.03.016

The COMBINE Study Research Group. (2003). Testing combined pharmacotherapies and behavioral interventions in alcohol dependence: Rationale and methods. *Alcoholism: Clinical and Experimental Research, 27*, 1107–1122. doi:10.1097/01.alc.0000086765.46408.64

Dean, H. Y., Touyz, S. W., Rieger, E., & Thornton, C. E. (2008). Group motivational enhancement therapy as an adjunct to inpatient treatment for eating disorders: A preliminary study. *European Eating Disorders Review, 16*(4), 256–267. doi:10.1002/erv.851

Dennis, M., Godley, S. H., Diamond, G., Tims, F. M., Babor, T., Donaldson, J., . . . Funk, R. (2004). The cannabis youth treatment (CYT) study: Main findings from two randomized trials. *Journal of Substance Abuse Treatment, 27*(3), 197–213. doi:10.1016/j.jsat.2003.09.005

Flynn, H. A. (2011). Setting the stage for the integration of motivational interviewing with cognitive behavioral therapy in the treatment of depression. *Cognitive and Behavioral Practice, 18*(1), 46–54. doi:10.1016/j.cbpra.2009.09.006

Geller, J., & Dunn, E. (2011). Integrating motivational interviewing and cognitive behavioral therapy in the treatment of eating disorders: Tailoring interventions to patient readiness for change. *Cognitive and Behavioral Practice, 18*(1), 5–15. doi:10.1016/j.cbpra.2009.05.005

Grant, J. E., Donahue, C. B., Odlaug, B. L., Kim, S., Miller, M. J., & Petry, N. M. (2009). Imaginal desensitisation plus motivational interviewing for pathological gambling: Randomised controlled trial. *The British Journal of Psychiatry, 195*, 266–267. doi:10.1192/bjp.bp.108.062414

Hsieh, M-Y., Ponsford, J., Wong, D., Schönberger, M., McKay, A., & Haines, K. (2012). Development of a motivational interviewing program as a prelude to CBT for anxiety following traumatic brain injury. *Neuropsychological Rehabilitation, 22*(4), 563–584. doi:10.1080/09602011.2012.676284

Kertes, A., Westra, H. A., Angus, L., & Marcus, M. (2011). The impact of motivational interviewing on client experiences of cognitive behavioral therapy for generalized anxiety disorder. *Cognitive and Behavioral Practice, 18*(1), 55–69. doi:10.1016/j.cbpra.2009.06.005

Lambert, M., & Barley, D. E. (2001). Research summary of the therapeutic relationship and psychotherapy outcome. *Psychotherapy: Theory, Research, Practice, Training, 38*(4), 357–361. doi:10.1037/0033-3204.38.4.357

Laska, K. M., Gurman, A. S., & Wampold, B. E. (2014). Expanding the lens of evidence-based practice in psychotherapy: A common factors perspective. *Psychotherapy: Theory, Research, Practice, Training, 51*(4), 467–481. doi:10.1037/a0034332

Meyer, E., Souza, F., Heldt, E., Knapp, P., Cordioli, A., Shavitt, R. G., & Leukefeld, C. (2010). A randomized clinical trial to examine enhancing cognitive-behavioral group therapy for obsessive-compulsive disorder with motivational interviewing and thought mapping. *Behavioural and Cognitive Psychotherapy, 38*(3), 319–336. doi:10.1017/S1352465810000111

Miller, W. R. (2017). Foreword. In S. Naar & S. A. Safren (Eds.), *Motivational interviewing and CBT: Combining strategies for maximum effectiveness* (pp. vii–x). New York, NY: Guilford Press.

Miller, W. R., Benefield, R. G., Tonigan, J. S. (1993). Enhancing motivation for change in problem drinking: A control comparison of two therapist styles. *Journal of Consulting and Clinical Psychology, 61*(3), 455–461. doi:10.1037/0022-006X.61.3.455

Miller, W. R., & Rollnick, S. (2009). Ten things that motivational interviewing is not. *Behavioural and Cognitive Psychotherapy, 37*(2), 129–140. doi:10.1017/S1352465809005128

Miller, W. R., & Rollnick, S. (2013). *Motivational interviewing: Helping people change* (3rd ed.). New York, NY: Guilford Press.

Naar, S., & Safren, S. A. (2017). *Motivational interviewing and CBT: Combining strategies for maximum effectiveness*. New York, NY: Guilford Press.

Norcross, J. C., Beutler, L. E., & Goldfried, M. R. (2019). Cognitive-behavioral therapy and psychotherapy integration. In K. S. Dobson & D. J. Dozois (Eds.), *Handbook of cognitive-behavioral therapies* (4th ed., pp. 318–345). New York, NY: Guilford Press.

Norcross, J. C., Goldfried, M. R., & Arigo, D. (2016). Integrative theories. In J. C. Norcross, G. R. VandenBos, D. K. Freedheim, & B. O. Olatunji (Eds.), *APA handbook of clinical psychology: Theory and research* (Vol. 2, pp. 303–332). Washington, DC: American Psychological Association.

Norcross, J. C., Krebs, P. M., & Prochaska, J. O. (2011). Stages of change. *Journal of Clinical Psychology, 67*(2), 143–154. doi:10.1002/jclp.20758

Norcross, J. C., & Lambert, M. J. (2019). Psychotherapy relationships that work III. *Psychotherapy: Theory, Research, & Practice, 55*(4), 303–315. doi:10.1037/pst0000193

Norcross, J. C., & Wampold, B. E. (2011). What works for whom: Tailoring psychotherapy to the person. *Journal of Clinical Psychology, 67*(2), 127–132. doi:10.1002/jclp.20764

Prochaska, J. O., & Norcross, J. C. (2013). *Systems of psychotherapy: A transtheoretical analysis* (8th ed.). Boston, MA: Cengage Learning.

Westra, H. A., Arkowitz, H., & Dozois, D. J. A. (2009). Adding a motivational interviewing pretreatment to cognitive behavioral therapy for generalized anxiety disorder: A preliminary randomized controlled trial. *Journal of Anxiety Disorders, 23*(8), 1106–1117. doi:10.1016/j.janxdis.2009.07.014

CHAPTER 5

Integrating MI and CBT With Diverse Clients

There is strong evidence to support that therapy is more effective when it is responsive to cultural and other individual differences (Norcross & Wampold, 2018). In the provision of counseling services, we can no longer mindlessly subscribe to the Eurocentric, monocultural ways of the past. The beautiful reality is that we live in a diverse world that is full of unique individuals who experience distress and growth within the context of diverse identities and cultures. Identities are complex and intersecting (see Crenshaw, 1989), which inherently results in various degrees of privilege or marginalization (Ratts, Singh, Nassar-McMillan, Butler, & McCullough, 2015). Diversity can include race/ethnicity, income/socioeconomic status, religion/spirituality, values, education, sexual identity, gender identity, language, ability, and other characteristics. Diversity must also be considered within the ecological context of the individual's environment. Ecological contexts are a culmination of environmental and systemic factors, including cultural values and community resources. For instance, clients will experience mental health–related concerns very differently if they are in a culture that does not value mental health treatment and fail to acknowledge these as "real issues," compared to a culture that values compassion and help-seeking from mental health professionals. To the former point, if clients' family members and friends act as if they are to blame for the mental health–related concerns, and when they mention the possibility of seeing a therapist they feel stigmatized, these can serve as barriers to help-seeking. The ecological context also includes viable resources for treatment, such as accessibility of services (e.g., long wait lists, very few providers in a rural area) and having the financial means to pursue them (e.g., providers who use sliding fee scales). These brief examples can quickly help us see the importance of culturally responsive services. Through culturally responsive methods, we strive for clients to feel as though our services are for them and that they will be provided services that are appropriate for and helpful to them, with consideration to their unique identities and ecological contexts.

Thus far in this book, we have discussed the benefit of using integrative practice to better meet the counseling needs of clients in general. This benefit also applies to diverse clients (Jones-Smith, 2016). In this chapter, multicultural competencies will be reviewed to emphasize our responsibility to provide culturally competent and responsive services. We then review the literature that supports the use of MI and CBT with diverse clients as separate approaches, as well as presenting a rationale for integrating MI and CBT to benefit diverse clients. Brief case examples are used throughout the chapter to illustrate how MI, CBT, and MI+CBT can be used with diverse clients to foster culturally responsive practice.

Culturally Competent Practice

Historically, counseling and psychology focused on the individual as functioning poorly within society. There was minimal attention paid to diversity or the environment in which the person experienced distress (West-Olatunji, 2010). More recently, with an emphasis on multiculturalism being embedded into counseling, including in our ethical codes (e.g., American Counseling Association, 2014), our training standards (e.g., American Psychological Association, 2018; Council for Accreditation for Counseling and Related Educational Programs, 2016), and our practices, professional counselors have been expected to acknowledge and seek to understand the impact of oppression, discrimination, and social marginalization on our clients, especially those from historically marginalized and oppressed groups. In essence, counselors gain an understanding of clients' environmental contexts, community support and resources, and strengths from an ecological perspective (West-Olatunji, 2010). To this aim, the American Counseling Association endorsed the Multicultural and Social Justice Counseling Competencies (MSJCC; Ratts et al., 2015) as a framework for counselors to provide culturally competent services. The MSJCC consists of four developmental domains in which counselors first strive to become self-aware of their own identities and worldviews. For instance, I currently have the identities of someone who is white, cisgender, English-speaking, and heterosexual, all of which grant me tremendous privileges in the United States (I was born into these privileges and did nothing to earn them). On the other side, as a woman, I may find myself at a disadvantage in environments and social contexts that subscribe to patriarchies or misogyny. In the second domain, counselors become aware of the client's worldview, including understanding the factors of diversity and the unique intersections of identity for this individual. These first two domains are essential to the third, which involves focusing on the counseling relationship, including understanding how the relationship is impacted by the counselor's and client's various privileged and marginalized positions. In the fourth and final domain, counselors identify and employ counseling and advocacy interventions with consideration to the three previous domains Thus, counselors are encouraged to integrate the MSJCC into their work with clients, as well as on system levels. As the authors of the MSJCC, Ratts, Singh, Nassar-McMillan, Butler, and McCullough (2016) stated,

> MSJCC acknowledge the following as important aspects of counseling practice for both counselors and clients: (a) understanding the complexities of diversity and multiculturalism on the counseling relationship, (b) recognizing the

negative influence of oppression on mental health and well-being, (c) understanding individuals in the context of their social environment, and (d) integrating social justice advocacy into the various modalities of counseling (e.g., individual, family, partners, group).

(pp. 30–31)

In addition to the MSJCC adopted by the American Counseling Association, other models have encouraged that factors of diversity be taken into consideration, such as D'Andrea and Daniels's (2001) RESPECTFUL model and Hays's (1996, 2016) ADDRESSING model. Both of these models seek to aid counselors in increasing their self-awareness of their own identities and of their biases and inexperience with cultures other than their own, as well as to consider the salience of these factors among their clients. D'Andrea and Daniels's (2001) RESPECTFUL model consists of religious and spiritual identity, economic class background, sexual identity, psychological maturity, ethnic/cultural/racial identities, chronological/developmental challenges, trauma and threats to well-being, family history and dynamics, unique physical characteristics, location of residence, and language differences. Hays's (1996, 2016) ADDRESSING model serves as an acronym for age (including generational influences), developmental or other disability, religion/spirituality, ethnicity and racial identities, socioeconomic status, sexual orientation, indigenous heritage, national origin, and gender.

In addition to competencies and models that can be integrated into counseling and therapy, there has also been a confluence of evidence-based practices and multicultural counseling through the development of specific cultural adaptations of evidence-based treatments. Adapting treatments (compared to developing brand-new treatments for diverse clients) is appealing because we start with an already empirically-supported treatment and then modify the full treatment or an intervention to better fit the client's culture, language, and context (Bernal, Jiménez-Chafey, & Domenech Rodríguez, 2009; DeAngelis, 2015; Maríñez-Lora & Atkins, 2012). Maríñez-Lora and Atkins (2012) noted that critics of cultural adaptations believe that the changes jeopardize the fidelity of these rigorously tested methods; however, they reported several meta-analyses that found support for cultural adaptations (i.e., Benish, Quintana, & Wampold, 2011; Smith, Domenech Rodríguez, & Bernal, 2011). Further, despite progress being made with culturally adapted treatments demonstrating effectiveness, the American Psychological Association (2013) reported the following:

> Many underserved communities can continue to benefit from specific adaptations or demonstrated effectiveness of evidence-based psychotherapy practice. For example, current psychotherapy research suggests that racial/ethnic minorities, those with low socioeconomic status, and members of the LGBT community may face specific challenges not addressed by current evidence-based treatment.
>
> (p. 323)

These considerations apply to both MI and CBT, as they are evidence-based approaches. Next, we explore how MI and CBT can be applied separately to meet the needs of diverse clients and then as an integrated approach.

MI and Diverse Clients

MI is a humanistic approach that is grounded in a person-responsive style. Central to this approach are the values of compassion, respect, fairness, human potential, prizing of differences, and collaboration (Miller, 2013). The spirit of MI allows this approach to be a natural fit for work with diverse clients, as it requires clinicians to approach each and every client with *acceptance* and the belief that each individual possesses the possibility of change within him or her. For clients who are experiencing ecological contexts that are marginalizing or oppressive, the MI spirit provides powerful components on which to develop a therapeutic relationship. As Miller (2013) stated,

> It is, I believe, no accident that motivational interviewing has usually found its home first among some of the most despised, rejected, and marginalized members of society: people with alcoholism, drug addiction, psychoses, HIV, and AIDS; the homeless, sex workers, and criminal offenders—those for whom humane treatment is most unexpected, most welcome, and most impactful.
>
> (p. 15)

With the engaging process and emphasis on reflective listening, an essential goal of MI is to hear and connect with people who might otherwise lack connection or do not have a place for their voice to be heard, people who lack the privileges inherently held by others, people who have been harmed by—or at least have not benefited from—social systems that can further oppress members of already marginalized and disadvantaged groups. MI emphasizes operating from an accurate understanding of the client's unique perspective and experiences, including their culture, contexts, and environments. Being based on these values and using the spirit and skills of MI in a client-responsive fashion enables MI to be well suited for use with diverse persons.

Research has supported the use of MI, including demonstrating that MI has had positive effects with persons of diverse races and ethnicities, different ages (adolescents and adults) and genders, as well as those who experience a variety of presenting concerns (Hettema, Steele, & Miller, 2005; Lundahl, Kunz, Brownell, Tollefson, & Burke, 2010). Hettema et al.'s (2005) meta-analysis showed that when MI was used with clients of diverse races, it had twice the effect size compared to white clients. In addition to research support for the use of MI with diverse clients, MI has been translated into 45 different languages (Miller, 2013), and it has been adapted for specific cultures, such as a culturally and linguistically relevant web-based intervention for Spanish-speaking clients with a first-time DUI charge (Osilla, D'Amico, Díaz-Fuentes, Lara, & Watkins, 2012) and being used to improve safety planning outcomes with adolescents who were hospitalized for suicidality (Czyz, King, & Biermann, 2018). Lee and colleagues (2011) adapted an MI intervention using assessment feedback to address heavy alcohol use with Latino clients. Cultural considerations included an increased focus on social context, including immigration stress, emphasizing consequences to family compared to the individual alone, considering social support as well as family support, and understanding the client's health literacy. These are among many examples of MI's ability to be adapted for use with diverse clients. Using MI in a culturally responsive manner, as illustrated in the case example that follows, is a specific implementation of being client responsive overall. In general, culturally *responsive* MI can be readily integrated with CBT. Culturally *adapted* interventions involve intentionally using information gained through focus groups and other research to adapt an existing empirically supported intervention (Feldstein Ewing, Wray, Mead, & Adams, 2012).

Case Example

Consider a client, a 19-year-old man, James, who identifies as gay and Jamaican American. He grew up in a Christian home where it was preached that "homosexuality is a sin." Therefore, he hides his sexual identity from his family and community. He feels ashamed, and he has internalized these beliefs to develop a self-hatred. In coming to counseling, James finds his therapist, Todd, is accepting of his identity. Further, Todd expresses compassion in his desire to help James discover his ways of navigating this complex dilemma. Although Todd is a gay man himself, he avoids pushing his own beliefs on James. Todd is aware of his own journey in coming out in his context of being white and growing up in the Catholic Church with a single mother. He practices self-awareness, which prevents him from using undue self-disclosures or imposing his experiences on James. Todd also understands that James's journey is different than his, largely due to cultural and family differences. Todd values and promotes James's *autonomy* (part of the MI spirit) in regard to deciding if, when, how, and to whom to come out, and Todd reinforces that only James truly understands the complex repercussions of doing so. Todd listens to James explain his thoughts, feelings, behaviors, and physiological responses in order to gain an accurate understanding of James's worldview and expresses empathy that is accurate to James's experience within his ecological context. Implementing the core skills of MI, Todd uses reflective statements to express his developing understanding, and he is open to James's corrections. For instance, consider the following exchange in which Todd erroneously reflects the meaning in James's statement:

James: I'm having the hardest time at Sunday service. Every week, I go with my parents and sister, but I feel like I shouldn't be there, you know? Like I just want to run out, like I don't belong.

Todd: You're questioning your Christian faith considering your understanding that it condemns people of the LGBT community. [*erroneous reflection*]

70   The Foundations

James: Oh no! I'm Christian for sure. I just don't feel like I belong in church. I guess it's hard to explain.

Todd: Ok, I apologize for misunderstanding there. Tell me what you mean by feeling like you shouldn't be there, that you don't belong. [*ownership of misunderstanding, open question to gain a better understanding of James's perspective*]

James: I just feel like such a liar. I feel like I'm being dishonest by not telling them. And God knows the truth. He sees it.

Todd: You've always valued honesty, and in other areas of your life, you've been honest with your family. This feels very different and uncomfortable to you, to hide this part of yourself. [*accurate reflection after making further effort to understand the client's worldview*]

James: Yes, I hate feeling like I'm lying.

In this exchange, the erroneous reflection may have been delivered from Todd's own worldview. For instance, let's imagine Todd removed himself from the Catholic Church to find a more congruent spiritual practice. By receiving James's feedback that this was not the case for him, Todd can increase his self-awareness to avoid further impositions of his worldview into his conversations with James and instead remain focused on gaining an accurate understanding of James's worldview. The core skills of MI assist in this process as open questions are used to gather information without limiting or directing the client's responses. Reflections and summaries are used to express empathy and understanding of the client's worldview, which helps to develop a counselor-client relationship that is grounded in a culturally responsive *partnership*. Todd is also focused on using *evocation*, another component of the MI spirit. Todd understands that James knows much more about this concern than he does, because it is James's concern and he is living it. Therefore, Todd elicits information about the problem and possible solutions from James first. He listens for what James values most (e.g., honesty) and gains an understanding of his goals. He assists James in cultivating his motivation based on James's values and goals without any preexisting ideas about how James "should" resolve his dilemma.

The four processes of MI (engaging, focusing, evoking, planning) also lend themselves well to culturally responsive practice. As illustrated earlier, by creating an atmosphere of acceptance and compassion that is rooted in the client's worldview, the client is more likely to *engage* in the counseling process. When transitioning to the *focusing* process of MI, Todd will not assume what the focus of their work will be. For instance, he will NOT determine that the focus is to improve communication with James's family with the goal of eventually coming out to them. Instead, he and James will collaboratively determine the focus of treatment. He will move at James's pace and allow the focus to evolve as they continue to work together. When exploring his options for change (in whatever form a "change" may take place), Todd will *evoke* James's values, goals, and overall motivations for making a change. In the *planning* process, James and Todd will co-create a comprehensive plan for James to engage in the change. The planning process will also be consistent with culturally competent practice because Todd first elicits James's ideas for the plan, and he respects James's autonomy in choosing what to include or not include in the plan based on his knowledge and experience of what might work, and what might not work, for him. If Todd makes a suggestion for the plan, he does so in an MI-consistent way, such as using EPE, and then James determines whether to include the suggestion in his plan.

CBT and Diverse Clients

CBT emphasizes cognition, emotion, behavior, physiological reactions, and to varying degrees, environmental influences (Beck, 2011; Greenberger & Padesky, 2015). With these components as the basis for change, CBT relies on clients valuing rational thinking, meta-cognition, and verbal communication, which are inherently rooted in dominant cultural perspectives (Hays, 2019). Clinicians must work to avoid pitfalls related to culture when using CBT, such as discounting alternative factors (e.g., spirituality, cultural norms) or causing the client to feel responsible for his or her distress caused by systemic problems within their environment, such as racism, sexism, ableism, and so on. For instance, Hays (2019) commented on CBT, "When a therapist does not consider the possibility of minority or cultural identities, it is more likely that the therapist will use language and engage in behaviors that reflect this lack of consideration" (p. 4). She included examples of clinicians who use CBT assuming clients subscribe to European American culture and using heteronormative terms, which can cause rifts in the counseling relationship and process. Although cultural considerations are not necessarily built into CBT, and the history of CBT is largely grounded in Eurocentrism in training, research, and practice (Hays, 2019), more recently there has been strong encouragement for CBT clinicians to attend to culture. Whereas MI is perhaps culturally responsive as a natural outcome of its emphasis on listening, accurate empathy, evocation, and partnership wherein the client is the "expert" on his or her own life, clinicians practicing CBT might need to be even more conscientious in order to practice in a manner that is culturally responsive.

To guide such practice, Iwamasa and Hays (2019) recently published a second edition of their book entitled *Culturally Responsive Cognitive Behavior Therapy: Practice and Supervision*. They explained that culturally responsive CBT practice begins with the clinician being self-aware, especially of biases, and engaging in honest reflection of his or her identities, including those that are of the dominant culture and those that are of the minority. When engaging in assessment, conceptualization, and treatment, clinicians using CBT should strive to understand the reciprocal influences of the client's culture and identities with their environment as well as their cognitions. Clinicians should also identify strengths clients derive from their culture and identities.

To illustrate, let's apply these concepts of culturally responsive CBT to Todd's work with James. James is experiencing distress due to conflicts between his sexual identity (i.e., identifying as gay) and the preaching of his religion and Jamaican culture, which state that being gay is sinful and ultimately unacceptable. James is also experiencing this conflict as a young man in the context of these cultures, which Todd learns further impacts James's distress. Without attending to these cultural components, Todd's understanding of James's distress would be severely lacking and likely inaccurate. As James describes it, a change in his environment is unlikely—according to James, the values of this family and church are inveterate, rigid, and steadfast, and he would likely be ostracized by both if he were to come out. Therefore, Todd and James might decide to focus their work on James's cognitions to help him develop a healthy schema of self despite the negative influences of his environment, including the cultural components, as well as develop methods to cope in his current environment. Long-term work might include exploration of environments that are more accepting of his identities. When pursuing these goals, Todd can also draw on James's cultural strengths, such as the emphasis on perseverance and resilience through struggle.

Similar to MI, in addition to being implemented in a culturally responsive manner, CBT has also been formally adapted for various cultures and tested for effectiveness. Overall, adapted interventions have been found to be efficacious (Benish et al., 2011). In most cases, the adaptation occurs in the methods in which the intervention or treatment is delivered or in how it is contextualized, or additional components were used to make the treatment more salient to the client's culture (e.g., cultural examples and themes are used in treatment) or to the client's circumstances (Chu & Leino, 2017). For example, a school-based counseling group for sexual minority youth who were ethnically and racially diverse incorporated components to address self-esteem, social connectedness, and proactive coping specific to the experiences of being a sexual minority and an ethnically diverse youth (Craig, Austin, & McInroy, 2014). In another example, a Latino parent training program included grandparents as well as parents in the program to include cultural values of *familismo* and the importance of extended family members who play essential roles in the children's lives (Calzada, 2010).

Culturally Responsive MI+CBT Practice

Thus far, we have looked at MI and CBT applied to work with diverse populations separately. In the example of Todd's work with James, culturally responsive MI described in this chapter could perhaps act as a prelude to the culturally responsive CBT described. However, let us explore what a seamless blending of MI and CBT might look like, paying specific attention to culturally responsive practice. Figure 5.1 illustrates the centrality of client identity and culture to the overall counseling process, and Practice Box 5.1 provides you with an opportunity to apply these concepts to a client case.

In Figure 5.1, each of the five surrounding circles represents an essential component of the counseling process: (1) establishing a therapeutic relationship, (2) assessment and conceptualization, (3) planning for change/treatment planning, (4) implementing change/active treatment, and (5) maintaining change. The client's identities and culture should be considered in each of these components of

Integrating MI and CBT With Diverse Clients 73

Figure 5.1 Centrality of Client Identity and Culture in Counseling

counseling and influence how each of these components are implemented. Ideas for how to do so within the scope of MI+CBT practice are provided as follows:

1. Establish a Therapeutic Relationship
   - Engage the client in the counseling process by initiating an authentic relationship that acknowledges and respects cultural differences and diverse identities.
   - Listen to and express empathy and understanding related to the client's culture, including how it influences his or her presenting concern.
   - View the client holistically, including intersecting identities, and remember that the client is the expert on him/herself.
   - AVOID assumptions; be mindful of your biases and work to mitigate them.
2. Assessment and Conceptualization
   - Seek to understand cultural and environmental influences on motivation as well as client's thoughts, emotions, and behaviors.
   - Use culturally appropriate instruments and tools for assessment.
   - AVOID attributing erroneous thinking or problematic behaviors to the client without considering environmental/cultural influences.

3. Plan for Change
   - Elicit ideas from the client: What has worked for him or her in the past? What has the client tried that did not work? What does he or she believe will be helpful?
   - Account for readiness for change and expect this to vary for different presenting concerns (e.g., client is ready to take action to be a better father, but not willing to stop using marijuana).
   - Collaborate on treatment planning to ensure what is included is applicable to and appropriate for the client, within his or her cultural context.
   - AVOID directing the client toward specific plans/actions/treatments without client input.
4. Implement Change
   - Adapt materials (worksheets, card sorts) to be applicable to the client.
   - Use metaphors and illustrations that suit the client's culture and identities.
   - In addition to verbal feedback, observe client's body language and other nonverbal sources of feedback.
   - If an intervention or treatment does not appear to be achieving the desired outcomes, use EPE to elicit the client's experiences and provide information about your observations. Then be open to modifying, adapting, or scrapping the intervention, based on the client's input.
   - AVOID using a "one-size-fits-all" approach.
5. Maintain Change
   - Seek to understand the client's perspective of setbacks and expectations for maintaining progress.
   - Understand threats to maintenance that are influenced by the client's culture, including those that affect motivation, thoughts, emotions, and behaviors.
   - Discuss the client's perceptions of termination of treatment and collaboratively develop a plan for termination when appropriate.
   - AVOID assuming the client has the same ideas as you do for maintaining change and terminating treatment.

Practice Box 5.1

Kiara is a 13-year-old student in the eighth grade. She identifies as African American and Muslim, and she is an only child who lives with her mother, father, and grandmother. Her parents have noticed that Kiara's grades have been dropping, and she seems sad. She has mentioned that "no one likes me" in regard to her classmates at school. Kiara has been complaining of stomachaches daily and has frequently gone to the school nurse instead of going to recess within the past two weeks. Kiara attends a public school in a middle-class community. Although her school is fairly diverse, with African American students and Arab Muslims, she is the only African American Muslim in her class. When Kiara's parents met with her teacher, the teacher was dismissive of their social concerns for Kiara and instead focused solely on her academic achievement. The teacher questioned whether Kiara had a learning disorder. Kiara had always been a bright child who had a love for learning, until this year. They had Kiara tested anyway and found that she did not have a learning difference, and in fact it confirmed their belief that Kiara was very intelligent and advanced in her knowledge for her grade level. The psychologist who administered the testing suggested that Kiara talk with a counselor about the social concerns as well as her decline in academic performance.

Imagine you are the counselor meeting with Kiara to help assist her with her social and academic concerns. How would you blend MI and CBT in a culturally responsive manner to be helpful to Kiara? Try completing the following activity by considering the suggestions presented earlier in this chapter.

1. Establish a Therapeutic Relationship
   a. How would you blend MI and CBT to establish a therapeutic relationship with Kiara?
   b. How would you ensure that this approach is culturally responsive?
2. Assessment and Conceptualization
   a. How would you blend MI and CBT to gather information from Kiara and conceptualize her concerns?
   b. How would you ensure that your approach to assessment and conceptualization is culturally responsive?
3. Plan for Change
   a. How would you blend MI and CBT to establish a plan for change, including developing a treatment plan with Kiara and her parents?
   b. How would you ensure that this approach is culturally responsive?
4. Implement Change
   a. How would you blend MI and CBT in your working sessions with Kiara to assist her with implementing change? What interventions and strategies might you use?
   b. How would you ensure that the approaches you use in treatment are culturally responsive?
5. Maintain Change
   a. Once Kiara made progress on her goals, how would you blend MI and CBT to help Kiara maintain the gains she made in counseling?
   b. How would you ensure that these approaches are culturally responsive?

Voices From the Field 5.1

Implementing a Culturally Tailored CBT and MI Skills Group in Primary Care

Written by
Brittney C. Brown
Clinical Psychology Doctoral Student
Mercer University

I was a part of a team of behavioral health clinicians who developed a culturally tailored intervention using MI to deliver CBT skills to clients who were African American. The intervention focused on individuals diagnosed with mild cognitive impairment (MCI), a stage between expected cognitive aging and dementia.

African Americans are an underserved population and have poor health outcomes due to a lack of accessibility to health-care resources and the impact of racial stress on physical health. In addition, African Americans are twice as likely to be diagnosed with dementia than European Americans and have less knowledge about dementia. Due to poor health behaviors, cognitive functioning may decline.

African Americans often report medical mistrust and racial discrimination in health-care settings, which may lead to a sense of being ignored. Therefore, MI was used to improve their sense of being heard and that their voices were respected. MI is a modality that decreases power differentials between providers and the individuals they treat. As a result, trust between patients and providers was facilitated through MI's emphasis on autonomy, collaboration, empathy, and affirmation.

Using cognitive behavioral therapy (CBT) skills, such as cognitive restructuring, implementing exposure to decrease avoidance, behavioral activation, problem solving, and coping skills, participants were encouraged to improve health behaviors while practicing self-care.

MI increases the ability to acknowledge discrepancies in behaviors, goals, and values. Therefore, using MI to deliver CBT skills helped to improve the implementation of these skills by focusing on change talk during group sessions. Because MI helps to acknowledge discrepancies in behaviors, goals, and values, we were able to emphasize how using CBT skills can align clients' behaviors with their goals and values.

Reported outcomes from group members' feedback included their ability to make long-lasting changes in health behaviors, improved relationships and interpersonal skills, unintentional weight loss, improved health, and their ability to join and trust the interventionalist, who was European American.

Summary

Diverse cultures and identities are indivisible from clients' presenting concerns in counseling. Clients never experience distress in a vacuum, and therefore, as helping professionals, we must strive to understand the influences of the clients' environment and culture on their identities and presenting concerns. In this chapter, we examined MI and CBT in regard to culturally responsive practice and cultural adaptations for diverse clients. Without attending to cultural components and clients' unique identities and adjusting our methods accordingly, we risk failing to provide services that are relevant and applicable to our clients. We also explored how intentional use of MI and CBT together can result in a practice that attends to clients holistically, including their culture, intersecting identities, and environment, and in which the methods are tailored to suit the individuality of clients as well as their particular environments, contexts, and circumstances.

References

American Counseling Association. (2014). *ACA code of ethics.* Alexandria, VA: Author.

American Psychological Association. (2013). Recognition of psychotherapy effectiveness. *Journal of Psychotherapy Integration, 23*(3), 320–330. doi:10.1037/a0033179

American Psychological Association. (2018). *Standards of accreditation for health service psychology.* Washington, DC: Author. Retrieved from www.apa.org/ed/accreditation/about/policies/standards-of-accreditation.pdf

Beck, J. S. (2011). *Cognitive behavior therapy: Basics and beyond* (2nd ed.). New York, NY: Guilford Press.

Benish, S. G., Quintana, S., & Wampold, B. E. (2011). Culturally adapted psychotherapy and the legitimacy of myth: A direct-comparison meta-analysis. *Journal of Counseling Psychology, 58*(3), 279–289. doi:10.1037/a0023626

Bernal, G., Jiménez-Chafey, M. I., & Domenech Rodríguez, M. M. (2009). Cultural adaptation of treatments: A resource for considering culture in evidence-based practice. *Professional Psychology: Research and Practice, 40*(4), 361–368. doi:10.1037/a0016401

Calzada, E. J. (2010). Bringing culture into parent training with Latinos. *Cognitive and Behavioral Practice, 17*(2), 167–175. doi:10.1016/j.cbpra.2010.01.003

Chu, J., & Leino, A. (2017). Advancement in the maturing science of cultural adaptations of evidence-based interventions. *Journal of Consulting and Clinical Psychology, 85*(1), 45–57. doi:10.1037/ccp0000145

Council for Accreditation of Counseling and Related Educational Programs. (2016). *CACREP Standards.* Alexandria, VA: Author. Retrieved from www.cacrep.org/wp-content/uploads/2017/08/2016-Standards-with-citations.pdf

Craig, S. L., Austin, A., & McInroy, L. B. (2014). School-based groups to support multiethnic sexual minority youth resiliency: Preliminary effectiveness. *Child and Adolescent Social Work Journal, 31*(1), 87–106. doi:10.1007/s10560-013-0311-7

Crenshaw, K. (1989). Demarginalizing the intersection of race and sex: A Black feminist critique of antidiscrimination doctrine, feminist theory and antiracist politics. *University of Chicago Legal Forum, 1989*(1), 139–167. Retrieved from http://chicagounbound.uchicago.edu/uclf/vol1989/iss1/8

Czyz, E. K., King, C. A., & Biermann, B. J. (2018). Motivational interviewing-enhanced safety planning for adolescents at high suicide risk: A pilot randomized controlled trial. *Journal of Clinical Child & Adolescent Psychology*, 1–13. doi:10.1080/15374416.2018.1496442

D'Andrea, M., & Daniels, J. (2001). RESPECTFUL counseling: An integrative model for counselors. In D. Pope-Davis & H. Coleman (Eds.), *The interface of class, culture and gender in counseling* (pp. 417–466). Thousand Oaks, CA: Sage.

DeAngelis, T. (2015). In search of cultural competence. *Monitor on Psychology*, 46(3), 64–69. Retrieved from www.apa.org/monitor/2015/03/cultural-competence

Feldstein Ewing, S. W., Wray, A. M., Mead, H. K., & Adams, S. K. (2012). Two approaches to tailoring treatment for cultural minority adolescents. *Journal of Substance Abuse Treatment*, 43(2), 190–203. doi:10.1016/j.jsat.2011.12.005

Greenberger, D., & Padesky, C. A. (2015). *Mind over mood: Change how you feel by changing the way you think* (2nd ed.). New York, NY: Guilford Press.

Hays, P. A. (1996). Addressing the complexities of culture and gender in counseling. *Journal of Counseling & Development*, 74(4), 332–338. doi:10.1002/j.1556-6676.1996.tb01876.x

Hays, P. A. (2016). Understanding clients' identities and contexts. In P. A. Hays (Ed.), *Addressing cultural complexities in practice: Assessment, diagnosis, and therapy* (3rd ed., pp. 79–99). Washington, DC: American Psychological Association. doi:10.1037/14801-005

Hays, P. A. (2019). Introduction. In G. Y. Iwamasa & P. A. Hays (Eds.), *Culturally responsive cognitive behavior therapy: Practice and supervision* (2nd ed., pp. 3–24). Washington, DC: American Psychological Association. doi:10.1037/0000119-001

Hettema, J., Steele, J., & Miller, W. R. (2005). Motivational interviewing. *Annual Review of Clinical Psychology*, 1, 91–111. doi:10.1037/a0016830

Iwamasa, G. Y., & Hays, P. A. (2019). *Culturally responsive cognitive behavior therapy: Practice and supervision* (2nd ed.). Washington, DC: American Psychological Association.

Jones-Smith, E. (2016). *Theories of counseling and psychotherapy: An integrative approach* (2nd ed.). Thousand Oaks, CA: Sage.

Lee, C. S., López, S. R., Hernández, L., Colby, S. M., Caetano, R., Borrelli, B., & Rohsenow, D. (2011). A cultural adaptation of motivational interviewing to address heavy drinking among Hispanics. *Cultural Diversity and Ethnic Minority Psychology*, 17(3), 317–324. doi:10.1037/a0024035

Lundahl, B. W., Kunz, C., Brownell, C., Tollefson, D., & Burke, B. L. (2010). A meta-analysis of motivational interviewing: Twenty-five years of empirical studies. *Research on Social Work Practice*, 20, 137–159. doi:10.1177/1049731509347850

Maríñez-Lora, A. M., & Atkins, M. S. (2012). Evidence-based treatment in practice-based cultural adaptations. In G. Bernal & M. M. Domenech Rodríguez (Eds.), *Cultural adaptations: Tools for evidence-based practice with diverse populations* (pp. 239–261). Washington, DC: American Psychological Association. doi:10.1037/13752-012

Miller, W. R. (2013). Motivational interviewing and social justice. *Motivational Interviewing: Training, Research, Implementation, Practice*, 1(2), 15–18. doi:10.5195/MITRIP.2013.32

Norcross, J. C., & Wampold, B. E. (2018). A new therapy for each patient: Evidence-based relationships and responsiveness. *Journal of Clinical Psychology*, 74(11), 1889–1906. doi:10.1002/jclp.22678

Osilla, K. C., D'Amico, E. J., Díaz-Fuentes, C. M., Lara, M., & Watkins, K. E. (2012). Multicultural web-based motivational interviewing for clients with a first-time DUI offense. *Cultural Diversity and Ethnic Minority Psychology*, 18(2), 192–202. doi:10.1037/a0027751

Ratts, M. J., Singh, A. A., Nassar-McMillan, S., Butler, K., & McCullough, J. R. (2015). *Multicultural and social justice counseling competencies*. Retrieved from www.counseling.org/

docs/default-source/competencies/multicultural-and-social-justice-counseling-competencies.pdf?sfvrsn=20

Ratts, M. J., Singh, A. A., Nassar-McMillan, S., Butler, S. K., & McCullough, J. R. (2016). Multicultural and social justice counseling competencies: Guidelines for the counseling profession. *Journal of Multicultural Counseling and Development, 44*(1), 28–48. doi:10.1002/jmcd.12035

Smith, T. B., Domenech Rodríguez, M., & Bernal, G. (2011). Culture. *Journal of Clinical Psychology, 67*(2), 166–175. doi:10.1002/jclp.20757

West-Olatunji, C. (2010). ACA advocacy competencies with culturally diverse clients. In M. J. Ratts, R. L. Toporek, & J. A. Lewis (Eds.), *ACA advocacy competencies: A social justice framework for counselors* (pp. 55–63). Alexandria, VA: American Counseling Association.

SECTION II
Methods of Integration

CHAPTER 6

MI as a Precursor to CBT

In this chapter, we will explore some of the specifics concerning *how* MI and CBT can be integrated in practice. We will discuss MI as a pretreatment or prelude to CBT. This approach is sequential, MI before CBT, as opposed to the approaches being used together. The goal of psychotherapy integration—to enhance the effectiveness of therapy by providing an additional component to better meet the client's individualized needs and circumstances (Norcross, Goldfried, & Arigo, 2016)—resonates with this approach, as using MI as a prelude to CBT is intended to enhance the effectiveness of treatment. However, in contrast to the other methods described in this section, when using MI as a prelude, MI and CBT are applied one approach at a time, with MI occurring first and then CBT, unaccompanied by MI, and often by different clinicians. Implementing MI and CBT in a sequential manner can be especially useful to agencies and practitioners who wish to add MI to a preexisting CBT treatment protocol. Let us begin by exploring the purpose and value of MI as a pretreatment to CBT and then examine research findings related to the impact of adding MI as a precursor to CBT on client outcomes. At the end of this chapter, Practice Box 6.1 provides a case study for you to consider the application of MI prior to CBT.

Purpose of MI as a Pretreatment

Many, if not most, CBT treatments assume that clients are ready to engage in therapeutic conversation and activities. They often approach clients with the assumption that clients are motivated to reach their goals, including reducing distressing symptoms. Implementing MI prior to CBT "as usual" can mitigate this limitation of CBT. Figure 6.1 illustrates the process of using MI, then CBT, and the therapeutic processes or tasks associated with each. MI as a prelude can include the four processes of MI: engaging, focusing, evoking, and planning. In the engaging process, the counselor strives to establish a working partnership with the client while gathering information about the client's perception of the problem and relevant background information. In the focusing process, the client and counselor negotiate the focus of treatment. The evoking process involves exploring the client's ambivalence in an effort to cultivate and strengthen motivation for change as well

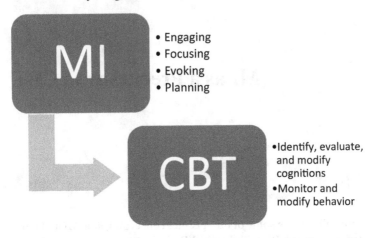

Figure 6.1 MI as a Prelude to CBT

Table 6.1 Summary of MI Sessions Prior to CBT Treatment as Described by Hsieh et al., (2012)

Session	Overall Goal	Objectives	MI Strategies
1	Increase readiness to change	• Assess readiness for change • Consider personal meanings of change • Support and affirm	• Open questions to elicit change talk • Elicit successful changes in the past
2	Explore and resolve ambivalence	• Normalize ambivalence • Hear and understand change talk • Elicit and reinforce change talk	• Cost/benefit analysis • Value card sort
3	Strengthen commitment to change and increase confidence	• Reassess readiness for treatment • Elicit commitments based on personal motivations • Emphasize autonomy	• Importance and confidence ruler • Discuss possibilities from which the client chooses

as to participate in CBT treatment. The client and counselor then collaboratively plan for CBT treatment, including addressing maladaptive thoughts and behaviors. Once the plan is developed and agreed upon, the client transitions to CBT treatment, which can occur with the same or a different provider.

Although each of the processes of MI is essential, the evoking process occurs when the client's motivational dilemmas are addressed. For example, Hsieh et al. (2012) described how practitioners used three MI sessions to address ambivalence and enhance readiness to change prior to engaging in treatment for anxiety following a traumatic brain injury. Table 6.1 provides a summary, including the broad focus of each session, specific objectives, and MI strategies described by Hsieh et al. (2012), all of which involve the evoking process of MI.

Within the evoking process, client motivation can be explored in regard to (1) readiness to change, (2) readiness to engage in treatment itself, and (3) understanding how treatment can result in the desired changes. Let's explore each of these in further depth.

Readiness to Change

Assessing readiness to change is an essential component of therapy. Norcross, Krebs, and Prochaska (2011) reinforced the fact that many clients will present for treatment in the earlier stages of change (precontemplation and contemplation). Through the lens of MI, we do not pathologize ambivalence. Instead, we consider how the behavior might be purposeful for the client, and we understand that there are often personal, private reasons the client continues to engage in the behavior of concern. For instance, consider Charlie, a 38-year-old single white man who was experiencing debilitating anxiety, panic attacks, and intensifying agoraphobia that caused him to be recently fired from his job. Although it would be easy to assume that, due to the consequences, this client was ready for change, in reality he was ambivalent about changing his anxiety. His ambivalence was evident even in the fact that he scheduled and canceled his intake appointment twice before walking through the door of the counseling clinic. When exploring his motivation to change, Charlie described how the anxiety was useful to him as a child in that he believed it protected him from his father's abusive rages. Now, as an adult, he viewed the anxiety as part of his identity and a strength that helped him survive threatening situations in his childhood, despite the fact that he was no longer in abusive environments. For these reasons, the client was reluctant to change his behaviors to reduce his symptoms.

When using MI, the client's "sustain talk," or client statements that are in favor of the status quo or against change (e.g., "I have been this way for so long, it would be like taking a part of me away," or "I still feel like I cannot let my guard down") are heard, understood, and accepted. For instance, in Charlie's case, the counselor would not argue to try to "get him" to see the consequences incurred because of his anxiety. Instead, the counselor would conceptualize these statements as evidence of the client's ambivalence about change and respond with paraphrases/reflections to express empathy and to encourage the client to explore the usefulness he finds in the anxiety more deeply. In doing so, the counselor would facilitate the client's verbalization of his awareness of the against-change side of his ambivalence—a side that exists and that has maintained the status quo but to which the client has likely given very little conscious attention or thought. In Charlie's case, the counselor would understand that his ambivalence is complex given the history of trauma and the perceived protection he believes is offered by the anxiety and related behaviors. The counselor would affirm Charlie's effort in considering these facets of his experience and disclosing them in session. Upon having a comprehensive understanding of how the anxiety has been useful to

Charlie, the counselor would then summarize the sustain talk, demonstrating her clear understanding of this side of Charlie's dilemma. Then the counselor would begin to elicit change talk or the pro-change side of Charlie's ambivalence. The following is an example:

Counselor: Charlie, thank you for sharing with me. It's clear that you've found the anxiety useful to you in the past, even helping you survive the abuse you experienced as a child. And now your father is gone, and yet it still seems risky in some ways to let your guard down. You're always kind of waiting for the next threat, and the anxiety and staying in your room seem to protect you from any potential threat. [*summary of sustain talk*]

Charlie: Yeah, right. So I can't just let it go, you know? I mean it has been part of me for nearly all of my life.

Counselor: This is the only way you know to be. [*reflection*]

Charlie: Exactly. And I don't really want to risk changing it.

Counselor: It feels like a big risk. [*reflect sustain talk*] And then there are the things you would like to be doing—you mentioned going back to school and your need to attend classes to achieve your goal of going into a business position. [*double-sided reflection to begin to draw out the pro-change side of his ambivalence*]

Charlie: Ugh, yeah. I just can't do classes right now. It was all I could do to come here today. I canceled two appointments before I made it in.

Counselor: It was a struggle to come to counseling, and yet you made it happen, and you walked through that door to make it here today. [*reflection and affirmation*] It seems something told you that it was important for you to get to counseling. [*reflection to elicit change talk*]

Charlie: Well, yeah. I know I can't keep on like this. I just lost my job, and I really don't know what to do next. [*change talk!*]

Counselor: And that bothers you, the fact that if you look into the future and continue as you have been, you do not see yourself accomplishing what you had hoped. That's not ok to you. [*reflection of meaning of change talk*]

Charlie: I mean, I have to get another job. There's a job my cousin told me about that I want; I just need to take a few classes. So that's where I'm stuck.

Counselor: You already have another job in mind. Tell me more about the classes you'd need to take and what this means to you in regard to the job that is waiting for you. [*open question to elicit further change talk*]

At this point in her work with Charlie, the counselor would continue to use OARS in the evoking process of MI to help Charlie cultivate and strengthen his motivations for change. The counselor would use reflections intentionally to help Charlie hear his motivations through her and strengthen them in a way that is meaningful to him.

Eventually, Charlie makes the statement, "I am going to take that job, so I need to get to class somehow; I just don't know how." This statement begins with a statement of commitment "I am going to," but the latter part includes sustain talk, "I just don't know how." The sustain talk speaks specifically to a perceived lack of ability, in which case Charlie may have sufficient motivation to change, but he is missing the knowledge and skills to know how to implement the changes. At this point in the conversation, the counselor might begin to discuss options for treatment, taking us to the next section in which we assess and respond to the client's readiness to engage in treatment.

Readiness to Engage in Treatment

In addition to addressing readiness to change the presenting or related concerns, readiness to engage in treatment can appear as a separate issue. Clients often drop out of CBT treatment prematurely or do not complete treatment fully, such as not completing homework or other therapeutic components (Westra, 2004). In treatment that is mandated by a third party, it is not uncommon for clients to "go through the motions" and complete treatment superficially without investing the necessary energy and effort required for meaningful changes to occur. For these reasons, discussing the client's readiness to engage in therapeutic activities before embarking on CBT treatment can be beneficial to improve outcomes. Similar to addressing the client's motivation for change, the client's readiness (or lack thereof) to engage in CBT treatment is received by the counselor with acceptance and without argumentation. The counselor avoids eliciting discord (formerly known as "resistance") by using reflective listening to hear and express understanding about the client's reservations or hesitations related to engaging in treatment. By listening empathically to the client's explanations, we gain a valuable understanding about potential barriers to treatment for this particular client. We might learn something about the client we did not know before, such as a client had a negative experience with a therapist in the past or is a single father and literally has no time for therapy, or perhaps the client has never discussed the depths of his or her pain with anyone before. Using MI, the counselor hears these concerns and affirms the client's disclosures without coercion or judgment.

Client descriptions of such barriers to treatment are examples of sustain talk related to engaging in treatment. By hearing these concerns, counselors further facilitate the accepting and nonjudgmental environment that is necessary for trust to develop in the therapeutic relationship. Similar to sustain talk surrounding change, MI practitioners hear and understand the sustain talk about treatment and conceptualize it as part of the client's ambivalence. Ambivalence is normal and often resolved through the client's explorations of the reasons, needs, abilities, and desires on each side, and connecting the treatment to the client's overall goals and values. In reality, this can be much easier said than done. When hearing the client's reservations about treatment, it is important for the counselor to avoid taking the client's perceptions of treatment personally. Instead, counselors should remain focused on the client's experiences and the meaning he or she is making of those experiences. This information can be helpful to inform the provider's approach in moving forward in treatment, but it should not elicit defensiveness on behalf of the therapist.

In many cases, clients will have options for treatment. Clients might choose from group counseling or individual counseling, for example. There might also be various approaches to treatment to choose from. For example, clients who experience posttraumatic stress disorder might choose from evidence-based treatments such as cognitive processing therapy, prolonged exposure therapy, eye movement desensitization and reprocessing, and/or an evaluation for medication. When presenting such options for treatment, the planning and evoking processes of MI can overlap. The counselor can use EPE to continue to foster client engagement and collaboration while providing information about various treatment options. Consider the following exchange between Charlie and his counselor:

Counselor: Charlie, I'm curious if you've tried any type of treatment before or receive any type of assistance for the anxiety you experience? [*eliciting the client's previous treatment experience, if any*]

Charlie: I was in therapy a lot as a kid. But the last time was when I was in high school, so it's been a long time.

Counselor: Yeah, it's been a while then. If you remember, what, if anything, did you find to be helpful about those counseling experiences? [*eliciting the client's experience about what was most helpful*]

Charlie: Nothing really. They just talked about my grades and taking tests, because I had issues with tests. And when my dad died, they tried to get me to talk about that, but I didn't have much to say. I was so glad he died. I mean he was hardly in my life then anyway, so who cares if he died.

Counselor: I see, you weren't interested in talking about your dad at that time. And it doesn't seem there was much attention paid to the anxiety or abuse you experienced as a child.

Charlie: No, not that I remember.

Counselor: Well, I have a few ideas for moving forward to address the concerns we've been discussing —the anxiety, classes, and not wanting to leave your apartment. Would you mind if I shared them with you? [*asking for permission before providing information*]

Charlie: Yeah, sure.

The counselor would then provide information about various options for treatment and ask Charlie what questions he had about the information provided to ensure he understood each option. Once each option was presented and understood, the counselor would then ask Charlie, "Which of these options sounds like it might be the best fit for you, if any of them?" Then they would discuss his reactions and thoughts. Once they collaboratively identify a treatment option that seems to be a good fit for Charlie, the counselor would address any ambivalence, as evidenced by sustain talk, she heard from Charlie in regard to pursuing the treatment he chose. For instance, let's imagine that Charlie opted for contracting to complete ten CBT sessions focused on anxiety and agoraphobia. If his body language and tone continued to suggest that he was hesitant about treatment, and he made a statement such as, "I just don't know if it can help me," the counselor would elicit discussion about any additional reluctance to pursue treatment by saying something like, "This course of treatment seems like it will be the best fit for you, and yet you're concerned about whether it will actually work." [*double-sided reflection*] Just as with readiness to change, readiness to engage in treatment can be fluid, and if we recognize ambivalence resurfacing at any point during the planning process, it can be beneficial to return to the evoking process of MI to give the client the time and space necessary to explore and resolve his or her ambivalence about engaging in treatment. For some clients, understanding the rationale for CBT by helping them understand the connection between treatment and their overall goals can help solidify their commitment to treatment.

Understanding the Connection Between Treatment and Change

Clinicians who use CBT understand the foundational theories of how change occurs on which CBT is based. CBT practitioners use these conceptualizations to develop treatment plans and to select specific interventions. Most of our clients, however, will not have these understandings and conceptualizations. Therefore, it can be helpful to provide clients with information that will help them understand how CBT treatment can lead to change and result in clients reaching their goals. Providing this information in an MI session prior to starting CBT treatment can help boost client motivation further for engaging in CBT treatment and set the client up for success. Consider the following dialogue between Charlie and his counselor:

Charlie: I just don't know if it can help me.
Counselor: This course of treatment seems like it will be the best fit for you, and yet you're concerned about whether it will actually work. [*double-sided reflection*]
Charlie: Right, I mean, I've just been this way for so long, I don't really understand how therapy can help, you know?
Counselor: It seems a little unbelievable to you that treatment can work. [*reflection*]
Charlie: Yeah, I guess I'm skeptical.
Counselor: I wonder, would it be helpful if I explained a little about how the treatment works and the expected timeline? [*asking for permission before providing information*]
Charlie: Yeah, maybe.
Counselor: Ok, well in CBT treatment, we will focus on how your thoughts and beliefs affect your emotions, such as anxiety, and behaviors, like not leaving your apartment . . . . [*continues providing information*]

90   *Methods of Integration*

From here, the counselor illustrates the cognitive model on paper and uses other examples to help Charlie understand the model. Then the counselor explains the cognitive conceptualization in general terms (not specific to Charlie) and presents the plan for treatment, in which session one is focused on understanding the cognitive model, session two is used to identify and log automatic thoughts, sessions three and four focus on evaluating and reformulating automatic thoughts, in session five the client learns guided relaxation and positive coping skills, sessions six and seven are focused on coping skills and intermediate beliefs, sessions eight and nine target core beliefs, and session ten is intended to consolidate skills and plan for the future. The anticipated outcomes of this course of treatment—significantly reduced symptoms of anxiety and agoraphobia and enhanced functioning—are made clear to Charlie, and he understands how the work he will be doing in CBT treatment can lead to these outcomes. The counselor also makes it clear that assessment of his symptoms and his progress will be ongoing, with formal assessments taking place prior to the first session and after every three subsequent sessions, and that the plan for treatment can and will likely change once he experiences progress and/or he encounters areas in which flexibility is needed in the plan (e.g., more time to address core beliefs). Throughout providing this information, the counselor asks for questions to ensure that Charlie understands the basic premises of CBT and the plan for treatment. After the information is given, the counselor would then ask an open question, such as, "How are you thinking about this treatment now that you have a better understanding of it?" Subsequent discussion could include using a scaling question to assess Charlie's current level of motivation (on a 0 to 10 scale) and any remaining ambivalence.

In this example, the connections between treatment and change are made after Charlie expresses some remaining ambivalence about treatment; however, this conversation could be a routine part of the MI sessions that precede CBT, even without the client expressing ambivalence. Using EPE could be an effective way to do so in that first the counselor asks an open question to elicit what the client already knows about how treatment will facilitate him or her achieving his or her overall goals ("As we talk about starting CBT next week, what are your ideas on how this treatment might help you?") and honors this knowledge. Then with the client's permission, the counselor can provide information that is new to the client, followed by a second open question to help the client consider and apply the information the counselor provided.

Practice Box 6.1

Use the following case example and questions as an opportunity to consider how using MI as a prelude to CBT might benefit the client.

Louis is a 22-year-old man who identifies as biracial, heterosexual, and cisgender. Louis grew up in an urban community, and he was exposed to marijuana as a child. He first used marijuana at age 10, and he has been using near daily since he was 14 years old. Nearly all of his friends used marijuana, and some went on to use other drugs. Although Louis experimented some with alcohol and crack cocaine, he preferred marijuana. Louis works at a factory, and he tested positive for marijuana on a random drug screen. His employer sent him to a treatment provider for an evaluation and to complete the recommended treatment. If Louis complies with treatment and tests negative for marijuana in 30 days, his employment will remain intact. However, if he does not comply with treatment or if he tests positive again in 30 days, he will be terminated from his employment. Louis's girlfriend is pregnant with their first child. He is excited to be a father, and this makes it even more important for him to be employed. However, Louis is aggravated that he got caught in the drug screen at work. He knows plenty of friends and coworkers who have experienced similar situations and who know ways around the urine drug screenings to test negative. Louis plans to go through the motions of treatment, but he plans to continue to use marijuana as usual and use "creative" ways to test negative on subsequent drug screens.

After his assessment, Louis is referred to an outpatient treatment center that uses an eight-week open group format. The group treatment implements a manualized CBT approach that includes a functional analysis, brief cognitive therapy, approach coping skills, refusal skills, and relapse prevention planning. Now, consider and discuss your responses to the following questions:

1. If MI was not used, and Louis presented to the open CBT group, how would you anticipate Louis's engagement in treatment to be? What might the outcomes of treatment be?
2. If you had the opportunity to use MI with Louis in two individual sessions prior to his first group CBT session, how might you implement the processes of MI (engaging, focusing, evoking, and planning) with Louis to help improve treatment outcomes? How might you consider and address Louis's readiness to change, readiness for treatment, and connections he is making between the two?
3. What struggles might you have in using MI prior to the CBT group with Louis? How might you manage those struggles and remain MI consistent?

Evidence to Support MI as a Precursor to CBT

Although there are some mixed findings, overall there is strong evidence to support using MI as a prelude to CBT treatment. For instance, in the treatment of anxiety, MI prior to CBT has resulted in higher engagement in treatment, greater homework compliance, and greater reduction in worry (Aviram & Westra, 2011;

92 Methods of Integration

Westra & Dozies, 2006; Westra, Arkowitz, & Dozois, 2009). Murphy, Linehan, Reyner, Musser, and Taft (2012) found that for men who inflicted partner violence, a two-session intake using MI resulted in better working alliance, treatment attendance, homework compliance, and treatment outcomes (no or reduced physical assaults on partner) when compared to the typical structured interview, especially when clients presented with higher levels of ambivalence and anger. Connors, Walitzer, and Dermen (2002) found that a 90-minute MI session prior to a 12-week program for alcohol use involving both weekly individual and group sessions resulted in better treatment attendance and reduced drinking, including more days abstinent early in treatment and fewer days of heavy drinking overall compared to participants who did not receive an MI pretreatment session. In each of these studies, there was a clear distinction between the MI pretreatment and the CBT treatment, ensuring that the CBT treatment did not include MI components. To illustrate, Aviram and Westra (2011) stated, "None of the CBT therapists had any formal training in MI and the supervisors ensured that interventions consistent with MI were disallowed during CBT" (p. 702), and Westra, Arkowitz, and Dozois (2009) stated, "Interventions consistent with MI were disallowed" (p. 1110).

Research is needed to further inform the dose of MI (e.g., number and length of sessions) for optimal outcomes. Studies have sought to inform this practice by asking, "How many MI sessions are needed prior to engaging in CBT?" Marker and Norton (2018) noted that one to four sessions are the most common, with as little as one MI session having a positive impact on symptom reduction; they noted, however, that this finding is tentative. In addition, further research is needed to address the notion that MI is not warranted for all clients, such as those who are already motivated for change and ready for treatment, and to investigate any adverse effects an MI pretreatment may have on clients who present with sufficient motivation for treatment and change (Marker & Norton, 2018; Murphy et al., 2012).

Practice Considerations

The feasibility of implementing MI as a pretreatment to CBT is a worthy consideration. Using MI as a prelude to CBT can be especially useful for agencies that already use CBT programs and protocols. To illustrate, let's consider an agency that provides an outpatient eight-week open group for substance use, such as in the case of Louis (from Practice Box 6.1). The program primarily serves clients who are mandated to treatment by third parties (e.g., the judicial system, child protective agencies). Many of the clients are on probation or parole and legal or other consequences are impending if they do not complete the recommended treatment, including established benchmarks (e.g., abstinence as measured by urine drug screens, weekly mutual help group meeting attendance). The program implements a manualized CBT treatment that is empirically supported, and the clinicians have been trained in this program and have experience delivering the treatment protocols. Although the agency leadership values evidence-based treatment and they would like to implement MI in services to further enhance the effectiveness of the program, this agency is state funded and does not have the resources to train the full clinical staff in MI at this time. Adding MI as an additional, brief pretreatment can be more feasible to implement compared to altering the existing treatment to include a true blending of MI+CBT, which would include all clinicians providing treatment to be proficient in both MI and CBT. Agency leadership might decide that its long-term goal is to have all clinicians trained, but as a short-term goal, the agency invests in three clinicians becoming trained in MI to proficiency. The role of these three clinicians then becomes to conduct two individual sessions with clients using MI prior to the clients going to the CBT group. The CBT group is not run by the three MI clinicians. Indeed, the model of treatment is being altered as the eight-week treatment that was solely CBT will become a ten-week program of MI followed by CBT. Although this ten-week MI+CBT model requires additional resources in order for the agency to designate three clinicians to provide two individual counseling sessions to each client prior to the client entering the open group, the agency feels confident in this investment given that research has shown the benefits of adding an MI precursor to CBT in that it can significantly improve treatment outcomes. For some agencies who are new to MI but well-grounded in CBT, adding MI as a prelude to CBT might be the starting point to introduce an integration of MI and CBT in practice without upsetting the existing treatment.

For individual clinicians who are familiar and well versed in CBT and who wish to add MI to their practices, adding MI in the assessment and intake sessions or the first session or two of treatment to address readiness to change, ambivalence, and personal motivation might be a productive first step, especially for clients who are struggling with low motivation or lacking active engagement in treatment. As a note for consideration, therapists who transition from MI to CBT and who do not retain MI as an underlying style might cause confusion for their clients. For example, if a therapist switches from a collaborative partnership focused on evocation in her use of MI to a directive educator in CBT, this could lead to the client being unsure of what to expect and even losing trust in the therapist. Although MI is no longer being used, and therefore the MI spirit need not be present, the therapist must be sure to maintain collaboration, which is also a component of CBT. Chapter 13 addresses this and other dilemmas that can be encountered when integrating MI and CBT in further depth.

Matching the intervention to client readiness is an important consideration when taking into account the dose and delivery of MI as a prelude to CBT. In order to implement a standard treatment, agencies may be tempted to prescribe a certain dose (e.g., number of sessions) of MI for all clients before they begin CBT work. However, we know that clients can progress through the stages of change at varying paces; some may resolve ambivalence in one session, but others may need more. Practitioners and agencies should also consider how MI is delivered in pretreatment. Using manualized MI makes the intervention uniform across practitioners; however, MI is client responsive by nature, which can be contradicted by a delivery method that emphasizes "follow the manual" instead of responding to the client. Hettema, Steele, and Miller (2005) noted that manualized MI can lead to lower effect sizes. Therefore, fidelity to MI, including responding to the client's current readiness for change, must be considered when using MI as a prelude to CBT.

Finally, the duration of the effect of MI as a pretreatment should be considered. In cases where the MI sessions are offered by providers other than the CBT practitioners (MI is not used beyond the MI pretreatment), the effects of MI may subside throughout CBT work (Marker & Norton, 2018). Therefore, Marker and Norton (2018) suggested incorporating MI into CBT work. They compared two studies: the first study (Barrera, Smith, & Norton, 2016) included one MI session, which resulted in greater improvements in symptoms of anxiety compared to the control group early in CBT treatment, but the differences were no longer significant, meaning the treatment outcomes resembled the control group, from CBT session five on. The second study (Merlo et al., 2010) included brief MI sessions (20 to 30 minutes) at systematic points throughout CBT, which resulted in symptoms being significantly reduced more quickly and to a greater degree throughout treatment. Therefore, as the implementation of MI as a prelude to CBT matures as a result of refining from outcome research, it might behoove agencies to consider MI booster sessions in the midst of CBT treatment, even if provided by therapists separate from the CBT treatment.

Summary

In this chapter, we explored MI as a prelude to CBT treatment. In this method of integration, the processes of MI are complete prior to the client beginning CBT. Examples were provided for both single practitioner's use and for implementation across providers in an agency setting. Strengths of this model include feasibility to begin to practice a combination of MI and CBT; however, considerations for how much MI, when to transition to CBT, and effects of the MI intervention subsiding are noteworthy when incorporating this method into practice.

References

Aviram, A., & Westra, H. A. (2011). The impact of motivational interviewing on resistance in cognitive behavioural therapy for generalized anxiety disorder. *Psychotherapy Research, 21*(6), 698–708. doi:10.1080/10503307.2011.610832

Barrera, T. L., Smith, A. H., & Norton, P. J. (2016). Motivational interviewing as an adjunct to cognitive behavioral therapy for anxiety. *Journal of Clinical Psychology, 72*(1), 5–14. doi:10.1002/jclp.22239

Connors, G. J., Walitzer, K. S., & Dermen, K. H. (2002). Preparing clients for alcoholism treatment: Effects on treatment participation and outcomes. *Journal of Consulting and Clinical Psychology, 70*(5), 1161–1169. doi:10.1037//0022-006X.70.5.1161

Hettema, J., Steele, J., & Miller, W. R. (2005). Motivational interviewing. *Annual Review of Clinical Psychology, 1*(1), 91–111. doi:10.1146/annurev.clinpsy.1.102803.143833

Hsieh, M.-Y., Ponsford, J., Wong, D., Schönberger, M., McKay, A., & Haines, K. (2012). Development of a motivational interviewing program as a prelude to CBT for anxiety following traumatic brain injury. *Neuropsychological Rehabilitation, 22*(4), 563–584. doi: 10.1080/09602011.2012.676284

Marker, I., & Norton, P. J. (2018). The efficacy of incorporating motivational interviewing to cognitive behavior therapy for anxiety disorders: A review and meta-analysis. *Clinical Psychology Review, 62*, 1–10. doi:10.1016/j.cpr.2018.04.004

Merlo, L. J., Storch, E. A., Lehmkuhl, H. D., Jacob, M. L., Murphy, T. K., Goodman, W. K., & Geffken, G. R. (2010). Cognitive behavioral therapy plus motivational interviewing improves outcome for pediatric obsessive—compulsive disorder: A preliminary study. *Cognitive Behaviour Therapy, 39*(1), 24–27. doi:10.1080/16506070902831773

Murphy, C. M., Linehan, E. L., Reyner, J. C., Musser, P. H., & Taft, C. T. (2012). Moderators of response to motivational interviewing for partner-violent men. *Journal of Family Violence, 27*(7), 671–680. doi:10.1007/s10896-012-9460-2

Norcross, J. C., Goldfried, M. R., & Arigo, D. (2016). Integrative theories. In J. C. Norcross, G. R. VandenBos, D. K. Freedheim, & B. O. Olatunji (Eds.), *APA handbook of clinical psychology: Theory and research* (Vol. 2, pp. 303–332). Washington, DC: American Psychological Association.

Norcross, J. C., Krebs, P. M., & Prochaska, J. O. (2011). Stages of change. *Journal of Clinical Psychology, 67*(2), 143–154. doi:10.1002/jclp.20758

Westra, H. (2004). Managing resistance in cognitive behavioural therapy: The application of motivational interviewing in mixed anxiety and depression. *Cognitive Behaviour Therapy, 33*(4), 161–175. doi:10.1080/16506070410026426

Westra, H. A., Arkowitz, H., & Dozois, D. J. A. (2009). Adding a motivational interviewing pretreatment to cognitive behavioral therapy for generalized anxiety disorder: A preliminary randomized controlled trial. *Journal of Anxiety Disorders, 23*(8), 1106–1117. doi:10.1016/j.janxdis.2009.07.014

Westra, H. A., & Dozois, D. J. A. (2006). Preparing clients for cognitive behavioral therapy: A randomized pilot study of motivational interviewing for anxiety. *Cognitive Therapy and Research, 30*, 481–498. doi:10.1007/s10608-006-9016-y

CHAPTER 7

Assimilating MI Into CBT

As described in Chapter 3, CBT is one of the most popular approaches to counseling. Its broad applications and proven effectiveness cause it to be very appealing to practitioners, clients, agencies, and third-party payors. Further, it can be implemented systematically, such as through treatment manuals, to readily evaluate treatment outcomes. Given its wide dissemination and use, it is not uncommon for seasoned practitioners who have extensive training and experience using CBT to be introduced to MI at some point. These practitioners might then consider the usefulness of MI in the context of their already established CBT practice, and they first begin to use MI with an assimilative stance, meaning they do not abandon or alter their use of CBT, but rather they use MI to supplement their existing practice of CBT. Fortunately, many CBT practitioners find MI compatible with CBT. For instance, Driessen and Hollon (2011) noted that CBT clinicians can appreciate that MI makes explicit certain aspects of therapy that might otherwise remain implicit in CBT, such as addressing ambivalence directly and in a manner that is compatible with CBT.

In this chapter, we begin by exploring the compatibility of MI with CBT and then describe specific ways in which MI can be used to enhance an existing CBT practice, including to diminish discord (formerly known as resistance) to establish a sound therapeutic alliance, to enhance clients' recognition of a problem, and to explore and resolve client ambivalence. Sample client-counselor dialogue is used throughout the chapter, and practice boxes are provided for opportunities for practice and application. Finally, practice considerations are discussed that are specific to assimilating MI into CBT.

Compatibility of MI with CBT

In many ways, MI is compatible with CBT. Some of the components of these approaches even resemble one another, although there are fundamental differences. For instance, Driessen and Hollon (2011) contended that the MI spirit itself is compatible with CBT, although variations will exist across CBT therapists' styles and approaches to clients in that some will be more directive (less MI consistent) than others. Being goal oriented and having direction in the conversation is part of both MI and CBT. However, MI makes explicit the relational components of therapy and counselor behaviors used to foster the therapeutic relationship, such as expressing acceptance and empathy, using reflective listening, and having compassion in addition to maintaining a partnership with the client. The relational components of therapy tend to be less explicit and can be vague in CBT. For instance, Beck (2011) described an effective therapeutic alliance, involving warmth, empathy, and genuine regard, as a main principle of CBT. She also noted that CBT cannot be conducted in a cold, mechanical manner. However, the skills necessary to provide a sound therapeutic relationship are not described as fully in CBT as they are in MI. The skills that are likely to foster a sound therapeutic alliance are woven into MI, and guidelines are established to assist clinicians in striving for competence in executing the relational components of MI (e.g., reflections to express accurate empathy and understanding of the client are used twice as often as questions in MI; open questions are highly preferred to closed questions; Moyers, Manuel, & Ernst, 2015).

Collaboration is another area of potential overlap between MI and CBT. In CBT, collaborative empiricism represents working together to identify, evaluate, and modify the client's thoughts and beliefs (Beck, 2011). However, in CBT, there is a natural hierarchy in that it is the therapist's role to educate the client about the etiology and treatment of the disorder or concern through the lens of CBT and then teach the client to become his or her own therapist (Beck, 2011). In contrast, collaboration in MI represents a partnership between client and counselor that is based on egalitarianism. As part of the spirit of MI, the partnership is maintained throughout therapy.

Beyond the relationship components, MI can also be compatible with CBT in regard to specific techniques. For example, Socratic questioning is often used in CBT to help clients identify the meaning of their thoughts and beliefs. This method is similar in nature to evocation, part of the MI spirit, in which the practitioner evokes from the client his or her own personal reasons for change, values, goals, and ideas for how to implement change. Socratic questioning in CBT and evocation in MI are both in essence guided by the therapist but driven by the client in that the therapist is not directing the client in what to do but rather creating opportunities for the client to consider these facets of change and to reach his or her own conclusions (Driessen & Hollon, 2011). Highlighting positives is another commonality between CBT and MI, although this can be executed differently across approaches. CBT commonly encourages practitioners to emphasize the positives, whereas affirmations are used in MI. Although both approaches seek to highlight positive components, affirmations in MI focus solely on *the client's* strengths, positive attributes, and efforts in treatment or toward change, whereas positives in CBT can include positives with the client's behavior or positives in the situation (Beck, 2011). Further, affirmations in MI are based on the therapist's observations and expressed through statements that typically begin with "you" (Rosengren, 2018), such as, "You are working hard here, despite the difficulty of the circumstances," whereas in CBT, the positives are discovered by asking questions of the client, such as, "What do you see as your strengths or positive qualities?"

In spite of the compatibility between MI and CBT, MI can be beneficial to add as needed to address motivational concerns when clinicians are practicing CBT as their primary therapeutic approach. This type of assimilative integration (Norcross, Goldfried, & Arigo, 2016) involves CBT as the foundation of therapy with intentional and selective intermittent incorporations of MI. For some clinicians, this method of combining MI and CBT might be a stepping stone to fully integrating MI and CBT (see Chapter 9). For others, assimilative integration may suffice. The remainder of this chapter focuses on when and how MI can be assimilated into CBT. We will begin by exploring the possibility of using MI to engage "resistant" clients in treatment, including practicing MI skills to diminish discord in order to develop and maintain a productive working relationship. We will then examine how MI can be used to address ambivalence or motivational issues that may arise during treatment. Finally, we will look at how MI can be implemented to address treatment noncompliance.

Implementing MI to Address Discord

Many therapists struggle with clients who present as "resistant." If you envision a "resistant" client, who do you see? Someone with his or her arms crossed and avoiding eye contact? Someone who gives one-word answers if the person speaks at all? Someone who is angry at having to come to counseling and who has no desire or intention to use the time productively? There are a range of approaches to address resistance under the scope of CBT. Some CBT sources briefly discuss people's natural hesitancy or reluctance to change and promote therapists' use of reflective listening and expression of empathy (Beck, 2005), whereas other sources encourage education and discussion about what the client may expect from the CBT process (Leahy, 2003) or restructuring the client's cognitive schemas that may be creating resistance to change (Leahy, 2008). CBT counselors may attribute client resistance to underlying irrational beliefs or cognitive distortions that are interfering with change (Arkowitz & Westra, 2004; Ellis, 2005). Therefore, in order to resolve client resistance, CBT counselors attempt to identify and restructure the disturbances in clients' cognitive processes that are causing the resistance (Arkowitz, 2002). However, as you can imagine, or perhaps as you may have experienced in your own work with clients, this can be a challenging process with a client who is unmotivated to address such cognitions.

Reactance is a term used to describe the lack of motivation clients experience when they perceive their freedoms to be lost or threatened as a result of the therapy environment, which then results in noncompliance (Beutler, Harwood, Michelson, Song, & Holman, 2011; Brehm & Brehm, 1981). According to Seibel and Dowd (1999), reactance involves client behaviors that establish boundaries between client and therapist, such as arguing, distancing, and limit setting, which they considered to be client attempts to control or reduce the therapist's influence. The theory of reactance accounts for the therapist's influence in that the therapist can cause or contribute to client reactance (Beutler et al., 2011). Similar to matching therapeutic approaches with the client's readiness to change, Beutler et al. (2011) found that clients who had higher levels of reactance responded better to nondirective treatments, whereas those with lower reactance levels responded more favorably to directive treatments.

The concept of reactance somewhat resonates with the conceptualization of "resistance" used by MI practitioners in that it considers the interpersonal dynamic between the client and the counselor. In MI, resistance is not considered to be a characteristic of the client but rather of the relationship. Due to the negative connotations and judgment inherent in the term "resistance" for how we consider clients (e.g., "He is being difficult," "She is not even trying here"), Miller and Rollnick (2013) recharacterized resistance as "discord" within the therapeutic relationship (p. 197). Instead of approaching discord as something that the client needs to fix, MI contests that the presence of discord is a signal for the *therapist* to respond differently. If discord is present in the first meeting with a client, it is very unlikely that the discord is solely due to this helping professional. More likely, clients are bringing their resentments, conflicts, and previous experiences with professionals into the developing relationship with the new therapist. For example, imagine you have a new adolescent client, Damon, who has been in foster care, juvenile detention centers, and drug treatment centers. This client has had a multitude of experiences with adult "helpers," most of whom he did not perceive as helpful at all. Damon has learned not to trust adults, and naturally he is expecting a similar dynamic with you. Therefore, he is defensive and shares very little with you. He tells you, "You are just like the others, I'm sure," and "You don't really care." Further, he remarks, "There is nothing you can do that is actually going to help me." These are hallmark signs of discord, as Damon is demonstrating a defensive tone and making negative comments that are directed to or are about the counselor and the services provided. An important distinction can be made here between discord and sustain talk, (which signifies ambivalence) in that the characteristics of discord are *not about a specific change*. Hence, discord is *not* ambivalence about change; instead, it is an interpersonal construct between the client and the therapist. As the professionals in therapeutic relationships, it is our responsibility to identify discord in these relationships and respond to it in a helpful way. Why? Research has shown that resistance/discord predicts nonchange and leads to poor outcomes, and yet optimistically, studies have shown that resistance/reactance/discord is highly responsive to the helper style (Beutler et al., 2011; Miller, Benefield, & Tonigan, 1993). More specifically, Aviram, Westra, Constantino, and Antony (2016) found that MI-consistent responses (e.g., expressing empathy, collaborating, supporting client autonomy) used to address discord early in treatment significantly reduced subsequent discord and improved outcomes related to anxiety (i.e., worry). However, it was essential that the therapist responded at the precise time when the evidence of discord arose (Aviram et al., 2016). In essence, what we say to clients (i.e., reflections that express empathy, statements that support the client's autonomy), the manner in which we say it (i.e., with the spirit of MI), and when we say it (i.e., responsive timing to the emergence of discord) has the power to diminish discord in the therapeutic relationship and enhance therapy outcomes. Now, let us focus on the strategies and skills used in MI to diminish discord.

100　*Methods of Integration*

The following describes and illustrates key approaches from MI to respond to discord in a relationship with a client. Practice Box 7.1 provides opportunities for you to practice these strategies.

1. *Maintain the spirit of MI.* Maintaining the spirit of MI can serve as a means to foster a productive therapeutic relationship as the spirit of MI contains the humanistic, Rogerian components of therapy that have been found to diminish discord (Beutler et al., 2011; Miller et al., 1993). Further, the remaining strategies in this list cannot be labeled MI unless they involve the spirit of MI. The spirit of MI involves *how* or the manner in which the strategies are delivered. By implementing the spirit of MI, we seek to develop a partnership with the client and avoid any notion of doing anything "to" or "on" the client. Instead, we strive to work "with" the client and serve as a guide through *the client's* process of change. We believe that each client has the ability to grow and change, and we strive to create an environment of acceptance and compassion to encourage client growth. Our actions are grounded in a desire to be of assistance to our clients and not for any personal gain or that of the agency in which services are provided or any third party. Finally, we honor the wisdom our clients have, and we use evocation to employ this wisdom in our work together.

2. *Avoid arguing.* In any relationship, arguing is often nonproductive. As professionals serving clients, it probably seems obvious that we should not argue with our clients. However, in practice, we may occasionally try to get clients to see a different perspective or help them understand something that we believe will benefit them, and yet our clients do not see it that way. It is not uncommon for clients who are accustomed to arguing with others in their lives to come to treatment or therapy seeking an argument with the therapist. For instance, if the client described earlier, Damon, says to you, "I have no need to be here. I have no issues with drugs. I don't even use drugs. All of this is totally stupid," you might be tempted to respond with, "Well, your JPO [*juvenile probation officer*] said that a teacher caught you using drugs at school, so yeah, you do need to be here." Although you may have a valid argument, what are the benefits of making this argument? What are the possible consequences of making the argument? Even if you are correct and armed with facts, the process of arguing can damage the relationship, reduce trust, and cause the client to further disengage from the therapy process.

3. *Recognize discord and respond.* As the professionals in therapeutic relationships, it is our responsibility to recognize discord and adjust our in-session behaviors to diminish discord. The first step in managing discord effectively is to recognize that it is there. To do so, we have to be in tune with emerging discord at any point during therapy, including the more subtle cues, such as withdrawing, tone, and gestures (Hara, Aviram, Constantino, Westra, & Antony, 2017). For instance, I remember using CBT with a young adult client who was struggling with feeling over-responsible for others' behaviors and relationships. In one session in particular, after several sessions together, I recall encouraging her to adopt an alternative perspective we arrived at collaboratively, and I felt

increasingly frustrated that she was not accepting the healthier perspective I was then attempting to install in her (however benevolently). I noticed her beginning to withdraw from the conversation and responding with "I don't know" an increasing number of times. The frustration I felt and my observations of the client's disengagement from our conversation served as signals for me to recognize the emerging discord in our relationship. "STOP! You're wrestling her," I told myself using Miller and Rollnick's (2013) analogy cautioning against figuratively "wrestling" clients and instead encouraged "dancing" with them (p. 15). In the moment, my frustration was rooted in my belief that the client should adopt the new belief and that she was being difficult by not doing so. My belief was erroneous. It was essential for me to recognize that *I was causing discord in our relationship* by attempting to push a new belief onto her. Once I recognized that my behaviors were resulting in discord, I reflexively took a step back and adjusted my behaviors to "dance" with the client in *her* process of change.

4. **Listen and express empathy.** Miller and Rollnick (2002) coined the phrase "*roll with resistance*" (p. 39) to capture the essence of a helpful response to discord. When rolling with resistance, we refrain from responding to clients with some opposing force. Instead, we listen. To show evidence that we are truly listening and gaining an understanding of the client's perspective, we primarily use reflective statements—including paraphrasing content, mirroring emotion, and reflecting underlying meanings. These statements express accurate empathy. If you are not quite accurate in your reflection, the client will often correct you, which can be helpful in that the client is expressing him or herself more fully, and you have continued to demonstrate your intention to truly understand. If you are correct, the client will feel heard and understood, thus diminishing discord in the relationship. Some therapists can struggle with formulating reflections or using them as the predominant skill. Miller and Rollnick (2013) describe various depths of reflection to differentiate simple reflections, which do not add to what the client already said, and complex reflections, which add a meaning or emphasis to what the client has said. Miller's (2018) book *Listening Well* can assist with grasping reflective listening more fully, including understanding the differences between parroting or repeating what the client already said in a superficial manner and effective reflective listening, which is used to express empathy. For many of us, when we find ourselves in an argument, we are often just trying to be heard. By truly listening and expressing empathy to our clients, we are providing them with the experience of being heard, which in itself is valuable and might be sufficient to move past discord to more productive conversations about change. Further, when clients hear your accurate reflections, they hear themselves through you. In this way, your reflections serve as an opportunity for clients to look into the figurative mirror. Let's look at what reflective listening might sound like with Damon:

Damon: I have no need to be here. I have no issues with drugs, I don't even use drugs. All of this is totally stupid.

Counselor: You're confused as to why you're even here. [*reflection—complex, added emotion*]

Damon: No, I know why; it's because my teacher saw me and my friends and made stupid assumptions about what we were doing.

Counselor: Your teacher saw you and believed you were doing drugs. [*reflection—complex, added that the assumption was using drugs*]

Damon: Yeah, because they don't care if we were or not; they're just looking for any reason to get us slammed.

Counselor: Hmmmm, so it doesn't seem to matter what you do really, drugs or no drugs, they're looking to get you in trouble. [*reflection—simple*]

Damon: Yeah, but what do you care? There's no way you're going to help me. You're just like all the others, I bet.

Counselor: Yeah, so we just met, but it seems you have had enough experiences in the past that cause you to believe we're all the same and that people like me—counselors and therapists—we don't really care. [*reflection—complex, added reference to past experiences*]

Damon: I haven't met one who has helped me yet.

Counselor: Yeah, so the counselors you've seen in the past have not been helpful to you. [*reflection—simple*] I wonder, what did you find that was not helpful to you so that I know not to repeat those same mistakes? [*open question*]

5. **Use OARS.** OARS represent the core skills of MI: open questions, affirmations, reflections, and summarizations. When navigating discord, I get a mental image of a therapist in a canoe using "oars" to work with the stream as opposed to going against it. One of the most common complaints therapists have of "resistant" clients is that they will not talk in session. So here we turn our attention to skills that, when used with the spirit of MI, can increase clients' engagement in the conversation, as well as in therapy overall.

    - *Open questions.* When we ask questions in MI, we typically use open questions to invite the client to share with us. Although closed questions have specific purposes in therapy, they inherently limit the client's responses. While it might be tempting to ask a client who presents as guarded and unforthcoming, "Have you had a bad experience in therapy before?," this is a closed question, and asking it in this way will limit the client's response. Instead, using an open question, such as "Tell me about your experiences in therapy before now," will more likely send the client the implicit message, "I'm not making any assumptions. I want to hear from you. Please share with me."

    - *Affirmations.* Many clients experience circumstances in which they frequently hear about their problems or their negative behaviors, and they might anticipate this same pattern with you. Providing affirmations can offset this dynamic by letting clients know that you see their strengths and their positive efforts. Affirmations have the potential to improve the therapeutic relationship as well as provide the opportunity for the client to become more aware of his or her own positives. In order to be effective, affirmations must be genuine and specific to a particular client. One-size-fits-all affirmations do not exist. They must be based on your observations of a client and then custom made for each individual. For some clients, the

positives are easy to identify. For others, especially those with whom you experience discord, the positives might be more challenging to identify; however, for those clients, highlighting their positive efforts or attributes might be even more meaningful and lead to diminished discord.
- *Reflections.* Reflections are described in #4, as this is the most essential skill to diminish discord. It results in clients feeling heard and understood, as well as clients hearing themselves through you. When we use reflections to roll with resistance, we are essentially eliminating anything in our relationship with the client for the client to resist. We are not pushing or pulling, judging or coercing, only listening and understanding. Using reflections well often results in clients talking more compared to when we ask questions.
- *Summaries.* Summaries serve as evidence that we have heard the client and that we care about what he or she said. We can follow a summary with a question to ensure our understanding is accurate or to inquire if we missed any essential element.

6. **Shift the focus.** When managing discord, summaries can be used to wrap up a conversation when it no longer appears productive or hits a "dead end." The summary is Then followed by an open question to *shift the focus* of the conversation to a potentially more productive area. See the following for example:

Client: You don't care about me. You don't know anything about me, and I don't believe for one second anything you say is actually going to help me.

Counselor: I'm very sorry that is the impression you are getting. [*apology*] It seems you're getting a sense that none of our services will be helpful to you and that I'm not caring about you as an individual, [*summary*] I'd really like to know, from your perspective, if we were able to provide some actual help to you, what would that look like? What do you think would be helpful to you? [*open questions*]

7. **Emphasize autonomy of the client.** It is not uncommon to experience discord in relationships with clients who perceive that their autonomy has been threatened, such as being mandated to treatment by a third party (i.e., parent, employer, judge). Although *you* perhaps have not directly reduced their autonomy, clients can perceive you as being in collaboration with those who have, and therefore, clients can bring that dynamic into the therapeutic relationship. In such cases, it can be helpful to emphasize client autonomy; however, this must be done in a way that is appropriate given the client's specific circumstances. The following suggestions outline specific methods to emphasize client autonomy:
- *Make explicit statements reinforcing personal choice and control.* Professional judgment is needed to make such statements appropriately when working with clients whose autonomy is genuinely limited, such as clients who are incarcerated, mandated to treatment, or children and adolescents. It would be disingenuous to make statements that suggest that these clients have complete independence and control over decisions that affect their lives. In order to be effective, these statements must be applicable to and resonate with the

client. For instance, consider Ms. T, who is mandated to complete parenting classes by a child protection services agency. Ms. T expresses to you that she feels forced to participate. A response such as "You have the choice to attend or not, and yet there would be consequences for not attending" would likely create further discord, as this statement directly counteracts the client's statement and could be perceived as arguing by an adversary. Instead, the counselor might respond using the previous suggestions, including emphasizing personal choice and control, as the following example illustrates:

Ms. T: The social worker told me I had to come in order to get custody of my kids. I don't need any of this. I'm just forced to be here.

Counselor: This was not a decision you made for yourself, to come to these classes. [*reflection*]

Ms. T: I have three kids! What is some class going to tell me that I don't already know about parenting? I bet I could teach you all a thing or two about parenting out here in the real world! Now that might be interesting!

Counselor: Yeah, so you're required to be here and that seems unnecessary to you. [*reflection*] Yet it sounds like you might have a lot to offer in a class like this. I really look forward to hearing what you have to say about the different topics we cover in the class. [*affirmation*]

Ms. T: Well, yeah, I mean, I have a lot of experience, right?

Counselor: Right. And despite the fact that you have to be here, only you can decide how you will use this time. As much as I might want you to participate in the class, I certainly cannot force you to do so. [*emphasizing personal choice and control*]

- *Reinforce that the client is the primary resource in finding answers and solutions to his or her problems.* This strategy is closely aligned with evocation in the spirit of MI in that we believe clients are the experts on themselves and their own lives. Therefore, they know much better than we do what solutions or change strategies might work for them as well as what might not work. Consider Ms. T, the client who is attending parenting classes from the earlier scenario. Ms. T is a mother of three children, and she feels confident in her parenting. Therefore, the parenting class required by the child protection agency is perceived as an insult to Ms. T, as in her mind it dismisses that she is already an effective parent. This dynamic can be mitigated in the class by the counselor reinforcing that the client is the best resource to herself. For instance, before presenting different strategies for disciplining children that do not include corporal punishment, the counselor can ask the class to make a list of all the nonphysical strategies they use. Or when discussing how to establish and maintain clear roles and boundaries with children, the counselor can first ask the clients, "What works for you?" and "What have you found does not work?" When presenting additional strategies, the counselor can make it clear that it is up to the parents to decide what might work for them and their families. By honoring what the clients know and the experience they have, we can reduce discord in the therapeutic relationship.

- *Ask for permission prior to giving information or making suggestions.* It is often a part of our job to provide clients with information. The manner in which we provide the information, however, is just as important as the information itself. Using MI, we provide information that is relevant to clients and directly applicable to their situations, but only after we have received their permission to provide such information. In this way, we respect clients' autonomy to choose to hear the information. For instance, consider if the counselor needed to provide Ms. T information about the law concerning corporal punishment of children, which was the charge that caused Ms. T to have to attend the parenting class. Before providing this information, the counselor would ask, "I wonder if it would be ok if we looked at the law surrounding disciplining children together?" In another example, after honoring what the client already knew about alternative methods to discipline children beyond physical punishment, the counselor might ask for permission to provide information about additional methods by stating, "These are some great ideas. I have a few others in mind that have worked for other clients of mine. Would you mind if I shared a few of them with you?" For the counselor, asking for permission might seem unnecessary at times; after all, providing information is often part of our job. However, we all know what it is like to receive information that we did not ask for, and we understand just how easy it is to tune out, even if we smile and nod politely, when someone is giving us information we did not ask for. Especially when discord is present in the relationship, the receiver of the information is even less likely to absorb unrequested information. By asking for permission, the client's autonomy is honored, and if he or she responds affirmatively, they are more likely to hear and assimilate this information compared to if they were not asked for permission.

Practice Box 7.1

Time for Practice!

A. Imagine you are Damon's counselor. For each statement, form a reflection and then choose an alternative strategy to practice, such as asking an open question, providing an affirmation, shifting the focus, or emphasizing client autonomy.
   1. "I have no need to be here. I have no issues with drugs, I don't even use drugs. All of this is totally stupid."
      Reflection:
      _____
      _____

106 *Methods of Integration*

      Alternative strategy:
      _____
      _____

   2. "What do you think you're going to do to help me?"
      Reflection:
      _____
      _____

      Alternative strategy:
      _____
      _____

   3. "Oh good, another touchy-feely therapist to make it all better. [*with sarcasm and eye roll*]"
      Reflection:
      _____
      _____

      Alternative strategy:
      _____
      _____

B. Now, imagine you are Ms. T's counselor. For each statement, form a reflection and then choose an alternative strategy to practice (open question, affirmation, shift the focus, emphasize autonomy, etc.):

   4. "There is nothing you all are going to tell me that I don't already know about parenting my babies. I birthed them, and I know them like the back of my hand!"
      Reflection:
      _____
      _____

      Alternative strategy:
      _____
      _____

   5. "This class is a waste of my time. I could be spending this time with my children, you know."
      Reflection:
      _____
      _____

      Alternative strategy:
      _____
      _____

6. "I bet you don't even have children, do you?"
   Reflection:
   _____
   _____

   Alternative strategy:
   _____
   _____

Developing Discrepancy to Increase Problem Recognition

Using CBT with clients who lack problem recognition can be a challenge. Expecting clients to engage in action-oriented interventions when they do not believe they need to change can be frustrating for the therapist as well as the client. Implementing MI can assist in meeting clients where they are in their process of change and responding to them in ways that can foster their readiness for change. Developing discrepancies is one strategy used in MI that can be an effective method to increase client awareness of a problem. The timing of this strategy is important to consider, as it might be most effective after discord in the relationship has mostly dissipated. Miller and Rollnick (2013) noted that most clients, even if they appear unmotivated, will begin to use change talk when the counselor is using MI. In these cases, the counselor would hone in on the change talk and use strategies described in the next section to further evoke and reinforce change talk. Some clients, however, may not use any change talk initially, and these clients might benefit from "instilling discrepancy," or discussing potential reasons why the client might consider change (Miller & Rollnick, 2013, p. 247). As with all MI work, these reasons are elicited from and grounded in the client's perspective.

In the examples used previously in this chapter, both Damon and Ms. T appeared to be precontemplative in that they did not see themselves as having a problem. To begin developing discrepancies, a counselor might use a value card sort with Damon in which Damon selects his top-five values after sorting a group of 20–30 values, each on its own card (e.g., Miller, C'de Baca, Matthews, & Wilbourne, 2001). After using OARS to explore Damon's top values, the counselor can develop discrepancies between what is most important to Damon and his current behaviors. For example, if Damon reported "loyalty" and "wealth" as his top values, the counselor can explore what these mean to him and then how his current troubles in school and being associated with substance use might be congruent or incongruent with these values. More specific discrepancies can be developed after the counselor and client complete the focusing process of MI in which they collaboratively determine the focus of their work together (i.e., improving compliant behavior at school, reducing/ceasing drug use).

The following dialogue illustrates how a counselor might develop discrepancies with Ms. T:

Ms. T: This class is a waste of my time. I could be spending this time with my children, you know.

Counselor: Spending time with your children is precious to you. [*reflection of client's value*]

Ms. T: Yeah, they grow up fast, you know? And I'm raising them right. I know CPS [*Child Protective Services*] has a lot to say about that; I'm not raising them to talk back and be foolish.

Counselor: It's very important to you to raise them well, and yet you mentioned that CPS maybe has a different perspective about that. [*instill discrepancy*]

Ms. T: Well, yeah, CPS says I can't discipline my children right. They say I have to learn their way.

Counselor: You and CPS don't quite agree on how to discipline children. [*reflection*]

Ms. T: Well, I mean, I don't beat my kids. I'm not trying to traumatize them. But they do need to show respect, and that's what I'm teaching them.

Counselor: Your goal is to teach them to be respectful, and yet the way it's been going led you to have to take a class like this. [*develop discrepancy*]

Ms. T: Yeah, and now they're tracking me, you know, with this case. If they see another instance, they're threatening to remove them. And now that's just ridiculous!

Counselor: If they see any more evidence of additional physical punishment, it seems like you'd face spending even more time away from your kids, even having them removed from your home, which is the opposite of what you want. [*further developing discrepancy*]

Ms. T: Yeah, so I guess I'll go through with all this. Again, I don't abuse my kids; it's just this is what my mother did with us, and it was fine at that time. This is how we discipline.

Counselor: This is all you've known, and yet you're in a situation where you're finding you might have to learn another way in order to live with and spend that precious time with your kids. [*double-sided reflection*]

Using MI to Address Ambivalence

Ambivalence can be defined as "simultaneous and contradictory attitudes or feelings toward an object, person, or action" (Merriam-Webster, n.d.). Norcross, Krebs, and Prochaska (2011) reported that approximately 40% of clients are in the contemplation stage of change, which is characterized by ambivalence. Within the scope of MI, we believe ambivalence is typical and expected in change, and yet we also understand that ambivalence is complex and often multifaceted. For instance, consider your own life for a moment and think about something that you have thought about changing, but that you have not yet changed. Common examples from students and trainees include getting more exercise, eating healthier, quitting smoking, spending time in a different way (e.g., less time on social media, more time with kids or aging parents), and managing finances differently. Once you have something in mind, ask yourself, "Why do I want to do this? How will it benefit me?" Your responses encompass your motivations for change, or your "change talk." Then ask yourself, "Why haven't I done this yet? What might it cost me?" These are your motivations for the status quo or against change, or "sustain talk." Ambivalence is composed of both of these together—motivations for change and motivations against change. Our clients experience ambivalence in this same way; it is not pathological but rather a very common experience of having contradictory motivations that juxtapose to create an impasse in the change process. Often, it's complicated, and various facets of change can take time to explore more deeply. Using MI provides clients with the time, space, and therapeutic environment for this personal exploration.

Another essential characteristic of ambivalence is that it is an *intrapersonal* construct. Considering again the behavior that you are ambivalent about, notice that you do not need anyone else to be involved in order to experience ambivalence; although, of course, others will influence your motivations (e.g., having a walking partner, family asking to spend time with you). Miller, Moyers, Amrhein, and Rollnick (2006) distinguished sustain talk (client statements that are against change or favor the status quo) from resistance (now known as discord). Miller et al. (2006) suggested that "sustain talk" should be used to describe client statements of desire, ability, reasons, and needs not to change or in favor of the status quo as well as commitment to the status quo, whereas "resistance" defined in-session client behaviors, such as defensiveness or negative comments directed to or about the counselor or services provided. With this distinction in mind, we now turn our attention to conceptualizations and skills used in MI to address client ambivalence. Chapter 6 described addressing ambivalence using MI prior to CBT. Here we will explore implementing MI in the midst of CBT. Although ambivalence may be resolved through MI sessions before embarking in CBT or some clients may not present with ambivalence initially, it is common for motivational issues to arise during the course of therapy as clients begin to embark on actual behavior change (Driessen & Hollon, 2011).

In the next section, we will explore using MI to address ambivalence related to CBT work specifically, including session attendance, participating in therapeutic activities, and completing homework (strategies to address ambivalence about change in general can be found in Chapters 6 and 9). For each of these areas, ambivalence can present as noncompliance—the client who is missing therapy sessions, who avoids participating in in-session interventions, and who returns to session with incomplete homework. In each scenario, using CBT we might be tempted to confront the behavior. When using MI, however, we aim to maintain the spirit of MI, and we focus on reengaging the client into treatment using the following strategies to evoke and strengthen change talk specific to CBT treatment:

110 *Methods of Integration*

1. ***Ask evocative questions.*** When exploring ambivalence, evocative questions can be extremely useful when used with the spirit of MI. Using this strategy, we elicit the client's explanations about what is stopping him or her from fully complying in treatment, and then we use open questions to evoke his or her motivations—specifically desires, abilities, reasons, needs, and commitments—to engage fully. In essence, we seek to understand both sides of the client's ambivalence. For instance, we might start with an observation or self-involving statement followed by an open question:
   - "I saw that you missed our appointment this week, and I was concerned. How is everything going for you?"
   - "I know sometimes it can be tough to try out new things in session together. What is it like for you to think about trying out these skills here with me?"
   - "It is not uncommon for clients to come in with incomplete homework from time to time. I wonder what got in your way of completing the homework this week?"

   After listening and seeking to understand the client's barriers to treatment compliance, we can evoke client change talk in regard to how compliance might benefit the client and the capabilities he or she possesses that would enable the client to be compliant. For instance, if Ms. T missed a parenting class, after the counselor inquired about the reasons why and then listened and understood her situation, the counselor might ask, "I wonder what information CPS has provided you about missing additional classes?" or "How do you imagine the missed class might affect your case with CPS?" In this way, Ms. T is considering the potential outcomes herself without the need for the counselor to "confront" or "warn" her of any potential consequences.

   For an example that focuses on engaging in therapeutic activities, let's imagine Damon came to a group counseling session in which the topic was refusal skills related to substance use. When it was his turn, Damon hesitated to get up and conduct the role play. In an individual conversation, you learn that Damon understands that he has to complete treatment, but he thinks the role play is "dumb." In response you might say, "It's actually super common for people to not be excited to act out these skills in group, so you're certainly not alone in that. What are your thoughts about why we include these role plays in treatment? What good do you think might come out of them? [*evocative questions*]?" In addition to eliciting the benefits Damon might incur from the role play, the counselor might also use evocative questions to ask about how he might use this information: "Tell me about a situation in which you might use these skills?" Or ask about his ability to engage in the role play: "How have you been able to refuse substances in the past?"

2. ***Use scaling rulers.*** Using rulers can be helpful to assist clients in scaling their motivation, commitment, readiness, confidence, or perceived importance of a change or therapeutic activity. For instance, a commitment ruler might be used to assess the client's commitment to attending ten weekly counseling sessions and then to evoke the client's motivations for why they chose that number and not a lower number (Naar & Safren, 2017). The following is an example of

using a commitment ruler with Ms. T for attending the parenting classes after she missed a class:

Counselor: Ms. T, on a scale from 1 to 10, where 1 is not at all and 10 is most definitely, how would you rate yourself in your commitment to attend the remaining parenting classes?
Ms. T: Oh, I'd say an 8 or 9 or so. I do plan to attend; it's just that stuff comes up, you know.
Counselor: Ok, so even when stuff comes up, you would rate yourself at an 8 or 9?
Ms. T: Yeah, I'm going to do my best.
Counselor: I really appreciate your effort, Ms. T. I wonder, what caused you to say 8 or 9 instead of a lower number, such as a 5 or 6?

The counselor asked why Ms. T was not a lower number to evoke her confidence and solidify her reasons for rating an 8 or a 9.

The following is an example of using a confidence ruler with Damon to focus on his ability to engage in refusal skills after completing the role play:

Counselor: Damon, you gave that role play a good shot! I'm curious, now that you've practiced these skills, on a scale from 1 to 10, where 1 is not at all and 10 is most definitely, how would you rate your confidence in your ability to use these skills outside of our group counseling session?
Damon: Oh, I don't know. Maybe a 4.
Counselor: Ok, a 4. And tell me what made you choose 4 instead of a 1 or a 2?
Damon: I did them once, and it felt really stupid, but I did them.
Counselor: I see, so you have a start on these skills, but it's still not super comfortable for you to do.
Damon: Yeah.
Counselor: So, what do you think would help you get to a higher number in your confidence, like a 6 maybe?
Damon: I'd have to say stuff that I would really say, you know, in real life.
Counselor: You'd have to use your own words and put your own spin on it.
Damon: Yeah.
Counselor: Well, I think this is a great place to try that out. Would you be willing to try another role play, but this time don't follow the activity so much as say what comes more naturally to you when refusing the drugs?

Rulers can also be used to address homework compliance. For instance, a therapist might ask, "On a scale from 1 to 10, where 1 is not at all and 10 is very important, how important would you say this homework is in regard to helping you make the changes you would like to?" If the client respond with a 2, the therapist can follow up by asking, "Why a 2 and not a 1?" to evoke the small amount of importance the client did attribute to the homework. Then it would be essential to flush out and understand the client's reasons for rating the importance of the homework so low and ask, "What would it take for the homework to increase in importance to you, perhaps going from a 2 to a 4 or

5?" Based on the client's responses, the counselor might adjust the homework to improve the relevancy of it to the client.
3. ***Asking about extremes, the past, and the future.*** Asking about extremes can be used to evoke the client's ideas about the positives that might come from engaging in or fully complying with treatment and negatives that might come with not completing or failing to comply, both of which result in change talk to further strengthen clients' motivation for treatment compliance and change. For example, if Ms. T was ambivalent about trying new strategies she learned in the parenting class with her children, then the counselor might choose from the strategies listed in Table 7.1 to help evoke Ms. T's motivation.
4. ***Connecting treatment to goals and values.*** As Miller and Rollnick (2013) emphasized, "No one is truly 'unmotivated'" (p. 177). All individuals have their own priorities in regard to what is most important to them. Often, however, clients' goals and values might be very different than ours or what we assume their values and goals to be. In addition to this discussion being relevant to encourage change overall, we can embark on exploring clients' goals and values and make connections to treatment. Consider Ms. T's explicit value of her children. The counselor might say something like, "It's so clear that you love your children deeply. It seems that taking this class, although inconvenient, is just another act of love for you—it's all for your kids." For other clients, we might explore more. For instance, we might ask Damon, "What is most important to you in your life right now?" Even if his response is "to get the school and JPO off my back," the counselor can make the connections between treatment compliance and his goal.

Table 7.1 Examples to Evoke Ms. T's Motivation for Treatment Compliance

Ask about extreme of consequences	• "Suppose you continued disciplining your children as you have been without implementing new strategies. What do you imagine is the worst that would happen?"
Ask about extreme of benefits	• "Imagine if you went home today and maybe this evening or tomorrow you tried this new way out. What good things might come of that?"
Looking forward	• "If you decide to try out these new strategies at home, what would you see happening in the future? What might that lead to?" • "If you look into the future and you do not change how you discipline your children, what do you see happening? What might that lead to?"
Looking back	• "It's very common for people to change for their kids, including adding new behaviors and stopping old behaviors. Of course, now we're talking about your behaviors related to disciplining your children, but I wonder if you've changed your behavior in other ways for your kids?"

Practice Considerations

Although there are many possible considerations for using MI to assist with discord and a lack of readiness to change or engage in CBT work, to close this chapter, I will address a few of these. First, clinicians who are seasoned in their use of CBT might be tempted to implement the MI strategies as a part of CBT. When using this type of assimilative integration, it should be clear what is MI and what is CBT or to be working toward a true blending of the approaches (see Chapter 9), but it should not be misunderstood that MI turns into or is in any way part of CBT. Miller and Rollnick (2009) clarified that MI is not a form of CBT and that it is not "practice as usual" prior to intentional training in MI. It is common for various components of MI to resonate with CBT clinicians, especially in regard to components that might overlap; however, Miller and Rollnick (2009) cautioned that although MI might seem familiar, MI-competent practice has not been found to be correlated with clinician's self-perceived competence, meaning intentional training in MI is necessary (see Chapter 14). Second, the timing of assimilating MI into CBT must be considered. When a single therapist is using both CBT and MI in this fashion, the therapist would determine when to switch from CBT to MI and vice versa. As Aviram et al. (2016) reported, it is essential that the therapist respond at the time when discord emerges in the relationship. More research is needed in this area to explore the impact of responsivity in addressing ambivalence. In other circumstances, such as when a CBT group is running without an MI component, it might be beneficial to assimilate MI at specified times, such as prior to the group and every three subsequent sessions, as a systematic way to consistently assess and address regressions in readiness to change (Marker & Norton, 2018).

Summary

Assimilating MI into CBT has the potential to mitigate some limitations of CBT, including addressing discord in the therapeutic relationship, enhancing problem recognition, and addressing ambivalence about therapeutic activities involved in CBT. In this type of integration, CBT is the primary treatment approach into which MI is incorporated only when discord emerges in the therapeutic relationship or when the client is not yet ready for or not complying with action-oriented interventions of CBT. MI has been found to assist with CBT treatment compliance, including treatment attendance, engagement in therapeutic activities, and homework completion.

References

Arkowitz, H. (2002). Toward an integrative perspective on resistance to change. *Journal of Clinical Psychology, 58*(2), 219–227. doi:10.1002/jclp.1145

Arkowitz, H., & Westra, H. A. (2004). Integrating motivational interviewing and cognitive behavioral therapy in the treatment of depression and anxiety. *Journal of Cognitive Psychotherapy, 18*(4), 337–350. doi:10.1891/jcop.18.4.337.63998

Aviram, A., Westra, H. A., Constantino, M. J., & Antony, M. M. (2016). Responsive management of early resistance in cognitive–behavioral therapy for generalized anxiety disorder. *Journal of Consulting and Clinical Psychology, 84*(9), 783–794. doi:10.1037/ccp0000100

Beck, J. S. (2005). *Cognitive therapy for challenging problems: What to do when the basics don't work.* New York, NY: Guilford Press.

Beck, J. S. (2011). *Cognitive behavior therapy: Basics and beyond* (2nd ed.). New York, NY: Guilford Press.

Beutler, L. E., Harwood, T. M., Michelson, A., Song, X., & Holman, J. (2011). Resistance/reactance level. *Journal of Clinical Psychology, 67*(2), 133–142. doi:10.1002/jclp.20753

Brehm, J. W., & Brehm, S. S. (1981). *Psychological reactance: A theory of freedom and control.* New York, NY: Academic Press.

Driessen, E., & Hollon, S. D. (2011). Motivational interviewing from a cognitive behavioral perspective. *Cognitive and Behavioral Practice, 18*(1), 70–73. doi:10.1016/j.cbpra.2010.02.007

Ellis, A. (2005). Rational emotive behavior therapy. In R. J. Corsini & D. Wedding (Eds.), *Current psychotherapies* (7th ed., pp. 166–201). Belmont, CA: Brooks/Cole.

Hara, K. M., Aviram, A., Constantino, M. J., Westra, H. A., & Antony, M. M. (2017). Therapist empathy, homework compliance, and outcome in cognitive behavioral therapy for generalized anxiety disorder: Partitioning within- and between-therapist effects. *Cognitive Behaviour Therapy, 46*(5), 375–390. doi:10.1080/16506073.2016.1253605

Leahy, R. L. (2003). *Cognitive therapy techniques.* New York, NY: Guilford Press.

Leahy, R. L. (2008). The therapeutic relationship in cognitive-behavioral therapy. *Behavioural and Cognitive Psychotherapy, 36*(6), 769–777. doi:10.1017/S1352465808004852

Marker, I., & Norton, P. J. (2018). The efficacy of incorporating motivational interviewing to cognitive behavior therapy for anxiety disorders: A review and meta-analysis. *Clinical Psychology Review, 62*, 1–10. doi:10.1016/j.cpr.2018.04.004

Merriam-Webster. (n.d.). *Ambivalence.* Retrieved from www.merriam-webster.com/dictionary/ambivalence

Miller, W. R. (2018). *Listening well: The art of empathic understanding.* Eugene, OR: Wipf and Stock.

Miller, W. R., Benefield, R. G., & Tonigan, J. S. (1993). Enhancing motivation for change in problem drinking: A control comparison of two therapist styles. *Journal of Consulting and Clinical Psychology, 61*(3), 455–461. doi:10.1037/0022-006X.61.3.455

Miller, W. R., C'de Baca, J., Matthews, D. B., & Wilbourne, P. L. (2001). *Personal values card sort.* University of New Mexico. Retrieved from http://www.motivationalinterviewing.org/sites/default/files/valuescardsort_0.pdf

Miller, W. R., Moyers, T. B., Amrhein, P. C., & Rollnick, S. (2006). A consensus statement on defining change talk. *MINT Bulletin, 13*(2), 6–7. Retrieved from https://motivationalinterviewing.org/sites/default/files/MINT13.2.pdf

Miller, W. R., & Rollnick, S. (2002). *Motivational interviewing: Preparing people for change* (2nd ed.). New York, NY: Guilford Press.

Miller, W. R., & Rollnick, S. (2009). Ten things that motivational interviewing is not. *Behavioural and Cognitive Psychotherapy, 37*(02), 129. doi:10.1017/S1352465809005128

Miller, W. R., & Rollnick, S. (2013). *Motivational interviewing: Helping people change* (3rd ed.). New York, NY: Guilford Press.

Moyers, T. B., Manuel, J. K., & Ernst, D. (2015). *Motivational interviewing treatment integrity 4.2.1.* Retrieved from https://casaa.unm.edu/download/miti4_2.pdf

Naar, S., & Safren, S. A. (2017). *Motivational interviewing and CBT: Combining strategies for maximum effectiveness*. New York, NY: Guilford Press.

Norcross, J. C., Goldfried, M. R., & Arigo, D. (2016). Integrative theories. In J. C. Norcross, G. R. VandenBos, D. K. Freedheim, & B. O. Olatunji (Eds.), *APA handbook of clinical psychology: Theory and research* (Vol. 2, pp. 303–332). Washington, DC: American Psychological Association.

Norcross, J. C., Krebs, P. M., & Prochaska, J. O. (2011). Stages of change. *Journal of Clinical Psychology, 67*(2), 143–154. doi:10.1002/jclp.20758

Rosengren, D. B. (2018). *Building motivational interviewing skills: A practitioner workbook* (2nd ed.). New York, NY: Guilford Press.

Seibel, C. A., & Dowd, E. T. (1999). Reactance and therapeutic noncompliance. *Cognitive Therapy and Research, 23*(4), 373–379. doi:10.1023/A:1018751817046

CHAPTER 8

Assimilating CBT Into MI

MI can be used as a stand-alone approach or in conjunction with other approaches (Miller & Rollnick, 2004, 2013); however, Miller and Rollnick (2009) explicitly noted that MI was never intended to be a comprehensive treatment. Instead, they described MI as a specific approach to address the distinct problem of ambivalence about change. As MI has evolved, it has been applied to each stage of change as well as to treatment initiation through maintenance (Miller & Rollnick, 2013; Naar-King, Earnshaw, & Breckon, 2013). As a style of counseling, use of MI can be sustained even when choosing to implement another approach.

In this chapter, we explore assimilative integration in which the therapist uses MI as the foundational approach and then incorporates CBT as needed, such as when the client has resolved his or her ambivalence and is motivated to change but does not know how. This type of integration might appeal to clinicians who are trained in and implement MI routinely in practice and who are considering complementary approaches to employ when clients appear ready for action-oriented interventions or if skills appear to be necessary for clients to make desired changes. Given that MI is a style of counseling, the spirit, skills, and processes of MI can be maintained while implementing CBT interventions. Figure 8.1 illustrates the process of assimilating CBT into MI work with clients.

Why Integrate CBT?

Research has shown that using nondirective approaches with clients who are motivated to change is not as helpful as using more directive approaches (Beutler, Harwood, Michelson, Song, & Holman, 2011). It is essential to match the readiness for change of these clients, just as it is to match the readiness of clients who are precontemplative or ambivalent about change. As a treatment that emphasizes action, CBT is effective with clients who are in the preparation or action stages of change (Norcross, Beutler, & Goldfried, 2019). Norcross, Krebs, and Prochaska (2011) noted that for many clients, awareness of the need for change is not sufficient to result in actual behavior change. Despite clients having sufficient motivation to change, this often does not equate to clients knowing *how* to alter their behaviors in ways that will be effective and sustainable. To draw an analogy, imagine that

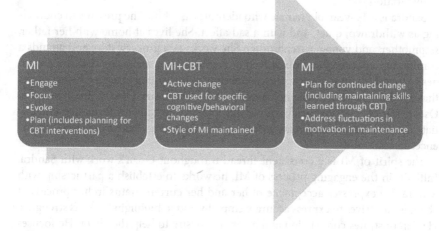

Figure 8.1 Assimilating CBT Into MI

you really wanted to engage in a new behavior, such as playing the piano. You might be very motivated and even purchase a piano. You might enjoy sounding out a few songs, but unless you are musically gifted, you will likely only get so far in your ability to play the piano without the guidance of a teacher. From a piano teacher, you can learn how to read music and how the musical notes on paper transfer to the keys on the piano. Similarly, when using CBT, the therapist in essence teaches the client new skills. These skills can target cognitions, such as the influence of thoughts on behaviors and emotions and replacing maladaptive cognitions with healthy, realistic cognitions, and target behaviors, such as effective communication skills and relaxation techniques. Therefore, the cognitive restructuring and behavioral skills included in CBT can be largely beneficial to clients who are ready for change but who are unsure of how to go about doing so. In their study of self-identified integrative psychologists, Norcross, Karpiak, and Lister (2005) found that most integrative treatments include CBT as one of the approaches incorporated. Although there is a dynamic range of treatments and strategies under the CBT umbrella from which to draw, in this Chapter we explore the value of CBT approaches in general and describe implementing several common CBT interventions in the midst of using MI as the foundational clinical approach. First, we examine MI as the foundation into which CBT interventions are incorporated and illustrate through a case example.

The MI Foundation

Assimilating CBT into MI is conducted in a manner that is responsive to the needs of the client. With MI as the foundation, this type of integrated practice would not be used with a manualized or a "fit the client to the treatment" approach. Instead,

118 *Methods of Integration*

CBT interventions are tailored to the client. The case of Sandra illustrates this type of integration.

Sandra is a 19-year-old female who identifies as white. She presents to counseling as withdrawn, quiet, and with a sad affect. She lives at home with her father, stepmother, and younger stepbrother. She works at a grocery store and attends a community college. She reports feeling depressed but expresses that she has no desire to talk about it. She came to counseling at the urging of a friend who knows that Sandra has been engaging in nonsuicidal self-injury (NSSI). The counselor, Oscar, uses MI as his primary counseling approach to gather information and initiate an effective working relationship with Sandra, who has no previous experiences in counseling.

The spirit of MI is a consistent thread throughout Oscar's work with Sandra. Initially, in the engaging process of MI, he works to establish a partnership with Sandra. He expresses acceptance of her and her current status in her process of change. He strives to express accurate empathy and to highlight Sandra's strengths. He demonstrates compassion and a genuine desire to help the client. He focuses on evocation to draw out Sandra's perspective of the problem. When exploring the client's ambivalence related to talking about her depression, the counselor learns that Sandra is afraid of bringing back hurtful memories. She describes being bullied in middle and high school and currently being treated poorly by her stepmother with whom she lives with her father and younger stepbrother. She notes her mother struggles with substance use and addiction, causing her to be in and out of Sandra's life. Sandra describes using NSSI to help her cope with all the negative that seems to surround her.

After Sandra is engaged in the counseling relationship and process, Oscar begins the focusing process of MI with her. When focusing, Sandra and Oscar agree that depression seems to be the overarching concern, and NSSI is a manifestation of the depression. As they enter the evoking process, they explore Sandra's ambivalence further. Sandra expresses that she does not want to feel depressed, and yet she is not excited to talk about it in talk therapy either. She uses NSSI as a means to cope with the depression, so without an alleviation of depression, she is not willing, nor does she believe she would be able, to stop the NSSI. The counselor uses evocative questions (e.g., "What would you like to change if you were able?") and a looking forward question (i.e., "If you look into the future, and you continue as you have been, not talking about the pain, what do you imagine happening? What might be some good things that can happen by talking about it?") and then reflects Sandra's responses. Sandra expresses further change talk in regard to addressing the painful experiences she has had. She describes the NSSI as being "not a great thing to do," and yet it is the only coping strategy she has found that works for her. She has been cutting consistently for about two years, and she does not plan to continue forever, as she dislikes the scars and having to cover her arms and legs to hide them. She is also getting fearful that she will cut too deep. Recently, the bleeding from one cut would not stop. She sought help from the friend who referred her to counseling. Continuing in the evoking stage of MI, the counselor starts to hear commitment language from Sandra: "I will talk about things with you. I really do want to get better if that's possible." But it is followed by, "But I just don't know how to stop cutting. That's going to take a miracle." With Sandra's commitment to pursue change, the counselor then guides Sandra into the planning process of MI. In doing so, he elicits her ideas about how to reduce or eliminate cutting behaviors. It becomes apparent that no matter how much motivation Sandra may have to no longer engage in NSSI, the motivation alone is not sufficient for Sandra to be able to change this behavior. After she has discovered and strengthened her personal reasons for *why* she will change, Sandra appears to need guidance on *how* to change, which is an indication that Sandra would likely benefit from incorporating CBT into their work together.

Assimilating CBT

CBT differs from MI in that it provides a theory about how change occurs. Therefore, when clients need guidance on how to implement change, CBT can pick up where MI leaves off and provide specific action-oriented interventions. CBT encompasses a wide umbrella of approaches that target cognitions, behavior, and affect. CBT is based on the crucial premise that changes in cognition influence changes in behaviors and emotions, and although targeting cognitions is a vital component of CBT, the ultimate goals are often to change behavior and mood. In the case of Sandra, she hopes to change her feelings of depression, hopelessness, and anger, as well as related behaviors, including NSSI and isolation. Here we will look at common elements of CBT, including the cognitive model, identifying and modifying cognitions, and behavioral skills training, and apply them to Oscar's work with Sandra.

1. ***Cognitive model.*** Implementing CBT interventions, especially those that target client's cognitions, often begin with teaching clients the cognitive model (Beck, 2011). In doing so, we inform clients that their thoughts influence their behaviors and emotions. Illustrating the model using a generic example first and then applying it to the client's situation can help clients understand and connect the model to how it can be useful to them. Figure 8.2 shows the cognitive model being explained using a generic example and then applied to Sandra's experience. Applying the model to the client's case should be done collaboratively in that the counselor is asking the client the questions that coincide with the model, as in Figure 8.2.
2. ***Functional analysis.*** Through the lens of CBT, functional analysis is used to examine the influence of contextual reinforcements and consequences related to the client's behavior (Drossel, Rummel, & Fisher, 2009). In other words, we aim to understand how the client's behavior is working in his or her favor and what the client is getting from engaging in this behavior (what is reinforcing it). On the flip side, we aim to understand the consequences the client is experiencing as a result of the behavior. Drossel et al. (2009) noted that a functional analysis must be understood within the client's unique context and should be a transparent process in which therapists share their conceptualizations with their clients.

120   Methods of Integration

Oscar used the following example to demonstrate how the cognitive model works. The counselor's dialogue is in italics with Sandra's responses next:

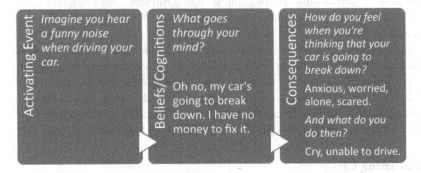

After Sandra understands the essence of the cognitive model, they collaboratively list the consequences Sandra has already described in the "consequences" column. Then they collaboratively identify the activating event and cognitions.

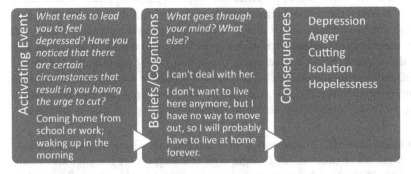

Figure 8.2 Explaining and Applying the Cognitive Model

When using a functional analysis with Sandra, Oscar learns that the antecedent, or the contextual factor that "triggers" her NSSI behavior, is being at home. When she is at home, her stepmother treats her poorly, often making negative comments to her about her appearance (i.e., "Why don't you wear clothes that actually fit you? Try a little!"), her ability in school ("I don't know why you're even going; you're not college material"), and treats her as if she is lower in status compared to her younger stepbrother. Within this context, Sandra experiences negative thoughts (which are rooted in her core belief that she developed from her history with her mother), which further intensifies her urges to cut. Being around her family is punishing to Sandra, and therefore, isolating in her room is a form of negative reinforcement. Cutting serves as a method of emotional release that is reinforced by her environment in that she can do it in isolation without anyone else involved, and it provides her with a needed emotional release. Over time and with repetition, the cutting has been reinforced in these ways, resulting in stronger associations between the antecedents, the NSSI behavior, and the emotional relief.

The counselor shares these ideas with Sandra, and together they further investigate how the NSSI behaviors are being maintained through the reinforcements and develop shared hypotheses (Drossel et al., 2009). Sandra also shares that seeing the drawer where she keeps her razors in her room is associated with the urge to use. The assessment aspect of the functional analysis works in conjunction with the intervention component as Oscar and Sandra work collaboratively to make her environment safer and to develop a plan to engage in alternative behaviors that are more adaptive and that can be readily reinforced given the client's context (e.g., removing the razors and replacing with a squeeze stress ball).

3. *Identifying, evaluating, and modifying cognitions.* When using CBT, therapists help clients increase their awareness of the influence of their thoughts and beliefs on their behaviors and emotions. In revisiting the cognitive model in Figure 8.2, counselors can instill hope by emphasizing to clients that changing the way they think (in the middle column) will enable them to change the way they feel and behave. Various levels of the cognitive hierarchy are of focus systematically during treatment, including automatic thoughts, intermediate beliefs, and cognitive schemas, as well as core beliefs. Not all treatment will address all of the levels down to core beliefs, and these decisions are often left to the therapist's clinical judgment (Naar & Safren, 2017).

After thoughts and beliefs are identified, they are evaluated for accuracy and helpfulness, often using Socratic questioning (Beck, 2011). For instance, using the example of the odd noise heard from the car when driving, we can evaluate the thoughts, "Oh no, my car's going to break down. I have no money to fix it." First, we evaluate the thoughts: Are these thoughts accurate? Where is the evidence that the car will break down? Unless I have previous knowledge of my car malfunctioning or I have mechanical knowledge about cars, I do not really know if the car is going to break down. Therefore, that thought might or might not be accurate, but I do not have the facts to know at this point. Second, if it is accurate, is the thought helpful? It might be accurate that I have no money to fix my car, but is that a helpful thought *at this moment*? Chances are that it is not a helpful thought at the moment, and it is something I can come back to later *if* the car breaks down. After evaluating the cognitions, we can use Socratic questioning to help clients develop alternative beliefs that are both accurate and helpful. For instance, we might revise these thoughts to focus on some problem solving, such as, "I'm not sure what that noise was. I will get to my destination safely and then think about getting it to a mechanic to learn if repairs are needed and how much they might cost."

In Oscar's work with Sandra, he can help her identify her cognitions and begin to evaluate them. Providing Sandra with information about cognitive distortions, or common errors in thinking, might be a helpful way to identify a pattern of maladaptive thinking (Beck, 2011). A list of common cognitive distortions, originally developed by Beck (1976) and further explicated by Burns (1980), is provided in Figure 8.3 along with examples. After guiding Sandra in identifying her cognitions and teaching her how to evaluate them and modify her thinking in session, the counselor collaborates with Sandra on how to continue to develop these changes in between sessions. They decide to use a self-monitoring worksheet in which Sandra will track the antecedents and her

Cognitive Distortions	Description	Example
All-or-Nothing Thinking	• Using black-and-white or dichotomous thinking. Viewing situations through polarization instead of on a continuum.	• "Change is either all good or all bad." • "I am either a total success or a total failure."
Overgeneralization	• Reaching a conclusion based on a single negative event.	• "My relationship ended poorly; therefore, I will never again enter another relationship because they are all bound to end poorly."
Mental Filter	• Using selective abstraction to see only the negative detail instead of all the positive that occurred along with the negative.	• A presentation goes well except for one audience member who asked an impossible question. The presenter focuses solely on the fact that she/he did not know how to answer that one question.
Disqualifying the Positive	• Believing the positive efforts, attributes, qualities do not count.	• Believing the audience clapped for me out of pity, not because my performance was good.
Mind Reading	• Believing you know what others are thinking without stopping to consider other likely possibilities.	• "They did not invite me because they do not like me." • "My boss did not train me in this task because she is setting me up to fail."
Fortune-Telling/ Catastrophizing	• Predicting a negative outcome, regardless of other possible outcomes.	• "It does not matter what I do, I will not pass the test." • "If I go to the party, I will feel stupid and not have anyone to talk to."
Magnification and Minimization	• Magnifying the negative and minimizing the positive.	• "I got nearly all As this term, but that's just because they were easy courses. I got one B because I'm really not smart."

Figure 8.3 Common Cognitive Distortions

Cognitive Distortions	Description	Example
Emotional Reasoning	• Believing something is true despite evidence to the contrary.	• "I know I will not get the job; I can feel it in my gut that they do not want to hire me."
Should Statements	• Using "should" and "must" to describe how self and others need to act and believing that there should be consequences if not.	• "How can they drive like that?! They should never cut me off, and they must obey the laws. They should get pulled over and get a ticket."
Labeling	• Placing a fixed label on self or others, despite evidence to the contrary.	• "He's a lost cause." • "I'm a loner."
Personalization	• Believing others' actions are because of or directed toward you, despite other possible explanations.	• "She is not looking at me because I did something wrong."

Figure 8.3 (Continued)

subsequent thoughts, emotions, and behaviors and then work to evaluate the thought, develop an alternative thought that is accurate and helpful, and track the related outcomes. By addressing her automatic thoughts that are associated with NSSI behaviors and modifying them, over time and with repetition, the associations will begin to change, as well as Sandra experiencing her negative emotions (depression, hopelessness, and anger) less intensely. Further, the alternative thoughts she developed are accurate and helpful in that they have activated some confidence in herself and initiated some problem solving, which in turn reduced the intensity of her feeling depressed and hopeless.

Using a cognitive conceptualization (Beck, 2011), Oscar helps Sandra identify her hierarchy of cognitions, including schemas and core beliefs. Historically, Sandra perceived her mother to love her drugs and alcohol more than Sandra. When Sandra's father remarried when Sandra was 9 years old, she was treated as a second-class child in the household. Through these experiences, Sandra developed the core belief "I am unlovable." Her ways of coping have been to isolate and inflict internalized self-hatred through self-harm. She has intermediate beliefs of "if I stay away from people, I will have less pain," and "no one cares." With this conceptualization, Oscar uses evocation and Socratic questioning to help Sandra modify these underlying beliefs by looking for evidence to support new beliefs, such as "I have friends who care about me" and "my grandmother really loves me." From a menu of options, Sandra decides to use a core belief worksheet and coping cards in between sessions to continue her progress (Beck, 2011).

Retaining MI as an underlying foundation while integrating CBT can assist in maintaining collaboration, honoring the client's autonomy, and evoking from the client as opposed to proscribing alternative beliefs that are grounded in counselor perspectives rather than that of the client. In other words, MI can assist in maintaining a productive working process with clients as opposed to solely focusing on content. For example, client autonomy is honored and respected when choosing whether a cognition needs to be changed. For instance, if Sandra stated she was not interested in altering her thought of "I can't deal with her," then the clinician respects that as her choice while possibly seeking to gain an understanding of her choice by asking, "What would that mean to you to change that thought?" When integrating CBT into MI, some of the techniques used in cognitive restructuring might be slightly adapted to allow for increased MI consistency. For example, when using Socratic questioning to implement guided discovery to help clients evaluate their current ways of thinking, practitioners can do so by using the core skills of MI to ask open questions instead of closed questions and reflecting a client's responses instead of asking multiple questions in a row (Naar & Safren, 2017). Further description of integrating MI and CBT in a blended fashion is provided in Chapter 9.

4. *Additional interventions.* In addition to the cognitive-based interventions described earlier, behavioral skills and emotional regulation are also often under the scope of CBT. These additional interventions would be selected as relevant to the client's concerns and desired outcomes of therapy. In the context of assimilating CBT into MI, they would only be chosen if there was evidence to suggest that the client currently does not have this skill set and such skills training would benefit his or her overall process of change to reach his or her goals. Behavioral activation, graded tasks, problem-solving skills, distress tolerance, relaxation and mindfulness skills, exposure, refusal skills, communication skills, and assertiveness skills are some of the common additional interventions used in CBT (Beck, 2011; Naar & Safren, 2017). Research and literature surrounding the client's presenting concerns or disorders should inform decisions about additional interventions chosen. For instance, behavioral activation has been shown to be vastly effective with clients who experience depression (Jacobson et al., 1996; Mazzucchelli, Kane, & Rees, 2009), and refusal skills and assertiveness training have been found to be effective components of substance use treatment (Witkiewitz, Donovan, & Hartzler, 2012; Witkiewitz, Villarroel, Hartzler, & Donovan, 2011).

In regard to Sandra, Oscar introduces the ideas of distress tolerance, mindfulness, and assertiveness skills based on the effectiveness of these CBT interventions with clients who experience NSSI (Andover, Schatten, Morris, Holman, & Miller, 2017). He introduces these ideas in an MI-consistent way as follows:

Counselor: I wonder if you have heard of "distress tolerance" or "mindfulness" before. [*closed question; first elicit in EPE*]
Sandra: I've not heard of the first one, but we had to do mindfulness or meditation or whatever in school.
Counselor: Oh really? Tell me about what you did in school. [*open question*]
Sandra: It was in high school; they had us close our eyes and breathe, and the voice on the recording told us what to do.
Counselor: What kinds of things did they tell you to do? [*open question*]
Sandra: You know, focus on your breathing. I don't really remember much else.
Counselor: Ok, would it be ok if I shared with you a little about distress tolerance and how it works with mindfulness? [*asking for permission before providing information*]
Sandra: Sure, ok.
Counselor: Distress tolerance means that you're increasing your level of acceptance and your ability to tolerate distressing situations and feelings. This can be done by distracting yourself, changing your thinking like we've talked about, or using relaxation techniques, such as mindfulness. How does that sound so far? [*providing information; open question*]
Sandra: So like when I get home and my stepmom's mean to me, I work to accept it?
Counselor: You would work to accept your response to her. For instance, you might say to yourself, "There she goes again, doing the same things that bother me. I am not going to let her get to me," or something else that helps you tolerate the distress you experience. [*providing information*]
Sandra: I see. So something like, "She's being an a-hole again. I don't care. I'll just leave"?
Counselor: That's a great start! What do you think about working further on increasing distress tolerance for these situations? [*encourager; open question to elicit Sandra's use of the information provided (EPE)*]
Sandra: Yeah, I think that might help.
Counselor: You feel hopeful about that. [*reflection of emotion*]
Sandra: Yeah.
Counselor: Ok, right now, when you feel distress, in a way it seems you're increasing your tolerance by cutting. I wonder about other physical ways you could distract yourself when you start to feel depressed when you're at home or when you have the urge to cut. [*linking summary; open question*]
Sandra: Ummmm, I don't really know. There's not much I can do in my room.
Counselor: I see, your room seems to limit you a bit. [*reflection*] (Pause) I have some ideas from other clients who I've worked with. Would you be interested in hearing them? [*asking for permission before making suggestions*]
Sandra: Yeah, sure.

From here, the counselor can introduce various distractions that are physical in nature but not harmful. Examples might include taking a shower, touching a plush pillow, squeezing a stress ball, putting on lotion, or eating a mint or chewing gum. After Sandra chooses activities that she is willing to try, the counselor then describes how to engage in each of the activities mindfully, meaning paying attention to the present moment as an observer without judgment. Oscar also introduced the idea of assertiveness skills to Sandra in the following dialogue:

Counselor: Sandra, for some people who are in situations where they feel like they are not being treated very well, kind of like how you feel at home, working on how to speak up for yourself can be helpful. I wonder what you think about that idea. [*providing information; open question to elicit client's input*]

Sandra: You mean like stand up for myself to my stepmom? Ha! No way.

Counselor: You feel strongly about that. Ok, tell me your thoughts about that. [*reflection; open question*]

Sandra: I used to try to do that. I gave up. My dad just jumps on her side. I end up feeling 1,000 times worse. That's why I started cutting in the first place. I tried to talk to my dad about what she was saying to me and how she treated me, and he just blamed me. No way I'm doing that to myself again. No way.

Counselor: Ok, so you've tried it, and it seemed to make things worse. And I commend you for looking out for yourself in this way—that you're going to avoid situations that would cause you further harm. [*reflection; affirmation*]

Sandra: Yeah, that would not put me in a good place.

Counselor: We will just leave that idea alone then, ok? [*honoring client's autonomy to choose*]

Sandra: Ok.

Oscar respects Sandra's decision to not work on communicating or asserting herself with her family. Instead of attempting to convince her, he listens and understands her perspective and affirms her decision to protect herself.

Resuming MI

After assimilating CBT, and the client has learned the skills necessary for change (e.g., cognitive restructuring, distress tolerance, mindfulness), the therapist resumes MI as the primary approach. The counselor would continue to meet the client in his or her current readiness for change. For instance, if the client remains in action, the therapist can support the client's efforts and reinforce the changes he or she is making. Evocation would be used to help guide the client to apply the strategies and skills learned in CBT in increasingly effective ways and to new situations. The client and counselor can develop an overall plan to promote sustained behavior change. As change is often a nonlinear process, it is common for ambivalence to resurface, especially as contexts change. For example, let's imagine Sandra has been successful in reducing her symptoms of depression, including eliminating NSSI. She moved out of her father's home and into an apartment with a friend. She was approaching four months without cutting when she received a call from her mother. Sandra was cautious but agreed to meet with her mother, who claimed she was just released from jail, and she wanted to apologize to Sandra for all that she has put her through. However, upon meeting with her mother, it became apparent that her mother was seeking money from Sandra. When Sandra refused to give her mother money, her mother became angry and accused Sandra of thinking she is "too good" to be her daughter. Sandra left in tears after her mother stormed out. She recognized her old ways of thinking resurfacing, and she went home and cut. In therapy the next day, she relayed this information to her therapist who listened, reflected, and expressed empathy. After Sandra stated, "Just because of her, now everything I've worked for went down the drain," the counselor summarized and reframed Sandra's relapse:

Counselor: This was a painful experience for you, and it is very natural for a stressor like this to bring back the old ways of thinking and old behaviors. I don't want you to think you're alone in this, as many people fall back into old behaviors after a stressor like this. You made such tremendous progress in the past several months, and although you might be feeling like "all is lost," the tools and knowledge that you've been putting to use are not gone. They are still there, within you. [*summary and reframe*]

Sandra: Yeah, but she just killed it, you know? She, once again, trampled on my success, squashed my happiness. It feels like I'm destined to have this life as long as she is my mother.

Counselor: To you, this feels inevitable, like it will continue no matter what you do. [*complex reflection*]

Sandra: I guess. [*silence*]

It is clear that Sandra's mother and the resurgence of old behaviors has resulted in Sandra's ambivalence reemerging. At this point, her clinical needs are the reverse of what they were prior to CBT—she now knows how to change, and she was successful in doing so for several months; however, she is now struggling with reigniting her motivation to reengage in change due to her perception that all progress is "down the drain." Oscar therefore uses MI with the focus being on reimplementing the skills she learned through CBT.

Counselor: What is it like for you to think about applying the techniques we used early in our work together to this situation? [*open question to explore motivation*]

Sandra: I just don't even know if I have the energy for it, you know? Like this sucked the life out of me.

Counselor: You feel completely deflated, and the work you put into therapy required a lot of energy and effort from you. [*reflection of emotion and sustain talk*]

Sandra: Yeah, I just don't know if I have it in me right now.

Counselor: [*Silence*] I'm curious, if you were to muster the energy to apply some of the strategies you used to, maybe not today but maybe in the future, what would be the first one you might try? What do you think would be most useful to you? [*open question to elicit change talk*]

Sandra: Probably distracting myself instead of cutting, you know? I had the pillow in my room that I used to touch and really pay attention to it, you know, mindfully, instead of cutting, but I didn't even think about it yesterday. I was just too mad. I grabbed a knife from downstairs and that was it.

Counselor: Yesterday, the anger and hurt you felt kind of took over, and you didn't think about alternatives. And yet if an urge comes again, you're thinking that using distraction might be another way to go. [*reflection; complex reflection of change talk*]

Sandra: Yeah, especially after talking it through and now seeing this cut on my arm. All my cuts were healing, going away, but now I have a brand-new one. It seems like starting all over again.

Counselor: You were successful the first time around; you stopped cutting for quite a while, and you felt proud of the work you'd done and the healing of your body. You're continuing to learn about how to keep these changes going, and it seems falling back into these old behaviors is not something you want to continue. [*summary to solidify change talk*]

Sandra: No, definitely not. I'll try again, I know I need to.

The counselor and Sandra would continue in the evoking and planning processes of MI to continue to enhance her motivation to apply the strategies she learned in CBT and plan for reengaging in active change. The counselor would again implement CBT if it seemed as though Sandra needed additional practice to modify her cognitions or if she needed to further develop behavioral skills, such as mindfulness or relaxation. In addition, CBT would be implemented if Sandra changed her mind and decided she indeed wanted to draw on assertiveness skills to have a conversation with her father or mother.

Summary

Integrating CBT into MI might be especially useful to clinicians whose primary approach is MI and who are seeking a compatible therapeutic approach to implement with clients who are ready for active change and who would benefit from cognitive or behavioral interventions. MI provides the foundation of an effective therapeutic alliance in which the therapist matches the client's readiness for change. The therapist begins with the assumption that the client has the wisdom and aptitude for change; however, CBT becomes indicated if the client is ready for and committed to change but appears to need additional skills in order to successfully implement and maintain change. Eventually, clinicians using this type of integration may move toward practicing fully integrated MI+CBT (see the next chapter). However, this may not always be the case, as some clinicians may continue to use MI as their foundational approach and integrate CBT (and other theoretical approaches) when appropriate in the manner of assimilative integration.

References

Andover, M. S., Schatten, H. T., Morris, B. W., Holman, C. S., & Miller, I. W. (2017). An intervention for non-suicidal self-injury in young adults: A pilot randomized controlled trial. *Journal of Consulting and Clinical Psychology, 85*(6), 620–631. doi:10.1037/ccp0000206

Beck, A. T. (1976). *Cognitive therapies and the emotional disorders*. New York, NY: New American Library.

Beck, J. S. (2011). *Cognitive behavior therapy: Basics and beyond* (2nd ed.). New York, NY: Guilford Press.

Beutler, L. E., Harwood, T. M., Michelson, A., Song, X., & Holman, J. (2011). Resistance/reactance level. *Journal of Clinical Psychology, 67*(2), 133–142. doi:10.1002/jclp.20753

Burns, D. D. (1980). *Feeling good: The new mood therapy*. New York, NY: William Morrow and Company.

Drossel, C., Rummel, C., & Fisher, J. (2009). Assessment and cognitive behavior therapy: Functional analysis as key process. In W. T. O'Donohue & J. E. Fisher (Eds.), *General principles and empirically supported techniques of cognitive behavior therapy* (pp. 15–41). Hoboken, NJ: John Wiley & Sons.

Hettema, J., Steele, J., & Miller, W. R. (2005). Motivational interviewing. *Annual Review of Clinical Psychology, 1*(1), 91–111. doi:10.1146/annurev.clinpsy.1.102803.143833

Jacobson, N. S., Dobson, K. S., Truax, P. A., Addis, M. E., Koerner, K., Gollan, J. K., ... Prince, S. E. (1996). A component analysis of cognitive-behavioral treatment for depression. *Journal of Consulting and Clinical Psychology, 64*(2), 295–304. doi:10.1037/0022-006X.64.2.295

Mazzucchelli, T., Kane, R., & Rees, C. (2009). Behavioral activation treatments for depression in adults: A meta-analysis and review. *Clinical Psychology: Science and Practice, 16*(4), 383–411. doi:10.1111/j.1468-2850.2009.01178.x

Miller, W. R., & Rollnick, S. (2004). Talking oneself into change: Motivational interviewing, stages of change, and therapeutic process. *Journal of Cognitive Psychotherapy, 18*(4), 299–308. doi:10.1891/jcop.18.4.299.64003

Miller, W. R., & Rollnick, S. (2009). Ten things that motivational interviewing is not. *Behavioural and Cognitive Psychotherapy, 37*(2), 129. doi:10.1017/S1352465809005128

Miller, W. R., & Rollnick, S. (2013). *Motivational interviewing: Helping people change* (3rd ed.). New York, NY: Guilford Press.

Naar, S., & Safren, S. A. (2017). *Motivational interviewing and CBT: Combining strategies for maximum effectiveness*. New York, NY: Guilford Press.

Naar-King, S., Earnshaw, P., & Breckon, J. (2013). Toward a universal maintenance intervention: Integrating cognitive-behavioral treatment with motivational interviewing for maintenance of behavior change. *Journal of Cognitive Psychotherapy, 27*(2), 126–137. doi:10.1891/0889-8391.27.2.126

Norcross, J. C., Beutler, L. E., & Goldfried, M. R. (2019). Cognitive-behavioral therapy and psychotherapy integration. In K. S. Dobson & D. J. Dozois (Eds.). *Handbook of cognitive-behavioral therapies* (4th ed., pp. 318–345). New York, NY: Guilford Press.

Norcross, J. C., Karpiak, C. P., & Lister, K. M. (2005). What's an integrationist? A study of self-identified integrative and (occasionally) eclectic psychologists. *Journal of Clinical Psychology, 61*(12), 1587–1594. doi:10.1002/jclp.20203

Norcross, J. C., Krebs, P. M., & Prochaska, J. O. (2011). Stages of change. *Journal of Clinical Psychology, 67*(2), 143–154. doi:10.1002/jclp.20758

Witkiewitz, K., Donovan, D. M., & Hartzler, B. (2012). Drink refusal training as part of a combined behavioral intervention: Effectiveness and mechanisms of change. *Journal of Consulting and Clinical Psychology, 80*(3), 440–449. doi:10.1037/a0026996

Witkiewitz, K., Villarroel, N. A., Hartzler, B., & Donovan, D. M. (2011). Drinking outcomes following drink refusal skills training: Differential effects for African American and non-Hispanic White clients. *Psychology of Addictive Behaviors, 25*(1), 162–167. doi:10.1037/a0022254

CHAPTER 9

Seamless Blending of MI and CBT

In this chapter, we explore a method of integration in which MI and CBT are used simultaneously in a seamless blending of these approaches. In this "theoretical integration" approach (Norcross, Goldfried, & Arigo, 2016, p. 306), neither MI nor CBT are the dominant or primary approach, but rather these approaches possess equal value, with the underlying foci of change and techniques melding together with the goal of creating an approach that is more effective than either approach alone. As described in Chapter 4, MI and CBT are complementary approaches in that MI compensates for some of the limitations that can accompany CBT (i.e., explicitly addressing motivational issues such as discord/resistance and ambivalence), and CBT picks up where MI can leave off (i.e., helping clients learn how to change). Integrated together, they allow for the provision of a comprehensive approach to treatment, with the potential for synergistic outcomes. How these approaches are implemented with clients largely depends on the client's needs, including the client's readiness for change and clinical focus in treatment. We will first examine an overview of the blending of MI and CBT and then discuss the process of how to deliver MI+CBT in practice starting with the initiation of counseling and ending with maintenance. This chapter concludes with considerations for practice.

Overview of the Integration of MI+CBT

The implementation of MI+CBT is tailored to each client's unique readiness to change, clinical needs, culture and identity, and contextual factors. Although guidelines may be provided, there is no "one size fits all" in regard to MI+CBT therapy. Decisions about how to implement the various components of MI+CBT can be guided by Figure 9.1. For instance, when clients present with low motivation and low coping skills, the implementation of MI and CBT would be relatively balanced, as the targets of each approach would need to be of focus; however, MI would likely precede CBT in order for the client to have sufficient motivation to learn and apply coping skills through CBT. If the client had low motivation for change, but had fairly effective and sufficient coping skills, the counselor's implementation of MI+CBT might be weighted toward MI to address the motivational issues. If the client was high in adaptive coping and high in motivation, the

132 *Methods of Integration*

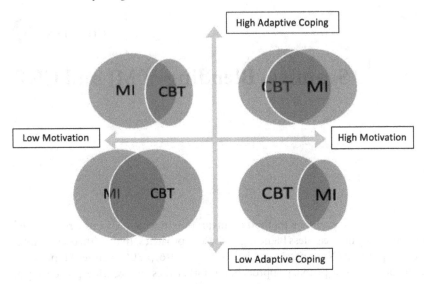

Figure 9.1 Client Responsive Integration

counselor's implementation of MI+CBT would be relatively balanced. Finally, if the client is motivated for change but has ineffective ways of coping, the counselor would implement CBT with MI in reserve. In this way, the client's stage of change also guides the counselor's approach to the therapeutic relationship (Norcross, Krebs, & Prochaska, 2011). Clients are expected to move across quadrants as therapy continues; hence, practitioners must consistently assess and respond to clients through an intentional integration of these approaches instead of relying solely on one approach or the other or using a rigid integrative approach.

Practice Box 9.1 Responsive Approaches to Using MI+CBT

Using Figure 9.1 as a guide, how would you approach each of the following clients?

Client A: A man whose doctor referred him to counseling for depression. In addition to medication, the doctor encouraged the man to attend counseling and to try a "lifestyle change," including changes in diet and physical activity. The man eats a diet that is high in sugar and fat, and he is sedentary most of the day. His job requires him to sit at a desk, and he states that when he gets home, he feels depressed and tired, so he eats fast food from a drive-through restaurant while watching TV. He does not believe anything he does will make a difference; he just wants medication to make him feel better.

Client B: A woman who has generalized anxiety disorder and who has been in treatment before is experiencing a resurgence of symptoms. She comes to counseling for a "refresher" to help her apply the cognitive modifications, breathing techniques, and mindfulness she has learned in the past.

Client C: A 19-year-old woman recently discovered she is pregnant. She wants to do what is best for her baby, but she is overwhelmed and in an unhealthy relationship with the father of her baby, and she wants to leave the relationship. She says, "I know I need to make some serious changes. I just don't know how."

Client D: A 52-year-old man came in for counseling at his wife's urging. The client has been abstinent from substance use for 15 years after completing drug treatment. Recent stressors, including the unexpected death of his brother, caused the client to return to cannabis use. He knows he should not be using, especially because he is a father to two teenage boys, but he tells his wife, "Who cares? Its only pot. We're all going to die anyway."

Process of Integrating MI+CBT

In this section, we explore how MI and CBT can be integrated as a blending of the two approaches throughout counseling. We will start by exploring MI+CBT in the initiation of counseling wherein the therapeutic relationship is established and pertinent information is gathered via assessment. Then the client's concerns are conceptualized and a plan for treatment is agreed upon by client and counselor. This is followed by partaking in mutually agreed upon treatment, with revisions made for progress and otherwise as needed. Latter counseling processes using a blend of MI and CBT are also described in this section, including evaluating progress and maintaining changes while working toward termination.

Initiating Counseling: Assessment and Establishing the Therapeutic Relationship

The onset of counseling essentially has two objectives for the counselor practicing an integration of MI and CBT: (1) to engage in assessment, including gaining an understanding of the client's presenting concerns and circumstances, readiness to address those concerns, and relevant history, and (2) to develop a therapeutic alliance with the client that is based on a humanistic connection and desire to help. These two objectives are not mutually exclusive—in order to have an honest conversation about one's presenting concerns, circumstances, and relevant history (objective 1), the clinician must simultaneously strive to establish a safe, nonjudgmental, and affirming environment in which the client feels heard and validated (objective 2). The engaging process of MI can resemble the collaboration CBT clinicians often strive for in developing an effective therapeutic alliance (objective 2); however, by integrating MI with CBT, the relationship between the counselor and client has an explicit humanistic core, grounded in empathy, compassion, and beginning with reflective listening with the goal of understanding the client's perceptions of the dilemma while gathering essential information to formulate a cognitive conceptualization.

In most settings in which counseling services are provided, the first meeting with a client involves an intake assessment (designed to achieve objective 1). According to Hunsley and Allan (2019), the following should be included in the initial CBT assessment: (1) the client's life contexts and circumstances; (2) client's general psychosocial functioning, social supports, and quality of life; (3) nature and history of the presenting concern and attempts to address the concern; (4) preliminary information about antecedents and consequences of the presenting problem; and (5) possible diagnoses (p. 132). In MI+CBT, these are combined with MI's emphasis on assessing the client's readiness for change and for treatment, as well as ensuring that a sound therapeutic alliance develops and remains intact (Naar & Safren, 2017). As such, the assessment is completed within an accepting and compassionate environment in which open questions are used in the assessment interview in tandem with reflections that express empathy and understanding of the client's responses. By conducting an assessment in this manner, we avoid the question-answer trap, which can discourage clients from sharing information or prevent them from feeling understood, which may result in client defensiveness or disengagement (Miller & Rollnick, 2013). For example, examine the differences in the two interview styles presented next when gathering information about the family history and relationships of a new client, Ricky, a 26-year-old man who is experiencing symptoms of depression, which are causing his work performance and social involvement to suffer.

Style 1: Not MI+CBT

Counselor: Does your family have a history of mental health concerns, such as depression, anxiety, suicide, or addiction? [*closed question*]
Ricky: Yeah, I guess so.
Counselor: Can you say a little more about who and what they experienced? [*closed question*]
Ricky: Yes, my grandfather killed himself before I was born, and I think my father is depressed, although he never talks about it.
Counselor: Has he ever been to treatment? [*closed question*]
Ricky: Not that I know of.
Counselor: Anyone else experience any issues? Substance use? [*closed question*]
Ricky: Well, my dad drinks too. That's how he deals with stuff.
Counselor: Do you talk with your dad? [*closed question*]
Ricky: Not often. Only on holidays, really.
Counselor: What about your mom, do you talk with her? [*closed question*]
Ricky: More than my dad.
Counselor: Do you have siblings? [*closed question*]
Ricky: I have two younger brothers.

Counselor:	Do you talk with them? Do they have any mental health or substance use concerns? [*closed question*]
Ricky:	I don't really know; I don't talk with them often.

Style 2: MI+CBT

Counselor:	Would you mind telling me about your family? [*supporting autonomy*] Who is in your immediate family and what are those relationships like? [*open question*]
Ricky:	Well, my parents are married still, and they live about 25 minutes from me. My mom and I have a pretty good relationship, and we talk sometimes, but not so much with my dad.
Counselor:	Ok, so you talk with your mom, but your dad, not so much. [*simple reflection*]
Ricky:	Yeah, he drinks a lot, and he's not a lot of fun to be around.
Counselor:	So you've learned to kind of stay away and not have much of a relationship with him. [*complex reflection*]
Ricky:	Right, when I was a kid, I didn't know better, but I learned pretty quick not to bother him. I mean, he wasn't abusive or anything, but I think he might be depressed. I don't know. But we've never been close.
Counselor:	You think he might be depressed, and that has affected how he interacts with you. [*complex reflection*]
Ricky:	Yeah, he doesn't really talk to anyone. I know that his dad died before I was born; he shot himself. From what I understand, my grandfather was really depressed and drank a lot. When he died is when my dad changed and started drinking more. And now I'm feeling depressed, so maybe its hereditary or something.
Counselor:	You've perhaps noticed a pattern in your family, between your grandfather, father, and now yourself as experiencing some depression, possibly. [*complex reflection*]
Ricky:	Yeah.
Counselor:	You seem to be aware that suicidal thoughts and behaviors often stem from depression, as what may have been the case with your grandfather. I wonder have you had any thoughts of suicide or wanting to harm or kill yourself in any way? [*closed question, assess risk for suicide*]
Ricky:	No, I haven't—and I don't want to get there either. I guess that's a big part of why I came in today. I don't want to end up like them. [*change talk, desire*]
Counselor:	You'd like to create a different path for yourself. To address the depression and start to feel better. [*reflection of change talk*]
Ricky:	Right, I don't want to just mask it with alcohol or whatever. [*change talk, desire*]
Counselor:	You're determined to find another way. [*affirmation*]

In the first style, the counselor is gathering information using primarily closed questions. It is not uncommon for counselors to have intake forms to guide these initial assessments, which can even promote the use of closed questions and lead to a question-answer trap with clients. However, the client is likely to share the bare minimum in response to the counselor's closed questions, with very little "alliance" or sense of partnership being developed between them. In the second style, using MI+CBT, the therapeutic alliance is being built in addition to the client's motivation being elicited. To do so, the counselor used open questions, reflections, and an affirmation to begin to develop a counseling relationship in which the client feels heard and understood, even when providing information about his background.

The following guidelines based on the recommendations of Naar and Safren (2017) can assist in maintaining MI consistency when using formal and informal assessment methods:

1. *Support client autonomy by asking for permission.* Although assessment is an essential component of counseling, we can support client autonomy by requesting the client's permission to engage in assessment in general as well as prior to administering specific assessments. For example, to describe and ask for permission for assessment in general, a counselor might say, "Today is the intake assessment, which means we will spend our time talking about what brought you to counseling and what you hope to get from coming to counseling. In addition, I will ask you about your background and history and other areas of your life so that I have a good idea of how I can best help you. How does that sound to you?" For a formal assessment, a counselor might say, "I have a questionnaire called the Beck Depression Inventory that can help me get a more objective understanding of the symptoms and severity of depression you're describing. It has 21 questions and usually takes about 5–10 minutes to complete. After clients complete it, I typically talk with them about the results. I wonder what you think about that. Would you be willing to complete that and then talk about it with me afterward?" By describing the processes and purposes of assessment and then asking for client permission to continue, we strengthen the therapeutic alliance by honoring the client's right to choose. If a client indeed says "no" (this is very rare), we seek to understand why ("What about this is offputting to you?" or "Tell me your concerns about this."), without involving our own defensiveness. If, after exploring the concerns, the client's answer remains no, we can collaborate to identify alternatives, including offering a menu of options.
2. *Reflect change talk.* As noted in the example with Ricky, by listening to clients' descriptions of their experiences and presenting concerns, we will often hear change talk. We want to hone in on clients' statements about their desires, abilities, reasons, needs, commitments, and actions toward change and reflect these statements back to the clients. Through these reflections, we aim to hold up a mirror to provide the opportunity for clients to see and hear themselves

through us to further develop their existing motivations for engaging in treatment and for pursuing change.
3. *Ask open questions.* As noted earlier, closed questions can lead to the question-answer trap and possibly elicit defensiveness and disengagement from the client. Asking closed question after closed question results in an "interrogation" feel rather than a helpful interview. Further, the client is restricted in what he or she is able to share, which can harm client engagement in the interview, as well as in overall counseling. By asking open questions, we send clients the implicit message of "I want to hear what you have to say. Please share with me."
4. *Reflect after each question.* This is one of the most helpful guidelines for integrating MI into assessment interviews—*after each question asked to gather information, reflect the client's response.* Reflection is the most used skill in MI, as it expresses empathy and understanding to foster a strong therapeutic alliance as well as provide the opportunity for clients to think more and talk more about their initial responses. Especially in assessment, some clinicians rely on questions to gather information. On the contrary, using more reflections than questions (in MI, we aim to have twice as many reflections than questions in a session) can often lead to gathering more information than asking questions.
5. *Reflect what is omitted.* Beck (2011) noted that assessment of general functioning should also include what clients are *not* doing. Instead of asking a question that might elicit defensiveness, reflections can be used to draw attention to that area (Naar & Safren, 2017). For example, the counselor might say to Ricky, "You've shared how the depression has affected your sleep and your ability to concentrate on your work, and those are areas that bother you, and your social life does not seem to be part of that." Without using a question, we would expect this reflection of omission to guide Ricky to describe his social life, or maybe the absence of one, as well as how his depression does or does not affect him socially.
6. *Use EPE when providing information.* There are many situations in which we might provide information to clients during the initial assessment. For instance, if a client arrives for her first appointment and states, "I'm bipolar," the counselor might follow up with, "Tell me how you know you have bipolar disorder." If the client has a previous diagnosis and treatment history, then there might not be a reason to provide information. However, if she describes symptoms that are not consistent with bipolar disorder and she has no previous clinical history suggesting bipolar disorder, then the counselor might ask for permission to provide accurate information about diagnosis in general, including that mental health professionals use published criteria based on rigorous research. After providing the information, the counselor might ask, "What do you think about going through a diagnostic interview and then we can talk more about how we might describe what you're experiencing?" By using EPE, the counselor is able to balance client engagement with providing corrective information.

Conceptualizing Client Concerns

Conceptualization is an essential linchpin between assessment and treatment. It involves applying theory to develop a functional understanding of the client's concerns, which is then used to select appropriate treatment and inform its implementation to alleviate the presenting concerns (Hunsley & Allan, 2019). Conceptualization begins with the first meeting with a client, and it serves as an ongoing hypothesis that is formulated with the information provided in the initial assessment and that is revised throughout treatment (Beck, 2011; Hunsley & Allan, 2019).

In addition to or as part of the initial assessment, it is recommended that assessment within CBT include a functional analysis to identify the causes of clients' symptoms (Hunsley & Allan, 2019). Traditional CBT also encourages case formulations to identify the cognitive mechanisms as well as contextual factors that influence behavior, emotional regulation and conditioned emotional responses, and skill deficits that cause and maintain clients' problems and symptoms (Persons, Brown, & Diamond, 2019). These are examined in light of the antecedents and origins of the cognitions (Persons et al., 2019) to begin to form a cognitive conceptualization (Beck, 2011). Figure 9.2 illustrates a sample conceptualization using the case of Ricky. The conceptualization presented is grounded in Beck's (2011) model for CBT, with the additional consideration for motivation. For instance, in the intake assessment session, Ricky used change talk about his desire to address his depression. Therefore, he might be ready for treatment, but before embarking on treatment, counselors using MI+CBT would also assess the client's readiness for change. These conversations can be facilitated through the focusing and evoking processes of MI prior to planning for treatment.

MI+CBT Case Conceptualization for Ricky

Relevant Childhood Data:
Client grew up with a father who largely ignored him, likely due to his father's own grief and depression after his father's death by suicide, which he coped with by drinking alcohol and withdrawing.

Core Belief:
"I'm not good enough."

Intermediate Beliefs:
"If I work really hard, I might get noticed."
"If I don't engage in social settings, then I cannot be ignored. It is better to stay home by myself."

Compensatory Strategies:
Striving to overachieve in school and work.
Avoiding social situations, isolating from peers.

Figure 9.2 Example of a MI+CBT Case Conceptualization

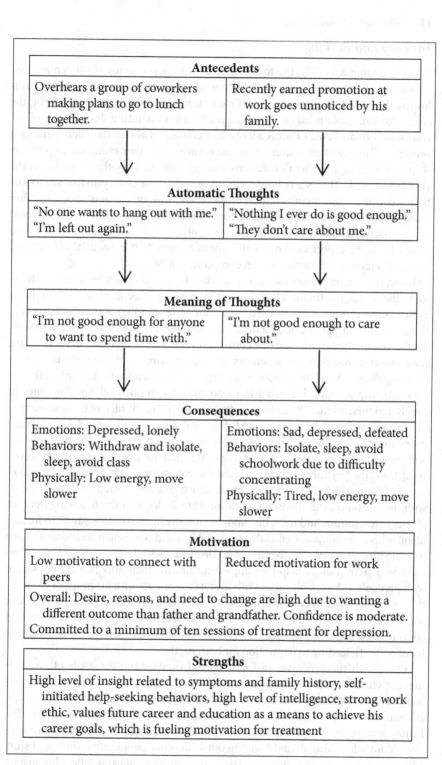

Figure 9.2 (Continued)

Focusing and Evoking

When blending MI+CBT, the focusing and evoking processes of MI can be used as a bridge from assessment and conceptualization to treatment planning. Following the initial assessment, in a collaborative conversation with the client, the counselor can explain his or her conceptualization including descriptions of the counselor's hypotheses of antecedents and consequences of the client's thought processes. Through this conversation, the counselor further establishes a partnership by soliciting the client's reactions and revising the hypotheses based on the client's feedback. This is a rich opportunity to refine the conceptualization to further account for the client's cultural contexts and unique circumstances. In other words, through this conversation, the conceptualization should be further tailored to this particular client and to evade any notion of a "one-size-fits-all" or "the counselor is the expert and knows all" type of approach. It is essential to *listen* and be *client responsive* throughout each component of MI+CBT.

Using the conceptualization as a basis, the client and counselor together determine the foci of treatment. MI-consistent strategies can be implemented to do so. For instance, evocation can be used to gain an understanding of the client's perceptions of what will be most helpful to address in treatment as well as what is a priority for the client when more than one concern is present. For example, in Ricky's case, the counselor would initiate a conversation about prioritizing the various facets of his symptoms of depression by summarizing his lack of motivation for and difficulty concentrating at work, his social isolation, and his strained relationship with his family and then asking, "What bothers you the most?" or "Which of these would you like to address first?" A focusing map (Miller & Rollnick, 2013; Naar & Safren, 2017) is a strategy that can be used in session to help evoke and then collaboratively discuss and prioritize various client concerns. Specific goals are then collaboratively developed from the pertinent concerns. Then the counselor might present a "menu of options" from which the client can choose which goal and related treatment to start with. For instance, the counselor could provide Ricky with the following options: (1) begin to examine and track his thought patterns in each of these areas to further identify his cognitions as well as their antecedents and consequences and then move to evaluating and revising cognitions he determines to be unhelpful, (2) focus on behavioral activation to help him implement healthy behaviors that are consistent with his goals, (3) work on social skills to start to connect with his peers, or (4) work on emotional regulation related to issues concerning his family of origin. Without specific, mutual attention to the focus and goals of counseling, we risk the client and counselor having different ideas about what the focus of treatment is (or what to focus on first), leading to frustration for both parties.

Along with the processes of focusing and establishing the goals of counseling, the client's readiness to engage in therapeutic actions to achieve these goals is assessed, including readiness to implement changes in daily life. Of course, it is common for a client's readiness to change to vary for different concerns. For instance, if we are examining the various foci for Ricky, and he states, "I just cannot see myself talking to and hanging out with other people after work and stuff. I just don't think that's going to happen," we can hear this and reflect his sustain talk in this area. He might place social isolation low on his priority list as a result of his ambivalence to address this concern. Therefore, evoking and focusing can go hand-in-hand in that counselors want to be in tune with how ambivalence might influence what clients are willing to address and when. Perhaps after addressing his top concern of not being able to concentrate and feeling low motivation for work, Ricky might agree to revisit social isolation as part of treatment. Then the client and counselor can plan accordingly, including revisiting the evoking process to address his ambivalence surrounding change in this area.

Planning for Treatment

Treatment planning is an essential component of CBT, whereas planning for change is an integral process of MI. In MI+CBT, these components can come together to strengthen the client's motivation toward treatment and change while formalizing the treatment plan. Collaboration is essential in this process, which brings together the fruits of the previous processes, including assessment, establishing the therapeutic relationship, focusing, and evoking. Figure 9.3 shows an example of a form that can integrate treatment planning from CBT with the planning process of MI. The information is personalized for this particular client's motivations for change, readiness for change for various goals, and cognitions and behaviors that will be of focus.

Treatment

Treatment in MI+CBT consists of a culmination of motivational strategies and change interventions that are tailored to the client. As MI is an underlying style of counseling, the MI spirit and processes should be present throughout CBT interventions, hence making the therapeutic relationship grounded in empathy and evocation a constant as the client embarks on the journey of cognitive and behavioral change with the counselor as the guide. In order to be most effective, treatment methods are tailored to the client's readiness for change. Therefore, for clients who are not yet ready for change, MI strategies may be in the forefront (see Figure 9.1); however, this is not to say that CBT is absent. Instead, the clinician using MI+CBT would continue to conceptualize using CBT and then introduce CBT when the client is ready for action-based interventions. When CBT interventions are introduced, they are approached in the style of MI and with the client's motivation consistently being assessed. For instance, self-monitoring can be introduced to a client using EPE, and after discussing self-monitoring in session, the counselor can assess the client's motivation and commitment to implement this strategy in between sessions. In doing so, the counselor can then address any ambivalence about participating in the intervention using the evoking process of MI. Naar and Safren (2017) described how MI can be incorporated in a range of common CBT interventions, including self-monitoring, cognitive restructuring, behavioral skills, and emotional regulation. Although the scope of this book does not allow for such breadth and depth, to illustrate in this chapter we will explore the MI+CBT approach to behavioral activation as

142 *Methods of Integration*

Plan for Change/Treatment Plan

The changes I want to make are:	My reasons for making these changes:
Stop being depressed.	*I want to be successful at work, and I want to be happier overall.*

In order to make these changes, I will engage in the following treatment:

Concern	Goal	Treatment
Depression	*Increase motivation for work*	• *Identify and revise cognitions that are interfering with motivation* • *Explore values and goals*
	Improve mood	• *Self-monitor mood and cognitions* • *Engage in activities that increase mood*
	Sleep less and replace with healthy coping	• *Behavioral activation* • *Identify healthy replacement activities*

Outside of treatment, I will also take these steps:

Talk with my mother once per month. Consider getting a dog.

How will I know if my plan is working?

If I have energy for and get excited about work again, if I get out of bed every morning and nap less, if I feel less depressed every day.

What might interfere with my plan?	What will I do if this happens?
If I don't have energy to go to therapy	*Call my therapist and discuss it*
If the depression is genetic and stays regardless of what I do	*Talk with my therapist and doctor about antidepressant medication*

Figure 9.3 Plan for Change/Treatment Plan for Ricky

applied to Ricky, and Section III of this text offers MI+CBT strategies for various presenting concerns.

Seamless Blending of MI and CBT 143

Behavioral activation is considered an essential and effective CBT intervention for clients who experience depression (Beck, 2011; Mazzucchelli, Kane, & Rees, 2009). However, when traditionally applied, Beck (2011) suggested that clients will need "to be provided with a rationale" and that "therapists will need to be gently persistent" (p. 99) as well as encourage behavioral experiments when clients are skeptical about participating in behavioral activation. Now, let's look at how this intervention might be approached using MI+CBT. First, this intervention would be chosen as a result of a collaborative decision between the client and counselor. The dialogue that follows illustrates an example of such dialogue between Ricky and his counselor. Considering that Ricky's major concern was his work performance, he chose to first focus on making changes to his behaviors and establishing a schedule to help him get to work on time and complete his work in a quality and timely fashion. The counselor's skills are noted in the dialogue including EPE, action reflections (reflections of what the client said in addition to introducing new ideas or potential evidence-based interventions; Naar & Safren, 2017), and reflections to emphasize mastery (through the lens of CBT, increasing activities that result in a sense of mastery or pleasure will help minimize depression; Beck, 2011).

Counselor: Ok, so it makes the most sense to you to begin focusing on and perhaps adjusting how you spend your time, and it seems this might be the most helpful in regard to the struggles you're having with getting to work and feeling motivated once you're at work. [*summary*]

Ricky: Yes, I think so. I'd like to start there.

Counselor: Ok, excellent. Before I share my ideas about how we might be able to do that, I'm curious if you've ever done something like behavioral activation or scheduling your time intentionally before? [*closed question; first "elicit" in EPE*]

Ricky: No, I haven't. I've always just kept my schedule in my head, and that's worked for me. But now, even when I know I have to get to work, I don't go, and I just stay in bed.

Counselor: I see, and what you're describing is very common for people who experience symptoms of depression. Would it be ok if I described one possible way for us to explore changing these behaviors that often works for clients who experience similar symptoms? [*asking for permission before providing information about the intervention*]

Ricky: Yes, that sounds good.

Counselor: Ok, we first begin by looking at how you currently spend your time. One way to do that is by using a chart that accounts for each day of the week. [*hand client an activity chart*] After you complete the chart with how you currently spend your time, then we can start to identify days and times were you'd like to change how you're spending that time. [*provided information*] Does that make sense? [*checking for understanding*]

Ricky: Yes, I think so.

Counselor: What do you think about trying something like this in the next week? [*open question; second "elicit" in EPE*]

Ricky: Well, if I were to fill that out with what I'm doing right now, it would be "sleep, sleep, stare, and sleep some more."

Counselor: Ok, so it might not be very helpful to start with what you're currently doing, but maybe you'd prefer to move directly to scheduling activities that you'd like to be doing. [*action reflection*]

Ricky: Yeah, I think so.

Counselor: You're ready to jump right in. I can see you're motivated to make these changes, Ricky. [*affirmation*]

Ricky: Yeah, I need to do something about work, and the sooner the better.

Counselor: Ok, so looking at a weekly schedule like this, what are some activities that are most important to you to do? [*open question; evocation*]

Ricky: Get to work on time on Monday through Friday.

Counselor: Getting there on time, that's an important one. [*simple reflection*]

Ricky: Yeah, my boss just promoted me. And I can't disappoint him or myself. I want to show him he made a good choice, but I just can't seem to get it together.

Counselor: Ok, getting to work on time will lead you to feel like you're doing a good job and reinforce his decision to promote you. [*reflection of mastery*]

Ricky: Yeah. And if I get there on time, then I don't have the thoughts that berate me while I'm there and distract me from getting any work done—"You shouldn't have been promoted; you're no good at this; he's going to catch on that you cannot do this."

Counselor: When you're late to work, those thoughts kick in and persist. [*simple reflection*] If you arrive on time, chances are you won't have those thoughts, and you'll be able to focus better on your actual work. [*reframe*]

Ricky: Right! That's what I need to do.

Counselor: Ok, would you like to write in getting to work Monday through Friday on your chart? [*honoring client autonomy; fostering partnership*]

Ricky: Yeah, sure. [*takes the chart and writes it down*]

This interaction would continue until Ricky had several activities on his chart that he deemed most important and that provided him with a sense of mastery or pleasure (Beck, 2011). The number of activities would be collaboratively determined, with consideration to the low amount of activity Ricky was accustomed to; he would not want to overwhelm himself with too much activity, and yet the counselor would honor Ricky's autonomy in choosing the activities and how many. The therapist would then assess Ricky's motivation and commitment to follow the new schedule for the week, perhaps by asking, "On a scale from 1 to 10, with 10 being 'absolutely' and 1 being 'no chance,' how confident are you that you will be able to follow this schedule this week?" If Ricky responds with "6," the counselor can inquire about and seek to understand why he chose a 6 instead of a 4. Ricky would then describe the factors that enable him to feel confident in following the schedule (i.e., change talk). Next the counselor asks, "What would it take for the 6 to become a 7 or 8?" Ricky responds with the possibility of addressing the interplay of his automatic thoughts that could interfere with behavioral activation:

Ricky: Well, I just know that it will be hard. I'll set an alarm to get up in the morning for work, but when it goes off, my mind will kick in, and I'm not sure I'll be able to ignore it.

Counselor: So you're imagining this in your mind, [reflection] and when the alarm goes off, what is the thought that comes into your head? [open question to elicit automatic thought]

Ricky: I can't do this.

Counselor: I can't do this. [simple reflection]

Ricky: I can't do this, and what's the point of even trying? No matter what I do, it will not make a difference.

Counselor: No matter what you do, it won't make a difference, so what's the point of trying. [simple reflection]

Ricky: Yeah, and then I won't get out of bed.

Counselor: Those thoughts then lead to you not being able to get out of bed. [reflection] And how do you feel then? [open question]

Ricky: Super depressed and just defeated and hopeless.

Counselor: And that kind of makes sense considering what we talked about before in how what we think affects what we do and how we feel. [reinforcing the cognitive model]

Ricky: Yeah, and I'm not sure a schedule is enough to overcome all that.

Counselor: The schedule is one thing, but it might be helpful to address those thoughts that might interfere with following the schedule too. [action reflection]

Ricky: (Nods) Yeah.

The counselor can then assist Ricky in evaluating the automatic thoughts that would interfere with behavioral activation and developing alternative thoughts. The alternative thoughts can be recorded on coping cards (Beck, 2011) for Ricky to reference outside of session. After addressing Ricky's ambivalence, the counselor might then return to the confidence scale to assess if the cognitive interventions affected his self-efficacy related to behavioral activation. If Ricky responds that his initial rating of 6 is now at an 8, the counselor might ask what resulted in the boost of confidence, which would elicit change talk and help solidify his commitment to implement the strategies learned in session.

Maintenance

After clients have been making active changes for at least six months, they enter the maintenance stage of change (Norcross et al., 2011). In maintenance, the client is working to consolidate gains made in action and avoid falling back into former ways of thinking and behaving. Naar and Safren (2017) encourage MI+CBT practitioners to avoid terms that might have negative connotations, such as "relapse" (p. 185) due to the "all-or-nothing" assumption this term can convey. The all-or-nothing perception can lead to the client succumbing to the abstinence or goal violation effect, which is a phenomenon in which small setbacks can cause the client to feel as though all is lost as opposed to learning from one's mistakes (Larimer, Palmer, & Marlatt, 1999). Beck (2011) noted that it is important for clinicians to prepare clients for potential setbacks. As such, counselors can introduce the notion of a plan for maintenance and normalize the reality of challenging situations and the potential for setbacks. Plans for maintenance can include identifying the client's triggers and high-risk situations, as well as ideal responses, including employing coping skills, social support, and other strengths to help the client maintain the changes he or she has made despite facing potential threats. In MI+CBT, planning for maintenance should be a collaborative process in which the counselor provides the structure and the client provides the content with the guidance of the counselor. The following dialogue is an example of introducing a plan for maintenance with Ricky after three months of therapy:

Counselor: Ricky, you've made a lot of successful changes over the past few months. You've been getting to work on time and completing your work; you're also sleeping more regularly, and you're using other methods to manage your emotions, and socially you have a new relationship that you seem very happy in. [*summary*] For many people, once they've made changes, they can benefit from talking about and even developing a plan for continuing these changes, especially if situations come up that might be challenging. What do you think about that idea? [*open question; elicit*]

Ricky: Well, yeah, I mean I feel pretty confident about things now, but I guess it can't hurt.

Counselor: Yeah, you're proud of these changes, and I know you want them to continue. [*reflection*] Looking ahead, it is very common for people to experience various bumps in the road after making different changes. Developing what we might call a maintenance plan can help people navigate or even prevent some of those bumps. [*providing information*]

Ricky: Well, yeah, that sounds good. I could see how things like going to my parents' for the holidays might be hard.

Counselor: Visiting your parents' might be one of those challenging situations for which we can plan how to manage it in a way to continue your success. [*action reflection*]

Ricky: Yeah, definitely.

After introducing the idea, Ricky and the counselor can continue to identify situations that are higher risk for setbacks and then collaboratively identify corresponding strategies that can help the client manage these situations. An example of a maintenance plan is provided in Figure 9.4 for Ricky (another example

Seamless Blending of MI and CBT 147

Maintenance Plan Example for Ricky

Goals
What changes do you want to maintain?

_____*Motivation, energy, getting work done well, being able to sleep and concentrate*_____

Identifying Triggers
What might be a threat to maintaining these changes?

_____*Vising my parents*_____

Coping skills
What do you do physically to engage healthy coping and wellness?

_____*Run, avoid too much sugar and caffeine, do not take naps so I can sleep at night, keep on my daily schedule*_____

What are the encouraging or helpful thoughts that help you stay on track?

_____*Lots of people appreciate what I do and who I am, even if my parents do not. Using the thoughts on my coping cards*_____

What are healthy and effective ways in which you can express your emotions?

_____*Use effective communication skills to talk with my parents, run*_____

Who can you talk to for social support?

_____*My girlfriend*_____

Figure 9.4 Maintenance Plan Example for Ricky

is provided in Chapter 10 for a substance use client). For instance, Ricky listed going to his parents' home as a potentially triggering situation for symptoms of his depression to return. Then he identified strategies to assist him with maintaining the changes he had made, such as employing coping cards, keeping a schedule when there, and practicing assertiveness skills as needed. This plan can be written in session so that Ricky can take it out of session and use it for reference when he is actually experiencing the situations identified. The plan can also be modified as needed. After regular counseling sessions are completed, booster sessions can be helpful to provide clients who are in maintenance with a designated time, often with weeks or months in between, to address difficulties that arose since the previous session and to provide guidance in revising the maintenance plan.

Practice Considerations

In order to practice MI+CBT as a seamless integration of these approaches, the therapist must blend the underlying theories and foci of change to produce unified conceptualizations, as well as integrating the techniques (Norcross, Beutler, & Goldfried, 2019). MI and CBT are no longer considered separate or stand-alone approaches in this type of integration. This can be a difficult practice to adopt for clinicians who are trained in and accustomed to practicing only one of these approaches, as both MI and CBT require intentional training and fidelity as separate approaches. Indeed, there are overlapping components (e.g., Socratic questioning mimics evocation), and yet there are many areas in which there can be vast differences (e.g., how discord/resistance is conceptualized and the interpersonal style in which it is addressed) and components that can even conflict (e.g., Socratic questioning typically uses multiple questions—often closed questions—in a row, which goes against MI-consistent practice). Given that this is an emerging integrated practice, few guidelines exist to assist clinicians using MI+CBT in navigating these areas of potential conflict. More information about these potential dilemmas and possible ways to address them: in practice can be found in Chapter 13.

Closely linked to the MI+CBT practice considerations are training considerations. Unfortunately, little is known about how to help clinicians who are accustomed to MI or CBT alone learn and integrate the other approach (Naar & Safren, 2017). For seasoned clinicians who are already experienced in one approach, blending these approaches conceptually and in practice would require intentional training in the other approach as well as training in their integration. Students and new professionals could learn the MI+CBT integration as a single approach. Naar and Safren (2017) offered a training plan that would be applicable for students and new professionals to learn the integration at the onset of their training, as opposed to learning the approaches separately and then learning to integrate them. This plan included seven steps as follows: (1) MI spirit and skills; (2) engaging process in the context of setting the agenda for counseling sessions; (3) focusing process, including in the context of treatment planning; (4) evoking process, including in the context of the rationale for self-monitoring; (5) planning process, including in the context of executing assignments; (6) using all four processes in the initial counseling session; and (7) implementing all four processes in cognitive and behavioral skill building sessions (p. 214). Additional information about training in MI+CBT is found in Chapter 14.

Summary

MI+CBT in the form of a seamless integration results in conceptualization and treatments that blend the philosophies and techniques of these approaches to essentially provide a more comprehensive and effective approach to therapy compared to one or the other used alone. The integration is steadfast from the onset of counseling through maintenance and transcends through assessment, conceptualization, planning for treatment, and treatment itself. As MI+CBT is an emerging area of integrated practice, there are limited guidelines to its practice and training for clinicians who wish to implement it. Therefore, clinicians using MI+CBT must use their clinical judgment when encountering dilemmas concerning the synthesis of these approaches.

References

Beck, J. S. (2011). *Cognitive behavior therapy: Basics and beyond* (2nd ed.). New York, NY: Guilford Press.

Hunsley, J., & Allan, T. (2019). Clinical assessment in cognitive-behavioral therapies. In K. Dobson & D. Dozois (Eds.), *Handbook of cognitive-behavioral therapies* (4th ed., pp. 120–144). New York, NY: Guilford Press.

Larimer, M. E., Palmer, R. S., & Marlatt, G. A. (1999). Relapse prevention: An overview of Marlatt's cognitive-behavioral model. *Alcohol Research & Health, 23*(2), 151–160. Retrieved from http://search.proquest.com.ezproxylocal.library.nova.edu/docview/619515347?accountid=6579

Mazzucchelli, T., Kane, R., & Rees, C. (2009). Behavioral activation treatments for depression in adults: A meta-analysis and review. *Clinical Psychology: Science and Practice, 16*(4), 383–411. doi:10.1111/j.1468-2850.2009.01178.x

Miller, W. R., & Rollnick, S. (2013). *Motivational interviewing: Helping people change* (3rd ed.). New York, NY: Guilford Press.

Naar, S., & Safren, S. A. (2017). *Motivational interviewing and CBT: Combining strategies for maximum effectiveness.* New York, NY: Guilford Press.

Norcross, J. C., Beutler, L. E., & Goldfried, M. R. (2019). Cognitive-behavioral therapy and psychotherapy integration. In K. S. Dobson & D. J. Dozois (Eds.), *Handbook of cognitive-behavioral therapies* (4th ed., pp. 318–345). New York, NY: Guilford Press.

Norcross, J. C., Goldfried, M. R., & Arigo, D. (2016). Integrative theories. In J. C. Norcross, G. R. VandenBos, D. K. Freedheim, & B. O. Olatunji (Eds.), *APA handbook of clinical psychology: Theory and research* (Vol. 2, pp. 303–332). doi:10.1037/14773-011

Norcross, J. C., Krebs, P. M., & Prochaska, J. O. (2011). Stages of change. *Journal of Clinical Psychology, 67*(2), 143–154. doi:10.1002/jclp.20758

Persons, J. B., Brown, C., & Diamond, A. (2019). Case-formulation driven cognitive-behavioral therapy. In K. Dobson & D. Dozois (Eds.), *Handbook of cognitive-behavioral therapies* (4th ed., pp. 145–168). New York, NY: Guilford Press.

SECTION III
Clinical Applications

CHAPTER 10

Substance Use and Addictive Disorders

MI and CBT are both popular and effective treatments for substance use and addictive disorders (Pilkey, Steinberg, & Martino, 2015). Meta-analyses have found CBT to be largely efficacious for treating substance use disorders with the strongest support for cannabis use disorders, followed by cocaine and opioid use, and with smaller effect sizes for multiple use substance use disorders (Magill & Ray, 2009; McHugh, Hearon, & Otto, 2010). MI was initially developed to assist people who had problems related to alcohol use and who were required to attend treatment (Miller, 1983). Lundahl, Kunz, Brownell, Tollefson, and Burke's (2010) meta-analysis found that MI was effective in addressing substance use as well as gambling behaviors. When compared to other treatments, MI's efficacy is on par with CBT and 12-step facilitation therapy but typically requires fewer sessions (Lundahl et al., 2010; Pilkey et al., 2015). In addition to these approaches being empirically supported separately, research has also supported the use of a combination of MI and CBT to further enhance outcomes related to substance use and addictive behaviors. For instance, the COMBINE study found that MI+CBT and medical management were found to be as efficacious as naltrexone and medical management in reducing drinking among clients with alcohol use disorder (Anton et al., 2006). A study conducted by Stea, Yakovenko, and Hodgins (2015) found that clients who implemented motivational, cognitive, and behavioral strategies were successful in altering cannabis use behaviors. The Cannabis Youth Treatment (CYT) series offers manualized approaches for five treatment protocols of varying length and foci, two of which incorporated MI and CBT (Sampl & Kadden, 2001; Webb Scudder, Kaminer, Kadden, & Tawfik, 2002). Research on the CYT found that clients who received motivational enhancement therapy (MET)+CBT had a 20% advantage for better outcomes at follow-up compared to those who did not receive a combination of MI+CBT (Donovan et al., 2008).

In this chapter, we explore MI+CBT applied to the treatment of substance use and addictive disorders, including during intake and assessment, goal development, making recommendations for treatment, treatment, and maintenance. In MI+CBT, we pay particular attention to the process of delivering the interventions as well as the content of the interventions and methods. Case examples are provided throughout the chapter to illustrate MI+CBT applied to specific client cases.

Overview of the Integration

Many clients present for substance use or addiction treatment due to the influence of a third party, including being judicially mandated to treatment (Bright & Martire, 2013; Tiger, 2011) or referred by employers, family members, or social service agencies (e.g., child protection agencies). Consequences are typically incurred when mandated clients do not follow through with treatment, such as incarceration or other consequences related to the criminal justice system, loss of employment, child custody restrictions, and other effects on family and friend relationships. Challenges involving motivation are common among these populations, and discord can be inherently present within the therapeutic relationship given the unique combination of extrinsic forces into treatment and high stakes for the client related to treatment outcomes. Even after clients acknowledge that there is a problem with the substance use or addictive behavior, ambivalence is a common barrier to embracing change. People often continue to have reasons why they should not change, including costs involved with change (e.g., "I can't give up my friends; they're my friends!" "If I'm in treatment, then I'm not working and my PO says I have to keep this job.") and perceived inability to change or need for the substance (e.g., "I can't fall asleep if I don't use." "I need to relax, and this works for me."). Therefore, the majority of clients will present in the earlier stages of change, including precontemplation and contemplation (Norcross, Krebs, & Prochaska, 2011). MI is a natural fit for this population given it was initially developed to enhance readiness to change and to address ambivalence. As Beck, Liese, and Najavits (2005) noted, MI differs from CBT in that it is a process-oriented method that is not focused on teaching new skills but rather on enhancing motivation. Through MI spirit and core skills, MI counselors seek to *engage* clients in conversations about potential change, collaborate with clients on what changes are of *focus* (including negotiating the goals of third-party referral sources with the clients' goals), *evoking* clients' own personal motivations for change, and then *planning* for change, all while moving at the client's pace.

In addition to concerns related to motivation and discord in the therapeutic relationship, substance use and addiction are typically accompanied by cognitions which lead to using or addictive behaviors. For instance, Wright, Beck, Newman, and Liese (1993) described three basic addictive beliefs:

1. *Anticipatory beliefs.* Expectations of use (e.g., "I will finally be able to relax." "I will have so much more fun than when I'm sober.")
2. *Relief-oriented beliefs.* Expecting the substance to remove discomfort (e.g., "This craving will not go away unless I use.")
3. *Permissive beliefs.* Justify substance use despite consequences (e.g., "I work really hard; I deserve this." "No one will know; it will be ok.")

Clients who are experiencing substance use or addictive disorders can benefit from learning the cognitive model, including how these common beliefs can lead to perpetuating substance use and addictive behaviors. MI+CBT treatment can involve increasing clients' awareness of current cognitions, evaluating them, and then working to revise them. These skills are learned in individual or group counseling sessions and then applied in between sessions. Further, addictive behaviors are often reinforced through repeated associations over the course of the addiction. For example, consider a client who drinks alcohol in social situations and over time, as he feels more confident and less inhibited, he associates social activity with drinking (let alone that many cultures associate social activity with drinking, such as happy hour or tailgating). A client uses opioid medication because she learned it is the only thing that sufficiently relieves her physical and emotional pain. Therefore, counterconditioning can be utilized as a behavioral tool to assist a client in diminishing the effects of a conditioned stimulus (Velasquez, Maurer, Crouch, & DiClemente, 2001). Using the functional analysis in CBT can help bring these associations to light and bring them into the focus of treatment. Behaviors are also a focus in CBT work in which clients learn new or strengthen healthy coping skills, such as relaxation techniques, assertive communication, and refusal skills. As both MI and CBT as separate approaches have a lot to offer clients who are seeking treatment for substance use and addictive disorders, the outcomes of MI+CBT can be synergistic. MI+CBT evokes and strengthens client motivation and addresses any discord in the therapeutic relationship, as well as offers clients cognitive and behavioral tools to enable changes in substance use and addictive behaviors. The case of Josie, a 14-year-old Latina girl who was brought to counseling by her mother for marijuana use, will be threaded throughout this chapter to illustrate how MI+CBT can be applied.

Voices From the Field 10.1

Integrating MI and CBT in DUI Drug Court

Written by
M. Scott Smith, M.S., LPC, CAADC
Doctoral Student, Clinical Psychology
Mercer University

As director of the DUI/Drug Court treatment program in Troup County, Georgia, I organized a two-day MI training not only for the clinicians on our team but also for the probation officers, staff members, and judge. I was particularly interested in how the MI training might affect the judge's relationships with participants since research suggests that this relationship is a mechanism that significantly affects treatment outcomes (MacKenzie, 2015; Rossman et al., 2011).

To evaluate the effect of the training, we recorded audio of court hearings before and after the training. We found that the judge asked more open-ended questions and used more reflections after the training. The judge's interactions with participants became much more of a dialogue than a one-sided conversation. Most significantly, the average hearing time increased from 1:43 before the MI training to 3:08 after the training. That may not seem like much of a change, but research shows that drug court programs where the judge spent at least three minutes on average with each participant during court hearings had 153% greater reductions in recidivism (Carey, Mackin, & Finigan, 2012). In the year following the MI training for our team, our program's retention rate increased from 73% to 80%.

Having our whole team complete the MI training changed the way we interacted with each other as well as with participants. We started to talk less about sanctions and more about affirmations. During every staffing, we brainstormed new open-ended questions to evoke change talk in the courtroom. The presiding judge commented, "The open-ended questions give us a focal point and help me to encourage reticent participants to talk more." A lead counselor observed, "When clients come to court, there's often a barrier between them and the judge. The MI approach takes down that barrier and allows the clients to build a relationship with the judge."

When the members of our drug court treatment team started to practice not only in the skills but also the spirit of MI, that laid the groundwork for the CBT interventions delivered in the substance use treatment groups. Strategies for changing thoughts and behaviors were more easily assimilated by participants when they were presented as part of a cohesive system that affirmed their efforts and empowered them with their own motivation rather than blaming, shaming, and shackling.

References

Carey, S. M., Mackin, J. R., & Finigan, M. W. (2012). What works? The ten key components of drug court: Research-based best practices. *Drug Court Review, 8*, 29. National Drug Court Institute. Retrieved from www.ndci.org/sites/default/files/nadcp/DCR_best-practices-in-drug-courts.pdf

MacKenzie, B. (2015). *The judge is the key component: The importance of procedural fairness in drug treatment courts.* American Judges Association. Retrieved from www.amjudges.org/pdfs/judge-key-component.pdf

Rossman, S. B., Roman, J. K., Zweig, J. M., Rempel, M., & Lindquist, C. H. (2011). *The multi-site adult drug court evaluation: Executive summary.* Urban Institute Justice Policy Center. Retrieved from www.courtinnwovation.org/sites/default/files/documents/MADCE_ES.pdf

Assessment and Establishing the Therapeutic Relationship

For most substance use and addiction treatment, the first in-person contact with a client is the intake assessment, in which the focus is on gathering information in order to inform treatment, including diagnosis, and to make recommendations for an appropriate level of care. While the content of the session is on gathering information, the process of the intake assessment is a ripe opportunity for the intake counselor to begin a relationship with the client. In many agencies, the intake counselor may not serve as the client's treatment provider, in which case it might be easy to focus solely on the content of the intake and dismiss the process. However, regardless of whether the intake provider will serve as the treatment provider, the experiences clients have during the intake assessment influence their impressions of help-seeking and their expectations of what is to come. Further, the counselor's approach to gathering necessary information can enhance or harm the client's engagement, including levels of resistance/reactance. MI+CBT can be applied during the intake assessment to achieve both objectives of developing a productive therapeutic relationship with the client and gathering necessary information to inform treatment.

Developing the Therapeutic Relationship

Given that many clients present for treatment due to some level of coercion (e.g., court mandate, family member, employer), it is not uncommon for discord to be present at the onset of the counseling relationship. Discord (formerly known as resistance) through the lens of MI describes conflict in the therapeutic relationship that can manifest in defensiveness, argumentative behaviors, or the client making negative comments directed to the counselor and/or about the services provided. When counselors recognize discord in the therapeutic relationship, as the trained professional, it is a signal for the counselor to approach the client differently. It is not uncommon for clients in substance use treatment to be disengaged, defensive, or argumentative at the onset—in these cases, it is important to not take this personally and to keep in mind that the client is likely lumping you in with the other components of the systems he or she has encountered, such as the judge, probation officer, the family member, or the employer who referred them, and the client expects you to meet him or her with similar judgment and directiveness that he or she experienced in these other relationships. And there lies the challenge *and the opportunity* to create a different environment for and relationship with the client—one that is grounded in empathy and compassion and focused on understanding clients' perceptions within their current contexts. Why? Because resistance has been shown to lead to poor outcomes in substance use treatment (Miller, Benefield, & Tonigan, 1993). In essence, the more resistant a client is in treatment, the more likely he or she is to continue or increase substance use. That leaves the question, "How do we establish a productive therapeutic relationship with clients?" By applying MI, we first embark on the process of *engaging*. This process guides MI+CBT practitioners to execute strategies to diminish discord (also described in Chapter 7), starting with *maintaining the spirit of MI*, or the humanistic, interpersonal "way of being" with clients. Clients who experience substance use disorders often have experiences that result in a "me against them" dynamic. Implementing the MI spirit can offset this dynamic by emphasizing partnership, acceptance, compassion, and evocation. Table 10.1 presents the components and descriptions

Table 10.1 Spirit of MI Applied to Engaging With Clients With Substance Use and Addictive Disorders

Component	Description Counselors' "Way of Being"	Antithesis Common Experiences of Clients	Applications Examples With Josie
Partnership	• Work *with* clients • Avoid "wrestling" with clients to "get them" to see a different point; instead, strive to "dance" together • Value client's wisdom and incorporate it into conversations about change • Enlist the client as an essential contributor to his or her change process	• Being mandated to or coerced into treatment • Feeling "forced" to change • Being told what to do by others who acted as if they knew best for the client • Going through treatment superficially, without authentic efforts	• "I've heard your mom's version of what is bringing you in today, but I think most important is your perception of all that's going on. Would you tell me what's bringing you in today from your perspective?" • "I understand that the school and your parents would like you to stop using. What would you like to get out of counseling?"
Acceptance	• Reinforce client's absolute worth and self-efficacy for change • Express accurate empathy to enable the client feeling heard and understood and to hear him/herself through the counselor • Emphasize autonomy • Affirm client strengths and positive efforts	• Experiencing the negative stigma surrounding substance use and addictive behaviors • Judgment from another's perspective • Others make decisions for him or her • Telling the client what he or she must do/prescribing treatment • Highlighting what the client is doing wrong • Focusing on pathology	• "You'd like to be part of a group of friends who you enjoy and who you like being associated with". [*accurate empathy*] • "Despite your parents and the school wanting you to quit, they certainly can't make that decision for you—only you can do that". [*supporting autonomy*] • "You've shared some important information with me today that will really help us as we move forward". [*affirmation*]

Compassion	• Genuine caring about the welfare of the client • Act in the client's best interest	• Being hardened to the struggles of the client • Acting in the best interest of the provider/agency	• "I can see that this is a tough time for you." • "Please let me know if you are finding our work together unhelpful, and then I can adjust my approach."
Evocation	• Evoke the client's personal motivations for change • Evoke the client's wisdom and perspectives	• Attempting to install motivation • Providing solutions	• "If you were to describe your ideal self and life, what would be most important to you?". *[eliciting values]* • "I wonder, what do you think might work in this situation?". *[eliciting possible solutions]*

of the spirit as well as antitheses that clients with substance use and addictive disorders commonly experience. Finally, examples of the spirit are illustrated through a counselor's dialogue with Josie.

In addition to maintaining the spirit of MI, counselors using MI+CBT can *recognize discord and respond* in a timely manner to diminish discord. MI+CBT counselors can recognize discord as client defensiveness, argumentation, or other negative comments made about the counselor or services (Miller & Rollnick, 2013). Discord is conceptualized as an interpersonal dynamic, and therefore, it is a signal for the counselor to respond differently. The first-line response includes *listening and expressing empathy*. When done well, this alone is often enough for discord to diminish. Once the client realizes you are not going to argue with him or her and you do not become defensive yourself, but instead you are consistent in your genuine striving to understand the client's experiences and ideas, there is no longer a need for "resistance," and discord in the relationship will diminish. *Reflections* are the most used skill to express empathy, and therefore, reflections are heavily relied upon when diminishing discord. However, there are opportunities to use open questions, affirmations, and summaries as well. *Open questions* let the client know that you want him or her to share, and when open questions are followed by reflections, this skill combination lets the client know you are listening and interested in hearing more. *Summaries* can be used to collect larger quantities of information to demonstrate listening and understanding, as well as to help organize or link information. When the discussion seems to hit a dead end or becomes nonproductive, counselors can summarize the previous content and then ask an open question to *shift the focus* to a more productive topic of conversation.

Affirmations can be especially meaningful for clients with substance use or addictive disorders due to the clients often hearing about all the things they do wrong and all the negatives about themselves and their behaviors from others. By highlighting the positives, clients can begin to see themselves in a more positive way, which can assist in further developing self-efficacy and strengthening a more positive self-image, as well as diminish discord. Finally, counselors can *emphasize client autonomy* by reinforcing personal choice and control (e.g., "As much as your parole office might want you to be in treatment, only you can decide how much effort you're going to put into this."), ensuring that the client is the primary resource in finding answers and solutions to his or her problems (e.g., "You've been in treatment before, and you've dealt with this issue for a while now. What have you found that works for you? What have you learned does not work?"), and asking for permission prior to giving information or making suggestions ("I have some assessments here that we use with all new clients. Would it be ok if I shared some information about them with you?").

Implementing strategies to diminish discord in the therapeutic relationship requires the counselor to practice with *responsivity and intentionality*. As with all MI+CBT practice, there is no single way to respond but rather a menu of options from which the practitioner can choose. Such decisions should be made intentionally, with consideration to the client's context, including social, cultural, and clinical considerations. Each decision is made based on a hypothesis about what might be effective in cultivating a relationship with this individual. If it does not result in the desired outcome (e.g., the client maintains defensiveness), then the practitioner listens and learns from the client's response to reformulate the hypothesis and try another strategy or revise his or her style to better match the needs of the client. The skills of responsivity and intentionality culminate in the art of the engaging process as well as in the remaining components of treatment. Practice Box 10.1 provides an opportunity for you to consider how you might develop a therapeutic relationship with an adolescent client, Josie, during the initial intake assessment session.

Assessment

Assessment in substance use and addiction counseling typically involves gathering detailed information about substance use and addictive behaviors, as well as historical and contextual information often gathered in a biopsychosocial spiritual assessment. The following components specific to substance use and addiction are typically included: current and past substance use and addictive behaviors; first and subsequent exposure to substances of use or addictive behaviors; context of use, including triggers, consequences, positive aspects, and expectancy, or the client's belief in the outcome of use (Stauffer, Capuzzi, & Aissen, 2015). In addition, the six dimensions identified by the American Society of Addiction Medicine are commonly used to guide assessment and then used to aid in determining the appropriate level of care for treatment (Mee-Lee, 2013). These include the following: (1) acute intoxication and withdrawal potential; (2) biomedical conditions and complications; (3) emotional, behavioral, and cognitive conditions and complications; (4) readiness for change/treatment; (5) relapse prevention and continued use or problem potential; and (6) recovery environment. It can be very tempting to use sequential closed questions when

---

Practice Box 10.1 Intake Assessment With Josie

Josie is a 14-year-old girl who was brought to counseling by her mother for marijuana use. Josie and her mother attend an intake assessment, and you are the assigned counselor. You have several pages of questions to ask from the agency's intake form that you must complete, as well as some formal assessments (Substance Abuse Subtle Screening Inventory-Adolescent Version; SASSI-A) the client must complete.

You meet with Josie's mother first and then with Josie alone. It quickly becomes apparent that Josie does not want to talk with you. She makes little to no eye contact and mutters "I don't know" or shrugs when you ask a question. What do you do? What strategies can you draw on to proceed with Josie?

gathering this information. However, the interpersonal style in which assessment is approached can impact the client's level of engagement. When using MI+CBT, we aim to avoid the question–answer trap and encourage client engagement by using OARS with added MI-consistent components, including reflecting the client's responses to our questions before asking the next question. In the following example, the counselor begins to gather information from Josie in the initial assessment after her mother has left the room.

Counselor: Josie, as you know, I just spoke with your mom about her concerns. And now I'd really like to hear about what's going on from your perspective. How does that sound? [*setting the agenda/partnership; open question*]

Josie: Fine.

Counselor: Ok, thank you. Would you tell me a little about what happened that led you to come in today? [*appreciation; open question*]

Josie: Like she told you, I'm sure. I smoked some pot. Big deal.

Counselor: Yeah, so your mom found out you smoked marijuana, and that was a problem to her but not necessarily for you. [*reflection*]

Josie: Yeah, they freak out about everything.

Counselor: They're upset about this. (Pause) [*reflection*] How did they find out? [*open question*]

Josie: Well, we smoked after school, right by the baseball dugout, and someone from the school saw and called the resource officer. We were all taken in then, and they called our parents.

Counselor: You were smoking with friends at school, and after you were caught, they notified your parents. [*summary*]

Josie: Yeah, like they had to come get us, and it was a whole ordeal (eye roll).

Counselor: You weren't happy about that part—your mom having to come get you and that it turned into a big deal. [*reflection*]

Josie: No, it's so dumb.

Counselor: Tell me about other times when you might have experienced something similar, getting in trouble when you didn't see it as an issue. [*open question*]

Josie: A couple of weeks ago, they caught me and my friend drinking when she was sleeping over. Before that, I came home drunk and high one night, and my mom was mad, but she didn't tell my dad.

Counselor: So there've been a few times recently that have caused your parents some concern, and it seems each time, you're thinking that there is no real problem; it's just your parents making a big deal out of nothing. [*summary*]

Josie: Yeah, I mean they're just, whatever . . . (silence).

Counselor: What happens when they make a "big deal" out of something? Are there certain punishments? [*open question*]

Substance Use and Addictive Disorders 163

Josie:	(Laughs) They try. They say I'm grounded and take stuff away, but they work a lot, so it's easy to get around it.
Counselor:	So they might say you're grounded and can't go out, but you don't feel obligated to stick to that. [*reflection*]
Josie:	No, I just go out anyway. But now the school is making me come here, which is a total waste of time.
Counselor:	I see that you're not real excited about being here, that you don't think it's necessary. (Pause) [*reflection*] What exactly do you think it is that your parents are concerned about? [*open question to elicit change talk*]
Josie:	Well, they don't want me smoking weed, ruining my future, getting expelled, blah blah blah.
Counselor:	You've heard these concerns before, it sounds like maybe more than just a few times. [*reflection*]
Josie:	Yeah, all the time. It's annoying.
Counselor:	Yeah, you don't like hearing their concerns. (Pause) So their concerns aside, how do you think about your drinking and marijuana use? [*open question to elicit change talk*]
Josie:	Like I said, it's not a big deal. Who cares?
Counselor:	Ok, would you mind if I asked you a few questions about your use then? [*shifting focus to gather further information*]
Josie:	I guess so.
Counselor:	Ok, despite you not wanting to be here, I do really appreciate your willingness to talk with me today. [*affirmation*] You've mentioned drinking alcohol and smoking marijuana. What other substances have you tried? [*open question for assessment*]
Josie:	That's it.
Counselor:	Ok, so you've only used alcohol and marijuana. [*reflection*] It seems lots of kids are finding different medicines around, pills and other things, I wonder if you or your friends have tried anything like that. [*providing information in context, closed question*]
Josie:	Oh, well, I haven't, but I know some people who do.
Counselor:	You've seen that happening around you, but it's not something you've chosen to do. [*reflection*]
Josie:	Yeah, people have offered them, but I don't mess with that. Too many people go to heroin or die.
Counselor:	Yeah, there's a big problem with drugs we call opioids right now—like heroin of some prescription pain medications. It seems you've heard about this or maybe seen some things about it. [*complex reflection*]
Josie:	I've heard about people dying on the news and stuff. We talked about it in health class, but lots of kids still take them.
Counselor:	Yeah, it's very easy to get hooked on those types of pills or opioids bought off the street, like heroin or fentanyl, and to overdose, which

	causes the deaths. Is it your plan to stay away from these types of drugs? [*closed question to solicit commitment to prevent opioid use*]
Josie:	Yeah, I've been offered them, but I'm not going to take them.
Counselor:	You've already made up your mind, and you're sticking to that. [*affirmation*]
Josie:	Yeah.
Counselor:	Ok, so tell me about your drinking and marijuana use. [*shift focus*] When did you first start using them? [*closed question*]
Josie:	Last year, when I was in eighth grade.
Counselor:	And now you're in ninth grade. [*reflection*] In a week, how much would you say you smoke? [*open question*]
Josie:	Most days, maybe 6–7.
Counselor:	Ok, nearly daily then. [*reflection*] What times during the day do you smoke? [*open question*]
Josie:	On the way to school sometimes, after school most days, weekends, parties, the usual stuff.
Counselor:	Sometimes several times a day, and it sounds like you're smoking with other people then. [*complex reflection*]
Josie:	Yeah, my friends.
Counselor:	It is something you do together then, something you enjoy. [*complex reflection; informing functional analysis*]
Josie:	Yeah, I mean everyone does it. And it's not like we're popping pills or shooting heroin so . . . (shrug).
Counselor:	It helps you feel connected to your friends, like this is something we all do together. [*reflection*]
Josie:	Yeah.
Counselor:	And you drink together too, with these same friends? [*close question*]
Josie:	Yeah.
Counselor:	And about how often do you drink? How many times in a week? [*open question*]
Josie:	Oh, not that often. I've only drank three to four times before.
Counselor:	You drink much less compared to smoking. [*reflection*] What was your experience like?
Josie:	I don't like it as much. And it's harder to get and to hide.
Counselor:	You prefer marijuana over alcohol. [*reflection*]
Josie:	Yeah.
Counselor:	How much alcohol would you guess you drank during those three to four times. [*open question*]
Josie:	I'd share a bottle of wine with friends, so hard to say, but it made me sick once.
Counselor:	You drank enough that it made you sick. [*reflection*]
Josie:	Yeah, that was gross.
Counselor:	That's not something you wish to experience again. [*complex reflection*]
Josie:	No! I hated it. So now I just take a sip or so, nothing big.

Counselor: You've learned that drinking small amounts doesn't make you sick, so you plan to stick to that. [*reflection*]

Josie: Yeah, my friends drink a lot more than I do.

In the transcript, the counselor begins to collect information about Josie's substance use while diminishing discord with a combination of OARS with some added components, including shifting the focus, providing information, and asking a closed question to solicit commitment. At one point, the counselor diverted the assessment somewhat to provide selective prevention related to opioid use, which is prevalent in her area and schools. Josie would be at higher risk for using opioids considering she is already using substances. The counselor is acting out of care and compassion, including taking the time to explore Josie's experience with this substance and elicit her commitment to avoid using it. Later in the transcript, the counselor elicits the times of day in which Josie uses alcohol and marijuana, which is a common component of assessment in CBT. They also begin to explore the social components of her use, which could be the start of a functional analysis, or understanding the purpose (i.e., the "function") of Josie's substance use. For example, what benefit does Josie experience by smoking marijuana in the morning before school? Once this is known, they can work to identify alternative behaviors to achieve the same or similar function. The counselor can also listen for cognitions that might be interplaying in the client's substance use. These would inform the counselor's conceptualization at the initial assessment stage and then be used to formulate a plan for treatment.

In addition to assessment interviews, formal screening and assessment instruments are also commonly used in substance use and addiction counseling. Common screening tools include the CAGE (Ewing, 1984), TWEAK (Chan, Pristach, Welte, & Russell, 1993), Alcohol Use Disorders Identification Test (Babor, Higgins-Biddle, Saunders, & Monteiro, 2001), Michigan Alcohol Screening Test (MAST; Selzer, 1971), Drug Abuse Screening Test (DAST; Skinner & Goldberg, 1986), and the Substance Abuse Subtle Screening Inventory (SASSI-4; Lazowski, Kimmell & Baker, 2016). Assessment tools include the Drinkers Inventory of Consequences (Miller, Tonigan, & Longabaugh, 1995), Stages of Change Readiness and Treatment Eagerness Scale (SOCRATES; Miller & Tonigan, 1996), and the Addiction Severity Index (McLellan et al., 1992), as well as many others. Although a full description of these instruments exceeds the scope of this chapter, here we will focus on the process of introducing and utilizing these tools with clients in a manner that is consistent with MI+CBT.

When using a verbal assessment tool, the counselor can ask the questions in a way that is client responsive, including adapting the questions to better fit that particular client, while preserving the integrity of the instrument. For example, Josie's counselor might choose to use the CAGE-AID (Brown & Rounds, 1995) due to its high sensitivity to detect problematic alcohol and drug use among adolescents (Couwenbergh, Van Der Gaag, Koeter, De Ruiter, & Van den Brink, 2009;

Table 10.2 CAGE-AID Verbal Screening With Josie

Counselor: Josie, I have a few questions I ask all the people I meet with for the first time who are using substances like alcohol and marijuana. Would it be ok if I asked you a few more questions specific to these substances? [*asking for permission*]

	Original CAGE-AID Question	*Sample Dialogue with Josie*
C	"Have you ever felt you ought to **C**ut down on your drinking or drug use?"	• "For some people, when they use substances like alcohol or marijuana, they consider using them less and even cutting back on how much or how often they're using. I wonder, have you ever thought about using alcohol or marijuana less since you starting using them [*counselor reflects Josie's response*]?"
A	"Have people **A**nnoyed you by criticizing your drinking or drug use?"	• "It seems you feel annoyed by your parents having concerns about your smoking marijuana and drinking alcohol. Is that right [*Josie responds affirmatively*]? What about others who have maybe criticized your drinking and smoking [*Josie responds, and counselor reflects her response*]? How did you feel about what he/she said?"
G	"Have you ever felt bad or **G**uilty about your drinking or drug use?"	• "You've mentioned that you feel as though your marijuana use is no big deal, but with alcohol, you didn't like how it made you sick. I wonder, have you felt bad or guilty about drinking [*Josie responds and counselor reflects the response*]? What about marijuana? Have you felt bad or guilty about using marijuana [*counselor reflects Josie's response*]?"
E	"Have you ever had a drink or used drugs first thing in the morning to steady your nerves or to get rid of a hangover?" [***E**ye-opener*]	• "Some people feel like they need to drink or use marijuana first thing after they wake up because they feel shaky or hungover. Have you used alcohol or marijuana right after waking up?"

Substance Use and Addictive Disorders 167

> ### Practice Box 10.2   Screening Practice
>
> Now it's your turn to practice! How would you ask the following questions from the DAST-2 when interviewing Josie?
>
> 1. "How many days in the past 12 months have you felt bad or guilty about your drug use?"
> 2. "How many days in the past 12 months have you used drugs other than those required for medical reasons?"

Meersseman et al., 2016). An example of introducing and delivering CAGE-AID questions in a manner that is consistent with MI+CBT with Josie is provided in Table 10.2. Then, you have an opportunity to practice using the DAST-2 in Practice Box 10.2.

Providing information with permission can be used to introduce formal screening and assessment measures as well. With Josie, the counselor chooses to use the SASSI-A (Miller & Lazowski, 2001), which was designed and validated to identify adolescents' (ages 12 to 18) probability of having a substance use disorder. To retain the therapeutic alliance while administering this pencil-and-paper screening tool, the counselor might introduce it as follows:

Counselor: Josie, I ask all clients who I see for the first time to complete a form for me. Would it be ok if I told you a little about this? [*asking for permission before providing information*]

Josie: Ok.

Counselor: Ok, thank you. It's a form that will ask you questions about your substance use, as well as about other things. It has a front and a back, and for each question, you will fill in the bubble of the response you choose. There are no right or wrong answers—this is not like a test at school—but it is important that you read each question and respond honestly. [*providing information*] What questions do you have about completing this? [*open question to check for understanding*]

Josie: How long does this take? Do I have to do it here?

Counselor: It should take about 15–20 minutes, but if you need more time, that is ok. I do ask that you complete it today while you are here. Then I will use this form, along with the other information we've talked about today, to help us determine possible next steps for you in regard to counseling. You and I, along with your mother, will discuss these possibilities when we meet again. [*providing information*] How does that sound? [*open question to elicit client input*]

Josie: Ok. Should I get started?

> **Practice Box 10.3   Case Example with Greg**
>
> Greg is a 41-year-old African American man who is a mechanical engineer. Greg is introverted and has always been shy. He was referred to counseling by his company's employee assistance program due to frequent absences, including disappearing for two- to three-hour lunches. Initially, Greg attributed his behavior to "depression." At intake, Greg explains he is not motivated at work; his sleep has been disrupted, and his mood has been low. After exploring Greg's concerns further, Greg discloses that he is at lunch too long because he is "hooking up." The counselor learns Greg has engaged in sex with men since he was 19 years old. Greg's sexual activity has increased over the last 18 months to the point that it is interfering with his work, social life, sleep, and eating habits. Greg is also embarrassed that he has never had a significant relationship, with neither a man nor a woman. This bothers him a good deal, but this is the first time he has said it aloud. You are considering using the PATHOS screening (Carnes et al., 2012) with Greg:
>
> - *Preoccupied.* Do you find yourself preoccupied with sexual thoughts?
> - *Ashamed.* Do you hide some of your sexual behavior from others?
> - *Treatment.* Have you ever sought help for sexual behavior you did not like?
> - *Hurt others.* Has anyone been hurt emotionally because of your sexual behavior?
> - *Out of control.* Do you feel controlled by your sexual desire?
> - *Sad.* When you have sex, do you feel depressed afterwards (p. 31)?
>
> How would you approach the process (e.g., the manner and tone) of gathering this information via screening? How might you deliver the PATHOS screening to Greg? Finally, what cultural and identity considerations would you have for your work with Greg?

Focusing and Evoking

Prior to making treatment recommendations based on the information gathered via assessment, the focusing process is essential to negotiate the goals for treatment. At some point during the assessment process, it is necessary to elicit the client's goals for treatment, which are separate from the goals *for* the client provided by the third-party referral source. For example, a counselor might ask, "I learned from your probation officer that the judge is requiring that you attend treatment based on our recommendations and that you test negative on all drug screens. Setting those ideas aside for a second, what do you hope to get out of treatment?" or "Your employer made it clear that drug use is not permitted, and they will require you to test more often now that you had a positive screen. So that is one thing that we can work on here in treatment, but before we do that, I'm curious about what you think about that and how it fits or maybe doesn't fit with your own goals in coming here for treatment?" If the counselor remains solely focused on the referral source's concerns and goals for the client, the counselor is potentially missing essential components of *the client's* concerns, which might include social (e.g., being bullied, relationships), mental health (e.g., symptoms of depression or anxiety), health (e.g., weight gain or loss, pain), academic/employment concerns (e.g., failing a class, difficulty concentrating), or other issues.

In the case of Josie, her parents and the school are concerned about the client's use of substances; however, the client does not see this as a concern. By having an explicit conversation about the foci and goals of counseling, client and counselor negotiate how they will spend their time in a collaborative fashion in which each member of the partnership is heard and valued. Consider the following example of focusing with Josie:

Counselor: So, we've talked a good deal about what your parents' concerns are and the school's concerns, which will be part of our focus in our work together here. [*summary*] But tell me what else are you concerned about, if anything, that we have not yet talked about? What other things do you think you might benefit from talking about here? [*open question*]
Josie: Hmmmm, I don't know.
Counselor: You're not sure. [*silence*]
Josie: Like anything?
Counselor: Anything that is troubling you that you might want help with.
Josie: Well, I feel like my parents hate me. [*becomes tearful*]
Counselor: [*Pause*] And that feels hurtful to you.
Josie: Yeah, [*cries*] they don't seem to care anymore, you know? They just yell at me and try to catch me smoking, but they don't actually seem to care about *me* anymore.
Counselor: Your relationship with them seems to have changed. It used to feel like they genuinely cared about you as a person, and now it seems like they only care about this trouble that you're in. [*complex reflection*]
Josie: Yeah . . . and I don't know what to do about it.
Counselor: So trying to improve your relationship with your parents could be another thing that we work on together here, especially in our individual and family sessions together.
Josie: Yeah, ok.

The conversation about goals for treatment and about the recommendations for treatment should be approached in a manner that is appropriate for the client's stage of change. Low motivation for treatment has been found to be one of the most common reasons for clients to drop out of substance use treatment, despite the fact that incarceration is a common consequence (Evans, Li, & Hser, 2009). On the bright side, although some inconsistencies exist, research has generally shown that client change talk leads to higher rates of behavior change and that counselors' use of MI-consistent skills—reflections in particular—enhances the frequency of client change talk (Magill, Stout, & Apodaca, 2013; Moyers, Martin, Houck, Christopher, & Tonigan, 2009). The evoking process of MI is designed to address motivational barriers to active change. Therefore, for clients who are in precontemplation, we can acknowledge their perspective and work to develop rapport, provide information, and develop discrepancies in a caring and compassionate environment to evoke ambivalence. When clients are in contemplation, counselors explore client ambivalence, including acknowledging their hesitations to pursue change while eliciting and strengthening change talk. For clients who are in preparation or even action, we can provide information while continuing to elicit client commitment to treatment and to maintaining active changes. Additional strategies for the evoking process are included in the "Targeting Motivation" section under treatment later in this chapter.

Planning for Treatment

When making recommendations for treatment, the interpersonal style of MI+CBT is maintained, including fostering partnership and supporting the client's autonomy. Substance use treatment providers commonly use assessment data to determine an appropriate level of care identified by the American Society of Addiction Medicine (ASAM): Level 0.5: early intervention, Level 1: outpatient treatment, Level 2: intensive outpatient/partial hospitalization, Level 3: residential/inpatient treatment, and Level 4: medically managed inpatient. Then treatment recommendations are provided to the client and often communicated to third-party referrals. A conversation about treatment recommendations might sound something like this with Josie and her mother:

Counselor: Thank you both for coming in today to talk about Josie's options for treatment. [*appreciation*] Before we begin, I wonder if you have any questions or anything that you think I might need to know from the last time we met? [*question to foster partnership*]

Josie's Mom: No, nothing else has happened, thank goodness.

Counselor: Ok, please do let me know if you have questions or if you think of anything along the way. If it's ok with you both then, I will go ahead and give you my ideas about what types of treatments might be helpful, and then you can let me know what you both think about that. How does that sound? [*asking for permission before providing information*]

Josie's Mom: Yes, that's good. The school wants to know.

Counselor: Yeah, the school is eager to know that Josie is following through, which she certainly is doing by being here today. [*reflection; affirmation*] Josie, is it all right with you if I give you my thoughts, and then you can let us know what you think about it? [*asking Josie's permission*]

Josie: [*Makes eye contact for the first time*] Yeah, ok.
Counselor: Ok, based on your experiences with substance use, Josie, I would recommend what we call an "intensive outpatient program," which means you would participate in group counseling three times per week, and you would also have one individual session per week and one family session per month.... [*providing information*]

After providing the information, the counselor would check for their understanding and respond to any questions. Then the counselor would explicitly ask Josie, the client, "What are your thoughts this?" The counselor would listen and respond to any concerns or questions Josie has about treatment. Reflections are (again) the most used skill so that Josie and her mother feel heard and understood. Open questions are also used to invite them to share information and to set the tone that their contributions are valuable. Also, the counselor takes special care to ensure Josie's autonomy is supported when it is appropriate to do so, such as seeking her permission for the counselor to give information even though her mother already responded affirmatively. Given that Josie is coming to counseling at the urging of her mother and the school and that she is an adolescent, it is especially important to support her autonomy to enhance the therapeutic alliance, increase her engagement in the conversation and in treatment overall, and encourage ownership of her change process.

Once they agree on the treatment modality, the treatment plan would be addressed, including the specific actions Josie would be completing in treatment. When possible, we can present clients with a "menu of options" (Miller & Rollnick, 2002). For instance, if attaining sober social support is part of Josie's treatment plan, then the counselor can use EPE to discuss with Josie ways in which she might wish to pursue this as follows:

Counselor: Josie, what are some of your ideas about how to connect with kids who do not smoke marijuana? [*open question/first elicit*]
Josie: I don't know. I guess I know some people who don't smoke, but not many.
Counselor: You know of some people. [*reflection*]
Josie: Yeah, my friend Lesa. We were like best friends in elementary school. She's big into gymnastics and stuff, so she doesn't smoke or anything.
Counselor: So one idea would be to reconnect with Lesa and see about spending some time together. [*reflection*]
Josie: Yeah, but I know she's busy a lot.
Counselor: Yeah, so that might work out when she has free time. [*reflection*]
Josie: Yeah.
Counselor: What about others? [*open question*]
Josie: I don't know.... [*shrugs*]
Counselor: I have a thought, based on what I've seen to be helpful for other kids in similar situations. Would it be ok if I shared it with you? [*asking for permission*]

Josie: Ok.

Counselor: Sometimes, it helps to think about what you're interested in—some kids are into different sports, like your friend Lesa, who spends her time in gymnastics, while others are into music and join the school band, or they like acting and singing, and they join the drama club or the choir. Others might enjoy writing and journalism and join the school's yearbook or media club. By pursuing their interests, they make friends with other kids with similar interests, and they're able to spend time together without worrying about getting in trouble for smoking or something like that. [*providing information*] I wonder, what do you think about that? [*open question/second elicit*]

Josie: I never really thought about it. I used to play soccer, but I stopped in high school because I didn't want to try out. But I do miss it. It was a lot of fun, and I still have some friends who play.

Counselor: Soccer could be a lot of fun. [*reflection of change talk*]

Josie: Yeah, I guess I could ask about joining them for the winter rec league—you don't have to try out for that I don't think.

Counselor: What do you think about putting that in your plan then? [*open question*] You will pursue playing soccer to engage in sober social activity. [*introduces commitment language*]

Josie: Yeah, I'll do that. [*commitment language*]

A sample treatment plan for Josie is provided in Figure 10.1.

Treatment

After the initial assessment and planning for treatment, the treatment phase begins. The transition to active treatment can be aided by a strong therapeutic alliance and enhanced motivation; however, clients will still commonly enter treatment with a healthy degree of skepticism and fluctuating motivation, especially when the service provider changes from intake assessment and treatment planning to the actual provision of treatment services.

Group counseling is the most common modality for treatment for addiction, but individual counseling and family components are also included, especially in higher levels of care (Substance Abuse and Mental Health Services Administration [SAMHSA], 2014). MI+CBT can be applied to group as well as individual counseling, and it can also play a role in family work. In a randomized clinical trial, Sobell, Sobell, and Agrawal (2009) found that a version of MI+CBT was as effective when delivered in a group therapy format compared to individual therapy. How MI+CBT is applied is contingent on client readiness for active change as well as the current coping skills (i.e., behavioral, emotional, and cognitive; intrapersonal and interpersonal). This section explores various ways to implement MI+CBT to match client needs for treatment, as guided by Figure 9.1 in the previous chapter.

Plan for Change/Treatment Plan

The changes I want to make are:	My reasons for making these changes:
Stop getting in trouble.	I'm tired of the school and my parents trying to punish me.

In order to make these changes, I will engage in the following treatment plan while participating in intensive outpatient group and individual therapy:

Concern	Goal	Treatment
Getting in trouble	Decrease and then eliminate marijuana use	• Functional analysis • Explore values and goals • Increase sober social activities
	Stop drinking alcohol	• Functional analysis • Explore values and goals • Increase sober social activities
	Improve relationship with parents	• Practice communication skills • Express self during family sessions

Outside of treatment I will also take these steps:

Register for the next soccer season; talk to my parents more; get all my schoolwork done.

How will I know if my plan is working?

Stop getting in trouble. Talk with my parents more. Get better grades.

What might interfere with my plan?	What will I do if this happens?
Friends ask me to smoke and I say yes	Talk to my counselor
If I miss my friends who I smoke with	Talk with my sober friends

Figure 10.1 Plan for Change/Treatment Plan for Josie

Targeting Motivation

Clients who present with low motivation for change will likely benefit from MI+CBT that is initially directed at the engaging and focusing processes of MI. This will involve creating a partnership to collaboratively explore client sustain talk, or their reasons for wanting to continue substance use or the addictive behavior or to avoid change. The counselor would largely draw on the use of evocation in these conversations. Open questions such as, "What do you like about drinking?" or "Tell me about what positives you get out of having frequent hookups?" are followed by reflections or summaries of the client's response. While doing so, the atmosphere of acceptance and compassion is retained, and the counselor can also begin to conceptualize the functional analysis. After clients express and feel as though their reasons not to change are heard, the counselor can elicit change talk and gain an understanding of the client's perception of the problem. Examples of questions to elicit change talk include, "I understand that marijuana use is a problem for your parents, but what do you see as possible problems with using it?" "What consequences have you seen others experience from using?" "If you were to continue to use, how might that affect you?" Additional evocative questions might include, "What do you dislike about drinking?" or "What do you wish was different about your sexual activity?" Counselors respond to client change talk by using OARS, including asking for examples and using reflections to strengthen clients' motivations. Consider the following example with Josie:

Counselor: Josie, it seems you really enjoyed smoking marijuana because it helped you feel connected to other kids, especially kids who were a little older than you and who might have boosted your popularity some. [*summary of sustain talk*]

Josie: Yeah, I was hanging out with juniors and seniors sometimes and that was pretty cool.

Counselor: So those parts of using made you feel pretty good about using and about yourself. [*reflection of sustain talk*]

Josie: Yeah.

Counselor: Even though you enjoyed some parts of smoking, it's really common for people to like some parts but not others, I wonder what aspects of smoking did you not like so much or that you wished were different? [*open question to elicit change talk*]

Josie: Ummm.... [*silence*] I guess I got really tired sometimes. There were a few times I'd just fall asleep—at school, at home, at parties—it didn't really matter where I was.

Counselor: It was like turning out a light; you'd fall asleep whether you wanted to or not. [*complex reflection*]

Josie: Yeah, it was really hard to stay awake.

Counselor: That seems like it could even be a problem, falling asleep at school, I'm guessing during class, and at parties when there are lots of other people around. [*complex reflection*]

Josie: Yeah, it's gotten me in trouble a few times in class.

Counselor: It's gotten you in trouble. [*reflection*]

Josie: Yeah, but classes are boring, so who cares?

Counselor: If you decided to continue to smoke, which led you to continue to fall asleep in these places, what do you see as possibly happening? [*open question to elicit change talk*]

Josie:	I'd get detention. And now with the whole school knowing I was caught smoking, they'd probably send me to the office.
Counselor:	Detention, being sent to the office. [*reflection*] What about at parties? [*open question to elicit change talk*]
Josie:	I don't know. People usually just leave me alone, but I don't know.... [*pause*]
Counselor:	So far, they've left you alone to sleep, but it seems like it might not be a situation you want to continue to put yourself in. [*action reflection*]
Josie:	Yeah, that's true.

Another strategy to cultivate client motivation is to encourage clients to identify their goals and values, and then the counselor assists clients in identifying discrepancies between what is most important to them and/or what they hope to accomplish and their substance use or addictive behavior. A value card sort (e.g., Miller, C'de Baca, Matthews, & Wilbourne, 2001) can be used to assist clients in identifying their values and to encourage discussion about what is most important to them in their lives. Further, this exploration can help reveal cognitions that perpetuate substance use/addiction. For instance, if Josie states that her friends are very important to her, yet her marijuana use resulted in her being undependable to them ("I forgot about plans I made with my friend last weekend because I went to go smoke with some people. My friend is still really mad about it."), the counselor can use double-sided reflections to draw attention to the conflict between her substance use and her value of friendship: "Although your friends are very important to you, they might be getting the impression that you put smoking marijuana ahead of them." Using the evoking process of MI, the counselor neither pushes nor pulls the client to action, but rather walks alongside the client, guiding the way in exploring and then resolving ambivalence and establishing a commitment to change.

As the client uses more change talk and less sustain talk, the counselor can work to elicit the client's commitment to change, which can range from committing to change ("I will stop using") to taking small steps ("This week I cut back on using") to comprehensive change ("I did not use this past week, and I went to my grandmother's house to spend time with her instead"). Research has supported an emphasis on change talk, as Magill et al. (2013) found that the degree to which the therapist focused on the client's commitment to change was associated with improved drinking outcomes, including more days abstinent and lower drinks consumed on drinking days. Similarly, Moyers et al. (2009) found that change talk led to improved outcomes related to drinking and that therapist behaviors, especially reflections, increased the amount of change talk clients expressed in session.

Targeting Cognitions That Affect Motivation

In addition to addressing motivation for change and treatment by eliciting and strengthening the client's change talk, MI+CBT practitioners should also listen for and conceptualize cognitive and behavioral factors that can be contributing to or causing ambivalence. For instance, consider the case of Greg from Practice Box 10.3.

Imagine that although the counselor empathized with Greg's sustain talk and elicited and reinforced his arguments for change, Greg remained ambivalent about changing his behaviors related to sex and relationships. Although Greg described that he wants a trusting and stable relationship (change talk), he also stated, "But I'm not worth it" (sustain talk). His counselor begins to conceptualize Greg's core beliefs that originated from his early childhood experiences—I'm unlovable and I'm unworthy—as causing his unwavering sustain talk. Therefore, it would likely behoove Greg if his counselor helped him address these cognitions that are resulting in his perpetual ambivalence.

Similarly, clients' perceived lack of ability to engage in new or alternative behaviors can result in enduring ambivalence. For instance, if Greg progresses to replace his negative core beliefs with new, healthy beliefs, such as, "I am worthy of love and an honest relationship," he might then begin to struggle with *how* to engage in this type of relationship, which he has never experienced. Therefore, he would likely benefit from skill development related to managing emotions, identifying and managing triggers, and participating in effective communication in relationships, as well as others. Greg might not be able to commit to making the changes he desires, such as pursuing a relationship instead of pursuing anonymous sex, if he continues to believe he is not worthy or capable of implementing these changes. Therefore, cognitive and behavioral interventions may need to precede commitment to change, in some cases.

Functional Analysis

A functional analysis brings to awareness the reasons why the client uses substances or engages in addictive behaviors and can result in the client understanding the antecedents or triggers to use as well as the consequences of use (Drossel, Rummel, & Fisher, 2009). Questions such as, "What does alcohol or drugs allow you to do or become?" and "What does alcohol or drugs allow you to avoid or escape from?" (Brooks & McHenry, 2015, p. 167) can be helpful in eliciting the benefits, roles, and functions substances and addictive behaviors have in the client's life. Once known, the client and counselor can work to address the purpose of the behaviors and eventually identify alternatives. For instance, if Josie believes that smoking allows her to be accepted by the older, more mature, desirable social group and helps her avoid being "a loner," she will likely feel compelled to say "yes" when older students ask her to smoke with them. Therefore, in treatment the client would likely benefit from addressing cognitions that perpetuate these beliefs and practicing refusal skills for when she is offered marijuana. She might also benefit from developing and strengthening social and family relationships (i.e., her parents) as part of solidifying new beliefs that she does not need to use marijuana in order to be accepted by others. Learning effective communication skills could also help improve her relationships with her friends and her parents.

Targeting Cognitions to Promote Behavior Change

Overall, cognitive interventions have been found to be effective when treating substance use and addictive disorders (Magill & Ray, 2009; McHugh et al., 2010).

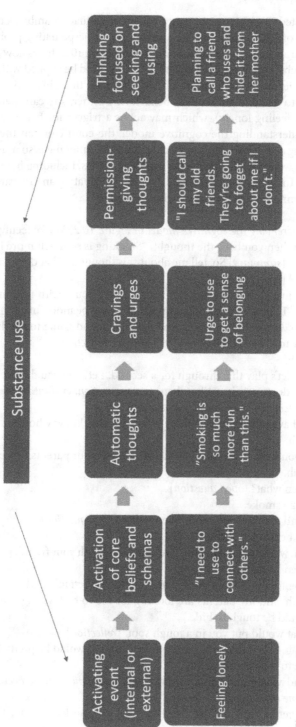

Figure 10.2 Cognitive Model for Addiction Applied to Josie

Source: Adapted from *Beck et al.* (2005).

178 *Clinical Applications*

As previously noted, cognitions can play a role in perpetuating ambivalence, and through the lens of CBT, cognitions are also culprits in perpetuating problematic substance use and addictive behaviors. To illustrate, Figure 10.2 shows how the cognitive model of substance use from Beck et al. (2005) could be applied with Josie.

In therapy, Josie can become aware of her automatic thoughts and how they affect her urges to use and subsequent behaviors. Further, she can identify the antecedents (i.e., feeling lonely), which may act as a trigger for her using. After applying and understanding the cognitive model, the counselor can then guide Josie in evaluating and revising her automatic thought, "Smoking is so much more fun than this," as well as exploring deeper-level cognitions, including her schemas and core beliefs. The dialogue that follows illustrates evaluating and revising Josie's thoughts in a manner that is consistent with MI+CBT:

Counselor: [*Referencing the cognitive model in Figure 10.2*] You're feeling lonely, and then you have the thought, "Smoking is so much more fun than this". [*summary*] So, tell me about this thought. What does it mean to you? [*open question*]

Josie: I'm just so bored when I'm sitting at my house with nothing to do. And I know that if I called up Tai, it would be more fun.

Counselor: Boredom is the concern. And calling Tai and going to smoke is one way to alleviate the boredom. [*complex reflections*]

Josie: Yeah.

Counselor: Ok, let's play this through for a second. Let's say you do call Tai, and you do go smoke. What then? [*open question; evaluating the thought for accurate outcome expectations*]

Josie: I'd have to hide it. I couldn't let my parents know who I was leaving with.

Counselor: If you were to do this, you'd have to lie to your parents. [*reflection*]

Josie: Yeah.

Counselor: Then what? [*open question*]

Josie: I'd go smoke.

Counselor: You'd smoke. [*reflection*] Then what? [*open question*]

Josie: It'd be fun for a while.

Counselor: You would have some fun while high and with your friend. [*reflection*]

Josie: Then I'd have to get home.

Counselor: Eventually, the fun would have to end. [*reflection*]

Josie: Yeah, and my parents are looking for me to be high right now, so it would be tough to hide.

Counselor: That would put you in a tough spot. [*reflection*]

Josie: Yeah, they'd find out. I know they would. It would be pretty impossible to hide at this point.

Counselor: And what would that mean? [*open question; eliciting accurate outcome expectations*]

Josie: I'd get in super trouble. They'd probably never let me leave the house again.

Counselor:	And that sounds like exactly what you do not want—for your parents to be even more on your case. [*complex reflection*]
Josie:	Well, yeah.
Counselor:	(Pause) So back to the thought, "Smoking is so much more fun than this." How true does that seem now? [*open question; eliciting Josie's evaluation of her thought*]
Josie:	Well, it would be fun for a while, but then it would lead to things being even worse.
Counselor:	"It would be fun for a while, but then it would lead to things being even worse". [*repeating client's revised thought*] With all this work you're doing, it sounds like you may have found a thought that might be very accurate. [*affirmation*]
Josie:	Yeah, that's the truth.
Counselor:	And if you have in your mind, "It would be fun for a while, but then it would lead to things being even worse," what do you think you would do? Would you call Tai? [*question; eliciting behavior response to revised cognition*]
Josie:	No, I wouldn't. I'd find something else to do.
Counselor:	You'd find something else to do that would not result in making your situation worse. [*complex reflection*]
Josie:	Right. I'd watch TV or something.
Counselor:	The next time you feel lonely, what do you think about recognizing and stopping the thought, "Smoking is so much more fun than this," and replacing it with, "It would be fun for a while, but then things would be even worse"? [*open question to evoke commitment to modify cognitions*]
Josie:	Yeah, I can do that. That makes sense.

MI+CBT can be used to help clients identify problematic cognitions (especially those beliefs that commonly accompany addiction), evaluate them, and then alter them to be conducive to recovery, as opposed to further perpetuating addiction. This example describes evaluating and revising beliefs that are related to Josie's anticipatory belief ("It would be more fun"). Specific to addiction, MI+CBT practitioners should also tune in to relief-oriented beliefs ("I will explode if I don't have a drink; I need to calm down") and permissive beliefs ("No one will know; it will be ok") (Wright et al., 1993).

Coping Skills and Relapse Prevention

The client's current level of coping skills will also factor into how MI+CBT is implemented. Clients with ineffective or lower levels of coping are likely to need more immediate skill development. For example, if Josie had strong intrapersonal (e.g., a healthy self-concept as an individual) and interpersonal coping strategies (e.g., being supported by strong family relationships and friendships outside of her friends who use substances), it would be easier for her to be motivated to move toward these other desirable and functional options and move away from substance use. However, if Josie lacked these coping strategies in that she does not have a healthy, autonomous self-concept and identity outside of the substance-using group of friends, and she lacked healthy, stable family relationships, she might need to develop sufficient coping strategies to increase the likelihood of her being able to move away from substance use. For many clients, it is not only a question of "What am I moving away from (i.e., substance use)?" but also "What am I moving toward?" or "What do I do instead?" For clients who have ample coping skills and higher levels of functioning, they will be more equipped to respond to the latter question. For those who do not, counselors can help clients develop coping skills and strategies that will work for them; however, clients will have varying degrees of motivation to develop and employ healthy coping. Therefore, the interplay of motivation in substance use and addiction treatment must be considered on various levels of treatment, including when addressing coping.

Figure 10.3 displays various factors that impact relapse prevention (Marlatt & Gordon, 1985) and coping skills commonly targeted in substance use counseling. Assessing these areas and then using MI+CBT interventions to target the areas in which the client is not strong (e.g., low motivation, low self-efficacy) can increase the likelihood of their success in treatment. However, it is not uncommon for clients to feel ambivalent about using different behaviors (e.g., refusal skills, avoiding high-risk situations) and changing their beliefs (e.g., considering the negative effects of substance use, addressing beliefs that perpetuate substance use). Therefore, motivational issues can surface and should be addressed in the midst of implementing cognitive and behavioral interventions. For instance, consider the following exchange between Josie and her counselor when addressing the high-risk situation she identified for smoking marijuana:

Counselor: So having your friend Tai pick you up in the morning before school seems to be a high-risk situation for you—you're likely to use when she picks you up. [*summary*]
Josie: Yeah, I will. For sure.
Counselor: It seems like a sure thing; you can predict that happening. [*reflection*] Ok, so in the effort of not using marijuana, what are your options here instead of Tai picking you up? [*open question, eliciting a menu of options from the client*]
Josie: Instead of her picking me up? I don't know . . . [pause] I guess I could ask someone else to get me, but I don't know who. I've never taken the bus, and I refuse to do that anyway. [pause] But I can't tell Tai not to pick me up. That's what we've done since the start of school. [*sustain talk*]
Counselor: It seems like you can't change the routine with her. This is the way it's been and the way she expects it to stay. [*reflection*]
Josie: Yeah. She'll think . . . I got weird or something.

Factors	Less Likely to Change	More Likely to Change
Motivation	• Low motivation to change, including using alternative coping skills "I can't because..." "That won't work..."	• High motivation to change, including using alternative coping skills "I will try that." "I will do that instead."
Social Support	• No sober social support "I don't know anyone who does not use."	• Ample sober social support "I have family and friends who do not use and who support me not using."
Self-Efficacy	• Low self-efficacy "I can't make all these changes."	• High self-efficacy "It's going to be hard, but I know I can do it."
Outcome Expectancies	• Use-promoting outcome expectancies "No one will find out if I use. I will have fun with my friends."	• Sober-promoting outcome expectancies "If I use, I could get in even more trouble. I might make poor decisions."
Emotional Regulation	• Low emotional regulation "When I get angry, I can't control it."	• High emotional regulation "When I get angry, I take some deep breaths and take a moment to think."
General Coping Skills	• Low coping skills "When I get upset, I lash out."	• Effective coping skills "When I get upset, I reflect on the reasons why. Sometimes I go for a run or write in my journal."
Responses to Craving and Urges	• Lacking information about cravings "I must use. This urge will not go away if I do not use."	• Helpful thoughts about cravings "This will pass. My body is getting used to being without it. It takes time, but it will get easier."

Figure 10.3 Factors That Impact Relapse Prevention

182 Clinical Applications

Counselor: She'll wonder what's going on that you're getting to school a different way. [*complex reflection*]
Josie: Yeah.
Counselor: How might you explain it to her? [*open question/evocation*]
Josie: I don't want to explain it to her. She'll think I'm totally weird if I tell her I'm not smoking right now.

Identifying the high-risk situation alone was not sufficient for Josie to change her behaviors to avoid the situation. Therefore, the counselor began to explore and hear Josie's reasons for avoiding this change. Considering the developmental stage of the client, telling a member of her peer group about her abstinence would be difficult. The counselor would need to continue to express empathy through accurate reflections to ensure that Josie continued to feel heard and understood. Instead of succumbing to the temptation to push Josie into an alternative (e.g., "Ask another friend or your mom to drive you") or to threaten the consequences (e.g., "If you go with her and smoke again, you might be expelled from school, let alone consequences with your parents"), the MI+CBT counselor would continue to focus on evocation and guide Josie to develop an alternative behavior that would avoid the high-risk situation and that Josie is also willing to and feels capable of implementing. The alternative behavior might include skills that she does not have yet, such as assertiveness and refusal skills, in which case the counselor would assist Josie in developing these skills, and then Josie would choose if and how to use them.

Maintenance

After six months of active behavior changes, clients enter the maintenance stage of change (Norcross et al., 2011). Maintaining cognitive and behavior changes over time can be challenging, and therefore, the tasks of maintenance include working to consolidate gains made in action and avoid falling back into former ways of thinking and behaving (Velasquez et al., 2001). From a CBT perspective, it is important for clinicians to prepare clients for challenges in maintaining changes and how to respond to potential setbacks (Beck, 2011). Actively planning for maintenance can support client success. Common strategies to promote maintenance include identifying the client's triggers and high-risk situations and then collaboratively developing a proactive plan that incorporates the client's coping skills, social support, and strengths to navigate difficult situations. Naar-King, Earnshaw, and Breckon (2013) described MI+CBT strategies that can be used to encourage maintenance over time. These are summarized in the list that follows. Figure 10.4 illustrates a sample maintenance plan applied to the case of Josie.

- *Set goals.* Similar to the focusing process, when planning for maintenance, we avoid prescribing the goals or the plan. Instead, we continue to evoke clients' goals for the short and long term. When clients need guidance in setting the

Maintenance Plan

Goals

What changes do you want to maintain?

Not smoking marijuana or drinking, getting along better with my parents

Identifying Triggers

What triggers you to want to use?

Boredom, loneliness, wanting to have friends, arguing with parents

When you have a craving or urge to use, what can you do to distract yourself, or delay yourself from reacting, until the urge subsides?

Watch YouTube, do homework. Write in my journal.

Coping Skills

What do you do physically to engage in healthy coping and wellness?

Play soccer, swim sometimes

What are the encouraging or helpful thoughts you have that help you stay clean?

If I keep not smoking, the school and my parents will stop tracking my every move.

I have other things to do and other friends.

What are healthy and effective ways in which you can express your emotions?

Use effective communication to tell my parents. Write in my journal.

Who can you talk to for social support?

My mom (sometimes), my sister, and my friend on the soccer team

Identifying High-Risk Situations

What are your high-risk situations?

Going to school with old friends, going to parties

What are ways in which you can exit these situations without using?

Parties: Say I don't feel well and have to go home and call someone for a ride.

What could you do instead?

Going to school: Ask my friend Lesa to take me.

Figure 10.4 Maintenance Plan Example for Josie

goals for maintenance, counselors might use EPE and offer a menu of options from which clients can choose.
- *Avoid the goal violation effect.* Naar and Safren (2017) encouraged MI+CBT practitioners to avoid terms that might have negative connotations, such as "relapse" (p. 185), due to the "all-or-nothing" assumption this term can convey. The all-or-nothing perception can lead to the client succumbing to the goal violation effect, which is a phenomenon in which small setbacks can cause the client to feel as though "all is lost." Therefore, we can engage in "maintenance planning" as opposed to "relapse prevention." Further, we can use terms such as "slip" (as opposed to "lapse") and assist the client in identifying responses that can prevent him or her from fully resuming old behaviors of substance use and addiction, should he or she experience a slip, such as calling the counselor, reaching out to a sponsor, or attending a mutual help group meeting.
- *Identify triggers and subsequent coping skills.* Evocation is essential when identifying triggers that pertain to the unique client and his or her particular circumstances. If needed, we can use EPE to provide information about common triggers and possible coping skills. However, clients' maintenance plans must be achievable in clients' lives, so we want to ensure that they are able to commit to implementing the actions chosen.
- *Managing cravings and urges.* Although cravings subside with sustained abstinence, they can occur in the maintenance stage of change. We can use EPE to help clients employ skills learned in treatment to their plan for maintenance. If clients have difficulty identifying strategies they can use, we can suggest "urge surfing" (Marlatt & Donovan, 2005) to ride out the urge as opposed to falling into it and using. This strategy is accompanied by the perspective that letting the urge or craving pass weakens it and will allow it to get easier while using in response to the craving or urge strengthens it, and it will likely increase in difficulty (Miller, Forcehimes, & Zweben, 2011).
- *Identifying high-risk situations and alternative behaviors.* Planning for contingencies to avoid high-risk situations can be helpful for clients in maintenance, as well as developing plans to exit or ways to endure high-risk situations if they cannot be avoided (Miller et al., 2011). The high-risk situations identified and the plans for avoiding, exiting, or enduring should be collaboratively developed with the client, because once again, this plan is only useful if the client is willing and able to implement it in his or her life.
- *Supporting self-efficacy.* Clients' belief that they are indeed capable of maintaining changes will impact their ability to do so. We can support clients' self-efficacy by reinforcing past successes and providing realistic planning for the future. We can assess self-efficacy by using a confidence ruler and elicit ideas from clients about what can increase their self-efficacy. Finally, we can make affirmations that reinforce clients' strengths, abilities, and positive efforts.

Of course, when discussing maintenance planning in each of these areas, if the client appears ambivalent, then the counselor should explore the ambivalence, including addressing motivation, as well as cognitions that might be interfering with maintaining change.

Practice Considerations

High rates of client dropout and relapse are common in substance use and addiction counseling. Common factors attributing to clients dropping out of treatment include low motivation, longer criminal records, and more severe psychiatric and employment issues (Evans et al., 2009). In this chapter, we focused on substance use and addiction specifically, and yet there is a high prevalence of concurrent mental health and substance use or addictive disorders (Lai, Cleary, Sitharthan, & Hunt, 2015). There is a dire need for comprehensive treatment in which both mental health disorders and addiction or substance use disorders are addressed simultaneously by a single treatment team. However, the majority of clients who experience concurrent disorders have never had both issues addressed in a treatment setting. Instead, clients often access serial treatment (treat one issue and then the other) or parallel treatment (both issues addressed simultaneously by different treatment providers) and, unfortunately, with dismal success rates (Doweiko, 2015). MI+CBT has been applied to treatment of co-occurring disorders and found to be successful. For example, Cleary, Hunt, Matheson, and Walter (2009) conducted a meta-analysis of 54 studies, randomized and nonrandomized trials, that included psychosocial interventions for people with a severe mental illness and substance misuse. Their findings showed that MI had the most quality evidence for reducing substance use over the short-term, while MI combined with CBT resulted in significant improvements in mental health, as well as reductions in substance use.

In addition to providing comprehensive treatment, MI+CBT applied to substance use and addiction counseling should be culturally responsive. Research has supported the use of culturally informed treatments for substance use compared to treatments that did not account for cultural components (Steinka-Fry, Tanner-Smith, Dakof, & Henderson, 2017). As described in Chapter 5, MI and CBT have both been formally adapted to account for culture. Clinicians using MI+CBT should at minimum ensure that their interventions, terminology, and counseling processes are responsive and inclusive of a client's culture, including cultural beliefs about substance use and addictive behaviors, as well as about how change occurs within the client's context and community.

Summary

As separate approaches, MI and CBT both have strong empirical support in the realm of substance use and addiction treatment. This chapter described implementing MI+CBT across the span of treatment from the intake assessment to maintenance. The MI+CBT combination provides clinicians with strategies to address discord and motivational issues in the earlier stages of change and cognitive and behavioral interventions for clients who are ready for active changes. The foundation of a strong therapeutic alliance fostered through continuing the spirit of MI persists throughout MI+CBT. Practice considerations include the need for comprehensive treatment that addresses concerns that interplay with substance use and addiction, such as mental health disorders, criminal records, and employment concerns, as well as the duty to provide culturally responsive treatment.

References

Anton, R. F., O'Malley, S. S., Ciraulo, D. A., Couper, D., Donovan, D. M., Gastfriend, D. R., . . . Zweben, A. (2006). Combined pharmacotherapies and behavioral interventions for alcohol dependence: The COMBINE study: A randomized controlled trial. *Journal of the America Medical Association*, 295(17), 2003–2017. doi:10.1001/jama.295.17.2003

Babor, T. F., Higgins-Biddle, J. C., Saunders, J. B., & Monteiro, M. G. (2001). *AUDIT: The alcohol use disorders identification test: Guidelines for use in primary health care* (2nd ed.). Geneva, Switzerland: World Health Organization.

Beck, J. S. (2011). *Cognitive behavior therapy: Basics and beyond* (2nd ed.). New York, NY: Guilford Press.

Beck, J. S., Liese, B. S., & Najavits, L. M. (2005). Cognitive therapy. In R. J. Frances, S. I. Miller, & A. H. Mack (Eds.), *Clinical textbook of addictive disorders* (3rd ed., pp. 474–501). New York, NY: Guilford Press.

Bright, D. A., & Martire, K. A. (2013). Does coerced treatment of substance-using offenders lead to improvements in substance use and recidivism? A review of the treatment efficacy literature: Coerced treatment for substance-using offenders. *Australian Psychologist*, 48(1), 69–81. doi:10.1111/j.1742-9544.2012.00072.x

Brooks, F., & McHenry, B. (2015). *A contemporary approach to substance use disorders and addiction counseling* (2nd ed.). Alexandria, VA: American Counseling Association.

Brown, R. L., & Rounds, L. A. (1995). Conjoint screening questionnaires for alcohol and other drug abuse: Criterion validity in a primary care practice. *Wisconsin Medical Journal*, 94(3), 135–140.

Carnes, P. J., Green, B. A., Merlo, L. J., Polles, A., Carnes, S., & Gold, M. S. (2012). PATHOS: a brief screening application for assessing sexual addiction. *Journal of addiction medicine*, 6(1), 29–34. doi:10.1097/ADM.0b013e3182251a28

Chan, A. W. K., Pristach, E. A., Welte, J. W., & Russell, M. (1993). Use of the TWEAK test in screening for alcoholism/heavy drinking in three populations. *Alcoholism: Clinical and Experimental Research*, 17(6), 1188–1192. doi:10.1111/j.1530-0277.1993.tb05226.x

Cleary, M., Hunt, G. E., Matheson, S., & Walter, G. (2009). Psychosocial treatments for people with co-occurring severe mental illness and substance misuse: Systematic review. *Journal of Advanced Nursing*, 65(2), 238–258. doi:10.1111/j.1365-2648.2008.04879.x

Couwenbergh, C., Van Der Gaag, R. J., Koeter, M., De Ruiter, C., & Van den Brink, W. (2009). Screening for substance abuse among adolescents validity of the CAGE-AID in youth mental health care. *Substance Use & Misuse*, 44(6), 823–834. doi:10.1080/10826080802484264

Donovan, D. M., Anton, R. F., Miller, W. R., Longabaugh, R., Hosking, J. D., & Youngblood, M. (2008). Combined pharmacotherapies and behavioral interventions for alcohol dependence (the COMBINE study): Examination of posttreatment drinking outcomes. *Journal of Studies on Alcohol and Drugs*, 69(1), 5–13. doi:10.15288/jsad.2008.69.5

Doweiko, H. E. (2015). *Concepts of chemical dependency* (9th ed.). Belmont, CA: Cengage Learning.

Drossel, C., Rummel, C., & Fisher, J. E. (2009). Assessment and cognitive behavior therapy: Functional analysis as key process. In W. O'Donohue & J. E. Fisher (Eds.), *Principles and techniques of cognitive behavior therapy: An introduction* (pp. 15–41). Hoboken, NY: John Wiley & Sons.

Evans, E., Li, L., & Hser, Y. I. (2009). Client and program factors associated with dropout from court mandated drug treatment. *Evaluation and Program Planning*, 32(3), 204–212. doi:10.1016/j.evalprogplan.2008.12.003

Ewing, J. A. (1984). Detecting alcoholism: The CAGE questionnaire. *Journal of the American Medical Association*, 252(14), 1905–1907. doi:10.1001/jama.1984.03350140051025

Lai, H. M. X., Cleary, M., Sitharthan, T., & Hunt, G. E. (2015). Prevalence of comorbid substance use, anxiety and mood disorders in epidemiological surveys, 1990–2014:

A systematic review and meta-analysis. *Drug and Alcohol Dependence, 154,* 1–13. doi:10.1016/j.drugalcdep.2015.05.031

Lazowski, L. E., Kimmell, K.S., & Baker, S.L. (2016). *The Adult Substance Abuse Subtle Screening Inventory-4 (SASSI-4) user guide & manual.* Springville, IN: The SASSI Institute.

Lundahl, B. W., Kunz, C., Brownell, C., Tollefson, D., & Burke, B. L. (2010). A meta-analysis of motivational interviewing: Twenty-five years of empirical studies. *Research on Social Work Practice, 20*(2), 137–160. doi:10.1177/1049731509347850

Magill, M., & Ray, L. A. (2009). Cognitive-behavioral treatment with adult alcohol and illicit drug users: A meta-analysis of randomized controlled trials. *Journal of Studies on Alcohol and Drugs, 70*(4), 516–527. doi:10.15288/jsad.2009.70.516

Magill, M., Stout, R. L., & Apodaca, T. R. (2013). Therapist focus on ambivalence and commitment: A longitudinal analysis of motivational interviewing treatment ingredients. *Psychology of Addictive Behaviors, 27*(3), 754–762. doi:10.1037/a0029639

Marlatt, G. A., & Donovan, D. M. (Eds.). (2005). *Relapse prevention: Maintenance strategies in the treatment of addictive behaviors* (2nd ed.). New York, NY: Guilford Press.

Marlatt, G. A., & Gordon, J. R. (Eds.). (1985). *Relapse prevention: Maintenance strategies in the treatment of addictive behaviors.* New York, NY: Guilford Press.

McHugh, R. K., Hearon, B. A., & Otto, M. W. (2010). Cognitive behavioral therapy for substance use disorders. *Psychiatric Clinics of North America, 33*(3), 511–525. doi:10.1016/j.psc.2010.04.012

McLellan, A. T., Kushner, H., Metzger, D., Peters, R., Smith, I., Grissom, G., . . . Argeriou, M. (1992). The fifth edition of the addiction severity index. *Journal of Substance Abuse Treatment, 9*(3), 199–213. doi:10.1016/0740-5472(92)90062-S

Mee-Lee, D. (2013). *The ASAM criteria: Treatment criteria for addictive, substance-related, and co-occurring condition* (3rd ed.). Chevy Chase, MD: American Society of Addiction Medicine.

Meersseman, P., Vanhoutte, S., Van Damme, J., Maes, L., Lemmens, G., Heylens, G., & Verstraete, A. G. (2016). A comparative study of screening instruments and biomarkers for the detection of cannabis use. *Substance Abuse, 37*(1), 176–180. doi:10.1080/08897077.2015.1037947

Miller, F. G., & Lazowski, L. E. (2001). *The adolescent substance abuse subtle screening inventory-A2 (SASSI-A2) manual.* Springville, IN: The SASSI Institute.

Miller, W. R. (1983). Motivational interviewing with problem drinkers. *Behavioural Psychotherapy, 11*(2), 147. doi:10.1017/S0141347300006583

Miller, W. R., Benefield, R. G., & Tonigan, J. S. (1993). Enhancing motivation for change in problem drinking: A control comparison of two therapist styles. *Journal of Consulting and Clinical Psychology, 61*(3), 455–461. doi:10.1037/0022-006X.61.3.455

Miller, W. R., C'de Baca, J., Matthews, D. B., & Wilbourne, P. L. (2001). *Personal values card sort.* University of New Mexico. Retrieved from www.motivationalinterviewing.org/sites/default/files/valuescardsort_0.pdf

Miller, W. R., Forcehimes, A. A., & Zweben, A. (2011). *Treating addiction: A guide for professionals.* New York, NY: Guilford Press.

Miller, W. R., & Rollnick, S. (2002). *Motivational interviewing: Preparing people for change* (2nd ed.). New York, NY: Guilford Press.

Miller, W. R., & Rollnick, S. (2013). *Motivational interviewing: Helping people change* (3rd ed.). New York, NY: Guilford Press.

Miller, W. R., & Tonigan, J. S. (1996). Assessing drinkers' motivation for change: Stages of change readiness and treatment eagerness scale (SOCRATES). *Psychology of Addictive Behaviors, 10,* 81–89.

Miller, W. R., Tonigan, J. S., & Longabaugh, R. (1995). *Drinker inventory of consequences* [Database record]. doi:10.1037/t03945-000

Moyers, T. B., Martin, T., Houck, J. M., Christopher, P. J., & Tonigan, J. S. (2009). From in-session behaviors to drinking outcomes: A causal chain for motivational interviewing. *Journal of Consulting and Clinical Psychology, 77*(6), 1113–1124. doi:10.1037/a0017189

Naar, S., & Safren, S. A. (2017). *Motivational interviewing and CBT: Combining strategies for maximum effectiveness*. New York, NY: Guilford Press.

Naar-King, S., Earnshaw, P., & Breckon, J. (2013). Toward a universal maintenance intervention: Integrating cognitive-behavioral treatment with motivational interviewing for maintenance of behavior change. *Journal of Cognitive Psychotherapy, 27*(2), 126–137. doi:10.1891/0889-8391.27.2.126

Norcross, J. C., Krebs, P. M., & Prochaska, J. O. (2011). Stages of change. *Journal of Clinical Psychology, 67*(2), 143–154. doi:10.1002/jclp.20758

Pilkey, D., Steinberg, H., & Martino, S. (2015). Evidence-based treatments for substance use disorders. In D. A. Kaye, N. Vadivelu, & R. D. Urman (Eds.), *Substance abuse: Inpatient and outpatient management for every clinician* (pp. 209–227). New York, NY: Springer.

Sampl, S., & Kadden, R. (2001). *Motivational enhancement therapy and cognitive behavioral therapy (MET-CBT-5) for adolescent cannabis users*. (DHHS Publication No. (SMA) 01-3486, Cannabis Youth Treatment (CYT) Manual Series, Volume 1). Rockville, MD: Center for Substance Abuse Treatment, Substance Abuse and Mental Health services Administration.

Selzer, M. L. (1971). The Michigan alcoholism screening test: The quest for a new diagnostic instrument. *The American Journal of Psychiatry, 127*(12), 1653–1658. doi:10.1176/ajp.127.12.1653

Skinner, H. A., & Goldberg, A. E. (1986). Evidence for a drug dependence syndrome among narcotic users. *British Journal of Addiction, 81*(4), 479–484. doi:10.1111/j.1360-0443.1986.tb00359.x

Sobell, L. C., Sobell, M. B., & Agrawal, S. (2009). Randomized controlled trial of a cognitive–behavioral motivational intervention in a group versus individual format for substance use disorders. *Psychology of Addictive Behaviors, 23*(4), 672–683. doi:10.1037/a0016636

Stauffer, M. D., Capuzzi, D., & Aissen, K. (2015). Introduction to assessment. In D. Capuzzi & M. D. Stauffer (Eds.), *Foundations of addiction counseling* (3rd ed., pp. 89–118). Boston, MA: Pearson.

Stea, J. N., Yakovenko, I., & Hodgins, D. C. (2015). Recovery from cannabis use disorders: Abstinence versus moderation and treatment-assisted recovery versus natural recovery. *Psychology of Addictive Behaviors, 29*(3), 522–531. doi:10.1037/adb0000097

Steinka-Fry, K. T., Tanner-Smith, E. E., Dakof, G. A., & Henderson, C. (2017). Culturally sensitive substance use treatment for racial/ethnic minority youth: A meta-analytic review. *Journal of Substance Abuse Treatment, 75*, 22–37. doi:10.1016/j.jsat.2017.01.006

Substance Abuse and Mental Health Services Administration. (2014). *National survey of substance abuse treatment services: 2013. Data on substance abuse treatment facilities*. Rockville, MD: Author.

Tiger, R. (2011). Drug courts and the logic of coerced treatment. *Sociological Forum, 26*(1), 169–182. doi:10.1111/j.1573-7861.2010.01229.x

Velasquez, M. M., Maurer, G. G., Crouch, C., & DiClemente, C. C. (2001). *Group treatment for substance abuse: A stages-of-change therapy manual*. New York, NY: Guilford Press.

Webb, C., Scudder, M., Kaminer, Y., Kadden, R., & Tawfik, Z. (2002). *The MET/CBT 5 supplement: 7 sessions of cognitive behavioral therapy (CBT 7) for adolescent cannabis users*. (DHHS Publication No. (SMA) 02-3659, Cannabis Youth Treatment (CYT) Manual Series, Volume 2). Rockville, MD: Center for Substance Abuse Treatment, Substance Abuse and Mental Health Services Administration

Wright, F. D., Beck, A. T., Newman, C. F., & Liese, B. S. (1993). Cognitive therapy of substance abuse: Theoretical rationale. In L. Simon Onken, J. D. Blaine, & J. J. Boren, (Eds.), *Behavioral treatments for drug abuse and dependence* (pp. 123–146). doi:10.1037/e495912006-008

CHAPTER 11

Mental Health–Related Concerns

In 2017, nearly 19% of adults in the United States met criteria for a diagnosable mental health–related disorder in the past year (SAMHSA, 2018). Despite the prevalence of these disorders, only a fraction of people receive treatment. Nearly one out four adults who had a mental health–related disorder and 44.2% of adults with a serious mental illness perceived that they had an unmet need for mental health care in the past year, and 44.8% of those who had a mental health–related diagnosis did not receive any mental health services in the past year. Dishearten123ingly, 16.1% of those with serious mental illness and 12.8% of those with a mental health–related disorder reported their belief that treatment would not help was a barrier to seeking services (SAMHSA, 2018). These statistics illustrate the importance of reinforcing the help-seeking behaviors of people with mental health concerns by providing effective services. Implementing MI+CBT is one method to serve this population, which includes establishing strong therapeutic alliances and providing therapeutic interventions that meet clients' clinical needs while accounting for their readiness to change. In this chapter, we explore applications of MI+CBT to three areas of mental health–related concerns, including anxiety, depression, and serious mental illnesses.

Of adults in the United States, an estimated 19.1% in the past year and 31.1% at some time in their lives experienced an anxiety disorder (Harvard Medical School, 2007). According to SAMHSA, in 2017, 7.1% of adults and 13.3% of adolescents experienced at least one major depressive episode in the past year alone. A major depressive episode with severe impairment— when depression causes inability to function at home, work, socially, or in relationships—affected 4.5% of adults and 9.4% of adolescents in the past year. Prevalence rates for major depressive disorder are 1.5 to 3 times greater for adults who are women and ages 18–29 (American Psychiatric Association, 2013). Depression that involves suicidality is especially concerning. SAMHSA (2018) reported that nearly 45,000 people in the United States died from suicide in 2016. Further, an estimated 4.5% adults experienced a serious mental illness in the past year, meaning they were diagnosed with a mental, behavioral, or emotional disorder that substantially limited or interfered with major life activities. Approximately 42.6% of people with any mental health diagnosis and 66.7% with a serious mental illness received mental health services in the past (SAMHSA, 2018). Here, we will explore MI+CBT as a viable and effective option for treatment.

Overview of the Integration

CBT is commonly applied to the treatment of mental health–related disorders, including anxiety, depression, and psychosis. Outcome studies have provided empirical support for CBT in the treatment of anxiety disorders (generalized anxiety disorder [GAD], panic and agoraphobia, and social anxiety disorder) and mood disorders, including major depressive disorder, suicide-related behaviors, and as an adjunct to medication in the treatment of bipolar disorder (Dobson, McEpplan, & Dobson, 2019; Tarrier, Taylor, & Gooding, 2008). Further, CBT for psychosis (CBTp) is considered to be the preferred intervention for psychotic disorders in addition to medication for clients whose symptoms warrant psychopharmacological intervention (National Institute for Health and Care Excellence, 2014). Despite empirical support for CBT across these disorders, Dobson and colleagues (2019) noted that there is room for improvement. For example, Hanrahan, Field, Jones, and Davey (2013) found that 43% of participants with GAD who completed cognitive therapy did not meet criteria for recovery at a 12-month follow-up. Dobson et al. (2019) also noted that the effectiveness of CBT in the treatment of depression has decreased in recent studies, and they speculated that this might be due to the studies including participants who present with complexities and challenges, such as having not responded to treatment in the past (Dobson, 2016). Treatments for serious mental illness, such as bipolar disorder and psychosis, often rely on pharmacotherapy, and CBT might be limited in effectively addressing medication compliance. Treatment adherence is also a factor in effect sizes when examining CBT efficacy (Karyotaki et al., 2017).

MI has also been applied and demonstrated success as a stand-alone or adjunctive treatment for anxiety (see Westra, 2012), depression and suicidality (Britton, 2015; Naar & Flynn, 2015; Naar-King, Parsons, Murphy, Kolmodin, & Harris, 2010; Zerler, 2009), and severe mental illness, including psychosis (Barrowclough, Haddock, Fitzsimmons, & Johnson, 2006; Cleary, Hunt, Matheson, & Walter, 2009; Craig et al., 2014; Fiszdon, Kurtz, Choi, Bell, & Martino, 2016; Hayward, Kemp, & David, 2000; Rubenstein, 2016). Following their review and meta-analysis, Romano and Peters (2015) reported that client engagement in treatment is a potential mechanism of change for clients with anxiety, mood, and psychotic disorders. Thus, integrating CBT and MI holds promise to improve the effectiveness of treatment by enhancing client engagement, improving treatment adherence including medication compliance, and tailoring treatment to each client while assisting clients with cognitive restructuring and behavioral skills training that have long-standing support for improving symptoms of depression, anxiety, and serious mental illnesses.

As with all MI+CBT practice, when used to treat mental health–related disorders, the humanistic spirit permeates the counselor's way of being with the client and sets the tone for the therapeutic relationship. MI+CBT practitioners strive to establish a partnership with clients and value the knowledge and experience clients bring to the therapeutic relationship. These relational components must be tailored to the client's level of functioning in cases in which a client is in crisis or unable to function in some areas due to a debilitating disorder. However, the foundational philosophy remains that practitioners cannot impose lasting change on clients. Even if clients are forced into change initially for safety reasons (i.e., involuntary hospital admission), the stabilization and progress achieved during this brief, acute treatment frequently do not last without additional comprehensive services. Despite it being necessary to protect the safety of clients and others, forced treatments such as involuntary hospitalization violate client autonomy. If the client's autonomy is not eventually acknowledged and supported, any progress made is likely only to appease the external force that brought the client to treatment, which no longer exists once the client is discharged or treatment is deemed complete. Flipping this script, once the client is stabilized and no longer posing a threat to anyone's safety, MI+CBT focuses on promoting client autonomy and sets the tone that clients are capable of lasting change, if they choose this. Approaching clients in a manner that is suitable for their readiness for change can partially offset any "force" or "push" to change. It also fosters more effective interventions. Further, using evocation, practitioners set the tone that clients are the best resource for their change process, including problem solving and employing coping skills. If clients would benefit from skill development or cognitive changes, these are learned in therapy to equip clients with additional effective methods to bolster their repertoire of strategies to manage their distress. Perhaps most importantly, treatment is approached from the perspective of the client. Empathy helps the client feel heard and understood, allowing trust to develop in the therapeutic relationship. Clients' values, goals, and perspectives actively shape the motivational, cognitive, behavioral, and emotional interventions used in therapy. Finally, the full therapy process is executed with compassion. The practitioner approaches clients with a genuine desire to learn about their distress and goals and to guide them through their unique process of change. With intense negative stigma surrounding mental health concerns, it is essential that mental health professionals treat clients with respect, dignity, and understanding.

In the following section, we briefly examine the evidence to support MI+CBT in the treatment of mental health concerns. Then we will explore the implementation of MI+CBT for anxiety, depression and suicidal ideation, and psychosis.

Evidence to Support MI+CBT in the Treatment of Mental Health Concerns

Although still relatively new in its development, multiple studies have investigated MI+CBT in the treatment of anxiety, especially generalized anxiety disorder (Westra, 2012; Westra, Arkowitz, & Dozois, 2009; Westra, Constantino, & Antony, 2016; Westra & Dozois, 2006), and applications of MI+CBT have been described to treat depression and suicidality (Arkowitz & Burke, 2008; Britton, Patrick, Wenzel, & Williams, 2011; Flynn, 2011; Naar & Flynn, 2015). Although research has been mixed in that some studies have shown MI+CBT to have no or limited effectiveness with clients with serious mental illness (Barrowclough et al., 2010; Barrowclough et al., 2014), others have found MI+CBT to be useful in treating and managing various aspects of serious mental illness, including addressing comorbid substance use, managing positive symptoms, and addressing sleep dysfunction (Chiu, Ree, Janca, & Waters, 2016; Cleary et al., 2009).

Anxiety

Stemming from her own work with clients with whom CBT seemed ineffective, Westra (2004, 2012) described various ways to combine MI with CBT for the treatment of anxiety and depression. By integrating MI and CBT, Westra (2012) sought to make the relational and contextual factors of therapy explicit when using cognitive and behavioral interventions, while also adding explicit attention to clients' motivation to change. She noted that many clients come to therapy reluctant to change, often due to ambivalence that commonly accompanies anxiety disorders, such as wanting to change but also fearing change, or seeing excessive worrying as a problem and yet also finding comfort and perceived protection from the worry. Studies have shown that MI has a positive effect when added as a prelude to CBT treatment (Westra, 2004; Westra et al., 2009; Westra & Dozois, 2006; Yang & Strodl, 2011) as well as when integrated throughout CBT for generalized anxiety disorder (Westra, 2004; Westra et al., 2016). Across studies, participants who completed MI+CBT benefited from greater reduction in worry, lower degrees of general distress, being more likely to no longer meet diagnostic criteria for GAD, and experiencing lower dropout rates compared to CBT alone. These gains were largely maintained at 6- and 12-month follow-ups. However, there is still a need to consider the individual needs related to motivation and coping skills to inform the amalgamation of MI and CBT (remember Figure 9.1). For instance, Westra and colleagues (2009) reported that four sessions of MI resulted in greater worry reduction compared to four sessions of CBT for individuals with high worry severity ($d = 0.62$). However, for those with moderate worry severity, they found a small effect ($d = 0.27$) favoring four sessions of CBT over four sessions of MI. These findings suggest that there is no one-size-fits-all MI+CBT. Instead, the practitioner must be responsive in his or her delivery of MI+CBT to suit the needs of the client or group.

In addition to outcomes related to symptomology, studies have also qualitatively explored client experiences of MI+CBT and CBT only. Kertes, Westra, Angus, and Marcus (2011) compared the experiences of participants who completed an eight-session CBT group for anxiety to participants who received four individual MI sessions prior to completing eight group sessions of CBT for GAD. They found that participants who had an MI pretreatment prior to CBT described the group therapist as an evocative guide and perceived themselves as taking an active role in therapy. Those who participated in the CBT group only described the same group therapists as directive and perceived themselves as taking a more passive role in therapy. Likewise, Khattra and colleagues (2017) compared the experiences of two clients who completed treatment for GAD. One client received four individual MI sessions followed by 11 individual CBT sessions integrated with MI and the other client received 14 individual CBT sessions. They found that the client who completed MI+CBT described increased confidence in her ability to maintain positive changes and that she attributed the progress she made in therapy to her increased awareness and confidence in her abilities. The client who completed CBT-only expressed confidence in her application of CBT tools and skills to maintain positive changes, and she attributed her progress to the therapist's expertise (Khattra et al., 2017). Although this study is not generalizable, it provides a case example of the impact that adding MI to CBT can have in that it resulted in not only improved symptomology and greater functioning but also a potential corrective shift of self-perception, increased confidence in self-agency, and empowerment.

Depression

Although multiple descriptions have been provided of MI+CBT in the treatment of depression and suicidality (Arkowitz & Burke, 2008; Britton, 2015; Britton, Patrick, Wenzel, & Williams, 2011; Flynn, 2011; Naar & Flynn, 2015), studies have not examined the efficacy of MI+CBT when treating depression alone. However, studies have explored outcomes of MI+CBT in treating depression along with substance use. Riper and colleagues (2014) conducted a meta-analysis of treatment outcomes for co-occurring depression and alcohol use disorder, and they found that MI+CBT was significantly more effective compared to treatment as usual. Further, Kay-Lambkin, Baker, Lewin, and Carr (2009) found that MI+CBT delivered via computer-based and traditional live formats improved depression, as well as improved alcohol and cannabis use outcomes. More research is needed to further inform the efficacy of MI+CBT to treat depression and suicidality.

Serious Mental Illness

Similar to depression, studies have investigated MI+CBT in the treatment of serious mental illness along with substance use. Barrowclough et al. (2006) conceptually supported the integration of MI and CBT to address psychosis and comorbid substance use, and yet subsequent research has demonstrated mixed findings. For instance, Baker, Turner, Kay-Lambkin, and Lewin (2009) found that ten sessions of MI+CBT resulted in comparable outcomes comparable outcomes as a single session brief intervention using MI, and Barrowclough et al. (2010) found that people with psychosis and substance misuse did not improve on outcomes related to hospitalization, symptoms, or functioning after completing MI+CBT treatment, but they did reduce substance use for at least 12 months posttreatment. In a meta-analysis of 54 studies that compared several psychosocial interventions for people with a serious mental illness and substance misuse, Cleary et al. (2009) found that MI had the largest effect for reducing substance use over the short term, while MI+CBT resulted in improvements in mental state as well as reductions in substance use. From their data collected from focus groups with individuals with schizophrenia on sleep dysfunction, Chiu et al. (2016) found that negative beliefs about sleep and behaviors that interfered with sleep (i.e., caffeine consumption, substance use, excessive napping) were common, and they suggested MI and CBT as potential treatments to improve sleep.

Despite being a relatively new integrated practice, existing research can be used to inform the practice of MI+CBT in the treatment of anxiety, depression, and serious mental illness. In the next section, we explore how MI+CBT can be implemented in the treatment of each of these mental health–related disorders, starting with assessment and beginning the therapeutic relationship through treatment completion.

Assessment and Establishing the Therapeutic Relationship

Anxiety

When using MI+CBT for anxiety, Westra (2012) noted that the components of the MI spirit can serve as antidotes to low self-efficacy that commonly accompanies anxiety. Clinicians model compassion in their work with clients, and they understand the possible purposefulness of symptoms of anxiety, which can then translate to the client practicing more self-compassion and diminishing possible pejorative self-understandings (Westra, 2012). Affirmations offered by therapists can help clients recognize their own strengths and validate their own positive efforts. The client-therapist partnership fosters client engagement and sharing of the client's expertise in regard to how the problems came to be and how to best approach them for relief. Evocation often results in clients sharing experiences that were key in developing the cognitions and behaviors in which anxiety manifests (Westra, 2012), which can begin to inform the cognitive conceptualization.

During the assessment, the spirit of MI is maintained while the symptoms of anxiety are assessed, including nature, intensity, and duration. One study with adults who were diagnosed with anxiety disorders found that an estimated 22.8% had serious impairment, 33.7% had moderate impairment, and 43.5% experienced mild impairment (Harvard Medical School, 2007). In addition to assessment interviews, formal assessments such as the Beck Anxiety Inventory (Beck, Epstein, Brown, & Steer, 1988) and the Subjective Units of Distress Scale are available and commonly used to more objectively assess the severity of clients' symptoms. Information collected via assessment is gathered using OARS (the core skills of MI: open questions, affirmations, reflections, and summaries), and formal assessments are administered with client permission. In addition to collecting information about symptoms of anxiety, practitioners using MI+CBT also assess clients' readiness and motivations to change. Readiness to change can be observed as well as inquired about (Westra, 2012). If a client appears to be disengaged or not willing to talk about his or her experiences of anxiety, the counselor should explore the meaning behind the disengagement and respond in ways to diminish any discord in the therapeutic relationship (i.e., avoid arguing, express empathy, emphasize client autonomy). However, counselors should distinguish discord from sustain talk in their assessments in that discord is specific to the relationship and can manifest in clients' negative comments about the counselor or services provided, whereas sustain talk is the against-change side of ambivalence. Sustain talk is a normal and expected manifestation of ambivalence—there are reasons to change, but there are also reasons to avoid change. During the initial assessment, counselors gauge client readiness to change and respond with acceptance and normalization. Then they employ strategies to enhance client readiness as needed.

Depression and Suicidality

When addressing depression and suicidality, we are literally talking about how we can save lives. Although most clients who experience depression will not be suicidal, we do not know unless we ask, and if we do not ask, we potentially miss a chance to intervene. Further, if we—the mental health professionals—do not ask, who will? It is our duty to ensure that we conduct risk assessments with each new client and ongoing assessments with clients who are at risk. Risk assessments are essential to understand the severity of the risk and to determine appropriate treatment. For instance, in 2017, 4.3% of adults in the United States had serious thoughts about killing themselves (SAMHSA, 2018). An estimated 33% of those who had suicidal thoughts made plans for suicide, and about one in eight adults who had serious thoughts of suicide attempted suicide (SAMHSA, 2018). As mental health professionals, we must be able to accurately understand clients' suicidal symptoms, as the implications of misunderstanding could risk a life.

In applying MI+CBT, we first create an environment that is grounded in acceptance and compassion. For some clients, disclosing suicidal thoughts can be extremely difficult, and our presence with the client must be empathic and focused on evocation. Clients who are depressed, feeling hopeless, and potentially suicidal could experience exacerbated symptoms if they are met with perceived judgment, rejection, or dismissiveness. Therefore, expressing accurate empathy in a nonjudgmental and supportive environment can encourage clients to disclose any thoughts, plans, or actions they might have taken. Open questions set the tone of encouraging client disclosure. Further, while clients are sharing their thoughts, MI+CBT practitioners can begin to conceptualize the case formulation that can be used to guide cognitive and behavioral interventions in treatment.

Before we can effectively assess or treat depression or expect clients to provide honest information about their symptoms, including suicidal symptoms, we must first recognize and address any discord in the therapeutic relationship. Discord is commonly present after clients are hospitalized involuntarily, they have had other experiences in which their autonomy was threatened, or they perceived being mistreated. Strategies consistent with MI+CBT to diminish such discord with clients who have been involuntarily hospitalized for suicidality are as follows:

- *Recognize discord and respond.* As the professional in the therapeutic relationship, it is our responsibility to recognize discord and adjust our in-session behaviors to diminish discord. If we notice the client acting with defensiveness, withdrawing, or complaining about services, we seek to understand the underlying causes. Responding with our own defensiveness will likely exacerbate the discord and discourage client engagement. Instead, we respond in ways that remain focused on the client and the meaning behind these behaviors (e.g., mistrust, protecting oneself).

- *Maintain the spirit of MI.* Instead of defensiveness, we seek to develop a partnership and to work "with" the client, including serving as a guide through their process of change. We strive to create an environment of acceptance and compassion and without judgment. Express through your words and actions your genuine desire to be of assistance to the client and not for any personal gain or that of the agency in which services are provided or any third party. Finally, honor the knowledge and experience clients have and use evocation to employ their wisdom.
- *Avoid arguing.* In the great majority of cases, clients were hospitalized to preserve their safety or the safety of others. This does not mean that clients see it that way. If you can develop enough rapport, clients will tell you their version of the events that resulted in the hospitalization. Listen to them and reinforce their disclosures using expressions of empathy. Their perception is their reality.
- *Listen and express empathy/use OARS.* Clients feeling heard and understood is going to strengthen the therapeutic alliance. Primary skills involved include expressing empathy by using reflections, gathering information using opening questions, organizing information using summaries, and highlighting clients' positives by using affirmations. Remember to use silence and to match clients' pace. Clients who experience depression might talk more slowly and quietly. Avoid the temptation to fill the silences with questions. Instead, use reflections (aim for the 2:1 reflection to question ratio) and allow the clients time to think and respond without being rushed to match your pace. Finally, avoid the question-answer trap. Clients will often experience this dynamic in medical settings, and avoiding this dynamic can reinforce that their experience with you can be different.
- *Emphasize autonomy of the client.* When clients' autonomy has been threatened in very real ways (such as involuntary hospitalization), we empathize with that. Then we can find organic and realistic opportunities to empower clients to regain their autonomy. For instance, "You were admitted to the hospital for three days, and that felt very unfair and unhelpful to you. Now that you're out of the hospital, you have much more control over what happens next."

Safety is of the utmost concern when assessing depression and suicidality. Although it is beyond the scope of this book, it is essential for every mental health professional to be able to assess the level of risk clients present with and the corresponding appropriate treatment. For example, SAMHSA (2009) offers the *SAFE-T: Suicide Assessment Five-Step Evaluation and Triage* to guide clinicians in assessing and responding to the determined level of risk. Britton et al. (2011) suggested assessing clients' motivation for treatment in addition to their motivation to live, as they can be very different, and motivations to live can even work against motivations to pursue treatment. For example, a client who values his autonomy and

> **Practice Box 11.1 The Case of Paul:
> An Untimely Medication Change**
>
> Paul, a 33-year-old white male who is diagnosed with major depressive disorder, is having suicidal thoughts daily. He is receiving treatment in a mental health facility, and he implements his plan for safety to avoid attempting suicide. The thoughts of death and suicide distract him from his graduate school coursework, and he is not able to interact socially or with his wife and two young children. He is taking antidepressant medication prescribed by his psychiatrist, but it does not appear to be working effectively. He is tearful as he describes his intense psychic pain and his assiduous efforts to escape suicidal thoughts. The therapist asks what Paul thinks about talking with his psychiatrist about a medication adjustment, to which Paul responds, "No, I cannot make any changes during this semester. I don't know how it will affect me, and I don't want a new medication to cloud my thinking because I have to do well on my qualifying exam." The therapist knows that Paul's education is extremely important to him. Therefore, one of Paul's major motivations for living, his education and future career, is standing as a barrier to Paul requesting a necessary change in his medication. Paul's decision is evidence of his impaired cognitive functioning due to depression and intense suicidal thoughts. How would you proceed in your work with Paul using MI+CBT?

the ability to manage his problems on his own may be less likely to seek help. In order to optimize client outcomes for the short and long term, it can be important to distinguish these different motivations and address them, including their interdependence and impact on risk for suicide. The case example of Paul in Practice Box 11.1 illustrates this type of concern.

Clients with severe depression and suicidal ideation can experience restricted cognitive functioning, which can further complicate their decision making and ability to apply cognitive techniques. For severe depression and suicidal ideation, pharmacological interventions are sometimes needed before other interventions can be useful and in some cases are more effective in diminishing thoughts of suicide (Dunlop et al., 2018). When the etiology of depression seems linked to neurobiological mechanisms or with severe depression, suicidal ideation, or nonresponsiveness to therapy alone, clients can benefit from an evaluation for medication in addition to psychotherapy.

Serious Mental Illness

Engagement and befriending, the first process of CBTp, involves establishing a therapeutic relationship and supporting the client in identifying a problem list (Hardy, 2017). Within the MI+CBT framework, the engaging process of MI would facilitate the establishment and strengthening of a therapeutic relationship. Skills such as asking open questions, listening and expressing empathy using reflections, and affirming the client's strengths and efforts can assist in the engaging process. When clients are initially reluctant to engage in conversation or change, the MI+CBT practitioner approaches the client with the goal of understanding and moves at a pace that is comfortable for the client. By not pushing or pulling clients into change, practitioners support client autonomy and respect their decisions concerning engaging in therapeutic activities and change.

CBTp acknowledges that the relational and engagement processes might need to be extended due to client reluctance to engage in therapy, especially due to having had negative experiences with helping professionals in the past or due to symptoms such as paranoia. The strategies employed in MI to diminish discord can be especially effective. MI+CBT counselors characterize discord as client defensiveness, argumentation, or other negative comments made about the counselor or services (e.g., "You can't help me. You're just like all the others. You'll just try to get me drugged up and on my way."). Discord is conceptualized as an interpersonal construct and a signal for the counselor to respond differently. As noted earlier, for the treatment of depression and suicidality, one option for responding to discord includes listening and expressing empathy. Once the client hears your expressions of accurate empathy and recognizes that you are not getting defensive yourself (e.g., "You've had some bad experiences with 'helpers' in the past, and you're concerned I'm going to treat you the same way."), the discord is likely to diminish. Reflections are the most used skill to express empathy; however, there are opportunities to use open questions, affirmations, and summaries as well. Open questions let the client know that you want him or her to share, and followed by reflections, the client knows you're listening and interested in hearing more. For example, "I'm very sorry you've had such experiences in the past. It seems the medications you were prescribed were part of the problem. What else did you not like or find unhelpful in your previous therapy experiences?" and "I wonder what sort of things you think might be helpful to you that we can perhaps incorporate in our work together?" Summaries can be used to collect larger quantities of information to demonstrate listening and understanding as well as to help organize or link information. Affirmations can be especially meaningful for clients with low self-efficacy and low self-esteem due to experiencing the negative effects of stigma surrounding serious mental illnesses. By highlighting the positives, clients can begin to see themselves in a more positive way, which can assist in further developing self-efficacy and strengthening a more positive self-image. Finally, counselors can work to diminish discord by emphasizing the autonomy of the client, such as by reinforcing personal choice and control (e.g., "The psychiatrist is going to prescribe you medication, but you can ask about your options and for information about different side effects. You can help your doctor find medications that work better for you."). To further emphasize client autonomy, you can ensure that the client is the primary resource in finding answers and solutions to his or her problems (e.g., "You've dealt with these concerns for a while now. What have you found that works for you? What have you learned does not work?") and asking for permission prior to giving information or making suggestions ("I have some ideas based on what has helped other clients. Would it be ok if I shared some information about them with you?"). Implementing these strategies to diminish discord in the therapeutic relationship requires the counselor to practice with responsivity and intentionality. Consideration must be paid to each client's context, including social, cultural, and clinical considerations. Each decision is made based on a hypothesis about what might be effective in cultivating a relationship with this individual. If it does not reap the desired outcome (e.g., client maintains defensiveness), then the practitioner listens and learns from the client's response to reformulate the hypothesis and try another strategy or revise his or her style to better match the needs of the client.

Formal assessments can be useful to gain more objective information about clients' experiences of delusions and hallucinations. For instance, when used throughout treatment, instruments such as the Psychotic Symptom Rating Scales (Haddock, McCarron, Tarrier, & Faragher, 1999) can provide baseline information about intensity of psychotic symptoms and then subsequent information to see if treatment is effective in reducing the severity and quantity of symptoms. When using formal assessments in the practice of MI+CBT, practitioners will present the instrument in a manner that preserves client engagement and maintains a strong relationship, including asking for client permission prior to administering the instrument (e.g., "There is a form I often ask new clients to complete. When clients complete it, it can help me understand some of your experiences even better. Would you be willing to look at the form and complete it if you're comfortable doing so?"), providing affirmations (e.g., "You've provided me with a good deal of information that will be helpful in guiding your treatment here. I can see the effort you're putting in"), and continuing to foster a partnership ("I'm happy to answer any questions you might have as you're completing the questionnaire).

Voices From the Field 11.1

Perspective on Using Motivational Interviewing With Cognitive-Behavioral Therapy in Private Practice

Written by
Jessica Melendez Tyler, PhD, LPC-S, NCC
Partner and Clinical Therapist at the Wandering Mind, Columbus, Georgia
Assistant Clinical Professor at Auburn University

When I reflect on my professional development, I immediately think of my mentorship relationships that helped me expand my humanistic qualities and clinical skills. My early career experiences in using cognitive behavioral therapy (CBT) were optimistic and uncoordinated at best, but learning about and how to integrate motivational interviewing (MI) helped me to focus on and understand the nature and dynamics of the therapeutic relationship and the change process while still feeling the direction and guidance of my CBT orientation.

Now, integrating MI and CBT into private practice helps me to increase investment in the therapeutic process for clients who are voluntary but may be uncertain or hesitant about engaging in therapy at the expense of their ego, work schedules, and finances. I am able to break from the common belief of a therapist doing a treatment *to the client* and instead have a healing experience *with the client*. Clients often come with the shame and guilt of being told by their loved ones that they "need help," so MI has greatly strengthened clients' motivation and their ability to work through defenses in a safe place that is free of direct confrontation and tension. My private practice clients particularly appreciate the engaging and focusing portions of a session, where this may be the first time they feel truly heard and understood versus being told what is best for them.

Particularly, most of my clients have experienced significant and multiple episodes of trauma, so the integration of MI and CBT helps to address their complex issues of trust, safety, disempowerment, and control. I help clients to rewrite their stories from victims to survivors and often for the first time consider and recognize change talk as they shed their old identities of people who felt fragile and fearful. With the spirit of MI, I feel like a guide and copilot in this human healing process and that there is less of a divide in the therapy room between the "expert" and client. I am grateful for the perspective that MI has provided me as a clinician, along with the tools of CBT to help guide my clients who feel stuck, suicidal, hopeless, worthless, and powerless.

Conceptualization

Anxiety

Anxiety can be debilitating, and yet for many clients, it often feels purposeful. Therefore, counselors must conceptualize the perceived functionality of anxiety and understand how it can lead to ambivalence about change. For instance, consider the case of Cristina, a 20-year-old biracial woman who identifies as queer and who was bullied in school as a child and teenager. Figure 11.1 illustrates a

---

Relevant History: Client was bullied in school, especially for her sexuality and differences.

Core Belief: "People are mean and dangerous." "I am not good enough."

Intermediate Beliefs: "If I keep to myself at all times, I will not expose myself to hurt or humiliation." "Never trust new people."

Figure 11.1 Case Conceptualization for Cristina

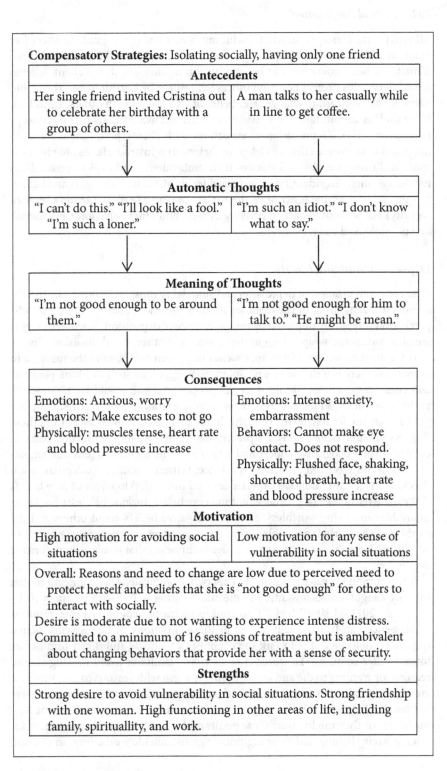

Figure 11.1 (Continued)

MI+CBT case conceptualization, including how Cristina's cognitions affect her emotions, behaviors, and physiological responses and how the perceived functionality of her anxiety reduces her motivation to diminish it. If a client believes her anxiety helps protect her from others who might be hurtful to her, she would naturally be reluctant to change. Her belief of "if I go out with others, I will look like a fool" is sustain talk that is evidence of her ambivalence. Using this conceptualization, MI+CBT practitioners empathize with clients' predicaments and do not pressure or coerce clients to let go of their worry. Instead, clients are given the space and time to explore all sides of their ambivalence and explore possibilities for change, including identifying and considering alternative thoughts and behaviors that serve the same function as the anxiety or worry (e.g., to provide a sense of security) but without the accompanying distress and other behavioral, emotional, and physiological consequences.

Depression and Suicidality

Case conceptualization of depression and suicidality must be informed by the clinician's understanding of the disorder itself. Motivation, energy, hope, and self-perception is typically impacted by the experience of depression. Suicidal thoughts are also commonly wrapped up in depression and other mood disorders. Therefore, we must move away from approaches that, even subtly, send the message to clients that there is a simple or easy solution. Suggestions such as "think positive" and comments such as "think of all the people who you would hurt," although perhaps well-intentioned efforts to deter someone from suicide, can instill further guilt and shame for having the thoughts in the first place. Moving away from these "layperson" approaches, MI+CBT practitioners conceptualize depression and suicidality through cognitive conceptualization with the additional lens that ambivalence is a common and expected experience. Within cognitive conceptualization (Beck, 2011), early childhood experiences lead to the development of core beliefs that can be reinforced over time. Common core beliefs include helplessness, being unlovable, and being worthless, as well as negative beliefs about others and the world (i.e., the world is a terrible place). An antecedent can trigger these beliefs to be activated, resulting in automatic thoughts surfacing that result in symptoms of depression.

It is common for suicidal clients to experience ambivalence about death in that they are caught between wanting to die and wanting to live with less pain (Britton et al., 2011). Using MI+CBT to conceptualize the cognitions that result in ambivalence can be especially useful in these situations. A perhaps instinctual response would be to try to talk the client out of suicide and direct him or her toward other solutions. However, if counselors dismiss or avoid hearing clients' reasons for wanting to die and instead provide them with reasons to live, they risk creating a situation in which clients feel as though their reasons for suicide were not heard. Clients might disengage from the conversation as a result of not feeling heard, or they might argue these points again, resulting in their argument for suicide strengthening and their argument against suicide weakening. In essence, ambivalence represents an internal conflict for clients. Both arguments—for and against suicide—exist with the client. If the therapist gives voice to one side of this argument (i.e., against suicide), the client will naturally give voice to the side of the argument that has not been expressed (i.e., for suicide). Therefore, when conceptualizing ambivalence using MI+CBT, therapists do not take a side of the argument. Instead, they facilitate clients' exploration of their own ambivalence, including eliciting and understanding clients' personal arguments for and against suicide, and then they evoke and strengthen clients' change talk in favor of living. Strategies to do so are described in the treatment section of this chapter.

Ambivalence can also be perpetuated through cognitions, including negative schemas ("I will never be 'normal' no matter what I do. I will always be this way, so what's the point in trying."). Therefore, clients may benefit from exploring what might bring them hope in regard to the possibilities of living with less pain, which can then ignite motivation to live. In other words, if clients do not believe change is possible (e.g., low self-efficacy), or they harbor another belief that maintains ambivalence, progress in enhancing motivation may be limited without addressing the interplaying cognitions. Cognitions that are addressed and modified (e.g., "I don't know what the future holds, but I can do what is in my power to feel better") can allow for further motivational enhancement for both living and for treatment. Generating possible ways for clients to live with less pain can be derived from the client via evocation or the clinician through the forms of cognitive restructuring and behavioral interventions (e.g., behavioral activation). We must remain open to the possibilities generated by clients and support clients in taking actions that will provide them with diminished symptoms, including suicidal ideation.

Serious Mental Illness

MI+CBT normalizes ambivalence among people with serious mental illness. Despite the struggles caused by these disorders, any number of factors can deter clients from embracing changes that would diminish or help manage symptoms of the disorder. For many, the medications prescribed to treat psychosis and severe mood disorders have undesirable side effects, and communication with prescribing providers can be limited. In other cases, clients may not be fully committed to letting go of the symptoms. For instance, clients with bipolar disorder can enjoy the energy and creativity that accompanies manic episodes. MI+CBT practitioners expect clients to harbor arguments for both sides of their ambivalence within them—their motivations to stay the same and not pursue change as well as their arguments to engage in treatment and pursue change. Within therapy, these arguments are elicited and explored from the client's perspective. In CBTp, the process of formulation development involves the client and counselor gaining an understanding of how early experiences, core cognitive schemas, unhelpful ways of thinking, and current symptoms, including behaviors and emotions that might be considered problematic, are connected by applying the cognitive model (Hardy, 2017).

Focusing and Planning for Treatment

Despite clients presenting with clear mental health–related concerns and mental health professionals having the ability to conceptualize and to address these concerns with evidence-based strategies, we should not proceed with treatment until we have an explicit conversation with the client about what to focus on in counseling sessions (or what to focus on first) and developing a plan for change/treatment plan. We should *avoid assuming* that clients' goals are what we think they should be. If we proceed based on our assumptions, we risk frustrating ourselves and the client as we focus on different goals in our work together. Instead, MI+CBT clinicians use the focusing process to collaborate with clients to reach concordance on the focus of their work together and develop a plan for treatment.

Developing a problem list in CBT can be likened to the focusing process in MI. This process relies on the partnership between the client and counselor as they collaboratively develop a problem list including the primary complaints of the client. Focus mapping (Naar & Safren, 2017) or agenda mapping (Miller & Rollnick, 2013) can be a useful tool in this process. Within MI+CBT, the focusing process will also often include negotiating the focus of counseling to include the complaints of others. For instance, a client with psychosis may have had run-ins with law enforcement, or feedback has been provided by case managers on issues such as medication compliance, social skills, or tasks of daily living that clients might not bring up themselves, but that might be beneficial to add to the problem list. Counselors and clients can discuss information received upon referral and from third parties (with a coinciding signed release-of-information) to negotiate various facets of impending treatment. If clients are hesitant to list concerns of others on a plan for treatment, we can enter the evoking process to explore clients' ambivalence and listen to their reasons. We can then evoke change talk that can mature into client commitment to addressing such concerns in treatment, if they indeed choose to.

Once the problem list is established, the client and counselor collaborate to identify goals to work toward for each of the problems included in the list. Through this process of focusing and planning for treatment, the counselor must be sure not to move too quickly or without taking the time to address ambivalence as it surfaces. Doing so would cause client disengagement and the treatment being one-sided. When addressing ambivalence as well as when gathering information about clients' experiences of their symptoms and related experiences, CBTp encourages the therapist to "drop the expert role" (Hardy, 2017, p. 3) and to be open to the perspective of clients.

The following dialogue demonstrates the focusing process in MI+CBT in which the counselor received information from the client's case manager about his interaction with the police and concerned neighbors due to his reactions to positive symptoms of psychosis. The client, Cam, is a 54-year-old African American man who experiences delusions about aliens taking over Earth as part of his experience of schizophrenia. Note how the focusing and evoking processes overlap as well as how the counselor avoids the "expert role" while still guiding the client by eliciting his goals and setting the structure of the conversation.

Counselor: I've talked with your case manager, and she let me know that the police were called over the weekend because you were outside your apartment yelling, and a concerned neighbor called them.

Cam: Yeah, I thought aliens were coming, you know? They were coming to take over, and I was screaming at them not to come. I was scared, you know?

Counselor: Yeah, you felt scared. You believed aliens were coming, and your defense was to yell at them. [*reflections*]

Cam: Yeah, but the cops were nice about it. They just called my case manager. I mean I wasn't harming anything. I just didn't want the aliens to come.

Counselor: And how are you feeling about that now? [*open question*]

Cam: Fine, I'm glad I didn't get in trouble for it.

Counselor: You're content with the outcome this time. [*reflection*] What do you think about adding something like "coping with beliefs" to your plan for treatment to provide you with some other ways to respond to these thoughts when you have them? [*open question; fostering partnership in focusing process*]

Cam: Nah, I don't think we need to talk about that anymore. Nothing happened so I can move past it.

Counselor: This time, it doesn't seem like a big deal. [*reflection of sustain talk*]

Cam: No, right.

Counselor: I wonder, has something like this happened before? [*closed question to evoke client's understanding of a possible pattern and possible change talk*]

Cam: Oh yeah, but this time, I didn't have to go to jail, and the cops were nice. You know, it's not always that way. They've not always been nice, and they put me in jail before, not that I was harming anyone or anything, but just disturbing the peace or something.

Counselor: I see, so this time it didn't seem to be a problem, but there have been other times that were a problem—you had to go to jail, the police were not always so understanding. [*reflection of change talk*]

Cam: Yeah, now I do *not* wish to go through any of that again.

Counselor: It sounds like you'd like to avoid it if you could. [*reflection of change talk*]

Cam: Oh yes.

Counselor: So if we were to work on developing other ways to respond to these beliefs you have, what do you think might happen? [*open question; fostering partnership in focusing*]

Cam: Well, I don't know.

Counselor: If you weren't going outside to yell or "disturb the peace," but instead you knew how to respond to these thoughts in other ways, what do you think would happen then? [*open question; evocation*]

Cam: I guess they wouldn't call the cops anymore.

Counselor: They would have no reason to call the police. [*reflection of change talk*] And how does that sound to you? [*open question to strengthen change talk*]

Cam: Very good. This last time they were nice, but man, I don't wish to have another bad run-in with them again.

Counselor: Now that we've talked about it a little bit more, what do you think about putting it on the plan for treatment—to respond to these beliefs in other ways—to help you avoid future interactions with the police? [*open question to elicit commitment language; continuing to foster partnership in focusing*]

Cam: Yes, that sounds fine. Especially if it will help me avoid any bad run-ins with the police or jail. That would be good.

When developing his problem list, Cam did not believe his behaviors in response to the delusions was a concern worth putting on the list. In his mind, there was no consequence this time, and therefore, no reason to address it in treatment. The counselor responded with empathy and understanding and then evoked change talk that was grounded in Cam's goal of avoiding additional negative experiences with law enforcement. After Cam came to realize these skills could help him reach his goal, he was in support of adding these therapeutic activities to the plan for treatment. If the counselor had not taken the time to listen to and understand Cam's ambivalence, Cam would not have had the opportunity to see the value in this therapeutic activity for himself. Now that he has, he would likely be more engaged and invested in treatment compared to if the goal was simply prescribed to him.

If it seems as though clients will need more time to resolve their ambivalence when we are planning with clients, we can include addressing ambivalence (revert to the evoking process or MI) as part of the treatment plan. For example, in the case of Cristina, she is ready to discuss her anxiety in session, but she is ambivalent about engaging in social activities outside of session. Therefore, instead of stating on her treatment plan, "Client will engage in one new social activity per week," a goal Cristina is far from committing to, her counselor might collaborate with Cristina to include, "Explore and resolve ambivalence about engaging in social activities" on the treatment plan instead.

Treatment

MI+CBT treatment for mental health–related disorders is going to be composed of ongoing assessments and conceptualizations of motivation, symptoms, and functioning, and then applying interventions to target cognitions, behaviors, emotions, and motivation accordingly. As treatment progresses, clients' needs will also change, although not always in a linear fashion, and treatment is responsive to the unique circumstance and needs of each individual client. In this section, synopses of MI+CBT treatment methods specific to anxiety, depression, and serious mental illness are provided. In addition to talk therapy, pharmacological treatments are common and often effective among clients with mental health–related disorders. Therefore, we will start with a description of how MI+CBT can be used to address medication compliance.

Medication Compliance

Pharmacological treatment is commonly used for anxiety, depression and suicidality, and serious mental illness. However, clients can struggle with consistently taking medications as prescribed. Balán, Moyers, and Lewis-Fernández (2013) offered several suggestions when addressing antidepressant medication nonadherence that are consistent with MI+CBT and can also be applied to anxiolytic and antipsychotic medications. First, practitioners can focus on clients' past successes with medication adherence to build self-efficacy and collaboratively develop strategies to overcome barriers to adherence. For example, open questions such as, "How were you able to remember to take your medication in the past?" "What worked for you?" and "What might work to help you remember now?" might be useful to evoke strategies that were successful for the client in the past and that can be applied currently. Client responses should be met with reflections, summaries, and affirmations. This will often lead to clients expressing change talk and increasing their motivation for medication adherence. If not, practitioners can elicit client change talk and commitment to adhering to pharmacological treatment by asking evocative questions such as, "What benefits did you experience when you were talking medication before that you would hope to experience now?" "What are reasons to take the medication that are important to you?" and "How might things change for the better if you do decide to take the medication as the doctor wants you to?" Using a commitment ruler might also be helpful in solidifying commitment to medication adherence. In the dialogue that follows, the counselor uses a commitment ruler with Cam:

Counselor: If you look at this ruler, how would you rate your level of commitment to taking the medication as Dr. X prescribes it"? [*shows ruler with 0 meaning "not at all committed" and 10 meaning "completely committed"*]
Cam: Oh, probably a 7.
Counselor: A 7. Ok, tell me about what made you choose a 7 instead of maybe, a 5? [*open question to elicit change talk*]
Cam: Well, I feel like I will remember to take it better by putting the meds by my toothbrush, like we talked about. That will make it easier.
Counselor: Yes, giving yourself that cue—when you brush your teeth at night, you take your pill—helps you feel committed to it. [*summary*]
Cam: Yeah, it's right there so I will remember.
Counselor: What else? [*open question to elicit further change talk*]

Cam: If I take them, I won't have the police called as much. And I really don't want to get put in jail or have a bad run-in. So I'm going to take them.

Counselor: Hmm, keeping on with the medication will lead to fewer run-ins with the police, and that's very important to you. [*reflection of change talk*]

Cam: Yeah, for sure.

Counselor: Ok, now I wonder what would help your commitment to taking the medication go from a 7 to maybe a 9? [*open question to further solidify commitment*]

By asking Cam about why his commitment was a 7 instead of a 5, the counselor elicited change talk. After reflecting these motivations, the counselor inquired about how Cam might move from a 7 to a 9. This could lead to Cam and the counselor collaboratively problem-solving obstacles he might anticipate while attempting to adhere to the pharmacological treatment as prescribed and to address any thoughts he may have about early termination from treatment. Finally, practitioners and clients collaboratively review medication as part of the treatment plan and mutually make decisions about future treatment (Balán et al., 2013).

Anxiety

MI+CBT for anxiety provides clients with opportunities to discover their solutions for themselves, often drawing on interventions and techniques already known and valued by the therapist (Westra, 2012). Treatment can begin by first eliciting from clients what they believe would be helpful steps to take to diminish their symptoms. Clients who have previous successes managing anxiety typically have their own ideas about what has, and what has not, worked for them. Examples of questions that can be used to elicit these ideas are provided as follows (Westra, 2012):

- What might be your first step(s)?
- You know yourself better than anyone. What has worked for you in the past?
- What have you found does not work for you? What might be helpful to avoid?
- If it was not you but a friend experiencing these concerns, what might you suggest your friend do about it?
- If you were to start tomorrow, what is one thing you would do differently to help reduce this distress?

Eliciting language speaking to activation and taking steps (Miller & Rollnick, 2013) might be sufficient with clients who already possess coping skills that are ready to employ. However, clients with lower levels of coping, including those who are novices at managing anxiety, might need to be offered cognitive, behavioral, and emotional management strategies. After all, if someone is in a therapy office seeking help, he or she is likely at a loss for how to manage his or her symptoms. Therefore, after eliciting clients' ideas about how to implement change, the MI+CBT therapist assesses if additional strategies are needed for the client to know how to initiate action. In other words, if eliciting and reinforcing activation and taking steps appears sufficient, then clients are able to identify strategies and skills to employ and then perhaps no additional cognitive, behavioral, and emotional management strategies are needed at this time. For other clients, cognitive, behavioral, and emotional management strategies may be necessary.

Using a cognitive conceptualization, the therapist will have ideas about what might be helpful to activate change, including diminishing distressing symptomology. However, these strategies are presented as a "menu of options" (Miller & Rollnick, 2002) from which clients can choose to implement based on the value and applicability clients find in them. When presenting a new strategy to clients, therapists can do so by providing a rationale and then asking for clients' permission before going further. For example, the therapist might say the following to Cristina:

> For many clients who struggle with these types of symptoms, targeting what goes through their mind can be very helpful. It is a common theory that what we think affects how we feel and what we do. Would you be willing to explore this idea a little further and see how it might fit, or not fit, for you?

Counselors' use of evocation and emphasizing clients' control over their changes would continue when applying the cognitive model and engaging in cognitive restructuring. Socratic questioning can be used to guide clients to evaluate their current ways of thinking and to find their alternative, more functional cognitions. In MI+CBT, Socratic questions can be followed by reflections and summaries to ensure that clients feel understood and that they hear themselves through the therapist (counselors reflect clients' emotions, meanings, etc., as if the client is looking in a mirror). By doing so, we avoid the question-and-answer trap that can cause clients to feel interrogated and disengage from the therapy process. The following dialogue illustrates how MI+CBT can be used to help Cristina explore the impact of her thoughts on her emotions and behaviors specific to a situation in which she was in line for coffee when a man behind her began to make conversation. Cristina experienced intense anxiety and did not respond. She has been ruminating on this event for days.

Therapist: What comment did he make to you? [*open question*]
Cristina: I don't remember, but it was something totally benign like, "Nice day, isn't it?" And my response was totally ridiculous. I panicked—my face got all red. I was sweating, and I couldn't even look at him. I was so embarrassed.
Therapist: At the time, the anxiety kicked in, and you weren't able to respond. [*reflection to normalize her response*] But now, you're thinking maybe it would be ok to respond. [*reflection of current awareness*]
Cristina: Right, and I feel silly. I feel stupid that I reacted like that.

Therapist:	What are you able to see now that tells you it would be ok to respond that you were not able to see in that moment? [*open Socratic question*]
Cristina:	There was nothing in what he said or did that was threatening or saying anything mean. He was just a man making totally normal conversation.
Counselor:	Just a man making totally normal conversation. There is no threat. [*simple reflection to solidify new thought*]
Cristina:	Right.
Counselor:	How do you feel when you think that way? "Here's just a man making normal conversation; there's no threat". [*open question to elicit affective response to new thought*]
Cristina:	Cautious still, like he might be a bad person underneath, but in that moment, I feel like kind of a normal person.
Counselor:	You feel calm, in control, yet remaining a little cautious. [*reflecting emotions*]
Cristina:	Yeah, I don't feel the need to run away or melt into the ground like I did the other day.
Counselor:	Ok, so with that thought, "Here's just a man making normal conversation; there's no threat," your emotions are quite a bit different. Instead of feeling intense fear or embarrassment, you feel cautious yet calm and in control. [*summary*] What about your behavior? What might you do if you had the thought "Here's just a man making normal conversation; there's no threat" in your mind at the coffee shop? [*open question to elicit behavioral response to new thought*]
Cristina:	Respond, you know, like a normal person. Say, "Yeah, it's a nice day."

In addition to cognitive interventions, strategies to manage anxiety will also often include behavioral strategies, such as relaxation skills, mindfulness, and assertiveness skills, in addition to eating a healthy diet (avoiding excessive caffeine and other substances that can induce or exacerbate anxiety) and using additional coping skills (e.g., exercise, music, social activities). These options can be included in the menu of options offered to clients as possible means for them to diminish their symptoms. Therapists avoid a "one-size-fits-all" approach and instead respond to clients' preferences and situational, cultural, and environmental contexts, as well as clinical presentation. For example, Cristina's therapist learned she is experiencing muscle tension and higher blood pressure as a result of her anxiety, so the therapist encouraged her to engage in progressive muscle relaxation or mindfulness practices (e.g., body scans). However, after introducing these techniques, Cristina explained that she is not comfortable doing these practices and that they do not work for her. The therapist hears and accepts this feedback and refrains from any type of persuasion for Cristina to engage in them. Although we might experience some frustration when clients do not latch on to interventions we highly value, we must remember that we are not of focus—the clients are—and the goal is to discover strategies that work for *them*. The therapist can proceed by using evocation that is grounded in the client-therapist partnership and continue to problem solve together. Even though Cristina declined to use the behavioral strategies presented thus far by the therapist, the therapist remains her guide in this process and retains compassion for the client:

Counselor: Cristina, these techniques work for some people, but no one thing works for all people. [*expressing acceptance*] Now that we've tried a few things, I wonder if something may have spurred other ideas for you about what might help you to physically relax to help with the muscle tension? [*question to elicit Cristina's ideas*]

Cristina: Well, I think these didn't work for me because when I do things like that, they're typically incorporated in my religion, like spiritual meditation and prayer. And I feel really weird doing it without including God.

Counselor: Hmm, I see. You're used to incorporating a reflective, meditative practice with your spirituality, and the spiritual component was missing in what we've already tried.

Cristina: Yeah, it just didn't feel right. I couldn't get into it.

Counselor: You're thinking you might benefit from a meditation that includes God and has spirituality within it.

Cristina: Yeah, that would be great.

Although we bring a lot of knowledge and expertise to the therapeutic relationship, MI+CBT therapists also value the importance of learning from our clients, which comes from listening to their cultural and individualized needs and readily adjusting interventions to better fit our clients. For Cristina, she would benefit from incorporating her spiritual beliefs into her relaxation or meditation practice. For others, they might need a community in which to recover, and a referral to group counseling or a support group might be warranted. In these ways, we tailor treatment to each individual client.

Voices From the Field 11.2

Integrating MI and CBT in Group Therapy for Anxiety

Written by
Dixie Powers, PhD, LPC, NCC
Assistant Professor, LaGrange College
Co-owner and Therapist, The Wandering Mind, LLC

When beginning a CBT group, MI is often utilized and usually essential to increase clients' interest and commitment and to begin the forming stages of group process. Working in a community agency setting, group was often hard to create and maintain; therefore, using MI was helpful to foster commitment to the change process and group cohesion. I have seen success when integrating MI and CBT with a closed CBT for anxiety group. I used MI initially to build motivation with clients in individual sessions to encourage them to attend the group sessions and to increase their intrinsic motivation and commitment to change in a group counseling setting. MI techniques, such as responding to sustain talk and eliciting change talk, were the primary counselor behaviors utilized to help foster positive behavior change. Once commitment to group therapy was elicited from six clients, the group began. I employed MI during the first meeting in the group setting to build motivation for the closed group, multisession intervention. For example, the spirit of MI was utilized in the first group meeting to foster group cohesion and a sense of hope and optimism for reducing their anxiety symptoms. The spirit of MI was paired with the first of the MI processes, engaging, to provide information about the treatment, describe the purpose of the group, and explore the group's goals in order to establish rapport and strengthen the forming stage of the group.

Throughout the ten-week group experience, MI was used at specific moments during the group when client discord or ambivalence arose. After introducing CBT and educating the group on the ten-week treatment plan, the MI process, focusing, was used to set an agenda and guide the group through the weekly exercises as well as to increase motivation to complete homework outside of the group setting. Using the MI processes from the start of the group helped build a strong group cohesion, and group members were apt to hold each other accountable for attendance and homework assignments. When the group appeared to waver in commitment to change, engaging was revisited and then a focus map was implemented to help the group rebuild alliance and motivation to modify anxiety symptoms. This helped the group continue to engage in behavioral activation exercises and renewed hope for their ability to change. As the group remained motivated and focused on changing target behaviors, CBT was utilized to clearly identify maladaptive thoughts and how these thoughts were influencing behaviors. As the group leader, I used MI intentionally to reflect and highlight change talk with each group member and help the group move through the storming stage into the performing stage. This led to the planning process of MI where the group confidently implemented CBT techniques to reduce anxiety and progress forward, where they developed a plan of maintenance to promote continued change outside of session and reduce reoccurrence of increased anxiety symptoms.

Depression and Suicidality

Concerning ambivalence related to suicidality, counselors must consider the timing and sequence of exploring both sides of the ambivalence (Britton et al., 2011).

As mentioned earlier, first counselors listen to clients' experiences and seek to understand their reasons for considering suicide. When clients appear ready to move beyond this discussion, counselors can then begin to elicit clients' motivations for wanting to live. However, if the counselor moves to eliciting reasons to live too quickly, before clients are ready for this discussion, clients will likely bring the conversation back to their motivations for suicide. Evocation is essential because this leads clients to essentially talk themselves into living using their own personal motivations. If the therapist gives voice to one side of clients' ambivalence (e.g., against suicide), clients will often respond with sustain talk, which can cause the alternative side (e.g., for suicide) to be reinforced.

Methods to elicit motivations for living include using an importance of living ruler (Britton et al., 2011), using open questions to evoke change talk, and eliciting clients' values and goals. The importance of living ruler was adapted from the readiness ruler commonly used in MI. It asks clients to rate on a 0 (not important at all) to 10 (extremely important) scale how important living is to them right now. Then the counselor asks their reasons for choosing that number and not a lower number. By asking about why not a lower number, clients consider why living is that important to them and express these motivations. Even if a client initially rates importance of living at a "2," by asking "Why a two and not a zero?," the client is prompted to consider the factors that allowed for the rating of 2, and he or she explores these reasons further in conversation with the counselor, likely strengthening these motivations. In addition to using the ruler, open questions can be used to evoke clients' motivation for living, and client responses should be met with reflections to facilitate clients hearing their motivations again through the therapist and allowing them the opportunity to consider their motivations further. Values and goals can be explored through conversation (e.g., "What are some of the most important things to you in your life?" "What do you hope to accomplish in your life?"), and then discrepancies can be developed between their stated values and goals and suicidal behavior or attending treatment, depending on where their ambivalence lies. When clients might benefit from additional structure or prompts to identify their values, tools such as the Personal Values Card Sort (Miller, C'de Baca, Matthews, & Wilbourne, 2001) can be implemented. After clients sort the cards according to level of importance to them, they can then explain the values and how they manifest in their lives. Finally, the counselor can ask about how the target behavior (i.e., suicidal behavior, treatment engagement, reducing symptoms of depression) is consistent or inconsistent with clients' top values as they described them.

After clients' ambivalence has been resolved in favor of living, a safety plan can be established. When developing a plan for safety, the content might resemble the example for Paul in Figure 11.2. However, the process in how counselors develop the plan with clients is also essential to consider. The plan must be collaboratively developed by first eliciting clients' ideas for each component. Despite your knowledge gained from doing 10, 100, or 1,000 safety plans with clients, planning for safety must result in a set of activities that *this particular client* is willing, able, and committed to implement, and therefore, the bulk of

Safety Plan

I want to keep myself safe because:

I want to live. I'm not going to give up.

Warning signs (thoughts, images, behaviors, emotions) that I might be approaching a crisis:

Obsessive thoughts about death and suicide, isolating myself from everyone, not being able to get myself feeling better, and having no hope it will ever end

Actions I can take to distract myself when I am alone:

Play video games, draw, and listen to music

Actions I can take to distract myself when I want to be around others:

Go to the gym, play with my kids, spend time with my wife

People I can ask for help:

My wife, my therapist

Professionals I can seek help from:

Student Counseling Center: (555) 555-5555
Local emergency room: (234) 567-8910
Suicide hotline: 1-800-273-8255
Emergency: 911

Ways I make my environment safer:

Ask my wife to hide the key to the gun safe from me and to get rid of unused medications or lock them up

Figure 11.2 Sample Safety Plan for Paul

Source: Adapted from the Safety Planning Guide provided by the Western Interstate Commission for Higher Education (2009).

the plan should come from the client. If clients struggle to develop content for any of the areas, the therapist can make a suggestion by first asking for permission, making the suggestion, and then eliciting the client's thoughts about the feasibility of the idea for him or her specifically. After completing the plan for safety, it is important to assess the client's commitment to following the plan. If clients are unable to commit, they could be at risk for suicide and likely need a higher level of care, including the possibility of pharmacological interventions or a controlled environment.

In addition to addressing motivation to live, counselors should also address clients' motivation for ongoing treatment. Engaging in treatment can reduce long-term risk for suicidal behaviors, and if clients are reluctant to pursue ongoing treatment, counselors can evoke and explore client ambivalence surrounding treatment engagement and help clients understand how making cognitive and behavioral changes in ongoing treatment can lead to diminished depression and suicidality in the long term (Britton et al., 2011).

When clients are ready for active changes, cognitive and behavioral interventions are likely to be effective. Cognitive interventions employed to address symptoms of depression include applying the cognitive model and restructuring cognitions, including automatic thoughts, intermediate beliefs and schemas, and core beliefs. Behavioral interventions include behavioral activation, relaxation skills, social skills, and assertiveness skills. Motivation is assessed throughout cognitive and behavioral interventions, and ambivalence should be addressed as it surfaces in regard to engaging in the various interventions (Flynn, 2011). Client autonomy is honored in that clients choose which interventions they engage in and how they will transfer these skills to their lives in between sessions.

In some cases, pharmacological interventions may be needed initially to help the client stabilize and to function well enough to engage in therapy, including to understand and apply cognitive and behavioral interventions. After some progress is made in therapy and the client has begun to employ different ways of thinking that allow for more functional behavioral and emotional responses, the client can consult with his or her prescriber about the implications for continuing or discontinuing the medication.

Serious Mental Illness

For clients who experience a serious mental illness and who are not yet ready for active change, interventions that target motivation should be of focus. In addition to the strategies described in the previous sections to evoke, explore, and resolve ambivalence (e.g., asking evocative questions, using scaling rulers), the Personal Goals and Values Card Sorting Task for Individuals with Schizophrenia (Moyers & Martino, 2006) can be used to facilitate conversation with clients about their goals and values and then to develop discrepancies to help motivate clients to move toward making healthy changes. When clients are ready for active change, we can draw on CBTp in which the final two processes are the application of interventions and skill building and then consolidation of skills. Cognitive and behavioral interventions are selected based on the conceptualization and implemented to address the concerns on clients' problem lists and to assist clients in achieving their goals. Common interventions specific to psychosis include developing and strengthening coping skills for managing voices, evaluating distressing beliefs, and addressing negative symptoms. In MI+CBT, each intervention would be implemented in a manner that contains the spirit of MI (partnership, acceptance, compassion, and evocation). For instance, consider that Cam is working on exploring the evidence for his delusion that aliens are coming to invade and control Earth. Indeed, his belief tells him that this is true. Upon hearing this, the MI+CBT counselor empathizes with this side of Cam's belief. The counselor does not argue or push Cam to see contradicting evidence from the counselor's perspective. Instead, the counselor uses evocation and *asks Cam for evidence that would contradict this belief*. If he struggles to identify contrary evidence, the counselor can provide information with permission (e.g., "I have a few ideas about this. Would it be ok if I shared them with you?") and then elicit Cam's reaction to the information (e.g., "What do you think about that?"), as well as evoke how Cam might apply this information (e.g., "How might thinking about these aspects instead of or in addition to your current belief change the way that you behave and feel?"). Counselors can also support clients' autonomy by encouraging them to choose which coping skills, alternative thoughts, or other methods they would like to intentionally apply in between counseling sessions and then checking in with them to see how the applications went and adjusting treatment interventions as needed to enhance effectiveness for this particular client. In doing so, we can enhance clients' self-efficacy to maintain these changes over time as well as increase their likelihood of seeking support in the future if they do slip back into old patterns or develop new concerns.

Practice Considerations

There are many complexities that can accompany the practice of MI+CBT for mental health–related concerns and disorders. First, clients will often present with more than one disorder. Comorbidity is common, especially among the three types of concerns described in this chapter as well as with substance use and addictive disorders. Therefore, clinicians are often challenged to apply MI+CBT to more than one disorder. Fortunately, some of the interventions can have overlapping effects, such as treating anxiety can help alleviate depression as well (Weitz, Kleiboer, van Straten, & Cuijpers, 2018). In other cases, assessment findings can indicate that specific symptoms need attention before the others can be addressed. This is common when clients experience a crisis and need to achieve safety and a sufficient level of functioning by diminishing suicidality or psychotic symptoms before other concerns can be treated. For clients using substances, mental health–related concerns frequently accompany the effects of intoxication (e.g., paranoia when using cocaine) and post-use (e.g., onset of depression during stimulant or cannabis withdrawal, experiences of anxiety during alcohol and sedative withdrawal). Therefore, clients may need to address the effects of substance use on their mental health concerns. As noted in Chapter 10, ideally treatment for co-occurring disorders addresses both disorders simultaneously using a treatment team approach, and as noted previously in this chapter, MI+CBT has shown to be an effective approach in the treatment of co-occurring disorders.

Another consideration related to using MI+CBT in the treatment of mental health–related concerns is the role and process of homework. Homework is often considered a hallmark of CBT, as it assists with clients applying the concepts and skills learned in session to activities and events that occur in between sessions. However, homework noncompliance is common (Helbig & Fehm, 2004). In the practice of MI+CBT, it is important to discuss clients' motivation surrounding homework—both at the onset of treatment and as specific homework activities are derived from in-session work. By addressing client motivation for homework explicitly, including eliciting and strengthening change talk in favor of homework, compliance can increase. However, this is another area in which we should be cautious about using a "one-size-fits-all" approach, starting with the term "homework." This term is academic by nature, and clients may harbor negative connotations with it (Naar & Safren, 2017). Younger clients who are in school will likely associate it with their school-based homework. Instead, therapists might use alternative terms, such as "between session activities" or another term that is collaboratively developed with the client. Beyond the term used, the content and process of homework should include clients' input and be mutually agreed upon. Cognitive and behavioral interventions lend themselves very well to a variety of logs, worksheets, and other monitoring instruments that are readily produced and disseminated. The question is then, "How well does this activity fit this particular client?" The more homework is tailored to clients, the more relevant it will be to them, given their unique identities, contexts, and environments. Developing activities for clients to complete in between sessions should be a collaborative effort, with the therapist as a guide and the client as a partner. After all, it is the client, not the therapist, who we hope will complete this work, and therefore, we should ensure that it is an activity that the client perceives to be relevant and achievable.

A final consideration I will present for this chapter is when it is appropriate to express our concern to clients (Rosengren, 2018). Mental health–related concerns can pose serious and foreseeable harm to clients or others. There are occasions in which clients' autonomy is limited for safety reasons—for instance, when clients are suicidal, homicidal, threatening other imminent harm, or they are not able to care for themselves. In MI+CBT, we strive to elicit clients' perceptions of the problem and potential solutions. We do our best to enhance client motivation to enhance their own safety and that of others. There are times when this is not enough, and the client remains a risk to him/herself or others and other action needs to be taken. This can be consistent with MI+CBT if it comes from a place of compassion. For instance, if Paul became actively suicidal, and he refused to voluntarily go to the hospital, I might say, "Paul, I am concerned for your safety. I want you to live to see tomorrow, and it is my ethical and legal obligation to ensure your safety as best I can." If Paul continues to refuse hospitalization, then I must facilitate involuntary hospitalization. However, my attitude toward Paul remains one of care and concern. For another example, consider if Cam refused to take psychotropic medications and my efforts to evoke his motivations to do so were consistently unsuccessful, I might say, "Cam, I am concerned about what it might be like for you to continue to have these beliefs and to continue to act on them as you are. I worry about what might happen to you." Again, these expressions of concern are grounded in compassion. Tones that convey an accusation, judgment, or disappointment are missing the mark of MI+CBT. Instead, this is a genuine expression of concern about the welfare of another human being who is struggling. Such expressions of concern should only be used as essentially a "last resort" when all other attempts to evoke motivation for safety or positive change have been exhausted and relatively unsuccessful.

Summary

This chapter explored ways in which MI+CBT can be applied to mental health–related disorders including anxiety, depression and suicidality, and serious mental illness, such as psychosis. The possibilities for such applications are vast, and this chapter offered a foundation and an instigation from which you can begin to implement these ideas in your own practice while allowing you to expand beyond what is written here to best meet the needs of your specific clients. By targeting motivation, as well as cognitive, behavioral, and emotional interventions, MI+CBT in the treatment of mental health–related issues has some sound empirical support and immense potential to have synergistic effects with a vast range of presenting concerns among diverse populations.

References

American Psychiatric Association. (2013). *Diagnostic and statistical manual of mental disorders* (DSM-5, 5th ed.). Washington, DC: Author.

Arkowitz, H., & Burke, B. L. (2008). Motivational interviewing as an integrative framework for the treatment of depression. In H. Arkowitz, H. A. Westra, W. R. Miller, & S. Rollnick (Eds.), *Motivational interviewing in the treatment of psychological problems* (pp. 145–272). New York, NY: Guilford Press.

Baker, A., Turner, A., Kay-Lambkin, F. J., & Lewin, T. J. (2009). The long and the short of treatments for alcohol or cannabis misuse among people with severe mental disorders. *Addictive Behaviors, 34*(10), 852–858. doi:10.1016/j.addbeh.2009.02.002

Balán, I. C., Moyers, T. B., & Lewis-Fernández, R. (2013). Motivational pharmacotherapy: Combining motivational interviewing and antidepressant therapy to improve treatment adherence. *Psychiatry: Interpersonal and Biological Processes, 76*(3), 203–209. doi:10.1521/psyc.2013.76.3.203

Barrowclough, C., Haddock, G., Fitzsimmons, M., & Johnson, R. (2006). Treatment development for psychosis and co-occurring substance misuse: A descriptive review. *Journal of Mental Health, 15*(6), 619–632. doi:10.1080/09638230600998920

Barrowclough, C., Haddock, G., Wykes, T., Beardmore, R., Conrod, P., Craig, T., . . . Tarrier, N. (2010). Integrated motivational interviewing and cognitive behavioural therapy for people with psychosis and comorbid substance misuse: Randomised controlled trial. *BMJ: British Medical Journal, 341*(7784), 1–12. doi:10.1136/bmj.c6325

Barrowclough, C., Marshall, M., Gregg, L., Fitzsimmons, M., Tomenson, B., Warburton, J., & Lobban, F. (2014). A phase-specific psychological therapy for people with problematic cannabis use following a first episode of psychosis: A randomized controlled trial. *Psychological Medicine, 44*(13), 2749–2761. doi:10.1017/S0033291714000208

Beck, A. T., Epstein, N., Brown, G., & Steer, R. A. (1988). An inventory for measuring clinical anxiety: Psychometric properties. *Journal of Consulting and Clinical Psychology, 56*(6), 893–897. doi:10.1037/0022-006X.56.6.893

Beck, J. S. (2011). *Cognitive behavior therapy: Basics and beyond* (2nd ed.). New York, NY: Guilford Press.

Britton, P. C. (2015). Motivational interviewing to address suicidal ideation. In H. Arkowitz, W. R. Miller, & S. Rollnick (Eds.), *Motivational interviewing in the treatment of psychological problems* (2nd ed., pp. 193–218). New York, NY: Guilford Press.

Britton, P. C., Patrick, H., Wenzel, A., & Williams, G. C. (2011). Integrating motivational interviewing and self-determination theory with cognitive behavioral therapy to prevent suicide. *Cognitive and Behavioral Practice, 18*(1), 16–27. doi:10.1016/j.cbpra.2009.06.004

Chiu, V. W., Ree, M., Janca, A., & Waters, F. (2016). Sleep in schizophrenia: Exploring subjective experiences of sleep problems, and implications for treatment. *Psychiatric Quarterly, 87*(4), 633–648. doi:10.1007/s11126-015-9415-x

Cleary, M., Hunt, G. E., Matheson, S., & Walter, G. (2009). Psychosocial treatments for people with co-occurring severe mental illness and substance misuse: Systematic review. *Journal of Advanced Nursing, 65*(2), 238–258. doi:10.1111/j.1365-2648.2008.04879.x

Craig, T., Shepherd, G., Rinaldi, M., Smith, J., Carr, S., Preston, F., & Singh, S. (2014). Vocational rehabilitation in early psychosis: Cluster randomised trial. *British Journal of Psychiatry, 205*(2), 145–150. doi:10.1192/bjp.bp.113.136283

Dobson, K. S. (2016). The efficacy of cognitive-behavioral therapy for depression: Reflections on a critical discussion. *Clinical Psychology: Science and Practice, 23*(2), 123–125. doi:10.1111/cpsp.12151

Dobson, K. S., McEpplan, A. M., & Dobson, D. (2019). Empirical validation and the cognitive-behavioral therapies. In K. S. Dobson & D. J. Dozois (Eds.), *Handbook of cognitive-behavioral therapies* (4th ed., pp. 32–63). New York, NY: Guilford Press.

Dunlop, B. W., Polychroniou, P. E., Rakofsky, J. J., Nemeroff, C. B., Craighead, W. E., & Mayberg, H. S. (2018). Suicidal ideation and other persisting symptoms after CBT or antidepressant medication treatment for major depressive disorder. *Psychological Medicine*, 1–10. doi:10.1017/S0033291718002568

Fiszdon, J. M., Kurtz, M. M., Choi, J., Bell, M. D., & Martino, S. (2016). Motivational interviewing to increase cognitive rehabilitation adherence in schizophrenia. *Schizophrenia Bulletin, 42*(2), 327–334. doi:10.1093/schbul/sbv143

Flynn, H. A. (2011). Setting the stage for the integration of motivational interviewing with cognitive behavioral therapy in the treatment of depression. *Cognitive and Behavioral Practice, 18*(1), 46–54. doi:10.1016/j.cbpra.2009.09.006

Haddock, G., McCarron, J., Tarrier, N., & Faragher, E. B. (1999). Scales to measure dimensions of hallucinations and delusions: The psychotic symptom rating scales (PSYRATS). *Psychological Medicine, 29*(4), 879–889. doi:10.1017/S0033291799008661

Hanrahan, F., Field, A. P., Jones, F. W., & Davey, G. C. L. (2013). Corrigendum to "A meta-analysis of cognitive therapy for worry in generalized anxiety disorder." *Clinical Psychology Review, 33*(3), 500. doi:10.1016/j.cpr.2013.01.001

Hardy, K. (2017). *Cognitive behavioral therapy for psychosis (CBTp)*. NASMHPD Publications. Retrieved from www.nasmhpd.org/content/fact-sheet-cognitive-behavioral-therapy-psychosis-cbtp

Harvard Medical School. (2007). *National comorbidity survey (NCS): Data table 2: 12-month prevalence DSM-IV/WMH-CIDI disorders by sex and cohort*. Retrieved from www.hcp.med.harvard.edu/ncs/index.php

Hayward, P., Kemp, R., & David, A. (2000). Compliance therapy: A collaborative approach to psychiatric medication. In B. Martindale, A. Bateman, & F. Margison (Eds.), *Psychosis: Psychological approaches and their effectiveness* (pp. 50–67). London, England: Gaskell.

Helbig, S., & Fehm, L. (2004). Problems with homework in CBT: Rare exception or rather frequent? *Behavioural and Cognitive Psychotherapy, 32*(3), 291–301. doi:10.1017/S1352465804001365

Karyotaki, E., Riper, H., Twisk, J., Hoogendoorn, A., Kleiboer, A., Mira, A., . . . Cuijpers, P. (2017). Efficacy of self-guided internet-based cognitive behavioral therapy in the treatment of depressive symptoms: A meta-analysis of individual participant data. *JAMA Psychiatry, 74*(4), 351. doi:10.1001/jamapsychiatry.2017.0044

Kay-Lambkin, F. J., Baker, A. L., Lewin, T. J., & Carr, V. J. (2009). Computer-based psychological treatment for comorbid depression and problematic alcohol and/or cannabis use: A randomized controlled trial of clinical efficacy. *Addiction, 104*(3), 378–388. doi:10.1111/j.1360-0443.2008.02444.x

Kertes, A., Westra, H. A., Angus, L., & Marcus, M. (2011). The impact of motivational interviewing on client experiences of cognitive behavioral therapy for generalized anxiety disorder. *Cognitive and Behavioral Practice, 18*(1), 55–69. doi:10.1016/j.cbpra.2009.06.005

Khattra, J., Angus, L., Westra, H., Macaulay, C., Moertl, K., & Constantino, M. (2017). Client perceptions of corrective experiences in cognitive behavioral therapy and motivational interviewing for generalized anxiety disorder: An exploratory pilot study. *Journal of Psychotherapy Integration, 27*(1), 23–34. doi:10.1037/int0000053

Miller, W. R., C'de Baca, J., Matthews, D. B., & Wilbourne, P. L. (2001). *Personal values card sort.* Retrieved from www.motivationalinterviewing.org/content/personal-values-card-sort.

Miller, W. R., & Rollnick, S. (2002). *Motivational interviewing: Preparing people for change* (2nd ed.). New York, NY: Guilford Press.

Miller, W. R., & Rollnick, S. (2013). *Motivational interviewing: Helping people change* (3rd ed.). New York, NY: Guilford Press.

Moyers, T. B., & Martino, S. (2006). *"What's important in my life" the personal goals and values card sorting task for individuals with schizophrenia.* Retrieved from https://casaa.unm.edu/inst/Values%20Card%20Sorting%20Task%20for%20Individuals%20with%20Schizophrenia.pdf

Naar, S., & Flynn, H. (2015). Motivational interviewing and the treatment of depression. In H. Arkowitz, W. R. Miller, & S. Rollnick (Eds.), *Motivational interviewing in the treatment of psychological problems* (2nd ed., pp. 170–192). New York, NY: Guilford Press.

Naar, S., & Safren, S. A. (2017). *Motivational interviewing and CBT: Combining strategies for maximum effectiveness.* New York, NY: Guilford Press.

Naar-King, S., Parsons, J. T., Murphy, D., Kolmodin, K., & Harris, D. R. (2010). A multisite randomized trial of a motivational intervention targeting multiple risks in youth living with HIV: Initial effects on motivation, self-efficacy, and depression. *Journal of Adolescent Health, 46*(5), 422–428. doi:10.1016/j.jadohealth.2009.11.198

National Institute for Health and Care Excellence (NICE). (2014). *Psychosis and schizophrenia in adults: Prevention and management.* Retrieved from www.nice.org.uk/guidance/cg178

Riper, H., Andersson, G., Hunter, S. B., de Wit, J., Berking, M., & Cuijpers, P. (2014). Treatment of comorbid alcohol use disorders and depression with cognitive-behavioural therapy and motivational interviewing: A meta-analysis: CBT/MI for comorbid alcohol use disorders and depression. *Addiction, 109*(3), 394–406. doi:10.1111/add.12441

Romano, M., & Peters, L. (2015). Evaluating the mechanisms of change in motivational interviewing in the treatment of mental health problems: A review and meta-analysis. *Clinical Psychology Review, 38,* 1–12. doi:10.1016/j.cpr.2015.02.008

Rosengren, D. B. (2018). *Building motivational interviewing skills: A practitioner workbook* (2nd ed.). New York, NY: Guilford Press.

Rubenstein, D. (2016). Application of motivational interviewing in working with psychotic disorders. In B. Pradhan, N. Pinninti, & S. Rathod (Eds.), *Brief interventions for psychosis: A clinical compendium* (pp. 103–118). doi:10.1007/978-3-319-30521-9_7

Substance Abuse and Mental Health Services Administration. (2009). *SAFE-T: Suicide assessment five-step evaluation and triage.* HHS Publication No. SMA 09-4432,

CMHS-NSP-0193). Rockville, MD: Substance Abuse and Mental Health Services Administration, Department of Health and Human Services.

Substance Abuse and Mental Health Services Administration. (2018). *Key substance use and mental health indicators in the United States: Results from the 2017 national survey on drug use and health* (HHS Publication No. SMA 18-5068, NSDUH Series H-53). Rockville, MD: Center for Behavioral Health Statistics and Quality, Substance Abuse and Mental Health Services Administration.

Tarrier, N., Taylor, K., & Gooding, P. (2008). Cognitive-behavioral interventions to reduce suicide behavior: A systematic review and meta-analysis. *Behavior Modification, 32*(1), 77-108. doi:10.1177/0145445507304728

Weitz, E., Kleiboer, A., van Straten, A., & Cuijpers, P. (2018). The effects of psychotherapy for depression on anxiety symptoms: A meta-analysis. *Psychological Medicine, 48*(13), 2140-2152. doi:10.1017/S0033291717003622

Westra, H. A. (2004). Managing resistance in cognitive behavioural therapy: The application of motivational interviewing in mixed anxiety and depression. *Cognitive Behaviour Therapy, 33*(4), 161-175. doi:10.1080/16506070410026426

Westra, H. A. (2012). *Motivational interviewing in the treatment of anxiety*. New York, NY: Guilford Press.

Westra, H. A., Arkowitz, H., & Dozois, D. J. A. (2009). Adding a motivational interviewing pretreatment to cognitive behavioral therapy for generalized anxiety disorder: A preliminary randomized controlled trial. *Journal of Anxiety Disorders, 23*(8), 1106-1117. doi:10.1016/j.janxdis.2009.07.014

Westra, H. A., Constantino, M. J., & Antony, M. M. (2016). Integrating motivational interviewing with cognitive-behavioral therapy for severe generalized anxiety disorder: An allegiance-controlled randomized clinical trial. *Journal of Consulting and Clinical Psychology, 84*(9), 768-782. doi:10.1037/ccp0000098

Westra, H. A., & Dozois, D. J. A. (2006). Preparing clients for cognitive behavioral therapy: A randomized pilot study of motivational interviewing for anxiety. *Cognitive Therapy and Research, 30*(4), 481-498. doi:10.1007/s10608-006-9016-y

Yang, W., & Strodl, E. (2011). Motivational interviewing changes the treatment trajectory of group cognitive-behavioral therapy for anxiety. In S. Boag & N. Tiliopoulos (Eds.), *Personality and individual differences* (pp. 237-248). Hauppauge, NY: NOVA Science Publishers.

Zerler, H. (2009). Motivational interviewing in the assessment and management of suicidality. *Journal of Clinical Psychology, 65*(11), 1207-1217. doi:10.1002/jclp.20643

CHAPTER 12

Criminal Behaviors and Correctional Settings

Both CBT and MI have been applied as separate approaches to assist clients in changing criminal behaviors to reduce recidivism. After administering offender risk assessments, CBT methods or programs are commonly used to address clients' criminogenic needs (Taxman, 2018), although treatment will vary depending on the setting in which treatment takes place (e.g., prison or jail, community corrections, residential reentry). MI is a relatively newer application in corrections; however, its use has been encouraged across correctional settings and services (National Institute of Corrections, 2012), including in probation and parole (e.g., Walters, Clark, Gingerich, & Meltzer, 2007) and reentry education (e.g., U. S. Department of Education, Office of Vocational and Adult Education, 2012), and there is evidence supporting its use (McMurran, 2009). In this chapter, we explore MI+CBT applied to the needs of clients who have engaged in criminal behavior, including incorporating MI and CBT into the existing risk-need-responsivity (RNR) model that is considered a best practice in correctional settings (Askew, 2016). More mental health professionals who are familiar with best practices in corrections are needed to serve these populations (Andrews & Bonta, 2010a). Further, advocating for the implementation of MI and CBT within the RNR framework can be part of a greater focus on rehabilitation compared to punishment.

Overview of Correctional Services

Correctional services essentially have two foci: punishment and rehabilitation. Andrews and Bonta (2010b) noted that an emphasis on harsh punishment has failed to reduce recidivism and in turn has caused greater strain on the correctional system. High recidivism rates have created a revolving door that contributes to overcrowding in correctional settings. According to the Department of Justice, 67.8% of offenders will be rearrested within three years, and 76.6% will be rearrested within five years (Durose, Cooper, & Snyder, 2014). Instead of focusing solely on punishment, Andrews and Bonta (2010b) encouraged increased efforts toward rehabilitation.

The model of RNR (Bonta & Andrews, 2007, 2010a) was developed in an effort to improve the effectiveness of correctional services and reduce recidivism. The risk principle involves assessing offenders' level of risk for reoffending and then matching the offender to appropriate treatment (i.e., high level of risk warrants more intense level of treatment). The need principle involves addressing criminogenic needs—or risks that lead to criminal behavior—in treatment through cognitive and behavioral interventions. The principle of responsivity involves assessing and responding to clients' motivation and readiness to change, as well as mental health–related issues and cognitive functioning. Responsivity also emphasizes an effective therapeutic relationship in which conversations about change often include problem solving, modeling, and reinforcement (Bonta & Andrews, 2007). The RNR model largely draws on cognitive and behavioral principles and methods, as well as social learning theory. Next in this chapter, we examine current practices of CBT and MI within the RNR model and then explore possible ways to implement a more explicit MI+CBT approach to promote rehabilitation among people with criminal offenses within the RNR framework.

Current Practice of RNR

The "needs" principle of the RNR model describes what should be addressed to reduce risk of recidivism (Andrews & Bonta, 2010b). The intensity and breadth of services provided is related to the perceived level of risk, and treatment interventions are used to target specific criminogenic needs (Andrews & Bonta, 2010b; Latessa, 2012). CBT has been at the forefront of such rehabilitation efforts (Lipsey, Landenberger, & Wilson, 2007). Successful treatment programs include a focus on the present circumstances and criminogenic needs, interventions that are action oriented, and interventions that include a structured social learning component to reinforce prosocial behavior (Latessa, 2012). Research shows that people with past criminal behaviors can indeed change, especially when given the opportunity to engage in evidence-based treatments (Andrews & Bonta, 2010b; Latessa, 2012).

Whereas the needs principle of the RNR model describes *what* to address, the "responsivity" principle describes *how* interventions are delivered (Andrews & Bonta, 2010b). Consistent with MI+CBT, Andrews and Bonta (2010b) acknowledged the importance of the therapeutic relationship while implementing structured cognitive and behavioral interventions within the context of social learning theory. They also explained the need for interventions to be tailored to each individual by taking into consideration client motivation, strengths, culture, gender, age, and individual characteristics, such as personality. Thus, the responsivity principle is naturally aligned with MI.

Despite the RNR model being well-defined and demonstrating successful outcomes, it can be difficult to disseminate among agencies and to ensure that it is practiced with fidelity, especially considering the number of clients served in the criminal justice system (Andrews & Bonta, 2010b). In order to implement RNR in correctional services, Andrews and Bonta (2010b) recommended training new staff in cognitive and behavioral interventions, including providing ongoing supervision for skill development. In addition to training new staff, staff who completed initial training should be provided booster courses, feedback from experienced staff, and encouragement from administration. However, if staff are only trained in cognitive and behavioral interventions, explicit training is still then needed to address the responsivity principle. Agencies that have implemented the RNR model have provided MI training for staff to cultivate an environment that promotes behavior change based on evidence-based practice (Stinson & Clark, 2017). Therefore, although inconsistent, to some degree MI is already being incorporated into services within the scope of the RNR model.

Implementing MI+CBT Within the RNR Model

When applied within the framework of RNR, CBT is used to address *what* should be targeted to change criminal behaviors, while MI can make explicit the responsivity principle by addressing *how* to interact with clients and *how* to deliver cognitive and behavioral interventions. In this section, we explore applying MI to develop an effective working alliance with clients in correctional settings and engage them in the process of change. Then we will look at how MI and CBT can be implemented in assessment and treatment services within the RNR framework.

Engaging: Developing and Maintaining an Alliance

For many reasons, it might seem difficult to establish an effective therapeutic alliance with clients who have criminal offenses. First, we continue to use pejorative terms that label people by their past behaviors. These labels are accompanied by institutions that are designed to instill punishment by using the forces of authority and power, which result in an inherent division between "us" and "them." Within its spirit and core skills, MI delineates attitudes and behaviors that professionals working in corrections can adopt to cross this chasm to establish meaningful, genuine helping relationships. After the relationship is established and the client is engaged, we can pursue the focusing, evoking, and planning processes of MI to cultivate client motivation for change and actively pursue such changes.

Table 12.1 shows the components of the spirit with their descriptions and then contrasted with common experiences of people with criminal offenses. Then examples are provided of how each component of the spirit can be executed with CJ. CJ is a 36-year-old man whose parents immigrated from Colombia. CJ has two children with his girlfriend of seven years. He has served three years of a five-year sentence for trafficking cocaine, and he will soon be released on parole. He has prior convictions related to assault and drug possessions. Growing up, his father was addicted to cocaine and drank alcohol heavily, which led to an unpredictable and violent childhood. CJ was physically and emotionally abused by his father until CJ began to fight back at age 15. CJ then dropped out of high school and turned to drug dealing to help his mother with paying rent and providing for his three younger sisters.

Table 12.1 MI Spirit Applied to Engaging With Clients With Criminal Offenses

Component	Description *Counselors' "Way of Being"*	Antithesis *Common Experiences of Clients*	Execution *Examples With CJ*
Partnership	<ul><li>Work *with* clients</li><li>Foster equality</li><li>Avoid "wrestling" with clients to "get them" to see your point</li><li>Value client wisdom from their experiences and incorporate it into conversations about change</li><li>Enlist the client as an essential contributor to their change process</li></ul>	<ul><li>Being told what to do and how and when to do it</li><li>One-sided, authoritarian relationships with professionals</li><li>Being mandated to or coerced into treatment</li><li>Going through interventions superficially, without authentic efforts</li></ul>	<ul><li>"You've been through this before, so you might even know better than I do about what you might need to do to not come back to prison again."</li><li>"Of course, the goal of parole is to help you stay on the right path. That's our goal though, and I'm really interested to hear about your goals. What would you like to accomplish that I might be able to assist you with?"</li></ul>
Acceptance	<ul><li>Reinforce client's absolute worth and self-efficacy for change</li><li>Express accurate empathy to enable the client feeling heard and understood and to hear him/herself through the counselor</li><li>Emphasize autonomy in genuine, appropriate ways</li><li>Affirm client strengths and positive efforts</li></ul>	<ul><li>Experiencing the negative stigma surrounding being in the criminal justice system</li><li>Judgment from another's perspective</li><li>Others make decisions for the person</li><li>Telling the client what he or she must do/ prescribing treatment or change</li><li>Highlighting what the client is doing wrong</li><li>Focusing on pathology</li></ul>	<ul><li>"You grew up surrounded by substance use and these types of criminal activities. You thought this was 'normal' behavior for men". *[accurate empathy]*</li><li>"Of course, I'd like to see you be successful and never come back to prison again. But I sure can't do that for you. Only you can decide what you're going to do that might help you stay out of prison". *[supporting autonomy]*</li><li>"I appreciate your efforts in coming here today and sharing this information with me". *[affirmation]*</li></ul>

(Continued)

Table 12.1 (Continued)

Component	Description Counselors' "Way of Being"	Antithesis Common Experiences of Clients	Execution Examples With CJ
Compassion	• Genuinely caring about the welfare of the client • Acting in the client's best interest	• Being hardened to the struggles and humanity of the client • Acting in the best interest of the provider/agency • Being solely concerned about public safety without considering the individual	• "I can see that you are concerned about some of these requirements of your parole." • "You're facing a lot right now, and it's hard to keep going with a good attitude."
Evocation	• Evoking the client's own personal motivations for change • Inquiring about and seeking to understand the client's values and goals • Evoking the client's wisdom and perspectives	• Attempting to install motivation • Threatening/warning • Providing solutions	• "If you were to live a life that allowed you to be a free man, what would that be like for you? . . . What would be the best part"? [*eliciting change talk*] • "I wonder, what do you think might be helpful to you in this situation". [*eliciting possible solutions*] • "If you were to leave prison and become the person you want to be, what would be most important to you". [*eliciting values*]

Using the MI spirit is one way to diminish discord that can be inherent in starting relationships with clients who are in correctional systems. Additional strategies applied to this population are described next using the case of CJ as an example:

1. ***Maintain the spirit of MI.*** As described in Table 12.1, maintaining the spirit of MI can foster a productive therapeutic relationship, as the spirit of MI contains the humanistic, Rogerian components of therapy that have been found to diminish discord (Beutler, Harwood, Michelson, Song, & Holman, 2011; Miller, Benefield, & Tonigan, 1993). Further, the strategies listed next must include the spirit of MI.

    MI requires practitioners to meet clients where they are in their unique process of change, including not assuming every client is ready for change. For example, it might be easy for me to assume that CJ would like to stop selling drugs and stop his violent behaviors to avoid further prison time; however, this is my hope for him, which is derived from my values, background, culture, and so on. The spirit of MI emphasizes empathy and eliciting the client's perspective. In doing so, I see CJ's behaviors through his perspective. He grew up with violence; he does not know a life without it. He grew up surrounded by the use and selling of illicit substances; this is not a world he sought out, this is the only world he knows. Selling drugs was not driven from malice; it allowed him to provide for his mother and younger sisters in the absence of his father, and it is the only way he has known how to provide for his family. Therefore, I gain the understanding that CJ's situation is not readily conducive to having a substance-free, violence-free, employment-ready life—it is just not that easy. Instead, I must help CJ create new possibilities for himself to avoid falling back into his former ways upon his release from prison, and CJ must perceive these new ways as feasible and valuable. CJ's self-efficacy to develop and act on these new ways would likely be low initially; however, the MI practitioner communicates a belief that every client has the potential to grow and change if he or she wants to. In using MI, the practitioner avoids using labels with stigma attached and instead sees the person with his or her strengths and potential. An illustration of this component of the MI spirit can be found in the following quote by Bryan Stevenson (2014) (whose legal and advocacy work to promote equal justice is unrelated to MI): "Each of us is more than the worst thing we've ever done" (p. 17). The components of the MI spirit that speak to absolute worth and compassion can serve as counterforces to policies that result in higher-risk clients being denied services due to the belief that they cannot change or should not be eligible for treatment. As Andrews and Bonta (2010b) stated, "It is the higher-risk offender who may benefit the most from treatment" (p. 50). Although it is true that treatment will not be effective for every person in the criminal justice system, it will make a difference for some. Instead of going through the motions of the traditional "us" versus "them" dynamic, we can flip the script to instead demonstrate that we see a human being with potential, even if that potential is buried under years of maladaptive behavior and beliefs.

228   *Clinical Applications*

2. ***Avoid arguing.*** Many clients in the criminal justice system will explain why they should not be there or why their circumstances involving the legal system should be different from what they are. Arguing with these statements will likely reinforce the "us against them" dynamic and result in a counterproductive relationship. Instead, we use strategies consistent with MI, including reflecting the statements to figuratively hold up a mirror for clients to hear and see themselves. If a client is lying to you or attempting to argue with you, give him or her an opportunity to hear the words and meanings again through your reflections. Let the client's struggles remain his or her struggles, and you can assist with those struggles as an objective guide rather than turning it into an interpersonal struggle with you against the client.
3. ***Recognize discord and respond.*** Many relationships with clients in the criminal justice systems will begin with inherent discord. Through the lens of MI, discord is conceptualized as an interpersonal dynamic that manifests in client defensiveness, argumentation, or other negative comments made about the counselor or services. Because discord is an interpersonal construct, it is a signal for the professional to respond differently. If we expect the client to adjust to create a productive relationship with us, we will be sorely disappointed and be less than helpful to the client. Instead, we take the responsibility as the professional to diminish the discord in our relationship with the client.
4. ***Listen and express empathy.*** Clients who are in the criminal justice system are typically accustomed to unidirectional communication with professionals (i.e., judges, officers): the other talks and they listen, unless they are asked a question. However, when using MI, we strive for the client to talk more than the professional. In cases where the client is sharing his or her discontent about us or services (i.e., evidence of discord), we avoid becoming defensive or taking this personally. Instead, we strive to hear and understand the client's perspective. Miller and Rollnick (2002) coined the phrase "*roll with resistance*" (p. 39) to capture the essence of a helpful response to discord. When rolling with resistance, we refrain from responding to clients with some opposing force. Instead, we listen. To show evidence that we are truly listening and gaining an understanding of the client's perspective, we primarily use reflective statements—including paraphrasing content, reflecting emotion, and reflecting underlying meanings. These reflective statements express accurate empathy. Further, when clients hear your accurate reflections, they hear themselves through you.
5. ***Use OARS.*** OARS represents the core skills of MI: open questions, affirmations, reflections, and summarizations (Miller & Rollnick, 2013). We use *open questions* to invite the client to share with us. Although closed questions have specific purposes, they inherently limit client responses. Open questions can help offset some of the power differential and client passivity by sending clients the implicit message, "I want to hear what you have to say." *Affirmations* are used to highlight client strengths and their positive efforts. Needless to say, clients in criminal justice systems have a lot of negativity surrounding them, including having

a stigmatized status in our society. Affirmations have the potential to improve the therapeutic relationship as well as provide the opportunity for the client to become more aware of his or her own positives. In order to be effective, affirmations must be genuine and specific. We highlight clients' potential, strengths, and positive efforts to help them begin to develop an alternative identity to their current status as "criminal," "convict," "locked up," and so on. If we wish for people to change their criminal behavior, we can help them by strengthening a positive identity that is congruent with behavior change. In addition, providing clients with affirmations can have a positive impact on the therapeutic relationship. *Reflections* are the most essential skill to diminish discord, as it results in clients feeling heard and understood, as well as clients hearing themselves through you (described further in #4). *Summaries* serve as evidence that we have heard the clients and that we care about what they said.

6. **Shift the focus.** In some cases, we will want to steer away from unproductive conversations with clients. An MI-consistent way to do this typically involves using a reflection or summary, followed by an open question to *shift the focus* of the conversation to a more potentially more productive area. The following provides two examples of shifting the focus:

Client: I haven't done anything wrong. I'm innocent, and yet here I am locked up. It's not fair!

Counselor: You don't feel you belong here, and that bothers you quite a bit. [*reflection*] Given that you are here for now, what do you think might be helpful to you to work on to ensure you don't end up back here again? [*open questions*]

Client: She [*another inmate*] was harassing me so I punched her.

Counselor: You punched her and now you're on disciplinary. [*reflection*] What could you consider doing next time someone harasses you so that you don't face additional consequences here? [*open question*]

7. **Emphasize autonomy of the client.** People in the criminal justice system have their autonomy limited in very real ways—they must abide by external controls of varying degrees, ranging from being in prison to having to report to a probation officer. When clients are in controlled environments, such as prison or jail, they are able to make very few choices for themselves. Therefore, it can be helpful to emphasize client autonomy when appropriate to offset possible learned passivity. In the dialogue that follows with CJ, the counselor diminishes discord by emphasizing CJ's autonomy, including reinforcing his personal choice and control, asking for his permission before providing information, and emphasizing that he is the primary resource in finding a solution that will work for him and his family:

CJ: I'm stuck in here while my kids and girlfriend are out there trying to survive. It's not right. I need to provide for them, but I can't, because I'm here. And now you want me to do this reentry stuff when it's not

	going to help me. If it's not going to send my girl money, it's not helping me.
Counselor:	You're not happy with how things are now. [*reflection*] And once you're out, you will decide how you will provide for them—to go back down the same road and sell drugs and risk coming back here again or to choose a different path that might have a different outcome. [*emphasizing personal choice and control*]
CJ:	Yeah, but working odd jobs, fast-food restaurants, and stuff, they don't make enough. I cannot support them on that.
Counselor:	You want to make more than that to do better for them. [*reflection*] It would be your choice, but you do have the option to enroll in job training as part of your reentry program. [*emphasizing personal choice and control*] You could look into job training that can lead to more lucrative careers, such as welding, plumbing, or auto mechanics. Would it be ok if I gave you some information about that? [*asking for permission before providing information*]
CJ:	I heard about that. It seems like a lot of work. I don't know .... [*shrugs*]
Counselor:	Well, you know yourself and your family best, and you know what might work out the best for you all in the long run. I'm more than happy to tell you about job training programs if you think that might be helpful to you. [*reinforce that the client is the primary resource in finding answers and solutions to his or her problems*]

By using the strategies noted earlier, MI can be used to diminish discord and foster client engagement. Most of what occurs in corrections is done without the client's input. Therefore, it can take some time to offset passivity that many clients have learned and have become accustomed to. Once the therapeutic relationship is established, grounded in empathy and compassion, clients are more likely to talk to you. Consider conversations in your own life that you enjoy—chances are you feel heard and as if the other person cares about what you are saying. Now think about conversations with people you avoid—are the other people judgmental? Distracted? Do they attempt to problem solve for you, even though their solutions will not work for you? It is natural to get defensive and avoid such conversations again. With clients in correctional systems, our job is to create a conversation in which the clients feel heard and understood and in which they have the opportunity to take an active role. Clients should be talking more than the professional in the conversations about change; after all, it is their change process. Partnership, acceptance, compassion, and evocation can be the keys to unlocking these conversations with clients who have criminal histories. These conversations can begin during the assessment phase, continue with treatment providers in the treatment phase, and carry into reentry and community corrections if all staff are trained to use MI as a permeating style. Practice Box 12.1 provides an opportunity for you to consider applying these concepts to develop a therapeutic relationship with CJ, a client who is involved in the criminal justice system.

> **Practice Box 12.1**
>
> Imagine CJ is your client as part of a reentry program. What might be some barriers you encounter when establishing a strong working alliance with CJ? Consider your differences in regard to demographics, background, and culture. How will you approach a therapeutic relationship with him in spite of these differences? How could implementing the spirit of MI assist in these efforts?

Assessment

When working with clients who are involved in criminal justice systems, offender risk assessments are commonly used to measure the individual's likelihood of reoffending (Latessa & Lovins, 2010). In addition to being used for public safety and to most appropriately place prisoners, offender risk assessments also provide information about a person's needs that lead to criminal behavior. Andrews and Bonta (2010a) described eight major risk factors associated with criminal behavior, the first four of which are commonly referred to as the "Big Four" due to having the strongest risk factors: (1) history of antisocial behavior (e.g., early arrests, large number of prior offenses, does not take criminal offenses seriously); (2) antisocial personality pattern (e.g., impulsivity, pleasure-seeking, aggressiveness); (3) antisocial cognitions (attitudes, beliefs, values, and identity favorable to crime); (4) antisocial associates (associates with others who are pro-crime; isolation from those who do not engage in criminal behavior); (5) family factors, such as family criminality or lack of caring and cohesiveness; (6) low levels of educational, vocational, or financial achievement; (7) lack of prosocial leisure activities; and (8) abuse of drugs and alcohol (pp. 58–60). From this list, dynamic factors are considered changeable, such as attitudes/beliefs, social affiliations, substance use, and educational and vocational achievement. These are also called criminogenic needs, which are strongly correlated with risk and recidivism. Criminogenic needs can be targeted in treatment that matches the level of need with an appropriate level of intensity of interventions.

Instruments used to assess dynamic risk factors can provide evidence of progress while in treatment. Many of the common assessment instruments (e.g., Youthful Level of Service/Case Management Inventory, the Level of Service/Case Management Inventory, and the Ohio Risk Assessment System) provide professionals working in corrections with an individualized "road map" to address the criminogenic needs of client offenders (Latessa & Lovins, 2010, p. 214). As such, the content of assessment when working with offenders is incredibly valuable. In the practice of MI+CBT, the information gathered via assessment would be used to guide the plan for treatment interventions. However, client engagement should also be of focus when conducting assessment. Not unlike other settings such as mental health and substance use counseling, the assessment *process* in correctional settings commonly involves sequential questions asked by the professional and answered by the client. This can set the stage of client passivity and limited gains in strengthening an alliance, especially if serial closed questions are asked (Stinson & Clark, 2017). Instead, when integrating MI into assessment processes, the spirit of MI permeates the interaction, creating an environment that promotes trust, acceptance, and understanding. Within this type of environment, clients will be more likely to share honestly and provide more information. The core skills of MI, including OARS, can be used as information-gathering and relationship-building tools. The professional can also provide information with permission or by using EPE. For example, with CJ the assessor might say, "It's nice to meet you CJ. Today, we will be doing your assessment. Before we get started, I'd like to tell you a little bit about this process. Does that sound ok?" This would show respect and establish a collaborative process. Upon CJ's response, the assessor describes the process and answers any questions CJ might have. Reflections and summaries should be used throughout the interview components of assessment in order for the client to feel heard and understood, as well as to ensure the assessor is accurately understanding the client.

Voices From the Field 12.1

Enhancing Rehabilitative Change in Prison

Written by
Rick Vest, M.A., LPC-S
Reentry Services, Ingram State Technical College
Reentry Director, Julia Tutwiler Prison for Women

In the United States, 68% of prisoners released in 2005 were rearrested within three years of release, and within nine years of release 83% had been rearrested (Alper, Durose, & Markman, 2018). The reasons prisoners recidivate at such alarming rates are varied, but the reason is never because no one told them what changes they needed to make.

Well-meaning people are always telling people in prison how to change. After all, the fact that prisoners are in prison means that they have made mistakes and more often than not a long series of mistakes beginning at an early age.

These mistakes are usually the result of skill deficits. Incarcerated people often lack decision-making and problem-solving skills. They have poor interpersonal skills and poor emotional regulation skills. They have low frustration tolerances, and they have beliefs and ways of thinking about the world that put them at risk for reoffending. They struggle with mental illness. They have trouble coping with life and often turn to substance abuse to manage painful emotions or to cope with the day-to-day stresses of life.

They resent authority, and like all of us, they resent being told what they should do.

CBT is well suited to address the skill deficits and has long been the treatment of choice for the incarcerated population. It is well researched, and there is strong evidence of its effectiveness. A 2017 review of the literature found that CBT reduces recidivism by 20% to 30% (Duwe, 2017).

When CBT programs are well designed, well implemented, and when the individual is receptive, they work. People learn better decision making. They learn to get along better with people and to resolve conflicts successfully. They learn to manage their emotions better, whether it be anger or anxiety or depression or any number of the emotions that either paralyze them from acting or drive them to act in socially unacceptable ways. It teaches them to evaluate how dysfunctional thinking puts them at risk and change how they think about the world. CBT is a powerful and effective tool, but to benefit, people have to be receptive to change.

It would seem that the need for people in prison to change would be obvious to them—after all, life has not gone well. But many are still ambivalent—no matter how bad things have been or are, there are still forces pulling them to the status quo. And many prisoners are inherently resistant when they believe someone is trying to control them or tell them what they should do.

People in prison are told what to do, how to do it, and when to do it. Prisons are often characterized by an "us against them" culture, with the inmates being on one side of the divide and everyone else being on the other side. And for most, someone telling them how to change began long before they came to prison. For many, opposition to change is automatic when they believe someone is trying to control them.

MI creates an environment for change by humanizing the inmate. By design, prison is dehumanizing. Inmates are numbers; they all dress alike, and any expression of individuality is restricted. But there is growing recognition that a new culture is needed if prisons are to be rehabilitative environments, and in 2012, the National Institute of Corrections published *Motivational Interviewing in Corrections: A Comprehensive Guide to Implementing MI in Corrections* for use by corrections facilities across the United States.

When I meet with incarcerated people for the first time, I attempt to engage them by asking about their life outside of prison. It takes them off guard. They are not used to being seen as people, and sometimes they have stopped seeing themselves as people. Because MI respects the inmate's history and experience, it helps creates a paradigm shift in how they think about and approach participating in treatment. Dictating change does not work. If it did, no one would ever come back to prison. When we engage inmates as autonomous people, when we ask them to participate in recrafting their own future, when we acknowledge their value and their humanity, then they are more open to change.

CBT alone works with some people, but I believe its effectiveness is limited by the nature of the relationship between the prisoner and the prison staff who implement CBT-based programs. By using MI, prison staff can create an environment that is more conducive to the inmate choosing change.

References:

Alper, M., Durose, M. R., & Markman, J. (2018). 2018 update on prisoner recidivism: A 9-year follow-up period (2005–2014). U.S. Department of Justice, Bureau of Justice Statistics. Retrieved from www.bjs.gov/content/pub/pdf/18upr9yfup0514.pdf

Duwe, G. (2017). *The use and programming for inmates on pre- and post-release outcomes.* National Institute of Justice. Retrieved from www.ncjrs.gov/pdffiles1/njj/250476.pdf

Focusing, Evoking, and Planning

Through the course of assessment, the foci of treatment are identified. The criminogenic needs of this particular person become the targets for treatment. In MI+CBT, the recommended foci and goals of treatment are discussed with the client. This conversation fosters continued client engagement as well as ensures the client understands the intended focus of treatment. If the client disagrees, this can be heard by the professional with the goal of understanding the disagreement. For instance, many people in the correctional system have participated in "classes" in prison or other treatment settings and had negative experiences. This does not necessarily result in the recommendation for treatment changing; however, it can do a world of good for the relationship to listen without defensiveness to the reasons behind the client's perspective. This understanding is essential for the therapeutic alliance and in order to tailor cognitive and behavioral interventions effectively.

The evoking process of MI typically occurs before planning for change. This process is dedicated to cultivating client motivation to change and for engaging in treatment, including learning cognitive and behavioral skills and putting them into action to make sustainable changes. When ambivalence is present, we can use MI-consistent strategies to elicit and strengthen client change talk to enhance motivation to pursue these changes (see Table 12.2). Often, ambivalence might be too complex to be resolved before treatment begins. Therefore, targeting motivation, including eliciting and strengthening change talk and identifying and modifying cognitions that interfere with motivation, can be of focus during treatment as well as prior to the evoking and planning processes.

After the foci for treatment have been determined and the client's readiness for change, including the presence of ambivalence, has been addressed, the client and counselor collaboratively develop a plan for treatment. The plan for treatment should

Table 12.2 Strategies to Elicit and Reinforce Change Talk

Strategy	Examples
Ask evocative questions	• "How do you want your life to be different when you are out of prison/off parole/done with probation?" • "What do you think you might be able to change? What are your reasons for considering this change?"
Use an importance or confidence ruler	• "On a scale of 0 to 10, how important is it to you to not come back to prison? Why a ___ and not a 0? What would it take to bump it up a couple notches?" • "On a scale of 0 to 10, how confident are you that you can (make change)? Why a ___ and not a 0? What would it take to bump it upto a (couple notches)?"
Looking forward/ back questions	• "If you decide to continue on this path as you were and not make any changes, what do you think might happen?" • "Tell me about a time when you didn't have these problems? What was different about that time?"
Explore personal values and goals	• "What is most important to you in your life?" • "What do you hope to accomplish in your life?"
Use OARS after hearing change talk to reinforce and strengthen it	• "Tell me more about that." • "Give me an example. What might that look like?" • What else?" • "Use affirmations, reflections, and summaries specific to client change talk."

be individualized and completed with the client to continue to foster client engagement. Plans that are prescribed to clients are more likely to be met with defiance and noncompliance. If we hope for clients to follow the plans, we need to elicit their input and assist them in developing plans they are willing and able to implement.

Treatment

Within the RNR framework, treatment in correctional settings applies CBT methods to address criminogenic needs, as cognitive and behavioral interventions are well supported by research to reduce recidivism. For instance, in a meta-analysis of 58 studies involving adults and youth with criminal offenses, Landenberger and Lipsey (2005) found that programs that used CBT reduced recidivism by approximately

Voices From the Field 12.2

Integrating CBT and MI With Parents of Juveniles Who Sexually Offend

Written by
Leigh Falls Holman, PhD, LPC-MHSP-Supervisor, AMHCA Diplomate and CMHS in Substance Abuse and Co-occurring Disorders, Trauma Counseling, and Child and Adolescent Counseling
The University of Memphis

When a juvenile offends sexually, the victim is often a family member, affecting the entire family system, so treatment needs to engage the entire system including parents. The following provides a sample dialogue of a counselor integrating CBT and MI with a parent whose son sexually abused his sister:

Parent: People like you *think* I don't even care about my daughter. [*cognitive distortion [CD]: jumping to conclusions*] Should I abandon my son? [*CD: shoulds*] His life's ruined! [*CD: catastrophizing*]

Counselor: It's heartbreaking to find out one of your children has been harmed by another. [*MI: expressing empathy; CBT: confronting CD*] You clearly care greatly about both and are torn. I'm wondering how we might work together to keep *both* your children safe. [*MI: rolling with resistance and values clarification*]

Parent: How?

Counselor: What would *you* like to see different about the current situation? [*MI: eliciting change talk*]

Parent: I want you guys off my back; keep my kids safe.... BOTH of them!

Counselor: You are really worried about something else horrible happening [*MI: expressing empathy*] and keeping your son out of jail. [*MI: values clarification*]

Parent: Yes!

Counselor: But you also want to protect your daughter. [*MI: values clarification; CBT: confronting CD*]

Parent: Of course.

Counselor: On a scale of 1–10, 1 being not important and 10 being the most important thing in life, how important is it to keep your daughter safe and your son out of jail? [*MI: importance ruler*]

Parent: Eight.

Counselor: Why an 8, not a 6? [*MI: eliciting change talk*]

Parent: Well, a 6 is average. Right now, all I can think about is the fact that the PO and this program want us to do all these things, like counseling, and groups, and putting alarms on doors. It's ridiculous! [*CD: filtering only the negative*]

Counselor: You're overwhelmed. [*MI: expressing empathy*] What are your concerns about treatment? [*Decisional balance*]

Parent: Time off work, figuring out completely different kid schedules, and maintaining my job—more money for door alarms and counseling! [*MI: identifying negatives to change*]

Counselor: Those all make sense. It's hard enough being a parent with a job and a busy life trying to make ends meet. Now you have a lot of new demands that you weren't bargaining for. [*MI: expressing empathy*] On the other hand, I'm wondering what might be some of the potential positive things about treatment? [*MI: developing discrepancy*]

Parent: My family would be home together, and maybe we could get past this nightmare. [*MI: developing decisional balance*]

Counselor: So on the one hand, you're concerned about cost and time involved, but on the other hand, you know this will keep your family together and potentially heal from everything. [*MI: double-sided reflection; CBT: reframe*]

Parent: Yes.

Counselor: On that same scale as before, how *confident* are you that you can work through these obstacles? [*MI: confidence ruler*]

Parent: Four?

Counselor: A 4, not a 3? [*MI: eliciting change talk*]

Parent: I know it's important. I think I can help both kids see this is how we'll heal.

Counselor: What can I do to help you get from a 4 to a 5?

Parent: Maybe just help me think through logistics? You know, how it'll all work? And resources to finance the alarms and where to get them.

Counselor: I can definitely help you with those things! Those are really "normal" concerns. [*CBT: normalizing/reframe*] It sounds like you want to do what you can to work together to help your family heal. [*MI: affirmation*] On that same scale, how committed are you? [*MI: readiness ruler*]

Parent: Eight?

Counselor: Great! Though you have concerns about how it'll work, but it sounds like you know it's important to commit to treatment. [*MI: supporting self-efficacy*]

25% but ranging up to 50% decreases. Treatments that included higher-risk offenders, high-fidelity treatment implementation, and anger control and interpersonal problem-solving components were associated with larger reductions in recidivism. Given CBT's efficacy, several CBT programs have been manualized for dissemination, such as Moral Reconation Therapy (Little & Robinson, 1988), Reasoning and Rehabilitation (Ross, Fabiano, & Ewles, 1988), and Thinking for a Change (Bush, Glick, & Tymans, 2016). However, Landenberger and Lipsey (2005) found that there were no significant differences between branded programs and generic CBT. In CBT for corrections, the therapeutic relationship is recognized as being as important as the interventions themselves (Milkman & Wanberg, 2007), and MI+CBT maintains explicit attention to the relationship, including client engagement in the treatment process while delivering cognitive and behavioral interventions.

Motivational interventions can behoove clients who are ambivalent about change or unmotivated to participate in recommended or required treatment. If we ignore these motivational issues and begin with action-oriented CBT, we risk losing client engagement and effectiveness of the interventions. Therefore, for clients who are experiencing ambivalence or other motivational issues, evoking client change talk to reinforce and strengthen client motivation should be done prior to client involvement in structured CBT treatment protocols. On occasion, clients' cognitions might need to be addressed in order to resolve ambivalence. For example, if CJ believes that "selling drugs is the only way to sufficiently support my family, despite the potential consequences," this belief can interfere with his motivation to enroll in a job training program. Therefore, CJ might benefit from evaluating this belief and acknowledging the nature of this belief through social learning. Upon developing a new belief derived from new social learning experiences, CJ's motivation for a job training program can be enhanced.

Cognitive conceptualization is based on the notion that clients have distorted beliefs that were socially learned and that led to criminal behaviors (Lizama, Matthews & Reyes, 2014). Therefore, CBT programs help clients identify how their thinking affects their emotions and behaviors and then work to change old beliefs that involved "risk thinking" and develop new ways of thinking within the context of social learning (Bush, Glick, & Tymans, 2002, p. 90). Clients then connect the new ways of thinking to new emotions and behaviors. Skill development is also of focus, such as anger management, social skills, and problem-solving skills (Bush et al., 2016; Lizama et al., 2014). Lizama et al. (2014) recommended that prior to their release, incarcerated clients who are nearing the end of their sentence should engage in CBT treatment groups twice per week for at least 16 weeks with a treatment provider who delivers the program with high fidelity. Further, they noted that educational and vocational programming, as well as substance use treatment, are essential to address common criminogenic needs, and faith-based and mental illness programs could be helpful adjunctive treatments, but more research is needed to determine effectiveness (Lizama et al., 2014).

Voices From the Field 12.3

Benefits of Combining MI and CBT With Offender Populations

Written by
Abigail Holder, M.Ed., NCC
Doctoral Student
Auburn University

The offender population is a very diverse group that has many intersectionalities of identities. This population brings a broad range of mental health and addiction concerns into the counseling room and is usually experiencing counseling for the first time in their lives. The population is marginalized in the United States and is often seen as a second-class citizen group. This marginalization is usually in addition to the discrimination they face due to their social location in society.

In my experience working with this population, I have found using a combination of MI and CBT to be effective. The basis of MI is to strengthen one's internal motivation to change, and CBT is traditionally meant to alter the person's unhealthy behavior through cognitive restructuring. These treatment methods reduce symptoms through increasing the individuals' own motivation to change maladaptive and troubling thoughts and behaviors. Those who are receiving correctional interventions are in need of change because their past decisions have led them to have maladaptive behaviors that caused them to break the law.

MI brings control and empowerment to the individual, which is effective with the offender population due to these individuals feeling as though they have no control over their lives. This lack of control may be a new feeling or a feeling they have had for a long time. MI allows clients to find empowerment and intrinsic motivation for changing aspects of their lives due to the person-centered nature of the theory. While moving through the processes of MI, CBT interventions can be implemented. These interventions look different depending on the client; for example, various interventions can be used during the focusing process in order to identify the client's goals for change. CBT interventions can also be used to gain a better understanding of a person's motivations and identify his or her ambivalence toward change. These interventions, when used in conjunction, have also been effective with those who struggle with the use of addictive substances, which is a common disorder seen in the prison system.

Overall, I have had positive outcomes with the combination of MI and CBT while counseling the offender population. Clients generally respond well to having the opportunity to take control in some part of their lives while incarcerated. They can benefit from having a space to talk, someone to trust, and a healthy relationship to model after. Most importantly, clients have been able to implement the changes they desire while in prison.

Practice Considerations

CBT involves structured interventions and programs with a natural hierarchy in which the professional is the "educator" and the client is the "learner." Therefore, CBT fits relatively well in structured, hierarchical correctional settings. On the other hand, MI can present quite a contrast to corrections as usual. In the MI trainings I have done with correctional professionals in various correctional settings and programs, including probation and parole officers, counseling providers, case managers, and educational staff, I commonly received feedback that MI is "too nice" and that clients will manipulate and take advantage of this type of approach. Indeed, there is a lot of manipulation occurring among this population for various reasons. My response to these comments was, "So, what are the options for professionals working with these populations?" and we talked through the possibilities. Many professionals choose to be directive and emphasize their authority over clients, resulting in the work with clients staying on the surface—the client will hopefully complete the program but will likely remain in a passive role and with the identity as "criminal." Another option is to overcorrect or to be nondirective and follow the client. This style can result in a loss of the overall structure and direction of work with the client. Stinson and Clark (2017) coined these two approaches as "muscle versus meekness" (p. 68). MI is a third option, which provides a guiding approach. For many professionals working in correctional settings, a directive style comes more easily than the guiding style of MI. Empathy and compassion, which are essential in MI, can be challenging for some professionals working in corrections, as the professional must step into the client's world through listening well and with a stance of care and concern. It is making the conscious choice to see the world, including reasons for criminal behavior, through the eyes of the client. It is suspending our assumptions from our own background and history, education, and other privileges we have and instead seeing the situation through the lens of the client, with his or her background and history, education, socioeconomic status, generational history, and so on. As one trainee put it as he grappled with the concept of empathy, "Here's me . . . . and here's the offender (he held up his hands an arm's width apart). There's a line here (motions in the middle). And you want me to cross it?!" Yes, yes, that's it! Figuratively, of course, and with the caveat that you always come back to your world after the conversation with the client. Empathy is indeed a challenge, but it can have great impact, along with the other components of MI. And expressing empathy is not exchanged for, nor does it negate the importance of, structure in treatment to assist clients in pursuing the overall goals, objectives, and interventions involved in treatment. Direction in conversations and in interventions is still present and is the responsibility of the professional, as are boundaries and ethical practice that permeate all work.

As mentioned previously, training and fidelity concerns are common when disseminating and implementing evidence-based or best practices, especially to such an expansive breadth of service providers in correctional settings.

Correctional staff have varying functions and roles, and training should be made relevant to their specific role. For instance, probation and parole officers and intake assessment staff will benefit from using MI more so than CBT. However, counselors who provide individual and group treatment would likely benefit from training in MI+CBT to ensure the therapeutic relationship is sound and the client is engaged in treatment, as well as that the criminogenic needs are being addressed through cognitive and behavioral interventions. Fidelity measures, such as the Behavior Change Counseling Index—Criminal Justice Version (Lane, 2002), are helpful to assess skill development as well as fidelity of MI. CBT programs offer varying degrees of training, and many come with manuals to promote consistent delivery of and adherence to the content of the program.

When training is provided to correctional staff, it can be helpful for trainers to address trainees' levels of motivation, especially when trainees are mandated to learn an approach and when they are expected to implement an approach that is drastically different than the current climate of the agency (i.e., MI being implemented in an agency that currently subscribes to a traditional "get tough" approach). For example, Doran, Hohman, and Koutsenok (2011) used a two-item Quick Readiness Measure to assess trainees' motivation to use MI and their beliefs about its usefulness, and Barrick and Homish (2011) developed the Readiness to Change Questionnaire–Clinical Skills Adaptation and the What I Want from Training instrument. For trainees with lower motivation, it can be helpful for the trainer to use MI strategies to enhance trainees' motivation to promote successful training outcomes (Iarussi & Powers, 2018).

Strategies grounded in implementation science are also important to consider to increase the success of implementing best practices. For instance, Powell et al. (2012) recommended that trainers meet and frequently communicate with the director of training to develop strategies and relationships and solidify buy-in. Alexander, VanBenschoten, and Walters (2008) suggested providing education before the trainings, such as a two-hour introduction to evidence-based practices. Identifying and training leaders to champion the dissemination and offering incentives for practice with fidelity could also be useful strategies (Powell et al., 2012), especially to balance the already demanding work staff members experience due to managing large caseloads and being asked to do "another thing" in learning and implementing MI or MI+CBT.

Summary

MI and CBT have both been applied to work with clients in the criminal justice systems and both can be integrated into the RNR framework. A more explicit integrated practice of MI and CBT within the RNR framework and structured deliberate training in these areas for professionals working in corrections could result in improved service provisions focused on rehabilitation for clients who have criminally offended to further promote sustained behavior change and reduce recidivism.

References

Alexander, M., VanBenschoten, S. W., & Walters, S. T. (2008). Motivational interviewing training in criminal justice: Development of a model plan. *Federal Probation, 72*(2), 84–90.

Andrews, D. A., & Bonta, J. (2010a). *The psychology of criminal conduct* (5th ed.). New Providence, NJ: LexisNexis Group.

Andrews, D. A., & Bonta, J. (2010b). Rehabilitating criminal justice policy and practice. *Psychology, Public Policy, and Law, 16*(1), 39–55. doi:10.1037/a0018362

Askew, L. (2016). Best practices for effective correctional programs. *Research in Action, 1*(1), 1–5. Retrieved from www.cmitonline.org/research/publications/documents/best practices_7_2016.pdf

Barrick, C., & Homish, G. G. (2011). Readiness to change and training expectations prior to a training workshop for substance abuse clinicians. *Substance Use & Misuse, 46*(8), 1032–1036. doi:10.3109/10826084.2010.546821

Beutler, L. E., Harwood, T. M., Michelson, A., Song, X., & Holman, J. (2011). Resistance/reactance level. *Journal of Clinical Psychology, 67*(2), 133–142. doi:10.1002/jclp.20753

Bonta, J., & Andrews, D. A. (2007). *Risk-need-responsivity model for offender assessment and rehabilitation (User Report 2007-06)*. Ottawa, Ontario: Public Safety Canada.

Bush, J., Glick, B., & Tymans, J. (2002). *Thinking for change: Integrated cognitive behavior change program*. Washington, DC: National Institute of Corrections.

Bush, J., Glick, B., & Tymans, J. (2016). *Thinking for change 4.0: Integrated cognitive behavior change program*. Washington, DC: National Institute of Corrections.

Doran, N., Hohman, M., & Koutsenok, I. (2011). Linking basic and advanced motivational interviewing training outcomes for juvenile correctional staff in California. *Journal of Psychoactive Drugs, 43*(1), 19–26. doi:10.1080/02791072.2011.601986

Durose, M. R., Cooper, A. D., & Snyder, H. N. (2014). *Special report: Recidivism of prisoners released in 30 states in 2005: Patterns from 2005 to 2010*. (NCJ 244205). Washington, DC: U.S. Department of Justice, Office of Justice Programs, Bureau of Justice Statistics.

Iarussi, M. M., & Powers, D. F. (2018). Outcomes of motivational interviewing training with probation and parole officers: Findings and lessons learned. *Federal Probation, 82*(3), 28–35.

Landenberger, N. A., & Lipsey, M. W. (2005). The positive effects of cognitive–behavioral programs for offenders: A meta-analysis of factors associated with effective treatment. *Journal of Experimental Criminology, 1*(4), 451–476. doi:10.1007/s11292-005-3541-7

Lane, C. (2002). *Behavior change counseling index—Criminal justice version*. Cardiff, Wales, UK: University of Wales.

Latessa, E. J. (2012). Designing more effective correctional programs using evidence-based practices. *Resource Material Series, 88*, 48–63. Retrieved from www.unafei.or.jp/publications/pdf/RS_No88/No88_10VE_Latessa_Designing.pdf

Latessa, E. J., & Lovins, B. (2010). The role of offender risk assessment: A policy maker guide. *Victims & Offenders, 5*(3), 203–219. doi:10.1080/15564886.2010.485900

Lipsey, M. W., Landenberger, N. A., & Wilson, S. J., (2007). Effects on cognitive-behavioral programs for criminal offenders. *The Campbell Collaboration, 6*, 1–27. doi:10.4073/csr.2007.6

Little, G. L., & Robinson, K. D. (1988). Moral reconation therapy: A systematic step-by-step treatment system for treatment-resistant clients. *Psychological Reports, 62*, 135–151. doi:10.2466/pr0.1988.62.1.135

Lizama, J., Matthews, V., & Reyes, S. (2014). *What works? Short-term, in-custody treatment programs*. Fullerton, CA: Center for Public Policy.

McMurran, M. (2009). Motivational interviewing with offenders: A systematic review. *Legal and Criminological Psychology, 14*, 83–100. doi:10.1348/135532508X278326

Milkman, H., & Wanberg, K. (2007). *Cognitive-behavioral treatment: A review and discussion for corrections professionals: (681162012–001)* [Data set]. American Psychological Association. doi:10.1037/e681162012-001

Miller, W. R., Benefield, R. G., & Tonigan, J. S. (1993). Enhancing motivation for change in problem drinking: A control comparison of two therapist styles. *Journal of Consulting and Clinical Psychology, 61*(3), 455–461. doi:10.1037/0022-006X.61.3.455

Miller, W. R., & Rollnick, S. (2002). *Motivational interviewing: Preparing people for change* (2nd ed.). New York, NY: Guilford Press.

Miller, W. R., & Rollnick, S. (2013). *Motivational interviewing: Helping people change* (3rd ed.). New York, NY: Guilford Press.

National Institute of Corrections. (2012). *Motivational interviewing in corrections: A comprehensive guide to implementing MI in corrections*. Washington, DC: Author.

Powell, B. J., McMillen, J. C., Proctor, E. K., Carpenter, C. R., Griffey, R. T., Bunger, A. C., . . . York, J. L. (2012). A compilation of strategies for implementing clinical innovations in health and mental health. *Medical Care Research and Review, 69*, 123–157. doi:10.1177/1077558711430690

Ross, R. R., Fabiano, E. A., & Ewles, C. D. (1988). Reasoning and rehabilitation. *International Journal of Offender Therapy and Comparative Criminology, 34*(1), 29–35.

Stevenson, B. (2014). *Just mercy: A story of justice and redemption*. New York, NY: Spiegel & Grau.

Stinson, J. D., & Clark, M. D. (2017). *Motivational interviewing with offenders: Engagement, rehabilitation, and reentry*. New York, NY: Guilford Press.

Taxman, F. S. (2018). The partially clothed emperor: Evidence-based practices. *Journal of Contemporary Criminal Justice, 34*(1), 97–114. doi:10.1177/1043986217750444

U.S. Department of Education, Office of Vocational and Adult Education. (2012). *A reentry education model: Supporting education and career advancement for low-skill individuals in corrections*. Washington, DC: Author.

Walters, S. T., Clark, M. D., Gingerich, R., & Meltzer, M. L. (2007). *Motivating offenders to change: A guide for probation and parole* (NIC Accession #022253). Washington, DC: National Institute of Corrections, U.S. Department of Justice.

SECTION IV

Clinical Practice Issues

CHAPTER 13

Reconciling Potential Dilemmas

When used as separate approaches, both MI and CBT possess their own tenents, processes, and foci. Although they are complementary approaches in many ways, clinicians who combine them can find themselves in relatively uncharted territory, especially when the clinician behaviors involved in each approach do not fully align or MI+CBT practice does not neatly fit into existing organizational processes. In most cases, there will be no clear right or wrong way to mitigate dilemmas that can arise in MI+CBT practice. Instead, practitioners largely use their clinical judgment, especially taking into consideration the particular client in front of them and the setting in which services are being provided. As Norcross and Wampold (2018) noted, integration is complex as it essentially involves creating a new therapy for each client as the practitioner makes clinical decisions about how to blend the approaches together. In this chapter, we explore potential dilemmas that can arise when integrating MI and CBT and review suggestions for how to manage these situations. This is not an exhaustive list of potential dilemmas, but rather challenges noted in the literature (Moyers & Houck, 2011; Naar & Safren, 2017) as well as from my experiences in clinical practice and in providing supervision and training to others. This chapter comes with the caveat that when challenges or dilemmas in integrating MI and CBT arise, your own clinical judgment is most important, as well as seeking supervision or consultation as needed.

Priority in Organizational Processes

The first process of MI is engaging, meaning the therapeutic relationship is of focus. The client is heard and understood, and therefore, engaging results in the client being interested in talking further with the provider about potential changes. However, many service agency protocols and providers who use CBT conduct initial assessments before therapy begins, including before the therapeutic relationship has a chance to be established. This initial assessment occurs first in order to gather information needed to determine if the provider can indeed provide the requested or recommended treatment considering the scope of practice of the provider or agency, the provider's competency in providing the desired treatments, and other situational (e.g., insurance or private payment) and clinical factors (e.g., comorbidity). If the provider will be serving the client, the initial assessment also informs conceptualization, goals, and treatment approaches. However, the information-gathering process that accompanies assessment often involves clients being asked serial questions, and the goal of "filling out the forms" can be prioritized over connecting with the human beings who are providing the information. Within the framework of MI+CBT, gathering information via assessment and establishing a therapeutic relationship are considered interdependent— if clients believe you are listening to and understanding them, they are more likely to share information with you—and therefore these tasks are equally important. Naar and Safren (2017) suggest spending 10 to 15 minutes solely on engagement prior to attending to any protocol requirements set forth by the agency. Practically speaking, clinicians typically have a limited amount of time to complete initial assessments, and therefore, it can perhaps be helpful to attend to each task simultaneously throughout the initial assessment sessions to engage the client and build an effective therapeutic alliance while gathering assessment information.

Ambivalence and Treatment Planning: What Is the Goal?

When the time comes to plan for treatment, and clients continue to be ambivalent about change, therapists might question whether to continue with MI or to push ahead with CBT (Moyers & Houck, 2011; Naar & Safren, 2017). Some suggest continuing with pure MI, in which case the goal becomes to address and resolve ambivalence. This approach resembles using MI as a prelude to CBT. An alternative approach that is more aligned with a true blending of MI and CBT would be to include addressing ambivalence with MI as part of the initial treatment plan. This might be uncustomary, as CBT typically includes observable outcomes compared to an abstract construct, such as resolving ambivalence. However, this approach would be consistent with MI+CBT and could be measured using readiness rulers or other readiness to change instruments, such as SOCRATES (Miller & Tonigan, 1996).

Figure 13.1 illustrates a treatment plan for Greg (from Chapter 10), a 41-year-old client who engaged in anonymous sex and frequent hookups since he was 19 years old and who more recently began to experience consequences due to missing work to have sex and feeling unfulfilled due to a lack of love relationships. After the intake assessment, Greg's ambivalence was not resolved. He is facing more than two decades of engaging in these behaviors, and it might be unreasonable for him to fully commit to changing immediately. Therefore, in a true blending of MI and CBT, Greg's treatment plan includes addressing his ambivalence and the cognitive and behavioral interventions he is willing to engage in at the time of completing the treatment plan. As time progresses and his motivation increases, the plan for treatment is collaboratively revised so that action-oriented cognitive and behavioral interventions can take the forefront of treatment. For instance, cognitive restructuring would likely be listed along with other action or change-oriented interventions. As a clients' readiness progresses in favor of change, the treatment plan can be revised to include more action-oriented cognitive and behavioral interventions.

Plan for Change/Treatment Plan	
The changes I am considering are:	My reasons for considering these changes:
Reduce hookups *Change approach to relationships*	*Sex is taking away from work and other areas of my life. I still feel alone. I put my health at risk.*

In order to make these changes, I will engage in the following treatment:

Concern	Goal	Treatment
Sexual behavior causing consequences to work and causing a lack of love relationships	*Explore and resolve ambivalence related to changing sexual behavior*	• *Enhance motivations to reduce sexual behaviors* • *Identify and evaluate cognitions that are interfering with motivation* • *Explore values and goals*
	Reduce sexual behavior	• *Functional analysis of sexual behaviors* • *Cognitive reconstruction* • *Coping skills training*
	Change approach to relationships	• *Identify and evaluate beliefs related to relationships* • *Provide psychoeducation on healthy relationships* • *Identify alternative activities that are congruent with values and goals*

Outside of treatment, I will also take these steps:

<u>*Try a Sex Addicts Anonymous meeting*</u>

How will I know if my plan is working?

<u>*I will feel like I can control my sexual urges and activities*</u>

What might interfere with my plan?	What will I do if this happens?
I don't fight the urges	*Think about whether it's worth it*
Continuing to connect with guys on hookup apps	*Delete the apps*

Figure 13.1 Sample Plan for Change/Treatment Plan for Greg

In this way, treatment plans are consistent with the premise of MI+CBT in that the plan for treatment matches client readiness for change.

Ambivalence About Treatment

In addition to ambivalence about change, client ambivalence about engaging in specific interventions can also present as a hiccup in MI+CBT. Ambivalence can present surrounding self-monitoring, cognitive interventions, emotional regulation, behavioral interventions, homework, or attending therapy sessions (Naar & Safren, 2017). There are several suggestions to address ambivalence directed toward specific therapeutic tasks. First, we can listen to clients' reasons for their hesitancy and work with them to remove barriers and enhance their motivation to engage in the intervention. When we listen to and seek to understand client sustain talk, we can sometimes find opportunities to modify interventions to better fit the client. For example, if a client is opposed to self-monitoring because stopping to write her experiences down does not work for her, perhaps we can collaborate with the client to discover a way to collect this data that works for this particular client, such as using a smartphone app or taking short videos to track her thoughts, behaviors, and emotions and bringing these into session as opposed to a paper log. Second, with clients' permission, we can provide information about the purpose and intention of the intervention and then elicit clients' thoughts about how the intervention might apply to or be helpful for them. We can also provide information about the empirical support of specific interventions pertaining to particular disorders or symptoms that clients might be experiencing. Finally, we can provide clients with a menu of options of therapeutic activities, each with a similar focus, from which they can choose. For example, if mindfulness is not working for a client, he or she might choose to try guided imagery or progressive muscle relaxation.

Harm Reduction

Tatarsky and Marlatt (2010) described harm reduction as "a framework for addressing substance use and other potentially risky behaviors, [which] aims to reduce the harmful consequences of these behaviors without requiring abstinence as a goal or a prerequisite of treatment" (p. 117). In the United States, abstinence-based outcomes are the norm in substance use and dual diagnosis treatment, and therefore, goals aligned with harm reduction are often not included. However, MI is consistent with harm reduction in the sense that both revolve around mutually agreed upon goals, with the aim of clients taking steps to reduce harm or consequences by modifying use, although not requiring or mandating that they abstain. Instead, harm reduction seeks to meet clients where they are in regard to their use, readiness to change, values, goals, and social and environmental contexts (Tatarsky & Marlatt, 2010). It also incorporates CBT as clients learn new ways to cope and enhance self-efficacy through harm reduction. Marlatt and Witkiewitz (2010) noted that many clients who start off with a harm reduction approach eventually progress to giving up substance use altogether; however, this is a client decision and not imposed. The harm reduction approach and aiming to reach harm reduction goals works very well if you are affiliated with an agency that supports this model. On the other hand, many of us work for agencies and organizations that only support abstinence, and any substance use is criteria for discharge from the program. This leaves therapists practicing MI+CBT in a tight spot—do we honor clients' current readiness to change and work at their pace, or do we honor the agencies' directives and persuade clients into abstinence (Moyers & Houck, 2011)? In some cases, clinicians lack flexibility and will uphold the goal of abstinence set forth by the agency. When this is the case, clinicians might offer clients the option of a referral for alternative treatment centers or therapy providers who support harm reduction. In other words, if the goals of the agency and of the client are not compatible, making a referral to a more appropriate provider might be in order. If offering referrals is not possible, clinicians can guide clients to make their choice using evocation and providing information with permission. The following examples illustrate using MI with a client whose probation officer is requiring him to attend abstinence-based treatment:

Clinician: Ok, so it seems like you're ready to address the cocaine use, and you have been abstaining from using it since your arrest, and yet it sounds like you're not interested in stopping drinking at this time.

Client: No, I mean I need to cut back, yeah. But stop altogether, nah. That's not going to happen. Especially with giving up cocaine right now. One thing at a time, you know.

Clinician: Yeah, stopping using cocaine is enough work for now, and you'd like to continue to drink. Would it be ok if I give you a little information about our agency and how we approach treatment?

Client: Yeah, sure.

Clinician: Ok, well, at this agency we run an abstinence-based program, meaning drug or alcohol use while you are in treatment is a violation that results in clients being terminated from the program. [*Pause*] I wonder what you're thinking as you hear that criteria to be treated here?

Client: You mean I have to stop drinking? I got arrested for cocaine, not alcohol. Why in the world would I have to stop drinking alcohol? It's legal!

Clinician: That can be really confusing sometimes. Would it be ok if I explained that a little?

Client: Well, yeah.

Clinician: With an abstinence-based program, like this one, it doesn't matter what substance brought you here. The treatment is designed to help clients maintain sobriety, including alcohol. Alcohol can often lead to other drug use, so the program is designed to help clients establish an alcohol- and drug-free life. That said, there are other programs out there that offer a harm-reduction approach, meaning that you would work with a therapist to determine your goals to reduce any harm experienced due to substance use, but it would not require abstinence. Would you be interested in more information about those types of programs?

Client: No, my probation officer said this program. I have to complete this program.

Clinician: Your PO wants you to complete an abstinence-based program.

Client: If I don't want to go to jail, I have to complete this program. Yes, she was clear about that.

Clinician: You seem committed to staying out of jail.

Client: Well, yeah. I mean, I knew I was going to have to stop using coke for a while, but this alcohol stuff is unreal.

Clinician: It's taken you by surprise.

Client: Yeah, but I mean, it's not worth getting locked up again for.

Clinician: So even though it's not quite what you expected, you're now thinking it might be worth not drinking in order to complete this program and stay out of jail.

Client: Yeah, for sure.

In the dialogue, the clinician only provides information with the client's permission to honor his autonomy. He declined to hear more about the choice for a referral due to circumstances related to his mandate. Then he mentions his motivation to stay out of jail (change talk), which the clinician responds to by reflecting this to strengthen it. Other evocative questions might be helpful to further solidify his motivation, such as looking forward (e.g., "If you continue to use while in this program, what do you envision happening?") or drawing on periods of abstinence from the past, if applicable (e.g., "How were you able to be abstinent in the past?"). Although harm reduction is a pragmatic approach, unfortunately many agencies will not support its use, resulting in clinicians having to assist clients in exploring their options so clients can make their decisions.

The Expert Trap: Who Knows Best?

In CBT, the practitioner educates clients about their symptoms, the process of therapy, and the cognitive model, as well as about other skills that might be useful to the client (Beck, 2011). This educative component is an aspect of CBT that sets it apart from other therapies (Dozois, Dobson, & Rnic, 2019). Contrarily, in MI practitioners avoid the "expert trap" (Miller & Rollnick, 2013, pp. 15–16) or the notion that they have the answer to the client's problem. Instead, MI practitioners develop a partnership with clients in which both parties have valuable wisdom to share. When integrating CBT and MI, the educational components of CBT can be delivered in a way that emphasizes client autonomy by asking for permission before providing information (e.g., "Would it be ok if I explained how we might be able to address these symptoms in therapy together?"). Client engagement can be preserved when providing information by using EPE or, at minimum, asking an evocative question following the information (e.g., "Tell me how you see that

> **Voices From the Field 13.1**
>
> *Training and Integration Insights*
>
> Written by
> Katie A. Lamberson, Ph.D., LPC, CRC, ACS
> Assistant Professor
> University of North Georgia
>
> When I am teaching or training in MI, one of the things I find to be difficult is helping students/trainees understand how MI and CBT can inform and enhance one another. I have noticed that students/trainees often struggle with the juxtaposition of a nondirective or person-centered approach with a more directive approach, seeing these as opposing forces in the world of counseling. This can create confusion for new counselors trying to develop an identity. Integrating MI and CBT as I am teaching and training can really help provide insight into how we can be concrete and directive while still maintaining the MI spirit, which can help students/trainees develop a holistic approach to working with clients.

possibly fitting or not fitting for you?" or "How do you see this applying to your situation?"). In addition, many CBT practitioners rely on clients' informing them about the meaning of their thoughts and approach clients as the expert on their own experiences (DeRubeis, Keefe, & Beck, 2019). This approach to CBT is naturally more aligned with MI's stance that clients are the experts on themselves (Miller & Rollnick, 2013).

In addition to the expert trap, MI practitioners strive to diminish their use of the "righting reflex" (Miller & Rollnick, 2013, p. 5). Although the righting reflex typically comes from a place of care and concern, it manifests in not listening to or eliciting from the client. Instead, it essentially results in attempts to "install" solutions or fix problems for clients. Therefore, MI practitioners do not jump to problem-solving clients' dilemmas or lead clients to a particular solution that the practitioner believes is best. This stance can be congruent with CBT's use of Socratic questioning as long as the CBT practitioner is not guiding the client to a specific "correct answer" or believing that he or she knows how the client "should" revise his or her beliefs. In other words, practitioners must keep in mind that every client is different, and each client has the right to decide which thoughts to evaluate, the outcomes of the evaluations, and how to revise his or her cognitions as he or she sees fit. The therapist should not be guiding clients to destinations that were predetermined by the therapist. Instead, we assist clients in discovering their own solutions.

Homework: Between Session Activities

Activities that clients engage in between sessions are encouraged in CBT. Clients are introduced to cognitive, behavioral, and emotion regulation skills in sessions with the therapist, and they continue these activities in between sessions to build these skills further and apply them in everyday life. As a goal of CBT is for the client to become his or her own therapist (Beck, 2011), in many cases these tasks are essential for the client to accomplish without the therapist prior to terminating treatment. Nonetheless, clients commonly do not complete homework. In Chapter 11, I described dilemmas specific to homework related to the treatment of mental health–related disorders. As homework completion presents a common dilemma, we will also explore this dilemma some here.

In MI+CBT, clinicians attend to the processes of introducing the purpose of homework, developing the content of what will be done between sessions, and learning from completed homework. Clinicians possess the spirit of MI (partnership, acceptance, compassion, and evocation) to introduce the idea of homework and collaboratively develop the task. To introduce homework, clinicians will likely want to avoid the actual word "homework," as it often is attached to negative connotations (Naar & Safren, 2017). An alternative description might sound like the following: "For most clients, they find they benefit much more from intentionally applying the content of our sessions to their lives in between sessions, as opposed to only thinking about this once per week while in therapy. What do you think about us talking more about how you might apply some of the strategies we discuss in session to your life in between sessions?" As such, the client's autonomy is preserved, as he or she is being invited to actively assess the value he or she might see in between session work. Then the clinician can use EPE to first elicit the client's input on how he or she might apply the tools learned in session to between sessions. Next, with permission, the therapist can make suggestions about what has worked for others, such as thought logs, activity scheduling, thought evaluation and replacement, and so on. The therapist then elicits the client's reactions to the suggestion and together they develop in-between-session activities that the client and counselor both see value in and that the client is willing to engage in. By assigning homework without attending to the process (e.g., "For homework this week, I want you to complete the thought log and bring it back to next session."), we risk losing client engagement and input, and the client will be less likely to put in the effort required to complete the "assigned" tasks.

These ideas are equally important after clients return with completed homework. In MI+CBT, therapists reinforce client efforts on between session activities by asking the client about his or her experience with the activity and the value he or she found in it. In doing so, the client's responses bring these important factors into his or her awareness and can influence subsequent motivation for homework. Further, the therapist listens to the client's experience of completing the homework to learn about any difficulties or need for adaptation to better fit this particular client. Finally, the content of the homework is collaboratively examined relative to therapeutic gain.

Switching Styles

When using MI as a prelude to CBT or a type of assimilative integration, therapists switching styles between approaches could be confusing to clients and risk disconnection in the therapeutic relationship. For example, if a client has two sessions of MI with a therapist as a pretreatment and then the client transitions to a different therapist who uses CBT in a directive fashion congruent with CBT, clients may not be getting what they expected from the CBT therapist given their preceding experiences with the MI therapist. This could be even more confusing if it was the same therapist who drastically switched styles from MI to CBT with the same client. Similar concerns are possible when assimilating CBT into MI. For instance, if therapists begin with CBT and then switch to MI, clients may not know which therapist style to expect next.

A full integration of MI+CBT mitigates this potential concern in that the spirit of MI is maintained throughout CBT interventions to guide the interpersonal style consistently. For example, when using Socratic questioning to guide clients to evaluate their current cognitions, MI+CBT therapists use open questions and reflections as opposed to serial closed questions (Naar & Safren, 2017). In other examples, cognitive and behavioral interventions are introduced with the clients' permission ("I have an intervention in mind that might be helpful for you. Clients with similar concerns have used it and found it useful. Would it be ok if I shared it with you?") and clients' input and ideas are valued and included in the development and execution of interventions.

Fidelity

Fidelity, or the degree to which the practitioner implements the approach as it is intended, has been addressed in both MI and CBT research. In outcome research, it is important to examine the fidelity of the approaches used in order to have confidence that the treatments intended were indeed delivered so that accurate conclusions can be made. Observational coding with trained coders and a coding manual is considered to be the gold standard for assessing treatment fidelity (Rodriguez-Quintana & Lewis, 2018), and both MI and CBT have respective manuals for coding. For example, the *MITI* 4.2.1 (Moyers, Manuel, & Ernst, 2014) is used to assess practitioner fidelity to MI, and the CTS (Young & Beck, 1980) can be used to determine the degree of CBT fidelity.

When integrating MI and CBT, fidelity becomes exponentially complex. How does the MI+CBT practitioner practice with fidelity to both approaches without losing one approach to the other? How is fidelity to MI+CBT measured? Given the relative infancy of MI+CBT, these are currently unanswered questions and a rich area for future research. For practitioners who wish to use MI+CBT, it is important to be conducting some measures of fidelity for each approach to ensure one approach is not being lost to the other without our awareness and to keep our MI+CBT practice on track. These methods are often incorporated in training efforts (further described in the next chapter).

Summary

Dilemmas are likely to arise in any integrated practice, including MI+CBT. This chapter provided some guidance to address common dilemmas in the integrated practice of MI+CBT. The practitioner's clinical judgment is essential when navigating such issues, and supervision or consultation should be sought as needed.

References

Beck, J. S. (2011). *Cognitive behavior therapy: Basics and beyond* (2nd ed.). New York, NY: Guilford Press.

DeRubeis, R. J., Keefe, J. R., & Beck, A. T. (2019). Cognitive therapy. In K. S. Dobson & D. J. A. Dozois (Eds.), *Handbook of cognitive-behavioral therapies* (4th ed., pp. 218–248). New York, NY: Guilford Press.

Dozois, D. J. A., Dobson, K. S., & Rnic, K. (2019). Historical and philosophical bases of the cognitive-behavioral therapies. In K. S. Dobson & D. J. A. Dozois (Eds.), *Handbook of cognitive-behavioral therapies* (4th ed., pp. 3–31). New York, NY: Guilford Press.

Marlatt, G. A., & Witkiewitz, K. (2010). Update on harm-reduction policy and intervention research. *Annual Review of Clinical Psychology, 6*(1), 591–606. doi:10.1146/annurev.clinpsy.121208.131438

Miller, W. R., & Rollnick, S. (2013). *Motivational interviewing: Helping people change* (3rd ed.). New York, NY: Guilford Press.

Miller, W. R., & Tonigan, J. S. (1996). Assessing drinkers' motivation for change: The stages of change readiness and treatment eagerness scale (SOCRATES). *Psychology of Addictive Behaviors, 10*(2), 81–89. doi:10.1037/0893-164X.10.2.81

Moyers, T. B., & Houck, J. (2011). Combining motivational interviewing with cognitive-behavioral treatments for substance abuse: Lessons from the COMBINE research project. *Cognitive and Behavioral Practice, 18*(1), 38–45. doi:10.1016/j.cbpra.2009.09.005

Moyers, T. B., Manuel, J. K., & Ernst, D. (2014). *Motivational interviewing treatment integrity coding manual 4.1*. Retrieved from https://casaa.unm.edu/download/miti4_1.pdf

Naar, S., & Safren, S. A. (2017). *Motivational interviewing and CBT: Combining strategies for maximum effectiveness*. New York, NY: Guilford Press.

Norcross, J. C., & Wampold, B. E. (2018). A new therapy for each patient: Evidence-based relationships and responsiveness. *Journal of Clinical Psychology, 74*(11), 1889–1906. doi:10.1002/jclp.22678

Rodriguez-Quintana, N., & Lewis, C. C. (2018). Observational coding training methods for CBT treatment fidelity: A systematic review. *Cognitive Therapy and Research, 42*(4), 358–368. doi:10.1007/s10608-018-9898-5

Tatarsky, A., & Marlatt, G. A. (2010). State of the art in harm reduction psychotherapy: An emerging treatment for substance misuse. *Journal of Clinical Psychology, 66*(2), 117–122. doi:10.1002/jclp.20672

Young, J. E., & Beck, A. T. (1980). *Cognitive therapy scale*. Philadelphia, PA: University of Pennsylvania.

CHAPTER 14

Training and Supervision

Learning to integrate MI and CBT in practice requires training and clinical supervision. Goals of such training include competence and preparedness to implement these approaches in ways that are responsive to the needs of clients. Even as separate approaches, learning MI and CBT requires time, practice, and practice feedback. Speaking for the need for competent practice, Hunsley and Allan (2019) stated, "Knowing about CBT and knowing how to provide CBT are very different matters" (p. 121). This notion also seems to hold true for MI, as MI training literature has noted that clinicians often believe they are practicing with more MI fidelity than they actually are and that MI is complex to learn and often requires in-depth training, including practice feedback (Miller & Mount, 2001; Miller, Yahne, Moyers, Martinez, & Pirritano, 2004; Schumacher, Madson, & Nilsen, 2014).

In this chapter, we explore various paths to learning to practice MI+CBT. The suggestions and models described might resemble components of your own path to learn MI+CBT, or there might be differences. In many cases, clinicians must be opportunistic in seeking out specific training on integrated practices, as these experiences are often not built into training programs. Overall, competency development typically includes the following components: (a) knowledge of the approach, (b) trying out skills in the training settings and receiving feedback, (c) practicing with clients under close supervision, (d) implementing fidelity measures, and (e) practicing with clients while using supervision or coaching to receive practice feedback. With these components in mind, educators and trainers can be intentional in offering such learning opportunities and informing students/trainees that gaining competence in MI+CBT from a single-shot learning experience (e.g., a single workshop) is unlikely. Instead, workshops or courses can form the foundational knowledge, after which skill development continues to be of focus, including ongoing practice and seeking feedback from a supervisor or coach.

Voices From the Field 14.1

MI as a Starting Point in Clinical Supervision

In the spirit of collaboration, this section was written by a clinical site supervisor, M. Scott Smith, LPC, at Counseling & Psychology Services, Inc. and two master's-level counseling students, Ratoya S. Cofield and Timothy J. Cook at LaGrange College.

At our clinic, new student trainees are introduced to MI on their first day of supe.rvision. Because our trainees work primarily with court-mandated clients, it is vital for them to understand the spirit of MI. We want our trainees to see clients as people first, before they even begin to conceptualize clinical issues. The humanistic, client-centered spirit of MI helps trainees to establish rapport, which lays the groundwork for subsequent CBT interventions.

The spirit of MI also helps to balance out the inherent power differential in the therapy room. Many court-mandated clients enter treatment with a bitter attitude toward change—because it was not their choice to enter treatment! These clients often feel unacknowledged and powerless. Then the clients are sent into a therapy room with a student clinician who, like it or not, could potentially jeopardize his or her clients' freedom with one negative report to the court. Imagine being in the clients' position—already vulnerable—and then being asked to share their innermost thoughts and feelings. If the trainee attempted to act as an authority figure or an extension of the court, then the clients probably would not be very motivated to share. However, if the trainee emphasizes the clients' autonomy and helps clients to see their own reasons for making changes in their lives, then the trainee becomes a true advocate for clients. By approaching therapy with a spirit of genuine concern and compassion for people, trainees can create a safe space where clients feel respected, empowered, and in control of their choices.

Once rapport has been established, then the work of changing maladaptive thoughts and behaviors can begin. Some trainees have struggled to integrate MI and CBT because they have thought of them as two separate interventions, but we have found that MI and CBT can be delivered seamlessly in the same session. MI is more about how the clinician relates to clients, while CBT guides the conceptual content of interventions. For example, a cost-benefit analysis or decisional balance exercise can be done in a way that enhances motivation with MI while also exploring more helpful thoughts and behaviors from a CBT perspective.

The student trainees at our site have found that the best way to learn MI is through role-play and practice. We encourage supervisors to draw upon their own clinical experiences to develop ambivalent client personas for use in role-plays. The point, though, is not to frustrate trainees but to show them that even the most ambivalent clients are people with their own values and hopes who have the power to change their lives if they are given the opportunity. Through our relationships and interactions with clients, we can contribute to creating that opportunity.

Finally, we have found that MI works well as a starting point in supervision because trainees and supervisors need motivation, too! We believe we all do our best work when we are provided with the tools we need, along with affirmation and compassion in a supportive environment. Therefore, we encourage supervisors to think of trainees as collaborators who benefit more from empowerment than expertise. As a bonus, when a clinical supervisor acts as a collaborator rather than as an authority figure, then the supervisor has the opportunity to learn just as much as the trainee.

Adding MI or CBT to an Existing Practice

Developing competence in MI+CBT is a ripe area for research due to this integrated practice being relatively new to the helping professions. As Naar and Safren (2017) stated, "We know little about how to train MI practitioners in CBT and how to train CBT practitioners in MI" (p. 214). Indeed, many clinicians have "grown up" with training in one of these approaches but not the other, and therefore, they are a seasoned practitioner in one approach while a novice in the other. Fidelity measures are used for MI and CBT as separate approaches, and these tools can be extremely useful in helping practitioners gauge, "Am I doing it right?" when first learning MI or CBT. Moving toward measuring fidelity in integrated practice, Naar and Safren (2017) developed a measure for MI fidelity in CBT sessions, which includes 12 defined components (cultivate empathy and compassion, foster collaboration, support client autonomy, etc.) of MI practice that are rated on a 4-point scale. This measure is especially useful to clinicians who are learning to integrate MI into their established practice of CBT, as the instrument does not measure CBT fidelity. A sample of measures that can be used to measure MI, CBT, or combination are listed in Resource Box 14.1.

Models for Learning MI+CBT

Norcross and Halgin (2005) provided a six-step model for training in psychotherapy integration in general. Suggestions about how to apply this model to learning the MI+CBT integration are provided in Table 14.1. In this ideal model, students are evaluated for mastery of the step prior to moving forward to the next step in the training module. In a preliminary study, Iarussi, Tyler, Crawford, and Crawford (2016) investigated the degree to which graduate students in a counseling program gained competency in practicing MI and CBT within their graduate training program. A stand-alone course in MI was not available or possible in the curriculum, so training in MI was integrated into the basic helping skills course due to the overlap of the course content with MI core skills and processes. We assessed for

Resource Box 14.1

Sample of MI Fidelity Measures

- *MITI 4.2.1* (Moyers, Manuel, & Ernst, 2014) https://motivationalinterviewing.org/sites/default/files/miti4_2.pdf
- *MISC* (Miller, Moyers, Ernst, & Amrhein, 2008) http://casaa.unm.edu/download/misc.pdf
- *Motivational Interviewing Sequential Code for Observing Process Exchanges MI* (Martin, Moyers, Houck, Christopher, & Miller, n.d.) https://casaa.unm.edu/download/scope.pdf
- *Motivational Interviewing Competency Assessment* (Jackson, Butterworth, Hall, & Gilbert, 2015) http://micacoding.com/manual
- *MI Target Scheme* (Allison, Bes, & Rose, 2012) https://motivationalinterviewing.org/sites/default/files/MITS_2.1.pdf
- *Video Assessment of Simulated Encounters—Revised* (Rosengren, Baer, Hartzler, Dunn, Wells, & Ogle, 2005) http://adai.washington.edu/instruments/PDF/VASERScoringManual_145.pdf
- *Behaviour Change Counselling Index* (Lane, 2002) https://motivationalinterviewing.org/library/BECCI
- *Assessment of MI Groups—Observer Scales* (Wagner & Ingersoll, 2017) https://motivationalinterviewing.org/sites/default/files/amigos_rating_form_v1.2.pdf

Sample of CBT Fidelity Measures

- *Cognitive Therapy Rating Scale* (Young & Beck, 1980) https://beckinstitute.org/get-informed/tools-and-resources/professionals/cbt-basics-and-beyond-patient-worksheets/
- *CBT for PTSD Fidelity Scale* (Lu et al., 2012) doi:10.1176/appi.ps.201000458
- *Comparative Psychotherapy Process Scale* (Hilsenroth, Blagys, Ackerman, Bonge, & Blais, 2005) doi:10.1037/0033-3204.42.3.340
- *A Fidelity Coding Guide for a Group Cognitive Behavioral Therapy for Depression* (Hepner, Stern, Paddock, Hunter, Chan Osilla, & Watkins, 2011) www.rand.org/content/dam/rand/pubs/technical_reports/2011/RAND_TR980.pdf
- *Cognitive Therapy for Psychosis Adherence Scale* (Startup, Jackson, & Pearce, 2002)

Sample of MI /CBT Fidelity Measures

- *Measures of MI fidelity in CBT Sessions* (Naar & Flynn, 2015) In W. R. Miller & S. Rollnick (Eds.), *Motivational interviewing in the treatment of psychological problems* (2nd ed.). New York, NY: Guilford Press
- *MI-CBT Fidelity Scale* (Haddock, Beardmore, Earnshaw, Fitzsimmons, Nothard, Butler, Eisner, & Barrowclough, 2012) doi:10.3109/09638237.2011.621470

Table 14.1 Norcross and Halgin's (2005) Six-Step Model for Psychotherapy Integration Applied to MI+CBT

Step	Application to MI+CBT Integration
1. Train in fundamental communication and relationship building skills	• Focus on skills learned in a basic counseling techniques or skills class, such as expressing empathy, positive regard, active listening, and goal setting. These skills are used in both MI and CBT. They are explicitly part of MI and essential to competent practice of this approach.
2. Be exposed to various theories of counseling	• Students are often introduced to CBT and MI through an introduction to theories course or other introductory coursework, in addition to a wide range of other theories. Exposure to other theories can enhance an understanding of the breadth of available therapies and help to begin to understand how MI and CBT compare to other theories conceptually as well as variations in research support.
3. Apply, compare, and integrate the various theoretical models in-depth and detail	• Compare and contrast CBT and MI to enhance understanding of similarities and differences between them as separate approaches, including how they can complement each other but also ways in which they have the potential to conflict.
4. Apply at least two theory-based treatments in clinical practice	• Apply MI and CBT to various cases to meet client needs. Practice the approaches separately to gain competence in each.
5. Take a formal course in psychotherapy integration	• Coursework or workshops specific to the MI+CBT integration is ideal; however, these opportunities can be sparse. Read about the MI+CBT integration, apply the integration to case studies, and engage in role play or mock sessions as part of training.
6. Practice the integration in an intensive, supervised clinical experience	• Identify a supervisor who is competent in and who practices MI+CBT and apply this integration with clients under his or her supervision.

MI competency using the MITI 3.1.1 (Moyers, Martin, Manuel, Miller, & Ernst, 2010) with recorded mock counseling sessions at the end of the course. The next semester, students completed a course in CBT, and we used the CTS (Young & Beck, 1980) with a recorded practice session to assess for CBT competency and the MITI to assess how MI fidelity changed after learning CBT. The semester after their CBT course, students completed a role-play session, and we used the MITI and the CTS to determine the level of MI and CBT competency demonstrated. We found that students executed CBT in the "good" range for general therapeutic skills per the CTS (an average of 4 on a 0 to 6 point scale, with 0 being poor and 6 being excellent). Using the MITI, we found that students maintained the spirit of MI in all three semesters, but their use of MI skills, including open questions, complex reflections, and MI-adherent behaviors (i.e., asking for permission, providing affirmations), diminished when learning CBT and then improved the following semester. Although the small sample and single cohort design limits the generalizability of this study, it did provide some evidence that student counselors can achieve beginning levels of competence in practicing MI and CBT in a graduate program. The training model used in this study only accomplished through step four of Norcross and Halgin's (2005) model, however. Formal education and supervised practice of using MI and CBT together are necessary to complete steps five and six. Therefore, faculty might consider adjusting the curriculum to include coursework specific to integrated practice and providing opportunities for supervision and fidelity evaluations.

More recently, Naar and Safren (2017) proposed a training plan specific to MI+CBT for practitioners who are new to both MI and CBT. This plan involves seven steps as follows: (1) MI spirit and skills; (2) engaging process in the context of setting the agenda for counseling sessions; (3) focusing process, including in the context of treatment planning; (4) evoking process, including in the context of the rationale for self-monitoring; (5) planning process, including in the context of executing self-monitoring assignments; (6) using all four processes in the initial counseling session; and (7) implementing all four process as in cognitive and behavioral skill-building sessions (p. 214).

Considerations for Training

If you currently practice with MI or CBT and you are interested in learning the other approach, it can be extremely beneficial to enter such training with an open mind. When conducting training in MI or CBT, I commonly hear the negative perceptions trainees have of the approaches (e.g., MI is too "nice" and CBT is too structured and sterile). When learning and attempting to integrate the other approach into your practice, we must expect that it will be different than your current approach in some ways. Your own sustain talk that surfaces related to applying the new approach can serve as gentle reminders that change can be difficult for us, too. And yet working through this challenge can be very worthwhile, as you will then be able to combine these approaches for synergetic effects for your clients.

When in such training experiences, it is essential that we remain open to feedback from the trainer, supervisor, or coach. Learning MI+CBT is a developmental process, and receiving and integrating feedback on our practice is integral to skill development. It is common for the supervisor to draw on MI and CBT as supervision techniques to aid in the supervisee's development as well as to model these skills (e.g., Voice from the Field 14.2). Using recordings (with a client's written and verbal permission) or other direct observations of our actual work with clients is optimal for training. Finally, self-evaluating our own work via recordings of sessions is valuable in our own reflection on our practice as well as growth in skill development.

Perhaps most importantly, your clients will provide you with feedback, both subtle and explicit, about how your methods are working for them. Looking for

---

Voices From the Field 14.2

Integrating MI and CBT Within Supervision

Written by
Jason Branch, PhD., LPC, ACS
Assistant Professor
Monmouth University

One of the most successful ways that I have integrated motivational interviewing (MI) and cognitive behavioral therapy (CBT) took place during my clinical supervision of a prelicensed counselor in training. A major goal that the supervisee expressed interest in was to raise her rates for counseling service in her private practice. The supervisee charged the same rate for individual counseling sessions for almost three years. The supervisee shared that she felt she was not worthy enough to charge more because she was not fully licensed. The supervisee also reported that she compared herself to other counselors in the field and doubted her own skills and abilities, which made her keep her rates the same for so long. Based on the information provided by my supervisee, my strategy was to challenge the supervisee's automatic thoughts, which led me to utilize a CBT approach in my supervision. Being mindful and cautious of not crossing the boundary of becoming my supervisee's therapist, I chose to integrate MI and CBT in order to maintain healthy ethical boundaries and balance for supervision.

Utilizing MI and CBT allowed me to enhance our working relationship while supporting, engaging, and empowering the supervisee to promote autonomy and accomplish one of the major goals that she was interested in achieving. I led with MI to elicit various perspectives on the issue from her. I challenged the supervisee to explore alternatives by considering the results from raising her rates, discussing the fears associated with raising her rates, and validating the unhealthy thoughts and feelings related to comparing herself to others. Using MI provided me with the rapport and connection with the supervisee to go further in later challenging her automatic thoughts and beliefs with CBT. I was intentional in my efforts to support the supervisee while using the combination of MI and CBT to guide the supervisee in being able to reach her own conclusion and decision to increase her rates.

After several weeks of using MI and CBT, the supervisee was able to reach a decision in raising her rates on a trial basis. The supervisee decided to challenge herself and explore her fears by raising her rates. The supervisee maintained a safety net of having the ability to return to her normal rate if she did not like the results of the rate increase. I continued using MI and CBT to support the supervisee's decision and process the thoughts and feelings with her throughout this period. After 30 days, the client was excited to report that she would maintain the increased rate because she felt more confident in herself and her abilities and stopped comparing herself to other clinicians. The supervisee also reported that her fears associated with increasing her rates dissipated because of a steady increase of clients in her practice without any complaints or concerns from new clients about paying the new rate. The supervisee was transparent in her response that her automatic thoughts and ideas were not based on factual information but beliefs she created herself, which were no longer valid. The supervisee was also able to shift her comparison thinking to others and focus more on becoming the best version of herself by using the information that she gained from MI and CBT within our supervision sessions. The integration of MI and CBT was a contributing factor in the success of my supervisee as well as an evidence-based practice that I now continue to use in clinical supervision.

or eliciting this feedback from clients can influence our skill development. For example, when I was first learning to primarily use reflections in my MI training, I struggled—hard. Questions were my default skill, and I loved them, and yet my supervisor was gently persistent as she repeatedly stopped my video-recorded sessions and helped me revise my questions into reflections. When I delivered reflections in session, my clients' reactions reinforced this skill for me. I saw my words resonate with them. I witnessed them looking in the mirror that I was holding up for them. I heard them continue their thoughts and go much deeper than they would have had I asked a question. In these ways, my clients taught me the value of reflections. Making changes to our routine clinical practice requires intentionality and diligence, as well as feedback from a coach or supervisor, but ultimately, our clients will let us know about the effectiveness of our integrated practice.

Summary

My hope is that this book has in some way ignited or perpetuated your practice of MI+CBT. The beauty of this integrated approach is in its wide applicability and flexibility to meet the diverse needs of clients in various settings. Learning new ways to practice counseling or psychotherapy is a journey that requires dedication and intentionality. Implementing MI and CBT together requires a certain artistry that you create with your client, and therefore, it looks different each time.

Through your efforts in learning and practicing this integration, I hope you witness the benefits to those you serve and relish in your role as their guide.

References

Hunsley, J., & Allan, T. (2019). Clinical assessment in cognitive-behavioral therapies. In K. Dobson & D. Dozois (Eds.), *Handbook of cognitive-behavioral therapies* (4th ed., pp. 120–144). New York, NY: Guilford Press.

Iarussi, M. M., Tyler, J. M., Crawford, S. H., & Crawford, V. C. (2016). Counselor training in two evidence-based practices: Motivational interviewing and cognitive behavior therapy. *The Journal of Counselor Preparation and Supervision, 8*(3), 1–24. doi:10.7729/83.1113

Miller, W. R., & Mount, K. A. (2001). A small study of training in motivational interviewing: Does one workshop change clinician and client behavior? *Behavioural and Cognitive Psychotherapy, 29*(4). doi:10.1017/S1352465801004064

Miller, W. R., Yahne, C. E., Moyers, T. B., Martinez, J., & Pirritano, M. (2004). A randomized trial of methods to help clinicians learn motivational interviewing. *Journal of Consulting and Clinical Psychology, 72*(6), 1050–1062. doi:10.1037/0022-006X.72.6.1050

Moyers, T. B., Martin, T., Manuel, J. K., Miller, W. R., & Ernst, D. (2010). *Motivational interviewing treatment integrity 3.1.1 (MITI 3.1.1)*. Retrieved from https://casaa.unm.edu/download/miti3_1.pdf

Naar, S., & Safren, S. A. (2017). *Motivational interviewing and CBT: Combining strategies for maximum effectiveness*. New York, NY: Guilford Press.

Norcross, J. C., & Halgin, R. P. (2005). *Training in psychotherapy integration* (Vol. 1). Oxford, UK: Oxford University Press.

Schumacher, J. A., Madson, M. B., & Nilsen, P. (2014). Barriers to learning motivational interviewing: A survey of motivational interviewing trainers' perceptions. *Journal of Addictions & Offender Counseling, 35*(2), 81–96. doi:10.1002/j.2161-1874.2014.00028.x

Young, J. E., & Beck, A. T. (1980). *Cognitive therapy scale*. Philadelphia, PA: University of Pennsylvania.

Index

absolute worth 20, 227
acceptance and commitment therapy 5
addiction *see* substance use and addiction
addictive beliefs 154
affirmation 24; *see also* OARS
ambivalence 13, 17, 108–10
  about change 58, 85–9, 116, 126, 234
  about treatment 248–50
  anxiety 60, 192
  cognitions 176–7, 202–3
  depression/suicidality 213–14
  discord 99
  evoking 29, 55, 84, 110, 141, 170
  serious mental illness 203–4
  substance use 154
anger 36, 92, 233
anxiety 192–4, 208–12
  see also mental health
arguing 98, 104
  against change 29, *see* sustain talk
  avoiding 100, 196, 228
assessment 8
  in CBT 35
  in correctional settings 231–2
  in integrated practice 134–8

  in mental-health-related treatment
    194–5, 199
  in substance use and addiction treatment
    156–7, 161–7
automatic thoughts 12, 37–8, 57–9
autonomy 20, 103
  asking permission 26, 136, 252
  collaboration between client and
    counselor 124, 258
  discord 194–6, 198
  personal choice 160, 215–16, 229
  reactance 49
  safety 191, 217

Beck Depression Inventory 136

change 18–21, 29, 48
  process of 74–5
  readiness for 41, 49, 61
  resistance to 98, *see* reactance, sustain talk
  stages of 6–7, 13, 49
  talk 29, 235
cognitions 37–8
  dysfunctional or distorted 34, 36, 42,
    121–23, 238

cognitive behavior therapy (CBT):
  history of 34–5
  interventions 38–40
  limitations 41–2
  processes 35–8
  plus MI, *see* integrative practice
  for psychosis (CBTp) 190, 197–8
  skills 39–40, 42–3
  training 42–3
cognitive hierarchy 37–8
cognitive model 36, 57; in CBT 119–20
  for addiction 177
cognitive restructuring 209
Cognitive Therapy Scale 42–3, 255, 260–1
collaboration between client and counselor
  see therapeutic alliance between client and counselor
common factors 5–6
compassion *see* empathy
conceptualization 36–8
  of mental health-related concerns 200–3
  treatment 89, 138–40
core beliefs 37–8
correctional services 222–3
counterconditioning 155
criminal behavior 222–4
  risk factors 231, 238
culturally responsive practice 52–53, 66–72
  social justice 66–7
  see also diversity

depression 193, 195–8, 202, *see also* mental health
  ambivalence 99
discord 98–105
  in coercive situations 157, 160, 195
  see also resistance
discrepancy 107–8
discrimination 66, 76, 239
diversity 65–70
  competency framework 66–7, 71

elicit–provide–elicit strategy (EPE) 26
  when providing information 88, 137
emotion:
  in the cognitive model 36
  regulation of 138, 238
empathy 20, 54
  listening 101
  to diminish discord 160
  in correctional settings 240
engaging 28
evidence-based practice 30–1, 61, 67
evoking 29
  in correctional settings 234–5
  as integration method 140–1
  as treatment of substance use and addiction 168–70
expert role 15, 71, 73, 104, 204–5
expert trap 47, 252–3

fidelity 255, 259–60
  measures of 241, 260–4
focusing 28–9
  in correctional settings 234–5
  as integration method 140–1
  in treating mental health-related concerns 204–6
  as treatment of substance use and addiction 168–70
functional analysis 35, 119–21, 176

Generalized Anxiety Disorder 190–2
  see also anxiety
goal violation effect 146, 182

harm reduction 250–2
homework 216–17, 254
  compliance 41, 111, 216

identity 65–7, 71–3, *see also* diversity
integrative practice:
  assimilative approaches 46–52
  atheoretical approaches 13–15
  challenges of 14–15, 247–56
  culturally responsive approaches 65–6
  history of 4
  methods of 4–9
  research support for 61–2
  seamless approaches 58–61, 147–8
  theoretical approaches 13–15, 52, 131–2
  training considerations 14–15, 148, 257–9
intentionality 160–1
intermediate beliefs 37–8
interventions 6–7, 215
  action-oriented 48–9
  cognitive and behavioral 38–40, 177
  culturally-responsive or adaptive 52, 69, 72

pharmacological 197
psychosocial 184–5, 193, 215
recidivism 235

listening 26–7, 68, 87
empathy 101, 198, 228

maintenance 145–7, 182–4
medication compliance 207–8
mental health 189–91
treatment planning 204–6
see also anxiety, depression, serious mental illness, suicide
mindfulness 5
as skill or intervention 11, 39–40, 124–6
motivation 17
in MI 18–19, 20–1
in CBT 41
lack of, *see* reactance
motivational interviewing (MI) 18–19
challenges in correctional settings 240
discord 98–9
diversity 68–9
history of 17–18
increasing in substance use and addiction treatment 173–6
plus CBT, *see* integrative practice
as precursor to CBT 83–5
processes 28–9
skills 21–4, 102, *see also* OARS
spirit of 19–21, 47, 258
as style of communication 17–18, 230
as supplement to CBT 96–8

noncompliance 98, 109
see also reactance

OARS 21–6, 102–3, 228–9

planning 29–30
in culturally responsive practice 70–4
in correctional settings 234–5
in MI+CBT treatment planning 141–2
for safety 213–14; in substance use and addiction treatment 170–2
in treating mental health–related concerns 204–6

posttraumatic stress disorder 88
Premack principle 39
problem recognition 107

questions: open versus closed 21–2, *see also* OARS
versus reflections 24, 137
evocative 29, 110
Socratic 97
question and answer trap 25

reactance 49, 98–9
see also resistance
readiness: measurement of 241, 248
for change 6, 41, 85–7
to engage in treatment 87–9
see also reactance
recidivism 222–3, 235–8
reflection 25–7
see also OARS
relapse prevention 179–80
resistance 98–9
see also discord, ambivalence
versus reactance 49
responsivity 160–1, 223–4
righting reflex 253
risk–need–responsivity (RNR) 222–4
risk principle 223
see also recidivism
Rogers, Carl 4, 19, 20
rulers 110–11, 213

serious mental illness 193–4, 197–8, 203, 215
see also mental health
substance use and addiction 153–5
screening and assessment 156, 161–8
treatment 172–81
suicide 195–7
see also mental health
summaries 26, *see also* OARS
sustain talk 29, 87
versus discord 99, 109, 194–5

technical eclecticism 6
therapeutic alliance between client and counselor 13, 18–19, 28–9, 97

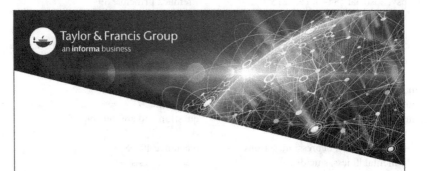